BEYOND PREJUDICE

BEYOND PREJUDICE

THE MORAL SIGNIFICANCE OF HUMAN AND NONHUMAN ANIMALS

EVELYN B. PLUHAR FOREWORD BY BERNARD E. ROLLIN

DUKE UNIVERSITY PRESS Durham and London

1995

© 1995 Duke University Press

All rights reserved   Printed in the United States

of America on acid-free paper ∞

Designed by Cherie H. Westmoreland   Typeset in Sabon

with Frutiger display by Tseng Information Systems, Inc.

Library of Congress Cataloging-in-Publication Data

appear on the last printed page of this book.

DEDICATION

For Werner—the human animal
I hold most dear

CONTENTS

Foreword by Bernard E. Rollin   ix

Preface   xi

1 HUMAN "SUPERIORITY" AND THE ARGUMENT FROM MARGINAL CASES   1
Candidates for Inclusion in the Moral Community/1   Frequently Held Views on Who Counts Morally: Homocentrism/10   Frequently Held Views on Who Counts Morally: The Full-Personhood View/57   The Argument from Marginal Cases: Two Versions/63

2 RESPONSES TO THE ARGUMENT FROM MARGINAL CASES   67
Failure to Address the Issue/67   Unsuccessful Attacks on the Argument from Marginal Cases/71   The Scope of the Argument from Marginal Cases/107   The Final Response/120

3 SPECIESISM AND FULL PERSONHOOD   124
The Speciesism Debate: A Brief History/125   Attempts to Show That Membership in a Species Characterized by Full Personhood Is a Morally Relevant Characteristic/140   Attempts to Show That Speciesism Is Justified Even if Species Membership Is Not a Morally Relevant Characteristic/171   Implications of the Failure to Justify Speciesism/177

4 UTILITARIANISM AND THE PROTECTION OF INNOCENT LIFE   179
Utilitarianism and the Full-Personhood View/180   Utilitarianism and the Charge of Inadequate Individual Protection/182   Utilitarian Attempts to Reject the Replaceability Argument/190   Rejection of the Extended Prior-Existence View/193   Preference Utilitarianism and

Replaceability/199 Return to the Case of the Wretched Child/212
Total-View Utilitarianism and Moral Rights/217

**5 JUSTIFICATION AND JUDGMENT: CLAIMING AND RESPECTING
BASIC MORAL RIGHTS 224**
Attempts to Provide Justification for the Moral Considerability and
Significance of Beings Who Are Not Full Persons/226 Justifying the
Rights View/240 Respecting Basic Moral Rights: Obligations and
Conflicts/268

Notes 303
Bibliography 349
Index 361

Contents

FOREWORD

When Evelyn Pluhar first embarked on the long intellectual voyage that culminated in this excellent book, she remarked to me that she saw herself as a "second generation" thinker in the area of ethics and animals. As one of the first-generation theorists, I thought it exigent in my work to establish rationally that nonhuman animals did enjoy significant moral status, and that such inclusion within the scope of moral concern needed to be "writ large" in social ethics and social policy. Although society had long acknowledged a minimalistic concern for cruelty to animals, it was growing increasingly obvious that the amount of suffering attributable to overt, deliberate cruelty was minute in comparison to the suffering unintentionally occasioned by such unchallenged pursuits as research, testing, and high technology agriculture. In the face of the sheer enormity of animal suffering to be found in society, then, I felt it most pressing to serve as an intellectual midwife to an emerging social ethic of concern about the treatment of animals in all areas of social use, and to attempt also to mitigate some of the most egregious practices.

In this crusade, the first-generation theorists have been very successful. Public concern about animals has resulted in many positive improvements in animal treatment, from laws mandating the control of pain and suffering in animal research to the voluntary abandonment of cosmetic testing by major companies. Animals have entered the moral arena, and now it is time to address a plethora of moral questions engendered by their presence therein. Most important perhaps, and certainly most vexatious, is the question of how much animal interests ought to be valued when they are in conflict with human interests and the interests of other animals. Furthermore, and inevitably, voices are being raised against the inclusion of animals in the moral arena, and these voices demand cogent—and devastating—responses. It is therefore imperative that the theoretical basis for animal moral status continue to be developed and deepened.

These tasks fall to the second-generation theorists, of whom Evelyn Pluhar is one of the best and the brightest. Her careful, cogent, deep, and eminently readable analyses of questions that I and others were pressed by circumstances to pass over far too quickly stand as exemplars for others working in this area. And her trenchant critique of recent neo-Cartesian rejections of an augmented moral status for animals should lay these positions firmly to rest—if not forever, at least for the foreseeable future. This provocative book is a major contribution to moving forward the field of moral theory about animals in a highly intelligent way, and should catalyze much valuable dialogue.

BERNARD E. ROLLIN

PREFACE

A PERSONAL INTRODUCTION

As far back as I can remember, I have been enchanted by animals. For much of my life, I have also been an unthinking consumer of their flesh and their products. In the mountains of southeastern Kentucky, where I grew up, we lived cheek by jowl with hunting dogs. (This is literally true, since at least one dog generally shared my bed.) I have seen my grandmother wring off the neck of the old laying hen who ended her days as Sunday dinner; despite my horror at her ghoulish death, I joined my family in eating her body. My father, one of the most wonderful men I have ever known, loved to hunt ducks and geese, and the walls of our home were decorated with trophy fish. I went fishing only once, as a very small child. I can remember being unwilling to impale a worm on a hook—Granny did it for me—and turning away as the small fish on the end of my line gasped and flopped in the air. This did not stop me from eating "Evelyn's fish," however, nor do I recall being upset by the corpses mounted in our living room.

At fifteen, I decided that nothing would please me as much as a career in philosophy. Imagine being able to earn one's living by reading, thinking, teaching, and writing about ultimate reality, truth, and justice! I left rural Appalachia for college in Colorado, graduating with a degree in philosophy, and went straight to graduate school at the University of Michigan. I learned a very great deal from teachers like William Alston, Richard Brandt, William Frankena, Alvin Goldman, and Jack Meiland, especially about uncovering and questioning presuppositions. We humans cling to these presuppositions, and we do not find their scrutiny a very comfortable experience. Engaging in such scrutiny despite our feelings is both the pain and the glory of philosophy. Any view worthy of one's belief, I became convinced, is a view that can be supported.

Even given my new skills and commitment to justification, however, I did not question my attitudes toward nonhuman animals. The love

I felt for my companion animals and the awe I felt toward wild animals coexisted with my patronage of Kentucky Fried Chicken and Long John Silver. I, who could never harm a rabbit, used cosmetics that ulcerated their eyes and wore a coat given to me by my mother that was trimmed with their skins. My attitudes did not begin to change until I learned about the conditions under which domestic nonhuman animals are raised for food and used to test products; the mistreatment of wild nonhuman animals by commercial trappers, hunters, and land developers resulted in further changes. The more I thought about how these actions were probably experienced by these animals, the less able I was to go on as before. I also began to doubt that "inhumane" treatment was really the problem. It was obvious to me that "humane" killing of other *humans* for food, skins, product testing, or research could not be justified: How, then, could it be right to do the same to sentient nonhumans? Further reading (see the next section) convinced me that the automatic assumption that members of other species are of little moral account in comparison to humans was just as indefensible as moral discriminations based on gender, sexual orientation, age, or race. I shared all these thoughts with my philosopher husband, Werner. We jointly concluded that major changes in our lives were in order, including rejection of the meat both of us loved to eat. We became vegetarians literally overnight. The campus picnic two days after our decision severely tested our resolve, but we did not succumb to the temptation of charcoal-grilled steaks: realizing what one would actually be eating does wonders for the appetite. When the meat section of a supermarket is perceived as a morgue, it is no hardship to focus on nonsentient produce!

A GLANCE AT MY WORK IN THE CONTEXT OF THE LITERATURE

So, my feelings have finally changed. So has my thinking. Why, indeed, have so many of us always presupposed that maximum moral significance accrues only to creatures like ourselves? I immersed myself in the new and expanding literature on this subject, and began contributing to it. Peter Singer, Bernard Rollin, and Tom Regan have argued very persuasively that attempts to restrict maximum moral significance to humans *either* lapse into unfounded prejudice *or* imply that even many *humans* are really not morally significant after all. Neither horn of this dilemma is particularly enticing. Other books soon began appearing. For example, Steve Sapontzis has argued for the extension of moral concern to sentient nonhumans in a rather different way from Singer, Regan, and Rollin; James Rachels has used philosophical biology to assault the presumption of human moral superiority; and Carol Adams has documented linkages between contemptuous exploitation of women and the same attitude toward nonhuman animals. After an initial period of silence, other philosophers have felt called upon to respond. Stanley Benn, Jan Narveson, Peter Carruthers, and A. I. Melden, among others, have taken issue with many of these arguments. Some have taken a different and very disturbing approach to the issue, holding that some sentient humans, for example, the very young and the mentally limited, actually have no moral right to life. R. G. Frey, for example, has argued that vivisection of some of these humans (as well as, of course, vivisection of nonhumans) would be justified, although he is far from gleeful about the prospect. One is tempted to dismiss this sort of response as the most desperate of attempts to exclude nonhuman animals from the realm of moral consideration, but such a dismissal would be unfair. Arguments deserve replies, and positions require justification.

In the current book, I try to accomplish both aims. I address and refute as yet unanswered critiques of views that accord moral significance to nonhuman animals, drawing upon relevant philosophical and empirical evidence. Contrary to the best attempts of several fine philosophers, there is no way to avoid the conclusion that if sentient, conative humans are highly morally significant, then many nonhuman animals are so as well. Further, I argue that these humans are indeed morally significant to the full extent. I offer a justification for the view that maximum moral respect is due any being, human or nonhuman, who is capable of caring about what befalls him or her. My argument differs from those of Singer, Sapontzis, and Regan. For—I hold—despite their great contributions to the literature, they do not ultimately justify the position that all such beings are worthy of significant moral consideration.

AN OVERVIEW OF THE BASIC ISSUES

Following is an overview of the basic issues involved in the debate over who counts morally and why. These issues are tremendously important, given their implications for the treatment of both humans and nonhumans.

Two questions are fundamental to moral theory: (1) What sorts of beings are morally considerable (i.e., proper subjects of our moral concern)? and (2) Are all morally considerable beings equally morally significant (i.e., due the same degree of moral respect from us)? In fact, although answers to these questions have been presupposed for quite a long time, the questions themselves were not posed until 1978, when Kenneth Goodpaster articulated the distinction between moral considerability and moral significance. For the most part, philosophers have only recently begun to address these foundational questions. Traditionally, it has been held that *full* moral significance is reserved for the members of the human species. However, this position has been subjected to devastating criticisms in recent years. For example, it has been argued that this traditional "homocentric" view implies that being human is itself a morally relevant characteristic. This implication appears to be just as objectionable as the assumption that one's gender or race is morally relevant. (By analogy to racism and sexism, the implication has been dubbed "speciesism.") It seems that moral considerability and significance must be linked in some manner to another characteristic or family of characteristics.

According to a number of philosophers, being a *person* is that characteristic. Following in the intellectual footsteps of Immanuel Kant, ethical theorists today defend the very popular view that full moral status is reserved for highly autonomous rational beings: "persons" in the richest philosophical sense of the term. Normal adult humans all qualify as such full-fledged persons. Yet, this is not a homocentric view, since nonhuman persons, if any (possible examples are whales, dolphins, or extraterrestrials), would be accorded full moral status by it. I call this position "the full-personhood view."

The full-personhood view faces two extremely serious difficulties: (1) Humans before birth, very young children, and the temporarily mentally disabled are not full persons. Is it justifiable to regard them as having no (or a reduced) moral status? Or should the fact that they are *potential* full persons have moral weight? This is, of course, one of the central issues in the problems of abortion and nonvoluntary euthanasia. (2) Humans who are permanently mentally incapacitated are not

and can never become persons in the Kantian sense. If full personhood or at least potential full personhood is necessary for basic moral
rights, none of these humans has a right to life. The implications are
staggering. It would follow that human nonpersons could justifiably be
confined, experimented upon, and killed just as nonhuman animals routinely are. This alone, in many eyes, is sufficient reason to reject the
full-personhood view. A number of ethical theorists who are committed
to that view have tried to defeat "the argument from marginal cases," as
it is known in the literature, but I contend that they have failed in their
attempts to do so.

Followers of the full-personhood view who cannot bring themselves
to exclude human nonpersons from significant moral consideration have
had to modify their position. They have developed a far more sophisticated version of speciesism than the homocentric variety mentioned
earlier. They have argued that being a member of a species *typified* by
full-fledged personhood is sufficient for full moral status. Thus, although
full persons would still be the primary possessors of basic moral rights,
in this view species norms could be used to justify the inclusion of other
humans in the moral community. I argue that even this most sophisticated form of speciesism is just as unacceptable as its homocentric
predecessor.

The only remaining alternative is to reject full personhood as the
primary criterion of maximum moral significance. If mentally limited
humans are to count as morally considerable and highly morally significant, as most of us believe they do, then we must acknowledge that
many nonhumans have the same moral status. Given the appropriate
theoretical basis, what characteristic or family of characteristics could
support the attribution of full moral status in these cases? There are
several possibilities. For example, sentience is one very plausible candidate. This would accord high moral significance to much of the animal
kingdom (including humans!). Alternatively, it has been suggested that
simply being alive is sufficient for moral considerability and significance.
Some have gone so far as to suggest that entire ecosystems are worthy
of direct moral concern. The explosion of literature in environmental
ethics bears witness to the new interest in such views. What arguments
can be mounted to support such positions? How is one to choose among
such alternatives? My book explores radically different suggestions, and

explains how a justified, nonarbitrary position can be defended. As I earlier indicated, I conclude that any being who is able to care about what happens to him or her should be included in the realm of moral concern. Each such being, in fact, should be accorded full moral significance. Taking such a position obviously requires us to rethink our assumptions about the appropriate treatment of human and nonhuman animals.

The issues I have sketched plainly lie at the very heart of ethical theory. Moreover, far from being "merely" theoretical, they have profound implications for the ways in which we should lead our lives.

AN OVERVIEW OF THE CHAPTERS IN THIS BOOK

Following is a brief sketch of the tasks undertaken in each chapter. Chapter 1, "Human 'Superiority' and the Argument from Marginal Cases," sets up the project and explores, using fresh philosophical material and current empirical findings, the many different attempts to justify a claim to human moral superiority. Homocentric appeals are shown to be resounding failures. However, the view that persons in the richest sense—autonomous moral agents or "full persons," as I call them—are the only "ends in themselves," as Kant puts it, cannot be dismissed so readily. At the end of this chapter, in response to the full-personhood view, I distinguish two forms of the famous argument from marginal cases: the categorical versus the biconditional versions. This distinction is entirely new. It sheds considerable light on the different positions that can be taken on moral considerability and significance. Clearly, advocates for the full-personhood view must respond to the argument: Can they escape the implication that humans falling short of full personhood are morally on a par with certain sentient members of exploited nonhuman species?

In chapter 2, "Responses to the Argument from Marginal Cases," I examine and refute numerous recent attempts to counter the argument in either of its two forms. I conclude that supporters of the full-personhood view cannot evade the unsavory implications their position has for the moral status of many sentient humans. They are logically required to throw out the baby with the nonhuman bath water. If they are unhappy with this, they can, at best, try to retain the *core* of their view by replacing it with a person-centered version of speciesism. However, as I show in the next chapter, this recourse to speciesism will be to no avail.

In chapter 3, "Speciesism and Full Personhood," I discuss speciesism and its relationship to racism and sexism, leading to its most plausible version: full-personhood speciesism (alluded to at the end of chapter 2). According to this version of speciesism, those who possess maximum moral significance, including what we call a right to life, are either (a) full persons or (b) members of a species *characterized by* full personhood. I then examine attempts to justify this position, exposing fatal flaws in each. I also offer my own arguments (which, I believe, are better than the ones that have been offered by speciesists themselves) in support of that position, and refute those arguments too. Speciesism, in short, does not survive this chapter. Anyone who continues to cling to the maximum moral significance of full persons but denies such significance to nonhuman animals *must* deny full moral significance to many humans as well. Anyone who *does not* want to accept that implication must give up the claim to superiority.

In chapter 4, "Utilitarianism and the Protection of Innocent Life," I discuss utilitarianism, particularly as defended by Peter Singer: this is an alternative to the full-personhood view (and the closely allied view of full-personhood speciesism). Many who *do* try to drop the claim of superiority have embraced some version of utilitarianism. I discuss the implications of utilitarian views for population policies (including contraception, abortion, and infanticide), food policies and farming methods, and research protocols. I examine perplexing attempts to compare in utilitarian terms the "value" of different lives: actual and potential lives, conscious and self-conscious lives, young and old lives, and so on. I show that, despite the most ingenious efforts that can be made by defenders of utilitarianism, this is not a view offering adequate protection for any innocent being's life, full person or otherwise.

The first few pages of chapter 5, "Justification and Judgment: Claiming and Respecting Basic Moral Rights," summarize what argumentative ground I have covered up to that point. I argue that further argumentation is needed to counter the positions of those who are not sufficiently moved by the horrific implications of the full-personhood view and utilitarianism. We must get beyond appeals to intuitions, however carefully considered those intuitions may be. After showing that Sapontzis and Regan do not succeed in decisively refuting key alternatives to their views, I offer a new argument for the maximum moral significance of all consciously conative beings. This argument is inspired by the work of one of the most important contemporary moral theorists, Alan Gewirth. However, it goes considerably beyond his own conclusions: although Gewirth believes that nonhuman animals have some degree of moral significance, he is in fact a homocentrist. I also show that the Gewirth-inspired argument I develop does not justify extending moral standing to entities with no capacity for consciousness or conation. I point out in this final chapter that if a more inclusive, environmental, ethic were to be justified, it would have to be so on other grounds (e.g., aesthetics). Indeed, such an ethic is entirely compatible with the argument that I advance. In the remainder of the chapter, I discuss the implications of my position for the treatment of morally significant beings, be they human or nonhuman, family or stranger, wild or domestic. Hunting for sport or survival, the raising of animals for food or research purposes, and the keeping and treatment of companion animals are all addressed. I explore the circumstances in which the killing of others, nonhuman or human, can be justified: not surprisingly, given the argument developed earlier in this chapter, those circumstances turn out to be rather limited. Other animals and the environment as a whole would benefit if human animals revised their attitudes and actions as suggested. We humans too would benefit in many ways if we were willing to resist prejudice in all its forms. Sometimes we would also lose, but that is the price of moral commitment.

ACKNOWLEDGMENTS

This book is indebted to a number of articles I have written in the past few years on the moral significance of humans and nonhumans. I want to thank the editors of the philosophical journals *Inquiry, Ethics and Animals, Between the Species, Philosophica,* and *The Journal of Agricultural Ethics* for permission to quote from my articles. For the most part, I have quoted rather little from myself. Material drawn from these articles has been thoroughly rethought and rewritten; in any case, most of the substance of this book is new. Two exceptions are "The Sentience Defense of Homocentrism" in chapter 1, and parts of chapter 4. The former is very close, though not identical, to "Arguing Away Suffering: The Neo-Cartesian Revival," *Between the Species* 9 (1), Winter 1993, pp. 121–28, and "Reply to Harrison" in the same journal, Spring 1993, pp. 77–82. Major parts of chapter 4 are based on "Utilitarian Killing, Replacement, and Rights," *The Journal of Agricultural Ethics* 3 (2), 1990, pp. 147–71; however, many new arguments and references have been added to the original material. Finally, a small part of chapter 5, "Is Moral Agency Mandated by Reason?" is closely based on "Reason and Morality Revisited," *Between the Species* 6 (2), 1990, pp. 63–69.

I began writing this book in the spring of 1990. I want to thank colleagues at the Pennsylvania State University for naming me the 1990 Helena Rubenstein Endowed Faculty Fellow in the Humanities: this fellowship released me from teaching duties during that semester. (The irony of my title did not escape me.) Thanks to a Pennsylvania State University Research Development Grant, I received a one-course release in the spring of 1991 to pursue my work. I also thank the Institute for Arts and Humanistic Studies for a grant that partially released me from teaching during the fall of 1992. I was able to complete the bulk of my book by late 1993: I am grateful to the university and to my campus for the one-semester sabbatical leave that made this possible.

My thanks also go to many of my students, who have debated ethics with me and with each other over the past several years. I also acknowledge with pleasure the support given to my project at various stages by Harlan Miller, Steve Sapontzis, Tom Regan, and Marc Bekoff. I am especially grateful to Bernard Rollin for his careful reading of the manuscript, his excellent comments, and his encouragement. I am honored by his offer to write the foreword to my book. Above all, I owe thanks to my philosopher-spouse, Werner, for his warm support and for his willingness to take time from his own work to debate issues with me.

Preface

HUMAN "SUPERIORITY" AND

THE ARGUMENT FROM MARGINAL CASES

We are moral agents. We are capable of understanding and acting upon moral principles. Unless we act under duress, we are responsible for what we do. Unlike small children and cats, we have moral obligations and can be held accountable for flouting those obligations. All moral codes are addressed to us. So are the following questions: Are we, as moral agents, all *morally considerable?* That is, are others (also moral agents) directly obligated to take our interests into account when their actions would affect us? Are we all equally morally significant, entitled to be treated as more than means to further others' purposes, or should some of us count more than others? Can any beings who are *not* moral agents be morally considerable? If such beings exist, are they equally *morally significant?* Are they as significant as we are? In short, who belongs in the moral community, and to what degree? These are all fundamental, extraordinarily important questions. They are also extraordinarily difficult to answer.

CANDIDATES FOR INCLUSION IN
THE MORAL COMMUNITY

Let us begin by considering the kinds of beings who may very well qualify for moral considerability and a high degree of moral significance. They will be considered in descending order of "plausibility." Not coincidentally, we humans tend to assume that we are the paradigms of moral significance. As other beings depart in greater and greater degree from our model, most of us find it progressively more difficult to accord them our moral concern. How much of this is bias and how much is warranted will occupy many of the later pages of this book.

Full-Fledged Persons

Normal adult human beings are obvious examples of full-fledged persons (or, as I shall usually call them, "full persons"). It will not have escaped the reader's notice that we ourselves are being described here! We have the intelligence, rationality, creativity, and communication skills required for moral agency. None but full persons can engage in debate about moral considerability and significance. A fully developed person is, in Paul Taylor's words, "a center of autonomous choice and valuation."[1] This high degree of autonomy makes it possible for such a being to forge a life plan and to interrelate that plan with the plans of others. If anyone is morally considerable and deserving of a right to life, we believe, such a person is. Many would add that thwarting such an (innocent) being's basic interests *may* be the only way for a sane, mature specimen of personhood to lose any moral significance.

Persons Lower on the Autonomy Scale

We do not normally restrict the concept of personhood to highly autonomous, mature beings. A good friend once shared his delight with my husband and me about the fact that his one-year-old daughter Katie had become "a little person." At first, he smiled, she was "all brain stem." Another friend beamed about how much fun it was to be with her toddler daughter: "Now Valerie's a person!" Anyone who has spent any length of time with small children in their second year of life can see that they have distinct "personalities," wants, goals, and even plans to achieve those goals (e.g., assembling corn chips in a row on the floor to play with; checking every glass with liquid in it in order to get a taste, then disgustedly tossing displeasing beverages on the floor, etc.). Those who know certain nonhuman animals "personally" commonly say the same about them. For example, our family boxer would whine while resting his muzzle on one's lap when he wanted to be fed. If we children didn't get the hint, he would take a hand gently in his massive jaws and lead his (by then) soggy-lapped victim directly to the refrigerator. We all took it for granted that Tiger was a person, although some philosophers and scientists would find this claim controversial at best.

The Argument from Marginal Cases

Joel Feinberg characterizes this less restrictive concept of personhood as follows: "In the commonsense way of thinking, persons are those beings who, among other things, are conscious, have a concept and awareness of themselves, are capable of experiencing emotions, can plan ahead, can act on their plans, and can feel pleasure and pain."[2] Feinberg adds that these traits *in combination* are not obviously present in humans until they are over one year of age.[3]

Tom Regan's category of "subjects-of-a-life" is the same as Feinberg's "commonsense personhood": "Individuals are subjects-of-a-life if they have beliefs and desires; perception, memory, and a sense of the future, including their own future; an emotional life together with feelings of pleasure and pain; preference- and welfare-interests; the ability to initiate action in pursuit of their desires and goals; a psychophysical identity over time; and an individual welfare in the sense that their experient[i]al [lives] fare well or ill for them, logically independently of their utility for others and logically independently of their being the object[s] of anyone else's interests."[4] Regan believes that all normally developed mammals over one year of age qualify as subjects-of-lives (commonsense persons).[5]

'Person,' however, is a notoriously slippery term with more than one meaning. Some simply equate 'person' with 'human being,' calling even a just-fertilized human egg a 'person.' Those who do not want to do this but share the same concept will deny that the fertilized egg is a human being, whereupon their opponents accuse them of biological illiteracy (many are the ways of muddying the abortion controversy's argumentative waters). Others simply use 'person' in an honorific way, meaning by it no more or less than 'deserving of basic moral rights.' Most of us, however, think of personhood in more descriptive terms, in the way which links 'person' to 'personality.' In this sense, it is an open question whether a dog, cat, ape, or human baby can be a person, let alone a being deserving moral consideration.[6]

Commonsensical though the commonsense concept of person may be, a number of contemporary philosophers reject it. For example, Paul Taylor,[7] H. J. McCloskey,[8] and Ernest Partridge[9] all restrict the concept of person to the group I have identified as *full-fledged* persons. Only the highly autonomous and linguistically sophisticated, who are capable of moral agency and able to act on principle, are awarded the accolade of "person." In my writing during the last few years on the

The Argument from Marginal Cases

subject of moral considerability, I have myself wavered on how high a standard to set for personhood.[10] I have since decided that this is not a merely terminological issue. The insistence that only relatively mature, highly autonomous beings can be persons suggests that all others, including four-year-old humans, are blanks, as lacking in "personality" as fertilized eggs. Calling the children "pre-persons" helps not at all: the same designation can be used for fertilized eggs. Calling them "near persons" is a bit better, but it still suggests that they will soon lose their "blankness" and become individuals (in more than the genetic sense). This seems outrageously unfair, not the least because the qualities so highly developed in the mature person did not spring full-blown into existence on that individual's eighteenth birthday. Those qualities had been present to a lesser but increasing degree for many years before.

Moral agency, for example, is a late stage in a complex, years-long process of moral development. The process begins in early childhood, according to psychologists who study this phenomenon.[11] Similarly, the ability to plan one's life many years in advance has its roots in the ability to make plans to achieve short-term goals. This ability manifests itself very early indeed, as any parent can tell you. Tom Regan calls the ability to act so as to satisfy preferences "preference autonomy." [12] Of course, eighteen-month-old Alex, who spies a bowl of peanuts on a high table, drags a nearby chair close to the table, climbs on the chair, then grabs the bowl of peanuts supposedly placed out of his reach, or the chimp who does the same to reach a tantalizing bunch of bananas, is not highly autonomous. Nevertheless, he has, even if to a primitive degree, the ability that is so much more highly developed in human adults (we drive to the grocery store to get the nuts, put them high on a shelf to discourage excess snacking, then climb on a stool at 4:00 A.M. to grab the darned things).

The more inclusive, "commonsense" sense of 'person' allows for these degree differences in autonomy and moral development. It remains to be seen whether those who are not, and perhaps never will be, full-fledged persons can be maximally morally significant. At least, however, our way of describing them does not load the deck against them by suggesting that they are less than individuals.

The Argument from Marginal Cases

Self-Conscious Beings Who Have Little or No Autonomy

Can beings with awareness of themselves fail to be persons or subjects-of-lives? Yes, if their ability to act (even with the most sophisticated mechanical aids) is severely diminished or nonexistent. Such beings may be either physically or mentally incapable of goal-directed action, and their sense of self may be rudimentary at best. Severely damaged humans or extremely young humans might qualify for inclusion in this category. Although at one point Regan claims that such humans are subjects-of-lives,[13] they are not, since they fail to satisfy (at the very least) his action requirement. However, they do have a *welfare:* their lives "fare well or ill for them logically independently" of the interest others have—or do not have—in them. Their lives matter *to them.* For this reason, many (although not all!) believe them to be morally considerable.

Merely Conscious Beings

Can beings be aware, in some sense, of their surroundings, but have no awareness whatever of *themselves?* Drawing on recent work by psychologist T. Natsoulis, ethologist Donald Griffin distinguishes between "perceptual consciousness" (being aware) and "reflective consciousness" (being aware that one is having a given experience).[14] This distinction seems natural and philosophically familiar, but those of us capable of thinking about such matters normally experience both types of consciousness, even if not always simultaneously. We have a difficult time conceiving of a consciousness that is *exclusively* perceptual. How is one to imagine a life that drifts from moment to moment with no hint of knowledge that anything is happening *to it?* How could beings with no sense (however undeveloped) of identity over time ever have preferences? How could their lives matter *to them?* Some believe that many nonhuman animals, even highly developed animals like dogs and cats, fall into this category.[15] If they are correct, the ordinary experiences of those of us who think we know such nonhuman animals well are riddled by misinterpretation. Many, many humans would also lack self-consciousness in that case.

On the other hand, Bernard Rollin has recently argued[16] that beings who could never be more than "merely" conscious, if they somehow came into existence, would have died off exceedingly quickly indeed (unless, presumably, cared for by those blessed with self-consciousness and preference autonomy). Natural selection would make very short work of them. If nonhuman animals truly were machines made of flesh, "hard-wired," as it were, to go through invariant sequences of behavior given certain environmental "triggers," perhaps they could survive even though "merely" conscious. However, those who closely study their behavior, as Rollin documents, cannot plausibly reduce it to a stimulus-response model. In a fascinating, positive argument for the contention that nonhuman (and human!) animals cannot have evolved as "merely" conscious beings, Rollin takes a leaf from Immanuel Kant, of all people. (This is a highly ironic move, since Kant took for granted that non-human animals have no mental lives.) In order for one to *experience,* as opposed to simply undergoing an onslaught of discrete sensations, one must synthesize one's sensory input. However, in order to do that, one must have an underlying sense of self. Without a "transcendental unity of apperception" (to give the sense of self its full Kantian title), one could never experience nor, a fortiori, learn from experience. In other words: "What this means is that in order for a being to have unified experience of objects in relations, it must be the same consciousness which experiences the beginning of an event [as experiences] the end, or the top of an object and its bottom . . . if it were not the same you that viewed the top of a tall building as the bottom and the middle, there could be no experience of 'the tall building.' But this same point must hold true for animals too; they must be able to realize that an event is happening to them in order to learn from it."[17]

We can summarize this argument as follows:

1. In order to learn from an event, one must recognize that the event is happening to one.
2. In order to recognize that an event is happening to one, one must be self-conscious.
3. Nonhuman animals learn from events.
4. *Therefore,* nonhuman animals cannot be "merely" conscious: they must be self-conscious.

A critic of this argument would probably not challenge the second premise. So long as 'self-conscious' is understood to imply no more than 'self-aware,' regardless of how peripheral that awareness may be, it is difficult to see how premise 2 could be false. Jean-Paul Sartre uses a stunning metaphor to describe the self-awareness most of us experience at every conscious moment;[18] it is a "horizon" bordering our awareness of the world, always there, seldom in focus, a boundary turning sensory chaos into lived experience. We need not mumble to ourselves, "Gee, I'm having an experience right this very minute!" in order to be self-conscious, nor do we need to do this to know that something is happening to us. No, a critic of the argument is more likely to attack the third or first premise.

Attacking the third premise, that is, denying that any nonhuman animals can learn from events, would be a singularly unpromising approach for a critic to take. I will have more to say about this later, but for now let us only pause to note that even psychologists who express very low opinions about the mental abilities of their nonhuman research "models" take for granted that those "models" can learn from events such as random electric shocks, food rewards, maternal deprivation, and more.

An attack on premise 1 inspired by recent developments in computer technology seems to be more promising. It can be pointed out that computers can "learn" from events, but they are assuredly not self-conscious. (Even the most ardent supporters of "artificial intelligence" do not claim that we have succeeded in creating self-conscious machines.) Might not some humans and perhaps all nonhumans be in the same boat? If so, the first premise of the neo-Kantian argument above is false.

I do not find this to be a convincing reply. There is a reason for our persistent use of quotation marks in discussion of the "mental" abilities of computers. The reason is that no one claims that we have succeeded in creating a *conscious* machine. Marvin Minsky of the Massachusetts Institute of Technology, who has devoted his life to the "artificial intelligence" field, does not hesitate to admit this.[19] They can be programmed to do amazing feats, but they are phenomenologically aware of nothing. Hence, they "see," but they do not *see;* they "learn," but they do not (yet!) *learn.* Hence, what they can be brought to do is not a challenge to premise 1 above. (As Rollin points out in *The Unheeded Cry,* some psychologists have used quotation marks when referring to nonhuman "experiences" as well. He argues convincingly that those who have done this have accepted the thoroughly discredited ideologies of logical positivism and behaviorism. We have the same excellent reason to believe that dogs are conscious as we have to believe that babies are.[20] By the same token, if "artificial intelligence" experts ever do succeed in creating genuine intelligence, we ought to drop our quotation marks in descriptions of computer activity.)

Rollin's neo-Kantian argument has not been discredited. However, it does not follow from it that no being could be "merely" conscious. I do not think that Rollin would deny that there could be humans who are so profoundly brain damaged or so extremely young that only the simplest kind of awareness would be possible for them. The same holds for non-humans. Of course, it is highly unlikely that such beings could survive without assistance from those who are better mentally and physically equipped: without that help, they would be "naturally selected out" in no time. It seems to me that it would also be possible for a relatively primitive organism to survive without having to organize sensations into perceptions, but this is an empirical question that others must try to settle. For our purposes, it is sufficient to say that "merely" conscious beings may very well exist. Would they be morally considerable? Many would deny it. Not surprisingly, the further we depart from our own characteristics, the less likely we are to extend our moral concern.

Living Beings with No Capacity for Consciousness

This is even more evident when we consider the next possible candidate for moral concern. Beings with *no* capacity for consciousness are not sentient. They can neither be aware of nor care about anything that happens to them, although they can live, flourish, deteriorate, and die. We may feel (justifiably or not) moral concern for humans who fall into this class, such as the irreversibly comatose, anencephalic babies born only with brain stems, and the brain-dead. However, many have no such moral feelings toward plants, sponges, or bacteria, who are quite far removed from the human form although much more apt to flourish in favorable conditions than the sad cases mentioned above. There are exceptions to the common notion that any human being counts more than any other living being, however. The view that all living beings are morally considerable has actually been accepted by some religions, most notably the Eastern religions of (strict) Buddhism and Jainism.[21] Some

The Argument from Marginal Cases

recent figures in environmental ethics strongly defend "biocentrism," which holds that all living beings are morally considerable. One environmental ethicist, Paul Taylor, even holds that all living beings, from bacteria to humans, are equally morally significant.[22] There may well be a legitimate moral distinction between the human and nonhuman cases, or it may be that all alike are deserving—or undeserving—of moral concern.

Natural Objects or Systems

Some environmental ethicists include natural objects or systems in the realm of the morally considerable. Many would agree with J. Baird Callicott's statement that "The land ethic may seem fatally promiscuous in its inclusion of 'soils, waters, plants, and animals,' individually and collectively,"[23] although Callicott does not believe this to be the case. It is difficult enough for most people to accord moral concern to living, nonsentient beings, but it is harder still to gather deserts, rivers, rock formations, and swamps into the moral community. We can and often do cherish these wild objects and systems, but it is not clear that we have obligations to them. With natural objects and systems, we are about as far as we can get from the autonomous human paradigms of moral considerability and significance.

Confusing These Views on Candidates for Moral Considerability

Plainly, many who are willing to countenance the moral considerability of all sentient beings balk at the prospect of including viruses, crabgrass, soils, and mountain ranges. Some firm opponents of the extension of serious moral concern to nonhuman sentient beings make use of this in their attacks on "animal rights." For example, in an editorial entitled "Animal Rights Nonsense,"[24] in the prestigious science journal *Nature*, defenders of animal rights are accused of being committed to the absurdity of "bacteria rights." Oddly, the editorial goes on to give the obvious rebuttal to this charge—namely that the movement *Nature* attacks draws the moral line at *sentient* beings—only to triumphantly

The Argument from Marginal Cases

assert: "At last, the *reductio ad absurdum* takes hold. They have been caught. But there is little satisfaction to be gained in skewering the animal rightists on their failure to stand up for bacteria."[25]

Philosopher A. I. Melden does somewhat better in his attack on animal moral considerability views than the piece of puzzling illogic above, but he too tries to associate these views with those commonly found less plausible. In his chapter entitled "Animal Rights?" in *Rights in Moral Lives*,[26] he begins correctly by saying that animal rights views base their rights claims on sentience.[27] In short order, however, the view is next characterized as one that requires us to grant rights to "any living creature."[28] Next we find him discussing "the view that animals, plants, etc. have moral rights" as well as "inanimate entities."[29] If Melden cannot be said to have committed the straw person fallacy in this chapter, he certainly can be accused of engaging in the "straw entity" fallacy! He quite naturally has an easier time dismissing views his readers are apt to find very implausible than he would in refuting his alleged target. In fact, he explicitly refuses to discuss that target's central contentions: "I shall not review here a variety of other considerations—such as the fact that animals have needs, desires, or interests—that have been adduced as grounds for the ascription of rights."[30] This sort of treatment of the issue is surely unfair to all of the views that depart progressively further from traditional beliefs.

Which of the candidates for moral considerability and significance discussed in this section has a chance of being justified? Let us now turn to some standard responses to the question of who counts morally, bearing in mind the sorts of beings we have just sketched.

FREQUENTLY HELD VIEWS ON WHO COUNTS MORALLY: HOMOCENTRISM

When philosopher Alan Gewirth claims that all basic moral rights are *human,* and that "for human rights to be had one must only be human,"[31] he is expressing the frequently accepted view of *homocentrism.* According to this literally human-centered view, all and only human beings can be maximally morally significant. Some would go even further, claiming that all and only human beings are worthy of any moral concern whatever, as St. Thomas Aquinas did. The eminent medieval synthesizer of Aristotle and the Scriptures assumed that humans alone were created rational, in the image of God, and that all other "nonrational" beings were fashioned purely for our use.[32] "Hence," he proclaimed, "it is no wrong for man to make use of them, either by killing or in any other way whatever."[33] Hunters and trappers who defend themselves against charges of cruelty by proclaiming "Animals were made for us to use!" are taking the same line of thought. The type of homocentrism most often expressed, however, is more moderate: we wrong nonhumans by "excessive" cruelty and killing, but their lives count for far less than ours, and there is no wrong in killing them for sport, food, clothing, product testing, or experimentation.

From the human point of view, homocentrism obviously has its merits. Indeed, compared to views (depressingly and disgracefully prevalent even now) that only humans of the "appropriate" race, creed, sex, sexual orientation, ethnic group, or political affiliation are maximally morally significant, homocentrism shines as a beacon of enlightenment. Nevertheless, it does not withstand careful scrutiny. Homocentrists are unable to explain why all and only human beings can be significant members of the moral community.

The Theological Defense of Homocentrism

Homocentrists frequently appeal to theology to support their view. As we saw, Aquinas was convinced that all other creatures were designed purely for human use. Humans alone, he held, are worthy of moral concern because they alone, as "intellectual creatures," resemble God.[34] One commonly hears less sophisticated versions of the theological argument: for example, "Only humans have souls," "God gave us these critters to eat and wear," and so on. Homocentrists who appeal to theology, however, run into multiple difficulties. Since religious traditions disagree on the value of nonhuman life, religious homocentrists must show that their views are "better" than, for instance, Buddhism or Jainism. Any "authorities" they quote are sure to be challenged by those who do not share their assumptions, including the "authority" of Holy Scripture. I have discussed this issue with theists who treat selected passages from

The Argument from Marginal Cases

the Bible as their ultimate trump cards in an argument: "Surely," they insist, "you aren't doubting God's word!" They are confident that an all-perfect being would never lead us astray. Unfortunately for their argument, they are unable to provide any convincing grounds for their claim of Scriptural infallibility. They are nonplussed when asked why one should believe the Scriptural passage of their choice expresses God's word. One of the few who even tried to answer the question thought he had won the argument for sure: "Of course the Bible is the inspired word of God! It says so right here in 2 Peter 1:21!" In short order, the circularity of this reasoning became painfully evident. (It is not just the untutored who make this mistake. Charles C. Ryrie, a doctor of theology and of philosophy and a highly regarded biblical scholar, wrote in an appendix to his annotated Old and New Testaments that the Bible, although occasionally historically inaccurate, expresses the infallible Word of God with regard to all important matters. Why? Because "The Lord" says so Himself in a number of passages in the New Testament!) [35] Homocentrists who base their claims on religion also find themselves unable to make any headway with atheists and agnostics. Much more can be said about the futility of a theological defense of homocentrism, but since others have already written much of value on this subject,[36] I will now turn to other defenses.

I will consider the following claims: (1) only humans can be sentient or conscious; (2) only humans are capable of intelligence, creativity, purposeful communication, and autonomy; and (3) only humans are capable of moral agency. Paradoxically, although the first claim seems the least likely, it will require the most space to explore and refute: it has recently gained sophisticated new defenders. I will then give briefer responses to the remaining claims. (Of necessity, my discussions of these three defenses of homocentrism will overlap.)

The Sentience Defense of Homocentrism

If sentience is restricted to humans, nonhumans would be no more deserving of moral consideration than bacteria. Unless a case could be made for the moral considerability of nonsentient beings in the environment, they would be due no consideration at all. Humans, on the

The Argument from Marginal Cases

other hand, would be prima facie excellent candidates for moral considerability—the only candidates, it would seem.

At first blush, this particular defense of homocentrism does not seem very promising. Generally, people who have had the opportunity to observe nonhuman animals, especially vertebrates, for any length of time take for granted that these beings are conscious and capable of suffering. If we are pressed to give a rational defense of our assumption that nonhumans can be sentient, we can have no better start than the inductive argument from analogy to other minds. Beings who are neurologically highly similar to me, who respond in complex, creative ways to stimuli that elicit similar responses in me, are probably conscious just as I am. This is an extraordinarily strong inductive argument, fulfilling all criteria for good two-case analogical reasoning, licensing one to infer that another, be the other human or nonhuman, is not merely a cleverly contrived "machine."[37] Those who are skeptical about induction as such are, of course, not persuaded by the argument, but they also cannot be persuaded about the existence of their own bodies, let alone anyone else's. Short of solipsism, one seems not to be irrational in putting one's confidence in the argument from analogy.

René Descartes, of course, had doubts about the extension of this argument to nonhumans: "This argument, which is very obvious, has taken possession of the minds of all men from their earliest age. But there are other arguments, stronger and more numerous, but not so obvious to everyone, which strongly urge the opposite. One is that it is more probable that worms and flies and caterpillars move mechanically than that they all have immortal souls."[38]

Philosophically, Descartes's counter to the argument from analogy is not plausible for many reasons,[39] including the fact that it is wedded to a version of mind-body dualism fraught with well-known difficulties. *Scientifically,* Descartes's counter (i.e., the machine model of nonhumans) has done considerably less well than the argument from analogy, which has grown even stronger since his day. The argument has been buttressed by centuries of observation, much of it done at great cost to nonhuman animals, that reveal complex, detailed similarities between human and nonhuman vertebrate nervous systems. We know that many nonhuman animals have the same pain mechanisms as we do, and their behaviors are consistent with this fact. Even some invertebrates appear

The Argument from Marginal Cases

to have some parts of this mechanism.[40] Moreover, as Bernard Rollin[41] and James Rachels[42] have argued, we fly in the face of the superbly confirmed theory of evolution if we assume that consciousness is a uniquely human trait. Logic, science, and common sense all point to the existence of nonhuman animal suffering.

Nevertheless, as Rollin (a professor of physiology and biophysics as well as a professor of philosophy) has painstakingly documented, some scientists even to this day persist in denying that animals can experience pain, relying implicitly on the philosophically long-discredited views of logical positivism and behaviorism. He is cautiously optimistic about the fact that it is becoming scientifically respectable once more to attribute conscious states to nonhumans in the social and natural sciences.[43] Ironically, if two current philosophers, Peter Harrison[44] and Peter Carruthers,[45] writing independently, are taken seriously, scientists might as well return to the practice of nailing research animals to boards for vivisection without benefit of anesthesia. Descartes's views are with us again, albeit in contemporary dress.

Now, quite a few of us regard it as screamingly obvious that nonhuman animals can suffer. Could any marginally reasonable homocentrist take arguments to the contrary at all seriously? Is critiquing such arguments merely a matter of (you should excuse the expression) beating a dead horse? The history of philosophy and science indicates that it is not. Philosophers have been enormously influential in shaping attitudes toward nonhuman animals. Descartes, a scientific experimentalist whose own interest in the issue of nonhuman animal treatment was not purely philosophical, had a profound effect on the practice of vivisection. Long before anesthesia became available, experimenters taking apart yelping animals in laboratories laughed at the sounds, comparing them to clocks striking the hour.[46] (Rachels notes that some researchers must have found all the noise distracting, however, finding it prudent to sever the animals' vocal cords. Some clocks do need to be muffled.)[47] Later, two hundred years after Descartes's death, Claude Bernard, a pioneer in experimental physiology, routinely vivisected complex animals, speaking of them in these terms: "It is necessary, so to speak, to take an organism to pieces in successive stages, in the same way that one dismantles a machine, in order to recognize and to study its working parts."[48] Although anesthesia was in practice then, Bernard never used

The Argument from Marginal Cases

it, any more than he would have tried to use it on a timepiece. (His wife and daughters found themselves unable to share his views; they originated the first European antivivisection society after coming home one day to discover that Bernard had vivisected the family dog.)[49] Even now, as Rollin reports, the occasional veterinarian (of all people) will publicly proclaim that anesthesia in operations on animals is merely a method of "chemical restraint," having nothing whatever to do with pain relief.[50]

As mentioned before, the philosophical movement of logical positivism has also had its influence on science: any discussion of conscious states in nonhumans (or, for that matter, humans) was ruled out as meaningless because such claims cannot be tested by observations. All claims about values fell by the wayside as well, reducing any ethical dilemmas a researcher might have to emotional, rationally irresolvable matters of taste. This view is no longer taken seriously by philosophers—for one thing, logical positivism cannot pass its own criterion of meaningfulness—but its influence can still be seen in psychology, biology, and physics. In short, philosophical views do matter in the conduct of science, particularly when these views have implications that some scientists find attractive. (They are hardly unique in this regard, to be sure.)

Some homocentrists will be pleased by Harrison's and Carruthers's contention that nonhuman animal suffering is fundamentally a myth. The two philosophers' arguments come at a time when many research scientists are mounting a counterattack on those who charge that their work with nonhumans is unethical. The articles in which their views were first presented appeared in journals of philosophy with very high reputations (indeed, Carruthers's piece was published by the journal with the top reputation in analytic philosophy in the world), and their influence is already spreading. Harrison's article has recently been excerpted in a popular anthology on nonhuman animal research.[51] Carruthers has expanded his views on nonhuman animals to book-length form (referring to his subjects as 'animals' rather than 'brutes'),[52] and he has begun to give invited lectures on the subject to varied audiences.[53] Defenders of factory farming, commercial hunting and trapping, and the use of nonhuman animals in product testing will likely also see these essays as contributions to their counterattacks. Both philosophers explicitly draw the obvious ethical consequences of their conclusions,

The Argument from Marginal Cases

Harrison only briefly—"Such causes as animal liberation may have to be rethought"[54]—and Carruthers at greater length. He expresses indignation at the charge that factory farming involves animal cruelty, terming this attack "morally objectionable" and going so far as to declare that we have a "moral imperative" to cease feeling sympathy for nonhuman animals.[55] In his 1992 book, he attacks not only "animal liberation" efforts but also any concern with *animal welfare,* judging even moderate concern to be "an irrelevance to be opposed rather than encouraged."[56] In addition to factory farming, Carruthers fully supports all manner of experimentation upon nonhuman animals, including testing of products acknowledged to be "trivial" (e.g., a new mascara blend). Carruthers, like many supporters of the commercial and academic use of nonhuman animals, refers to those who oppose these human enterprises as "animal lovers."[57] This phrase as commonly used is intended to have a patronizing, offensive ring ("brute lovers" would perhaps be worse). One cannot help but be reminded of the (alas, still sometimes used) epithet, "nigger lover," also employed to dismiss allegedly sentimental foolishness.

This position is quite consistent with the view that nonhuman animals are automata. It would indeed be absurdly misguided to devote time and energy to the equivalent of "typewriter rights." It is interesting that Carruthers devotes nearly 90 percent of his book, as opposed to his original article, to argumentation for dismissal of nonhuman moral standing *even if they could suffer.* He is much less successful here in drawing the conclusion that follows so evidently from the denial of nonhuman conscious experience. Briefly, he chooses a version of "contractualism" which excludes anyone who is not a highly autonomous rational agent from moral considerability. He argues that *such a theory is the most morally acceptable* because it coheres with the following allegedly "deeply embedded" attitude: "We find it intuitively abhorrent that the lives or sufferings of animals should be weighed against the lives or sufferings of human beings."[58] He then judges to be morally acceptable the view that nonhumans should continue to be used for product testing or the churning out of Chicken McNuggets, and so on, *even if the animals suffer and the products are trivial,* since important human interests in making a living and generating profits are at stake.[59] Why is such a view morally acceptable? Quite straightforwardly, because it follows from his version of contractualism, "the most acceptable framework for moral theory."[60] The reader will remember that the chief argument for the alleged moral acceptability of that framework was its coherence with the attitude that animal interests do not count in comparison with human interests—the very assumption made by the view above. As Steve Sapontzis has pointed out, we have here an example of "one of the tidiest circular arguments in the history of philosophy."[61]

If Harrison's or Carruthers's arguments against the possibility of non-human animal suffering succeed, however, the ethical implications are relatively clear without the "assistance" of any circular arguments. As we shall see, however, homocentrists who embrace this sort of argumentation do so at their own peril: *Very young and seriously mentally defective humans are denied sentience along with nonhumans.*[62] (I will return to this key point later.)

Thus, it is important on all counts to respond in as much detail as necessary to such philosophical argumentation. It is especially important that the response be rationally defensible. Otherwise, one is apt to be dismissed as a purely emotional anthropomorphic fantasizer (a.k.a. an "animal lover") when, for example, one objects to the rubbing of noxious substances into the eyes of immobilized, unanesthetized rabbits. I will argue that reason, not just emotion, severely undermines the denial of nonhuman animal suffering. Most of my time will be spent on Harrison's piece. Carruthers's article has already been ably attacked by philosophers Edward Johnson[63] and William Robinson,[64] so I will mostly confine myself to additional important problems with it. At the end of this discussion, it should be clear that these defenses of the nonhuman animal-as-machine model are no more successful than the one René Descartes proposed in the mid-seventeenth century. Homocentrists do their view no favors if they pursue this line of argumentation.

Harrison's Attack on Nonhuman Animal Suffering:
The Theological Context

Peter Harrison tries to turn the supporting evidence for the argument from analogy on its head. He argues that evolutionary theory actually undercuts the assumption that nonhumans can experience pain. He denies the relevance of the copiously documented similarities between human and nonhuman animals. Overall, he claims to be defending Descartes's conclusion without embracing the well-known difficulties of Descartes's metaphysics.

Harrison's overriding, explicit purpose in defending his thesis is theological. He believes that, while it is easy enough, allegedly, to reconcile human pain with the existence of a perfect God—such experiences are the price of free will and build character—nonhuman suffering (he assumes) cannot be explained in this way. Rejecting as "ad hoc" the theodicy proposing that fallen angels rather than God are responsible for natural evils, including nonhuman animal suffering,[65] Harrison embraces a version of Descartes's theodicy. According to that view, nonhuman animals are said to lack awareness of anything, including stimuli we find to be painful; thus, no experiences of theirs can be used as ammunition for the problem of evil. They are mindless bodies; humans are minds linked to bodies in this life. While accepting Descartes's conclusion, Harrison partially rejects the dualistic interactionism underpinning that conclusion. Apparently agreeing with Descartes's early critics that a nonphysical substance (mind) and a physical substance (body) could not directly affect each other, he amends the Cartesian position as Malebranche did, by proposing the theory of "occasionalism": "To work properly it [the Cartesian position] must assume God's activity in human beings, correlating bodily events (the flame burns my hand) with mental states (I feel pain). This 'occasionalism' is admittedly also ad hoc and mythological, but less so than attributing earthquakes, floods, volcanoes, disease and animal pain to demonic activity."[66]

In short, according to this view the flame that burns the hand, leading to nerve impulses that eventually reach the cortex, is not the cause of the pain: *God* sees to it that this "nonphysical" experience results. (Thus, ironically, part of the solution offered to the problem of evil is the proposal that the Almighty *directly* causes suffering!) Nonhuman animal suffering is literally explained away. (As we shall see, Harrison also must deny the existence of genuine suffering in very young children—a decided theological bonus). For those who do not share Harrison's religious presuppositions, it is important to note that the argumentation he goes on to give for his denial of nonhuman suffering can be cast in purely secular terms (in fact, the version of the article that has recently been anthologized is identical to the original *except* for Harrison's mentions of religion; all of these have been surgically excised).[67] In what

The Argument from Marginal Cases

follows, Harrison's theological views will be mentioned only when this is needed to shed light on his argument. My criticisms also do not presuppose the correctness of any one mind/body theory. (*Dualistic* mind/body theories interpret the mind as a nonphysical mental substance or states allied in some manner with physical bodies during life. Dualistic theories are quite varied: *Cartesian dualism,* often called "interactionism," holds that mind and body causally affect each other during life; *parallelistic* theories hold that nonphysical mental states and physical states are correlated but deny that any interaction occurs; *double aspect* theories maintain that nonphysical mental states and physical states are separate properties of the same substance; *occasionalism*—Harrison's view—holds that only God, not bodily states, can cause a mental state; *epiphenomenalism* proposes that mental states are causally inefficacious nonphysical by-products of a physical body; and *hypophenomenalism* maintains the opposite. *Materialistic* or *physicalistic* theories typically identify mental states with neural states.)

The argument Harrison gives to convince us that nonhuman animals are automata is, he warns us, not a "strict" argument against the existence of nonhuman animal pain, due to the fact that pain is essentially private,[68] but he does claim to make a plausible case for his contention. Let us now turn to his argument.

Harrison I: Why Nonhuman Animal Pain Does Not Exist

Harrison's argument can be summarized as follows:

1. Many kinds of pain could have no evolutionary value for nonhuman animals; quite the contrary. This includes frustration, anxiety, grief, and severe debilitating pain.
2. We know humans experience such pains (or that *we* do, at any rate!); we survive them because we are insulated by our cultures from the effects of natural selection.
3. Other, lesser pains would have no evolutionary value to nonhuman animals either, because:
   a. Nonhuman animals can make no choices. Survival-enhancing behavior can be determined without the "superfluous" experience of pain, as studies of reflex actions show.

b. The argument from analogy that leads us to believe otherwise is bad:

   (1) So-called pain behavior in nonhumans is no more than an adaptive response, as is shown by the different behaviors of, for instance, a wildebeest and a chimp in circumstances we would find painful.

   (2) The very minimal difference in physiology between humans and nonhuman animals has no bearing on pain: "It has long been recognized" (even by, for example, Aristotle, Spinoza, and Ryle) that pain is "associated with 'higher' faculties, the study of which is more properly psychological than physiological."[69]

c. Nonhuman animals could "learn" from experiences we would find painful, thus enhancing their survival chances, without having any conscious experiences at all, as is shown by studies of habituation in protozoa.

4. Humans experience lesser pains, as we know, not to ensure our survival (see 2), but to "free us from instinct" when we choose to endure or not endure pain.

In short, *all* pain is a complex phenomenon experienceable only by highly developed "conscious egos." Nonhuman animals lack the complexity required for consciousness.

The rationales for Harrison's major contentions will be discussed, followed by responses to those rationales.

The contention that evolutionary theory rules out severe, debilitating pain and "mental" pain such as anxiety, grief, frustration, etc., in nonhumans Harrison's first two premises rely on this contention. He makes this assertion on the simple ground that such pains *have no survival value.* In fact, pains of this kind often interfere with one's survival. Hence, "the canons of evolutionary dogma" do not permit the attribution of such experiences to nonhuman animals. Humans, on the other hand, do have such experiences, as one knows from one's own case. We have them despite their unhelpful consequences because we have "thwarted natural selection": human culture in general insulates us from the ravages of nature, keeping such painful experiences from threaten-

The Argument from Marginal Cases

ing human existence.[70] Thus, evolutionary theory is allegedly compatible with the existence of these experiences in humans but incompatible with their existence in nonhumans.

This contention is inadequately supported, for a number of reasons. First of all, Harrison misrepresents evolutionary theory. No evolutionary biologist would claim that every trait possessed by a typical member of a species has to have survival value. As Stephen Jay Gould puts it, "[the] imperfection of nature reveals evolution."[71] Colloquially speaking, a large part of inheritance is a crapshoot. Variation is due to mutations, which are copying errors in the genetic code, and most of these mutations are neither enormously helpful nor destructive. Individuals can survive and pass on their traits even if some of those traits are not particularly advantageous and might at times actually interfere with survival. As Niles Eldridge says, "[that] *some* of these biological mistakes may ultimately prove to be beneficial is all evolutionists have ever claimed."[72] It is *individuals* with their collection of more or less beneficial, neutral, and harmful traits who are subject to natural selection, not the individual traits themselves.[73] Harrison also does not consider the possibility that a trait may be harmful in some circumstances and beneficial in others (intelligence is one trait that comes to mind in this connection), or that it may be harmful in the short run but useful in the long run. For example, frustration might lead one to make beneficial changes in one's circumstances; grief is the consequence of caring, a trait that strengthens bonds with one's offspring; chronic pain may be destructive, but the mechanism responsible for it could be very constructive indeed in other circumstances.[74] Moreover, Harrison provides no independent grounds for thinking that nonhumans *cannot* experience grief, anxiety, frustration, or chronic pain. To Harrison, the behavior of a cat or dog who ceases to eat when a companion human or nonhuman dies must be inexplicable,[75] as would be the behavior of closely confined nonhumans in zoos, on farms, and in research laboratories. Even the most unsentimental nonhuman animal scientists are beginning to speak openly about such states in their subjects.[76] Porcine Stress Syndrome (PSS) and "mourning behavior" in tightly restrained sows are conditions identified and named by the pork industry itself. Psychologists whose research involves the induction of grief, anxiety, anguish, and psychosis in nonhumans would also disagree with Harrison.

The Argument from Marginal Cases

Harrison also gives us no good reason to believe that humans differ fundamentally from nonhumans in their experiences of "harmful" pains. No evidence whatever is given to support his contention that humans alone have escaped the strictures of natural selection. Did our forebears many hundreds of thousands of years ago have no such experiences? Or did they somehow "thwart" natural selection as modern humans allegedly have? Presently, one might say that in *some* societies medical care allows us to save those who would otherwise die before being able to reproduce, but this has only been so for a short while in human history, and not universally so even then. In many cultures, discrimination against and even killing of the handicapped has been more the rule than the exception. It is also simply false to say that debilitating pain, depression, anxiety, and so forth do not threaten *our* survival. Stress-related severe illnesses, cancer included, not to mention suicide, indicate otherwise. Harrison even quotes, *to support his own view,* a researcher's claim that chronic human pain interferes with human survival.[77] By his own argument above, employed against the possibility of such experiences in nonhumans, humans also should not be capable of them. If he were to reply that the human species as a whole is able to continue despite these individual deaths because most of us do not succumb to these very negative pains or are able to replace our deaths with the lives of offspring, why could this not also be true of nonhumans? Contrary to Harrison, evolutionary biologists see continuity rather than discontinuity between nonhumans and humans. Allan C. Wilson argues that "the brain of mammals and birds" can itself drive evolution by allowing members of a species to begin interacting with a habitat in new ways, ways that themselves expose members of the species to new selection procedures, leading to the perpetuation of individuals with different traits.[78] Wilson is hardly alone in attributing ingenuity, creativity, and intelligence to nonhumans.[79] Why should not "negative" traits also be shared by humans and nonhumans?

In short, Harrison has not shown that evolutionary theory supports his view that only humans could experience seriously harmful pain (premises 1 and 2). Instead, there is good reason to believe otherwise.

The contention that "lesser" pains would also have no evolutionary value for nonhumans Having rejected the view that nonhumans are capable of complex, counterproductive sorts of pain experiences, Harrison goes on to consider the claim that the ability to experience simple, useful pains would confer an adaptive advantage on nonhuman animals. He rejects this claim as well (premise 3 above), primarily on the grounds that the point of such a mechanism would be to allow the animal to make survival-enhancing *choices*. Since, in Harrison's view, no nonhuman is capable of making a choice, such a mechanism would be gratuitous at best: "If no 'choice' is involved in animal behavior, why should they suffer pain—to *compel* them to behave in certain ways? No, for surely their behavior is determined in a way that does not require the superfluous promptings of pain."[80]

This stage of Harrison's argument (premise 3a) is faulty for at least two reasons. First, he relies on the undefended assumption that the capacity to choose is incompatible with the deterministic thesis that all behavior is caused by events that are in turn caused, and so on. The classic problem faced by such a view is how to construe an *uncaused* choice in a meaningful way, not merely as an inexplicable, random event.[81] If we reject the view that choice and causation are incompatible (i.e., the view that all causation must be compulsion), it makes perfectly good sense to interpret pain as part of the causal sequence leading to a wolf cub's refusal to play with the next porcupine in her path. Why should the experience of pain be "superfluous" in this series of events? I can fathom but one reason for such a claim: *Harrison seems to be assuming that conscious experiences can have no role in nonhuman animal behavior.* Pain would be unnecessary because, allegedly, the nonhuman animal simply responds, puppetlike, to the external forces acting upon her.[82] Pain in these circumstances would not be survival enhancing. Yet, this is the very thesis that Harrison is trying to persuade us to accept: *the thesis that animals are machines.* He can hardly convince us of this thesis by appealing to it in his premises! This leads to the second and related major problem with Harrison's line of argumentation here. He simply assumes without argument that only humans can make choices. Since considerable respectable evidence to the contrary has been amassed by ethologists,[83] Harrison should at least address that body of information.[84]

Instead, Harrison now turns to the argument from analogy, rightly recognizing that it seems to provide powerful support for the contention that animals can experience at least simple pains. He rejects it for two reasons. First of all (premise 3b-1), he judges it to be scientifically unsupported fanciful thinking: "we tend to presume that certain animal behaviors are expressions of pain—an internal state—whereas they should properly be construed as adaptive behaviors which probably have some social significance."[85] Harrison asks us to consider a wildebeest being killed by wild dogs and a chimpanzee with a thorn in his foot. The chimpanzee screams pitiously, "as if in pain," but the wildebeest makes no outcry.[86] The chimpanzee behaves as we expect, the wildebeest does not, but each is responding in a generally "adaptive" way: it is to chimpanzees' advantage in thorny situations to get aid; it is not to wildebeests' advantage to expose the rest of the herd to predators. Neither, Harrison assumes, is really experiencing pain; they are simply doing evolution's bidding.

This is not a convincing attack on the argument from analogy. Harrison's claim that nonhuman animal behaviors are adaptive rather than expressions of pain is a clear instance of the fallacy of false dilemma. Behaviors can be expressions of pain *and* have adaptive significance. Harrison thinks not, presumably because he appears to believe that his wildebeest-chimpanzee example shows (a) the wildebeest experiences no pain and (b) there is no reason to think that chimpanzees differ from wildebeests in this regard. He considers the possibility that both might be experiencing pain, but turns it into a "straw possibility" by caricaturing that position. He describes the belief that the chimpanzee is being an oversensitive coward whereas the wildebeest is stoically enduring agony as "crudely anthropomorphic."[87] This may be so, but it does not show the belief that the two are expressing their pain *differently* to be anthropomorphic. We must indeed guard against using the argument from analogy in a simplistic way, but it is Harrison who is guilty of doing this here, not those who believe that nonhumans can experience pain. In fact, Rollin has argued that those who deny that nonhumans could be experiencing pain if they do not behave *exactly as we do* are the ones guilty of anthropomorphism.[88]

The view that vertebrate nonhuman animals can experience pain is consonant with the neurophysiological similarity of human and nonhuman species—a similarity Harrison fully concedes[89]—and with evolutionary theory. Humans generally yell, just as our close cousins the chimpanzees do, when we get large thorns in our appendages. We also happen to be experiencing pain when we do this; is it anthropomorphic to believe that chimpanzees do too? As for the wildebeest, who possesses the same nervous system that is linked to pain perception in *our* case, behavior that does not endanger the rest of the herd obviously does have an adaptive advantage; this is compatible with the suffering of the animal. There is yet another alternative. Humans have reported that *sometimes,* at times of great physical trauma, physical damage that one would expect to cause excruciating pain is somehow suspended. Later, if one survives the trauma, the pain comes roaring in. This phenomenon is known as "stress-induced analgesia." [90] A response of this kind would be advantageous, not only to the individual who is momentarily spared agony, who may then be able to concentrate on fighting for life or at least not die instantly of shock, but to the species as a whole. *Perhaps* the wildebeest, and others in similar circumstances, are being naturally anesthetized. While we can hope that this is so, such a possibility must remain speculative at this point.[91] Note, however, that this interpretation of the wildebeest's behavior is fully compatible with the argument from analogy: it grows out of human reports, is in line with our similar physiologies, and actually contradicts Harrison's claim that only humans are capable of pain perception (and hence of being anesthetized). Harrison has not shown his machine model of nonhuman animal behavior to be more plausible than either the suffering or the stress-induced analgesia hypotheses.

On the alleged disproportion between physical and mental worlds   At this point, it is highly relevant to consider some new arguments on Harrison's part. Since writing his article, Harrison has fashioned a general response to the criticism that he ignores the importance of the striking similarities between human and nonhuman mammalian physiology, especially the physiology of the much maligned chimpanzee mentioned above. He now claims that there is "no proportionality between physical and mental worlds." [92] He uses chimpanzees to illustrate his contention, noting that these closest of our physical relatives, who are 98.4 percent genetically similar to us and whose brains are so like ours, have not begun to equal human accomplishments: "There is in the animal world nothing to compare with the products of the conscious mind." He

The Argument from Marginal Cases

dismisses chimpanzees' ability to carry on simple conversations in sign language: after all, he observes, these communications would never be confused with Shakespeare's creations!

Does the fact that nonhuman animals have not created art works "98.4 percent" as good as our own show that there is *no* correlation between brain development and mental states, as Harrison would have it? Hardly! Contrary to his assertion that there are only "very small brain differences" between human and chimpanzee brains, modern humans' brains are *340 percent larger* than those of chimpanzees whose body sizes are roughly comparable to ours. The chimpanzee brain is almost as large as the brain of *Australopithecus,* members (as far as we know) of the first hominid genus.[93] One cannot expect *Hamlet* from a human-sized being with a 400 g brain (the vast majority of those of us with 1350 g brains could never manage it either).[94] We also know of no Australopithecine bards (if there were any, they failed to record their soliloquies); it does not follow from this that they were not *conscious.* In fact, there is excellent evidence that these ancient forebears used stone tools.[95] Not coincidentally, chimpanzees, who according to genetic evidence have been diverging from hominids for about five million years, also are known to fashion and use tools (I will have more to say on this point later). Contrary to Harrison, the correlation between relative brain size/structure and evidence of intelligence is just what one would expect.

Other mental states also have their physical correlates, including *pain.* PET scans of humans have revealed three different areas of the brain that are operative during painful experiences.[96] Much research now indicates that higher and lower thresholds of pain are related to *specific neural structures and activity.*[97] Moreover, autopsies of disease- and drug-free humans who had killed themselves after suffering from chronic pain and depression indicate that they had abnormal levels of certain brain chemicals as well as abnormalities in their opiate receptors. Researchers doing this latter study note that nonhuman animal experiments in which the subjects were exposed to high levels of stress and pain-producing stimuli (not just to "stress" and "pain"), resulting in dysfunctionality and often death, indicated that *the same brain abnormalities* were present.[98] Contrary to Harrison, we do not find a wild disproportion between physical states and mental states: quite the opposite. All of these findings, of course, are compatible with dualistic as well as materialistic theories

The Argument from Marginal Cases

of mind and body, and they are thoroughly in tune with evolutionary theory.

Harrison, however, after arguing extensively in his article that evolutionary theory counts *against* the existence of nonhuman consciousness, now claims that relating evolutionary theory to the emergence and development of mental states is "beyond the bounds of evolutionary theory," because "it is behaviours, not mental states, which adapt, and it is only physical entities which can be the subjects of natural selection."[99] This would come as quite a surprise to all the evolutionary biologists (Allan Wilson and Stephen Gould among them) who link natural selection to the development of intelligence, among many other mental traits. Harrison's claim, of course, presupposes that materialism must be false; anyone not already convinced of this will hardly be impressed. But, most importantly, even many dualists would find his claim to be highly misleading at best. *However* mind or mental states may be "connected" to the body, dualists hold that mental and physical states form some sort of unit during earthly life. What happens to the body is not unrelated to the mind or one's mental states. Interactionists have no problem with evolutionary processes' being correlated with mental changes; nor do epiphenomenalists or double-aspect theorists. Even parallelists could have no objection to increased mental complexity accompanying increased nervous system complexity; hypophenomenalists such as Schopenhauer, who believe that the mind drives the development of the physical world, would positively embrace the notion.[100] Only followers of *one* form of dualism could unequivocally accept Harrison's claim that mental states do not change in conjunction with the physical processes of evolution: occasionalists. If God is called upon to see to it that the appropriate mental states, whatever those are, occur in humans on particular occasions, we can see why there need be no mental parallel to the physical world. God is free to fashion any miracle that God chooses to fashion. Clearly, Harrison, an occasionalist, cannot use this argument to buttress his own position! The overwhelming evidence of correlations between "the mental and physical worlds" gives us independent grounds for rejecting Harrison's claims.

The psychological interpretation of pain   Let us now return to Harrison's original article for the launch of his second attack on the argument from analogy (premise 3b-[2]). A close look at pain perception, he argues, will show that physiological similarities between human and nonhuman nervous systems are for the most part irrelevant to an understanding of that phenomenon. He cites some twentieth-century psychological research to buttress his view that "pain is associated with 'higher' faculties, the study of which is more properly psychological than physiological."[101] He then leaps to the conclusion that pain is in large part a psychological phenomenon, joins it to the premise that psychological factors do not operate in nonhumans, and asserts that "[a]ll human experiences of pain, I have argued, are functions of our distinctive consciousness, and thus *cannot be shared* by our furry friends."[102] Harrison claims to be eschewing Cartesian dualism in drawing this overall conclusion: he holds that we, unlike him, commonly assume that nonhumans experience pain because we associate physical pain with the *body* and more complex pains such as frustration, anxiety, and so on with the *mind;* thus the common view is (supposedly) that nonhumans are capable of the former but not the latter.

This won't do. Despite his disclaimer, Harrison is the one who appears to cling to Cartesian dualism, construing *all* pain as part of the mind *rather than* the body. He provides no evidence sufficient to establish this sweeping conclusion (eminent as Aristotle, Spinoza, and Ryle were, they have been known to be wrong, and the psychological studies he cites from the 1950s are either thoroughly outdated by current research[103] or irrelevant to the dismissal of physiology in favor of psychology). As mentioned above, recent neurological research shows that Harrison is mistaken in assuming that individuals with the same neural structures and processes can apparently have very different pain thresholds.

Of course, no one these days denies that beliefs and emotions can affect pain perception. Clearly, it does not follow from this that pain is not also a sensation. Moreover, Harrison does not address the evidence that nonhumans apparently can also be affected by psychological factors when they are in situations we would regard as painful in our own cases (e.g., as is the case for humans, companion nonhuman animals show less "distress" when ill if they are treated kindly rather than coldly and clinically).[104] Once again, physiological similarities between humans and some nonhumans can explain these similar behaviors. One of the areas of the brain active during painful stimulation is part of

The Argument from Marginal Cases

the limbic system, often described as "the seat of emotions."[105] It is also known as "the *paleomammalian* brain": as the name suggests, this structure is shared by all mammals.[106] Note that parts of the limbic system become active in *all mammals* when stimuli we call painful are present.[107] As a pain researcher notes, "[p]ain is a perception colored by experience and particularly by emotions."[108] It is no wonder that many nonhumans as well as humans behave exactly as if their experiences are "colored" in these ways.

One final summary comment is in order. Harrison's use of a psychological interpretation of pain to rule out painful experiences in nonhumans is quite simply question begging: Pain is a state of the psyche rather than a sensation (a false dilemma); nonhuman animals have no psyches to speak of (the question at issue); thus nonhuman animals experience no pain. They are machines because they are machines.

Surviving and "learning" without pain   Finally, in his attempt to show that a pain mechanism would provide no evolutionary advantage to nonhumans, Harrison tries to show that they could "learn" from experiences that would cause pain to us without their being conscious at all (premises 3c, 3a). Harrison first argues that the experience of pain is "superfluous" for appropriate, survival-enhancing behavior. He appeals to facts about reflexes: when we touch a very hot surface, we instantly, *reflexively,* withdraw; the experience of pain comes *after* the withdrawal, so the experience has not caused us to act. Harrison believes this shows that conscious awareness of pain is unnecessary in evolutionary terms.[109] (He recognizes that this poses a puzzle for the existence of *human* pain. His way of trying to resolve that puzzle will be discussed below.)

Harrison himself seems to recognize the inadequacy of the reflexive model, for he cautions us that he is not claiming that all nonhuman animal behavior in "painful" circumstances is of this type.[110] In fact, rather little nonhuman animal behavior can be explained in terms of reflexes. Withdrawing from a flame is indeed a reflex action rather than a consciously motivated response to pain, but *avoiding the flame the next time* is another matter. Nonhumans are at least as likely as humans to avoid situations of this kind after their initial occurrence. This *learning* can hardly be construed as reflex action, and it is difficult to see how it would occur if a painful experience had no part in the prior incident.

The Argument from Marginal Cases

In one's own case, pain seems to be highly instructive, as humans who lack the pain mechanism discover (provided they live long enough to arrive at that realization). Nonhumans do not behave as if they could never experience pain; they behave as if they learn from it. As Harrison himself admits, nonhumans are used in pain research and can be, as he puts it, "conditioned by 'pain.'"[111]

To support his contention that nonhumans can survive quite well without any experiences, including painful ones, Harrison now gives us an illustration of learning without consciousness. Appealing to research on protozoa, he cites a study in which these presumably nonconscious one-celled beings exhibited habituation to a repeated stimulus.[112] Clearly, he thinks, this shows that learning ("learning"?) does not require consciousness.[113] Yet this sort of response by a one-celled organism bears no relation to a wolf's refusal to tangle with her second porcupine, a dog's cowering from a human who has beaten him but once before, or a goat's avoidance of an electrified fence that once gave her a shock. These are not acts of blind habituation. Once again, Harrison seems to recognize the weakness of his argument, claiming not to be saying that all nonhuman animal learning is like protozoan habituation.[114] Unfortunately, he neglects to give us more adequate models of the ways in which nonhuman animals seem to learn in circumstances we would term "painful."[115] Wolves and goats are a far cry from protozoa.

In reply to my earlier version of these criticisms of Harrison's illustrations, he has chosen to quote a physiologist rather than "multiplying examples beyond necessity."[116] The physiologist claims that the neural changes involved in memory and learning are simple and require no assumption of consciousness in nonhumans. Abundant research, however, shows that the neural mechanisms involved in short- and long-term memory and learning in humans are anticipated in nonhuman animals, especially the more complex ones.[117] Is it also not necessary to postulate consciousness in *humans?* (I must add that I find it a bit odd for an occasionalist, according to whom each human mental state is a miracle wrought by God, to regard the hypothesis that nonhuman animals are conscious as "superfluous." Surely Occam's razor[118] is double-edged!)

Harrison, therefore, has not shown that the capacity to experience pain would have no evolutionary advantage for nonhumans. What of the fact that humans, who have also evolved, do experience pain? Harrison turns to this question in his premise 4.

The Argument from Marginal Cases

The explanation of human pain "Why do we feel pain if animals do not?" asks Harrison.[119] He makes no attempt to relate the capacity for pain to an evolutionary advantage for humans, despite his admission that humans who lack the capacity are not long for this world.[120] Of course, it would be difficult for him to argue that the experience gives humans an adaptive advantage when he believes he has shown that it provides no such advantage to nonhumans. Moreover, his contention that humans are not subject to natural selection pressures (premise 2) would be in direct contradiction to such an attempted explanation. The explanation he does provide is rather curious. He holds that humans, unlike nonhumans, are capable of freedom of choice, and pain allegedly enables us to act deliberately rather than instinctively. Harrison believes that the capacity for pain is a necessary condition for freedom of the will: "What is distinctive about the human race is our ability to choose . . . We are free, in painful situations, to damage our bodies if we believe that there is a higher priority . . . Pain frees us from the compulsion of acting instinctively; it issues harsh warnings, but they are warnings which may be ignored. It is our capacity for pain which has given rise to those uniquely human attributes of courage, resignation, self-control, perseverance, endurance, and their opposites, and it is significant that we reserve these terms for ourselves . . . Free will is at the high cost of suffering, but it is a suffering which is rightly restricted to the human realm."[121]

This is a very puzzling argument. First of all, pain seems to be more a hindrance than a help to choice making as Harrison conceives it. Wouldn't it be a great deal easier to defy "instinct" if we were not subject to pain? We normally act to *avoid* being burned, stabbed, kicked, and so on, *just as many nonhumans do*. (In the world as it has developed this helps us one and all to survive, but this line of argument is not open to Harrison, as we saw above.) Now, I do not claim that such avoidance behavior is *unfree* (unlike Harrison, I do not think that freedom and causation are incompatible), but Harrison is reaching for a concept of freedom that is unique to human behavior. He has not shown us how pain "frees us [in his sense] from the compulsion of instinct."

Harrison might reply that only humans can act *despite* pain; that is, we are uniquely capable of courage, endurance, perseverance, and so forth. This is freedom in the highest sense, one might hold, the putting of other considerations over our own well-being. Without pain, Harrison could say, we have no barometer of well-being, and terms like 'courageous' become empty (as do terms like 'cowardly'). Nonhumans, however, sometimes behave *as if* they too defy pain. When we behave in these ways, we garner moral credit for ourselves; when they do, Harrison regards them as machines. He is not the only one to engage in double-standard thinking here: a human mother who attacks an armed criminal threatening her children, risking injury and death, is "heroic" and "courageous"; a harp seal mother who charges a seal hunter, finally throwing herself across her pup, taking the skull-shattering bashing intended for her offspring, is "just acting instinctively"![122] Harrison may take it for granted that we reserve praiseworthy terminology for ourselves, but it is far from clear that this is justified.[123]

Why, indeed, should humans be able to deliberately flout their own well-being and nonhumans be incapable of doing such a thing? What naturalistic explanation could account for such an alleged difference? Certainly, deliberate action requires some intelligence, but as Harrison concedes in a footnote,[124] nonhumans can display high degrees of intelligence too (even if Shakespeare is beyond them). Human children and some brain-damaged humans can also act in self-sacrificial ways, and their intellectual development may not differ significantly from the corresponding capacities of some nonhumans. I strongly suspect that Harrison has no naturalistic explanation of the difference he (and many others) believes to obtain between human and nonhuman behaviors. The language in his remark that "[f]ree will is at the high cost of suffering, but it is a suffering which is rightly restricted to the human realm" is redolent of a theological explanation. Harrison, remember, is grappling with and trying to defeat the argument from evil against the existence of God. As he sees it, human suffering *must* be good for us, make us better persons; since he seems to take for granted that nonhumans are not capable of such betterment, he finds it necessary to deny that they suffer at all. Those without Harrison's theological presuppositions will be left unconvinced by such argumentation.[125]

Finally, it is not difficult to conceive of a being who could make choices—including morally praiseworthy choices—without ever experiencing pain; God would be an outstanding case in point. Nor need we reach so high or so controversially for an example: surely Harrison would not claim that those few humans who lack the pain mechanism are unable to make choices.

The Argument from Marginal Cases

Thus Harrison has failed on all counts in his attempt to show that the experience of pain is a necessary condition for an allegedly unique human ability to make choices. Premise 4 has failed just as resoundingly as premises 1–3. Harrison's overall argument consists of a series of inadequately supported statements, hasty generalizations, and question-begging assumptions. The assumptions that nonhumans cannot (a) make choices, (b) consciously learn, or (c) have even undeveloped psyches already portray them as machines. Humans, by contrast, are portrayed as free, uniquely insulated from natural selection, potentially magnificent, brave, virtuous beings. Seldom since the days of Descartes has the deck been stacked so high against nonhumans.

Perhaps Harrison realizes that his argument is unconvincing. The second major part of his article now takes a stunning turn: *he appears to concede that nonhumans can experience pain, but denies that this pain could be significant.*

Harrison II: Why Nonhuman Animal Pain Is Insignificant

Harrison begins by providing us with thought experiments to help us imagine what it would be like to act as if one is in pain in response to stimuli that we normally find painful and "yet not feel pain." [126] However, the examples he goes on to sketch are really meant to support the conclusion that any pain felt by a nonhuman is experientially *and* morally insignificant. Long before Harrison's day, Descartes also appeared to be running both these lines simultaneously. Although he assured us that nonhumans could only be automata, he also claimed that they were capable of *sensation*.[127] Occasionally, an ambiguity hides the contradiction (e.g., Harrison's assertion that "animals do not experience pain as we do"),[128] but a contradiction it nevertheless is.

Harrison asks us to imagine three cases: a man who has violent nightmares that he never remembers, a drug that immobilizes one without anesthetic and makes one forget any pain that occurred under its influence, and our inability to remember any pain suffered as infants. The common thread in these cases is the inability to recall pain. Surely, Harrison presses, such experiences must be insignificant. Only experiences that we can sort in with our other experiences can be "owned" by us.[129]

However "insignificant" these allegedly unsorted experiences are, Harrison makes it plain that they are *painful*. "I assume, as a baby, that

The Argument from Marginal Cases

I had many painful experiences," he observes, adding that "we regard neonatal pain as less significant than pain which is experienced later in life."[130] The "nasty nightmares" of the forgetful dreamer, the "pain of surgery" forgotten by the amnesiac, are likewise genuine but "unowned" cases of pain:[131] "I am not implying here that painful experiences which are forgotten were never painful to start with."[132] However, significant pain—*suffering*—requires "a continuity of consciousness" open only to older humans (unless, of course, one is greatly mentally impaired— a possibility conspicuously absent from his entire discussion, although it poses well-known problems for theodicy). Homocentrists should by now be thoroughly uncomfortable: the attack on nonhuman suffering has now been broadened in a manner most disconcerting to them.

Now Harrison makes the link between his thought experiments and nonhuman animals. Singling out the case of infant pain, he states that: "This last example is crucial, because it is during our earliest stages of development that our awareness is most like that of the higher animals . . . [t]he force of these examples should now be apparent. *The 'awareness' of animals is like that of the sleeping Jones, the amnesia-esthetized patient, the neonate.* They encounter painful stimuli, they react to them, but there is nothing to which that pain can belong. The animal, and, dare I say it, the neonate, have no self, and their pains are rather successive states which lack the connection which would render them 'painful experiences.'"[133] Of course, Harrison spoke of human babies' "painful experiences" just a few lines up in his article. Presumably, he should have said "disconnected fragments of pain" instead. I take it, however, that he still maintains that the babies and his other examples have genuine pain. "Higher" nonhumans, we have just been explicitly told, are *like infants:* they "have no self," are mere bundles of discrete sensations, are incapable of doing any such sorting, of remembering that *they have been in pain.*[134] Pain that is fleeting, inchoate, or forgotten is pain nevertheless. Nonhuman animals are therefore *not* said to be unconscious automata, contrary to what we have been told in the first part of Harrison's article.

I first charged Harrison with inconsistency in my "Arguing Away Suffering," referred to earlier. He has responded that I have misinterpreted the last section of his article; he stands by his earlier total rejection of the nonhuman animal pain hypothesis. He now says that his sentence

The Argument from Marginal Cases

"I am not implying here that painful experiences which are forgotten were never painful to start with" obviously refers to *human experience only*.[135] It is true that this sentence referred to his three examples of humans who have pain but then forget it, as I indicated above. But it is also undeniably the case that Harrison explicitly goes on to claim that "[t]he 'awareness' of animals is like that of the sleeping Jones, the amnesiaesthetized patient, the neonate," and so on. As the reader can see from the quotes above, Harrison's own words make the charge of inconsistency inescapable. In fact, it is hard to see what point there would have been in his writing this final section, developing the particular examples he has posed, if he had meant to continue denying that nonhumans can have pain of any kind.[136]

For now, however, let us set aside the problem of inconsistency. Suppose, despite his later denial, that Harrison really has argued for the inconsequentiality of nonhuman animal pain in the last section of his article (as his own words force us to believe). Does Harrison make a better case for nonhuman animal pain's being *insignificant* than he has been able to make for his contention that it is *nonexistent?* His theological and ethical conclusions would still follow from this weaker claim.

No, the apparent turnabout in Harrison's argumentation does little to improve support for those conclusions. Harrison is not able to make a plausible case for the triviality of nonhuman *or* certain human pains, as will now be shown. First, he does not begin to show that nonhumans have insufficient continuity of consciousness to remember pain. Once again, the double standard clicks into place: When I avoid the bully who beat me senseless yesterday, I am remembering my painful experience and acting appropriately; when Beauregard Beagle cowers away from the human who kicked him yesterday, he is gripped by unconscious instinct![137] Second, even if Harrison were correct in claiming that nonhumans and some humans cannot remember pain, this could hardly render insignificant the pain that *he admits* takes place. I could beat you mercilessly, then give you a drug that would remove all your memories of the beating. Plainly, your suffering would still be immense and I would be wronging you by inflicting it. As Rollin points out in discussing a similar view, if it were really true that nonhumans could remember no past pain, during a time of suffering they would be incapable of remembering pain's *absence;* thus they would be trapped in

The Argument from Marginal Cases

an agonizing, unending present.[138] How could one be justified in focusing on the beings they will *become* in the future, when, as Harrison has it, they will have forgotten, rather than on the beings who are suffering right now? Surely one owes more to someone who is suffering than to someone who is oblivious to suffering, *especially* if we are ourselves inflicting the pain!

It is now necessary to speak for human infants, who have been tarred with the same brush applied to nonhumans. The degree to which infants have continuity of consciousness is debatable: their nervous systems are less well developed than the nervous systems of adult mammals. Still, the parts of the nervous system linked to pain perception are all functional. All the neurophysiological equipment necessary for pain perception in humans (and for vertebrates in general) is present in those humans well before birth, at twenty-five to twenty-six weeks after conception. (This also holds for many nonhumans during the last trimester of their gestation.)[139] Although Harrison asserts that "we regard neonatal pain as less significant than pain which is experienced later in life,"[140] we have excellent reason to believe that this pain can be very significant indeed. For many years, in fact, doctors assumed that infants felt little or no pain, or at least no serious pain, even during major surgery, which was routinely performed without anesthesia or (more recently) with only light anesthesia.[141] Neurologists no longer believe this to be the case. Carefully controlled studies have shown that human neonates who are deeply anesthetized during surgery have greatly reduced levels of hormones associated with stress in their blood afterwards, cry less in the days after the operation, and, most importantly, have a much better chance of surviving than traditionally treated infants. Even infants undergoing a relatively minor operation like circumcision show benefits from local anesthesia: they cry much less during and after the procedure and have lower levels of stress hormones than their unanesthetized counterparts.[142] In fact, pain researchers now think that babies and very young children may experience *more* pain than adults, because a "damping" mechanism that helps to cut down on the severity of pain experiences does not develop until later.[143] Only those who believe that mind and body are hermetically sealed compartments could think that physiology and appropriate behavior (e.g., crying) need have nothing to do with suffering. Being unable to verbalize one's pain makes it more

The Argument from Marginal Cases

likely that one's pain will be ignored or disavowed; this has been just as true for humans as it has been for nonhumans. Luckily, it does seem to be true that we are less able to remember pain occurring early in life than pain occurring later. That does not make the initial experience any less agonizing, or make the infliction of such pain any more permissible.

Thus, Harrison has failed to show that nonhuman (and human neonate) pain is insignificant, just as he earlier failed to show that no such pain exists. Whichever half of the contradiction one seizes, one is not rationally persuaded. Harrison provides no support whatever for his key claims about the distinction between humans (only some of them!) and nonhumans, namely, that only humans are not subject to the strictures of natural selection, are free, and possess continuity of consciousness. (How it is possible for nonhumans to be intelligent, creative, and even learn American Sign Language, as we have seen him admit in a footnote but not in his text, *without* a highly complex integrated consciousness is an impenetrable mystery.) Harrison is also utterly unable to show that this concatenation of allegedly unique qualities restricts suffering to normal adult humans. Opponents of the argument from evil will have to look elsewhere for a dissolution of nonhuman suffering; so will opponents of the ascription of moral status to nonhumans. Let us now turn to another participant in the neo-Cartesian revival.

Carruthers's Attack on Nonhuman Suffering

Peter Carruthers has his differences with René Descartes's vision of the *human* mind,[144] but he clearly subscribes to Descartes's machine model of nonhumans. Like Descartes, he claims to show that nonhumans— or "brutes," as he initially preferred to call them—cannot suffer. Unlike Harrison, he never wavers from this contention. Note, however, some potentially confusing terminology. He does ascribe "pain experiences" to nonhumans, but he denies that a "feeling" component is logically linked to the concept of *experience*.[145] For those of us who find the concept of an experience without a feeling component to be self-contradictory, Carruthers suggests we recast his conclusion in our own language: he is arguing for the nonexistence of pain experiences (*feelings* of pain)—or, in fact, *any* experiences—in nonhumans. Similarly, confusion should be avoided about his use of "consciousness" in reference to

The Argument from Marginal Cases

nonhuman animals. While Carruthers says in his book that these animals are sometimes "conscious," having sensations, beliefs, and desires,[146] *he doe not think that they ever feel anything*. To put it in his terminology, all their "experiences" are "unconscious." Presumably, they are "conscious" of heat in the way the heat-seeking missile is; any "beliefs" and "desires" must merely be biological programming, not dispositions to have certain conscious feelings or thoughts. Having said earlier in his book that insects, seemingly unlike more complex nonhuman animals, are *clear cases* of "automata" who would not feel a thing if their wings were pulled off,[147] he concludes in chapter 8 that *all* are alike in being "not genuinely sentient." When he goes on in this same chapter to muse about how "consciousness might have evolved," [148] he is speaking only of human beings, in direct opposition to his use of the term 'conscious' earlier in the same chapter. In the discussion below, I will use the least misleading terminology possible to sketch Carruthers's views. First I will summarize his argument, then I will turn to a brief evaluation of it, mainly covering ground unplowed by Johnson's and Robinson's recent fine critiques of Carruthers's work.[149] Some strong criticisms by these two authors will also be noted.

Why nonhumans cannot suffer

1. Humans have two types of "experiences": *conscious* and *unconscious* (Carruthers's examples are thinking about dinner while driving home and being unable to recall driving when one arrives; daydreaming about the article you are working on while, all unawares, washing and stacking dishes as usual; correctly identifying objects "shown" to one but denying that one sees anything, as a "blindsighted" person does); unconscious experiences *"do not feel like anything."* [150]

2. The best analysis of the difference between our conscious and unconscious experiences is based on suggestions by Daniel Dennett: the former and not the latter are "available to conscious thought," where *conscious thought* is itself "available to be thought about in turn." [151]

3. It is obvious that "brutes" cannot think about their experiences by acts of thinking that can themselves be scrutinized.[152]

4. Although one might think that the very nature of *pain* is to demand our conscious awareness (in normal circumstances), to stimulate our withdrawal, this cannot be true of nonhumans, as argued above; the

The Argument from Marginal Cases

mechanism of avoidance could be in place unaccompanied by any feeling of pain.[153]

5. If nonhumans, as has been argued, cannot suffer, even though they act as if they do, they are due *no moral concern* on our part (e.g., it is "morally objectionable" to criticize factory farming, or indeed to feel *any sympathy* for nonhumans).[154]

Carruthers and Harrison wrote their original articles independently and had them published in the same year, preventing one from responding to the other. They have much in common, despite their very different approaches. Clearly, both Carruthers and Harrison think that nonhumans' allegedly impoverished mentalities block awareness of pain: they follow Descartes by intellectualizing suffering. It is possible, though, that Carruthers would attack the last part of Harrison's article —the argument that nonhuman pain is insignificant—as being based on the confusion of conscious with unconscious states. Carruthers might say that if (to put it in Harrison's language) there is no continuity of identity, no self, no "owning of the pain," then the nonhuman is not *aware* of being in pain. Now, putting it in Carruthers's terms, this would mean that the nonhuman has no *conscious* experience of pain: according to him, *nothing hurts, even though the nonhuman behaves as if something hurts.* As Carruthers has put it rather succinctly: "while animals *have* pains, they do not *feel* pains."[155] We persist in thinking that suffering is taking place, he could say, because the argument from analogy distracts us from the vital distinction between conscious experience and machinelike behavior. This way of recasting the last part of Harrison's attack on nonhuman suffering would at least dispel the contradiction between that part and his case for the nonexistence of nonhuman pain. Harrison's overall argumentation remains as unconvincing as ever, however. Is Carruthers any more successful in making his own case for the nonexistence of nonhuman suffering? No, as I shall argue below.

Carruthers's inability to account for nonhuman animal behavior Carruthers gives us no account of how nonhuman animals can behave as they do if *all* of their "experiences" are unconscious (or, to put it in the more natural way, if they have no experiences at all). Indeed, the very examples he uses to illustrate the conscious/unconscious distinction, drawn of necessity from human experience, make no sense whatever in a context where no conscious experience has ever occurred. His dramatic, psychologically documented example of "blindsightedness" (having no conscious experience of seeing anything in one part of the visual field because of lesions in the visual cortex, but being able to catch balls or identify objects shown to the damaged part of the field, etc.) involves people whose abilities to identify visual stimuli were developed by conscious experience before their accidents; indeed, they still consciously see and correctly respond when other parts of their visual cortex are stimulated.[156] The same holds for the far more common examples of driving or washing dishes without being aware that you are. Complex habitual actions can certainly occur without our being aware of them, but we had to be consciously aware of performing such actions *in the first place* in order to learn to do them. You cannot be a driver or a dishwasher without this initial attention. Moreover, if we sometimes do not pay attention to these actions any more, it is because we are *aware* of something else that distracts us from the task at hand. What would it be like to perform complex tasks, behave appropriately in changing circumstances, and so on, without ever having any conscious experiences at all? Without ever *feeling* anything?

Carruthers does not say so, but perhaps he would respond as Harrison has in a different context, representing nonhuman behavior as largely a matter of reflex and "hard-wiring," that is, of fixed responses to stimuli. However, as ethologists have shown, much nonhuman behavior is far too complex, varied, and apparently creative to represent in this simple mechanical way. I cannot resist giving a personal example here. My husband and I have two feline companions, Callisto and Ganymede. Since kittenhood, the two have found the nearest bed and crawled under the blanket upon being exposed to loud thunder, firecrackers, or frightening strangers. It is hard enough to imagine them doing this while feeling nothing, but consider the next development. Just recently, in these same frightening circumstances, Ganymede began *spontaneously* to run to the hall closet's sliding door, work it ajar with his paw, and climb into its dark recesses. Neither cat had ever done this before, and we certainly didn't encourage them to do so (our shoes are always so hairy afterwards). At first, Callisto would follow him in at those times. Now she opens the door herself, using a different maneuver: at half her brother's size, she cannot manage the task with one paw, so she flings herself to

The Argument from Marginal Cases

the floor, lies on her side, and uses *both* paws. Sometimes Ganymede runs up in the midst of this project and shoves the door ajar before she can finish; then they both scramble in. Neither of them tries to open the closet under nonfrightening circumstances. Callisto, at first a follower, soon began to go in even more often than her brother: she, always the more fearful (how else can one describe it?) of the two, breaks into the closet whenever someone rings the doorbell; he curiously (so it seems!) waits to greet the visitor at the top of the stairs. All of this behavior is explicable if one assumes that the cats are afraid, are consciously trying to gain reassurance, believe that the closet is a safe place, and are bright enough to learn how to force the closet door ajar. Moreover, neither is a "copy cat." How can we begin to understand what is going on if we assume that they *feel nothing at all?*

If Carruthers could not plausibly attribute much nonhuman animal behavior to "hard-wired" responses to stimuli, would he do better to employ a computer model for that behavior? Again, he does not discuss this, but it would be natural for him to make such a comparison. Sophisticated computers can do amazing things, as we briefly discussed before; they can even be "creative" and "learn," after a fashion. Yet, as artificial intelligence experts agree, even computers with the most advanced hardware and software cannot now plausibly be construed as conscious. The computer model of nonhuman animal behavior is, at least, considerably less simplistic than the stimulus-response model. Nevertheless, the model is extraordinarily far-fetched. We are required to believe that nonhumans are "programmed" in extremely sophisticated ways. Indeed, the programming would have to be light-years beyond our current achievements in artificial intelligence, for we have yet to create a computer that acts as conatively as a cat. Behavior that in us is indicative of desires, beliefs, goals, and emotions would all have to be artfully simulated. There is no reason to believe that evolution has taken such a disjointed course, reserving sentience for the likes of us alone. Of course, the Cosmic Computer Programmer could be at work here, designing flesh-and-blood machines, but reason abhors such a deux ex machina. Perhaps this is why Carruthers does not draw such a comparison.

The hypothesis of nonhuman animal conscious experience, by contrast, accounts very economically for their complex behaviors. Cognitive ethologist Donald Griffin argues that conscious beings have an evo-

The Argument from Marginal Cases

lutionary advantage, because they are able to plan, to deliberate, and to learn from their errors.[157] Philosopher Dennis Senchuk essentially agrees, carefully arguing that consciousness and intelligence are not restricted to human beings.[158] If *flexibility* is the hallmark of consciousness, as Senchuk contends, many nonhuman *and* human animals can be said to behave *exactly as if* they are conscious. Why not assume that they *are*? The consciousness hypothesis, in contrast to the "hard-wired automaton" hypothesis, does not jibe with evolutionary theory. Ironically, this hypothesis, unlike the stimulus-response and computer models of nonhuman animal behavior, actually makes sense of the contention that they can have *unconscious* experiences. As I write this chapter, I am seldom aware of the placement of my feet (except for now!); there seems to be too much to be concerned about at any given time to open one's awareness to everything one is sensing. Nonhuman animal behavior is consistent with the same phenomenon. A cat asleep on one's lap may be bombarded by a variety of sounds: music, cars passing outside, the washing machine chugging away in the basement, the turning of book pages. None of these aural stimuli seems to demand his attention. If your spouse opens a can in the kitchen, however, the cat's ears suddenly swivel in that direction. When his name is called by the person in the kitchen, the cat flies off one's lap in the direction of the kitchen, for all the world as if his conscious awareness has just become fully engaged. Next, let us consider an example that directly involves behavior we call "instinctive." Cats who see prey "candidates" that they have no hope of attacking engage in an interesting series of behaviors. A cat watching a bird perched just out of reach will focus hard on the delectable item; she chatters and swishes her tail back and forth rapidly. Is she consciously aware of all this activity in her nether region? We do not know, but she seems to have eyes only for the "meal on wings." Now, gently putting your unshod foot on the cat's tail results in behavior we would call "confused" if it occurred in a human. She stops chattering at the bird, looks around at you, tries to pull away her tail, and may meow sharply at you. The intent wide-eyed look is gone, replaced by what appears to be a very irritated one. Carruthers's descrition of the writer planning his paper while mechanically washing the dishes comes to mind. If a dish breaks, the content of one's awareness shifts; if someone immobilizes your tail while you are lusting after the unobtainable, you try to yank it

The Argument from Marginal Cases

loose. All of this human and nonhuman behavior makes excellent sense when we assume that conscious experience is not an item inexplicably reserved for glabrous bipedal primates.

Carruthers has an especially difficult time explaining how "pain-like" behavior in nonhumans is to be understood. It is hard to fathom how a nonhuman whose paw is stepped on can scream, race away, and hide while feeling absolutely nothing. The only explanation Carruthers gives of such behavior is an attempted extension of the blindsightedness phenomenon. He argues that it is in principle possible for a being to act conscious when he or she is not. However, with regard to *pain,* he admits that there are no known human cases of having pain without feeling it, and he himself points out that the pain mechanism—*a mechanism shared by many nonhumans*—cannot be truncated in the way that the visual cortex is in blindsightedness. He even states that: "There is an obvious reason for [the lack of evidence that humans can have pain without feeling it], since part of the function of pain is to intrude upon consciousness, in order that one may give one's full attention to taking evasive action." [159] This excellent logic leads one to think that many nonhumans also feel pain, but Carruthers resists the implication. He is plainly convinced that his analysis of the difference between conscious and nonconscious states has already shown that nonhumans can feel nothing. Let us turn, finally, to that analysis itself.

A problem with Carruthers's analysis of the conscious/unconscious distinction   The problem can be stated very briefly. Carruthers gives no convincing defense of his analysis of the distinction between conscious and unconscious "experiences." After rejecting Descartes's implausible version of the view that consciousness is "intrinsic," that is, logically unrelated to any other state, he adopts a *relational* theory of consciousness.[160] In order for an experience to be conscious, Carruthers holds, it must be related to at least one other state. Building on a view espoused by Daniel Dennett, he maintains that a conscious experience is an experience that can be consciously thought about ("is available to conscious thought").[161] In order to avoid explicating consciousness in terms of consciousness, Carruthers adds that to consciously think about an experience is to have a thought which can be thought about in turn ("a conscious act of thinking is itself an event that is available to be thought about in turn").[162] *Unconscious* "experience," by contrast, would lack this double layer of potential scrutiny. This relational model of conscious experience is, however, supremely implausible. Why should one have to be able to think about one's possible thoughts about one's experiences in order to have the experience—to *feel* something—in the first place? As Robinson points out, it is hard to see how merely "being able" to think about one's experience, and "being able" to think about this *potential* thought in turn, would result in a conscious experience on Carruthers's account.[163] It would be more reasonable to call this "potential consciousness." It seems that one ought to be actively thinking about an actual thought about one's experience in order to have a conscious experience. But how often does anyone do this? Are we on "automatic pilot" unless we are engaged in multilayered introspection?

Even if we were to accept Carruthers's "double potentiality" view, quite a few humans would not qualify for what he calls "genuine sentience." Let us pause to dwell on this fact, so disturbing to homocentrists. At the very end of his article, Carruthers admits (like Harrison) that his view implies that infants and very young children must have no conscious experiences, including painful ones. Carruthers might be surprised to know about recent psychological research indicating that normally developed children as old as *six* might not count as conscious in his terms (the children had great difficulty reflecting upon their experiences, and could not consistently recall any thoughts they might just have had about an experience).[164] Never mind that these and other far younger children are perfectly able to tell you who they are, to verbalize feelings, and so on; they just don't yet have a sophisticated enough cognitive apparatus for Carruthers to count them as conscious! Can child abuse be tantamount to typewriter abuse? Carruthers would have to reply "yes" and "no." He expresses no concern about the implication that very young humans cannot be hurt, noting only that mistreating them would nonetheless be wrong because one would risk damaging the persons they will become.[165] As Edward Johnson has rightly recognized, this suggests that it would be fine to roast them alive on a spit if we already know that they will not survive infancy.[166] Carruthers also takes no note of the fact that many permanently brain-damaged humans would also be automata in his view.[167] As we have seen, even quite typical adult humans may not be able at a given time to think about their

The Argument from Marginal Cases

(possible? actual?) thoughts about their experiences; for example, they might be so overwhelmed by having a car crush their legs that anything but pure sensation is precluded. According to Carruthers's view, this would have to mean that they had nothing to think about in the first place![168]

All in all, Carruthers's relational theory of consciousness has little to recommend it as an account of human consciousness. An intrinsic theory of consciousness need not commit one to Descartes's full-blown mind-body dualism. In an intrinsic theory, thoughts (actual or possible) about one's experiences, let alone thoughts about one's thoughts about one's experiences, are not required for conscious experience.[169] Such a view in effect returns our minds to us; it also leads us to attribute minds to many nonhumans. Other *relational* theories of consciousness also avoid the problems of Carruthers's account. If one employs Occam's razor to prune Carruthers's analysis, requiring merely that experiences be thought about in some sense in order to be conscious, it is no longer implausible to imagine that nonhumans (and many humans!) can "think things consciously to themselves."[170] As Johnson very rightly points out, one would think this implausible only if one requires thoughts to be expressible in a language, and Carruthers himself denies that such a requirement is necessary.[171] Why shouldn't the cat be aware that she is afraid during a thunderstorm and take deliberate steps to feel safer? Carruthers's account is far less believable than the hypothesis that this is exactly what is happening.

Thus, neither Harrison nor Carruthers has succeeded in resurrecting the Cartesian machine model of nonhuman animals. Given that model, actual nonhuman animal behavior requires a cosmic puppeteer; otherwise, it is a bottomless mystery. The real mystery here is how clever, sophisticated philosophers can lead themselves so thoroughly astray. The ad hominem fallacy is indeed to be avoided, but one cannot help wondering if Descartes and his modern counterparts would have argued as they did, had they not had such powerful incentives to deny nonhuman suffering. Support for vivisection (Descartes), animal-exploiting enterprises (Carruthers), and a wish to get God off the hook by denying the suffering of innocents (Harrison) all seem to play a role. Most important, an overarching vision of human superiority unites the three. Homocentrists share that vision, but they would do well to reject the sentience defense of their view, since it throws out the human baby with the bathwater.

Let us now turn to a classic defense of ethical homocentrism: the appeal to human intellectual superiority.

The Homocentric Appeal to Human Intelligence, Creativity, Communication, and Autonomy

If sentience does not distinguish humans from all other creatures, what other morally relevant characteristic could justify the moral elevation of humanity over other beings? Homocentrists often cite rationality, creativity, intelligence, language use, and autonomy. Aquinas believed that we were favored by God because we alone were made in God's intellectual image; Descartes held that beings with minds are all capable of expressing thoughts linguistically. Again, however, as others have pointed out, none of these characteristics serves to distinguish all humans from all nonhumans. For example, the claim that no nonhuman can possess *any degree* of the above characteristics is highly dubious. A very great deal has been said on this matter by ethologists and philosophers,[172] and I have already given some illustrations of their contentions, so I will confine myself here to just a few additional "elevating" examples of nonhuman behavior.

Many sentient nonhumans apparently have the ability to learn from past experience, to anticipate future events, to change their behavior in the face of changing circumstances, to carry out short-term plans, and to solve problems in a creative fashion. Bernard Rollin reports George Romanes's study of rats and mice, published in *Nature*. Romanes showed that rats and mice, when confronted with food-filled containers too narrow for their heads, stick their tails into those containers, then either lick off their own tails or exchange tail licks with companion rodents.[173] It is also known that some nonhumans use objects as tools when they cannot use their bodies to attain what they want. Benjamin and Lynette Hart, animal behaviorists, recently documented tool design and use by elephants.[174] During the hottest and most fly-ridden part of the day, elephants will take whatever materials are "trunky" and turn them into "fly-swatters." They will shorten and trim tree branches as needed, and

The Argument from Marginal Cases

sometimes keep the tool for reuse. Donald Griffin tells us that polar bears will throw large chunks of ice at the seals they pursue, that vultures use stones to break open ostrich eggs, and that herring gulls crack clams by dropping them onto hard surfaces, ignoring sandy beaches in favor of parking lots and rocky walls (they fly lower over the walls than over the hard-to-miss parking lot surface).[175] Griffin is careful to point out that tool-using behavior varies in its complexity and even in its occurrence from individual to individual within a species.[176] The same holds for human beings. This is further evidence for the nonmechanical, nonprogrammed nature of tool-using behaviors among nonhumans.

A number of examples of remarkable tool-using behavior on the part of monkeys and apes have also been documented.[177] Mungo, a captive capuchin monkey, escaped from the zoo by using a split-off branch in his enclosure as a crowbar, systematically working it back and forth to rip open the wire mesh fencing him in. Chimps have been seen using twigs to pick locks in zoos, and they have also been observed piling boxes up and climbing upon them to reach bananas hanging high above their heads. Jane Goodall observed chimpanzees actually *making* tools out of leaves and branches, much as the elephants observed by the Harts did. For example, they will trim and bend stalks into the right shapes for termite and honey extraction. They build sleeping platforms from leaves and branches, and have been seen using leaves as we do toilet paper. They use particularly substantial rocks to crack exceedingly tough panda nuts, wedging the nuts between two strong tree roots before cracking them open. Griffin writes that European explorers of the Ivory Coast, hearing the loud cracks resulting from this common procedure, were convinced that unknown human tribes must be working in the rain forest.[178]

One of the most impressive examples of chimpanzees using stones concerns a youngster, Kanzi, born in captivity who has received a great deal of scientific attention. Known chiefly for his linguistic prowess, to be mentioned later in this chapter, Kanzi has also spontaneously made stone tools from flint, as early hominids did millions of years ago.[179] Faced with a tightly bound box of bananas, he created "knife chips" from flint by banging it against concrete, then, cutting toward himself, severing the cord binding the box. No one showed Kanzi how to proceed at any stage. He has refined his technique in subsequent trials,

The Argument from Marginal Cases

using more precisely aimed blows. Indiana University awarded Kanzi a prize for advancing our study of the origin of technology (one hopes the currency was bananas).

Jane Goodall also observed complex, evolving social relationships that appear to be anything but mindless. So did Japanese zoologist M. Kawai, who conducted a similar long-term study of a troop of macaques on the small island of Koshima. He observed an innovative monkey, Imo, initiate the heretofore unknown taste-enhancing practices of washing experimenter-provided sweet potatoes and handfuls of grain in salty ocean water. Other members of the troop spontaneously followed suit, and food washing is now a tradition on Koshima.[180]

One is not as surprised, perhaps, to read about amazing behavior on the part of our fellow mammals and our even closer primate relatives. After all, we share 98.4 percent of our genetic structure with chimpanzees, and nearly as much with gorillas (97.9 percent).[181] Although other mammals such as rats and rabbits are not quite so closely related to humans, they too are strikingly similar to us in many ways, just as one would expect given the fact of evolution. It would be astonishing if these physical similarities were unrelated to mental similarities. Two psychobiologists have recently done experiments (at great cost to several rats and rabbits) that confirm the theory that memory formation is correlated with physical changes in the brain. The researchers were not surprised by their results, and are confident that they apply to humans, because "The cerebellums of all mammals are remarkably similar."[182] This helps to explain how a sea lion, in a set of very carefully designed experiments, can consistently demonstrate a grasp of the basic logical relations of equivalence and transitivity.[183] (I assure "math-phobic" students daunted by learning the deductive inference rule, *hypothetical syllogism* [if *p* then *q*, if *q* then *r*; therefore, if *p* then *r*], that they can surely do at least as well as a sea lion.) Moreover, a growing new body of research indicates that Broca's area, the part of the human brain linked to language acquisition, has a less developed counterpart in the brains of other primates. This is viewed as a direct challenge to linguist Noam Chomsky's view that the "deep structures" required for language are uniquely human.[184]

We have known for some time that mammals are able to respond appropriately to certain human words. Everyone who lives with a dog or

The Argument from Marginal Cases

cat knows this to be the case. (Our neighbor has resorted to spelling in a deadpan way: "You-know-who has to be put in the b-a-s-e-m-e-n-t now." It did not take long for Ruby the Labrador retriever to learn that she must flee at the sound of this, however. She will win no spelling bee, but her associative powers are impressive.) Careful observers of nonhuman behavior have also been able to show that many species consistently use different vocalizations to send different signals. Griffin documents the fact that African vervet monkeys have three different alarm calls for leopards, snakes, and eagles (one needs to go to different places to escape such predators); and rhesus monkeys have five different alarm calls, depending upon who is threatening them.[185] Dolphins *appear* to communicate with each other by means of complex patterns of squeaks and clicks, but we have not deciphered these "messages," if any. (Instead, we seem to have succeeded in teaching them two artificial languages, one visual and one acoustic. The dolphins respond correctly over 80 percent of the time to new combinations of familiar signals, such as "Go to the hoop on the surface and take it to the basket at the bottom of the tank"; "Go to the Frisbee to your right and take it to the surfboard."[186] I doubt if I could perform as well as the dolphins, even in my own language.) Many other cases of animal communication (if not yet "language") have been documented by scientists.[187]

Many continue to doubt, however, that any nonhuman can master the semantics (vocabulary) and syntax (rules for meaningful combination) that are the hallmark of true language. Are dogs, cats, and dolphins comprehending the meaning of 'basement,' 'walk,' 'milk,' and 'Frisbee,' or do they merely think that these are the sounds we make when we are about to offer or do something? Their behavior indicates that they have a good grasp of what that something is, in any event, and if this is not judged as good enough to count as vocabulary acquisition, it does seem to be good enough to count as intelligence.

The famous experiments aimed at teaching ASL (American Sign Language) or an artificial computer language to apes like Washoe, Lucy, Lana, Koko, and others convinced many, including previously skeptical experimenters, that some nonhumans are capable of mastering at least the rudiments of a genuine language. Some, notably Noam Chomsky and Herbert Terrace, remain unconvinced, but even they are impressed by the young pygmy chimp Kanzi: he seems to have spontaneously picked up the rudiments of a computer language while experimenters literally were not looking. They have continued to leave him to his own devices and are astonished by his facility with the language.[188] The apes who have participated in the ASL experiments also reportedly amaze human visitors who are fluent in the language of the deaf. One ASL specialist experienced in working with deaf children and who had never met a signing chimp went to apply for a job at Ellensburg, Washington; Washoe and a number of other signing chimps, including chimps who got their only initial "instruction" in ASL from other chimps, reside in a colony there with humans who observe their behavior. During the walk from his car to the secluded compound, the job applicant was suddenly met by a very large unaccompanied chimp, who proceeded to ask the petrified visitor who he was, volunteered that his name was Dar, and invited him to play hide-and-seek![189] Now, if the visitor had met a signing child instead, would he not have been justified in assuming that the child was using language? Are we wrong when we think the eighteen-month-old who consistently cries "baba!" when he sees his bottle, simultaneously reaching for it with eager hands, has learned that this is the word for the beloved object? Do we err when, after the baby says "car!" upon seeing cars on the street, in the driveway, and on television, but not when he sees his puppy, we assume that he understands the word? If we do not err here, are we not erring if we deny that nonhumans like Kanzi and Dar can do the same? Once again, we find ourselves unable to cite a human ability unshared by nonhumans.

Even those nonhumans rather more removed from us in evolutionary terms exhibit behavior that we would not hesitate to call "rational," "creative," and "intelligent" in a human being. Consider the honeyguide birds of Africa. Local people and researchers have long been fascinated with these birds: not strong enough to break open a beehive, they apparently lead other animals (including humans) to hidden hives, wait for the "leadees" to breach the hives, then move in to feast on the remaining honeycombs. Honeyguides have even been known to imitate the sounds of the animals they wish to attract to the hive. The trek to the hive may take several miles, and the birds frequently double back for laggards. Attempts have been made to reduce this apparently highly goal-directed behavior to mere mechanical responses, but none of these explanations accounts for the nuances of honeyguide behavior.[190] Con-

The Argument from Marginal Cases

sider too the remarkable behavior of the blue tits (chickadees) of World War II Swathling, England.[191] At that time, milk and cream were delivered directly to porches and doorsteps. Some residents began noticing that their bottles were being opened. Those who woke early to catch the thieves discovered that they were birds! A few blue tits, in dawn attacks, were puncturing the foil bottle caps and partaking freely of the contents. The practice was soon taken up by blue tits all over town, similar to the way in which sweet potato washing spread among the macaques of Koshima. Eventually, other villages from miles away were reporting rampant milk sipping by lid-pecking birds. The milk company tried every ploy it could think of to stop this. First, it advised its many complaining customers to put stones out, so that the deliverers could put one on each bottle every morning. This worked for a while (days) but soon angry residents were finding opened bottles, stones lying unhelpfully beside them. The milk deliverers were cleared of the charge of laziness by early-rising villagers, who saw that the birds were pecking at the stones until they fell off, then availing themselves of the milk and cream. Next, towels were draped over the bottles every morning. Once again, it seemed the blue tits were foiled, but not for long: discarded towels were soon found next to opened bottles. Mystified villagers discovered the tactic by catching the birds in the act: the blue tits were going into group formation and actually lifting the towels up in their beaks, removing them from the bottles, then pecking open the caps as usual. Finally, the milk company triumphed over the inventive (what other word applies?) birds by delivering milk in crates to (by now) several villages. Although the birds then flew into the open milk trucks to open uncrated bottles when they could, their raids, diverting as they probably were to the wartime English, were essentially over. However, studies in 1984 and 1990 have shown that chickadees will learn to obtain milk in the same way, if given the chance.[192] Having a "bird brain," apparently, is nothing to be ashamed about. (Irene Pepperberg of Northwestern University would agree. She has worked with an African gray parrot for eleven years. Alex is able to identify five different shapes, seven different colors, and numbers of items up to six. He can also tell you what the difference is between a blue and a green triangle.)[193]

Much of this information was not known in the days when René Descartes proclaimed that nonhuman animals were automata, although

The Argument from Marginal Cases

those who lived with dogs or cats would not have found Descartes's view plausible even then. Nonetheless, despite all the evidence gathered and all the argumentation done since 1637, some continue to express considerable skepticism about the possibility of nonhuman creativity, intelligence, and rationality. The Cartesian view that thought requires linguistic ability has been revived in a highly sophisticated way by R. G. Frey.[194] He denies that nonhuman animals can have desires (and thus that they can act purposefully) on the grounds that beliefs are required for desires and linguistic ability is required for beliefs (an ability he assumes nonhumans lack). This view has been skillfully refuted by others on a number of grounds,[195] and although Frey says "I am not persuaded by the adequacy" of the criticisms,[196] he has apparently not yet replied to them. I will not pursue Frey's neo-Cartesian view further here, except to make one observation. Those homocentrists who, like Descartes (but unlike Frey, as we shall later see), refuse to extend their skepticism about nonhuman mentality to human beings, would have us accept the following rather dubious contrast: A child who goes placidly on her first trip to the doctor but who screams and struggles upon being dragged back for her second shot has *beliefs* about what is in store for her and *desires* to stay home instead, but a cat who behaves in the same way in the very same circumstances is just mindlessly exercising her limbs and vocal cords!

Once again, it is difficult to avoid the conclusion that a double standard is being employed here. Those who deny that nonhumans can be persons, even in the least stringent sense of 'person,' frequently appear to be committing that fallacy. Loren Lomasky provides a case in point. He holds that the ability to *pursue projects* does not require a *high* degree of autonomy (in the sense that one can direct and redirect one's entire life).[197] Indeed, he believes that goal pursuit can be entirely unreflective, as can be the case in humans rigidly conditioned by their parents or community.[198] One would think, then, that some nonhumans could be included in the ranks of less autonomous "project pursuers" (the blue tits come to mind). But no: Lomasky flatly asserts that "[n]o animal is a project pursuer, a prospective project pursuer, or an erstwhile project pursuer."[199] On this basis, he denies that they can have rights. One wonders why even the most unthinking, "brainwashed" humans can be termed "project pursuers" (hence members of the moral com-

The Argument from Marginal Cases

munity, in Lomasky's view) when wolves coordinating a hunt, a chimp fashioning a straw from twigs to suck up termites, or birds outwitting humans to obtain access to bottled cream cannot. Behavior dismissed as "merely instinctive" when performed by nonhumans is described in cognitive terms when performed by humans.

We would do well to question the "instinct/intelligence" dichotomy, even apart from the commonly prejudicial application of these terms. Stephen Clark suggests, in fact, that what we call "practical intelligence" may have a basis in "instinct," and that "instinctive" behavior typically involves intelligence.[200] The nest-building bird must locate an appropriate site, find the relevant building materials, fit them together properly, and so on. Female plovers will typically defend their young by giving every appearance of having a broken wing, drawing potential predators away from the nest. One can argue that this is merely preprogrammed behavior with a decided evolutionary advantage, but the fact is that the birds must determine when such behavior is appropriate. Controlled studies with wild nesting plovers have shown that the defensive reaction occurs only when the intruder has displayed "dangerous" behavior; subsequent encounters with "dangerous" and nonthreatening individuals, who took the same path near the nest and employed the same neutral manner on that later occasion, elicited different responses.[201] The birds appeared to gauge the probability of danger by remembering past encounters and recognizing specific individuals.

Now consider another avian example. Mallard females "instinctively" lead their newly hatched young to the nearest body of water, where the family group will spend the first several weeks of life. There the ducklings become proficient at swimming and at feeding on the seeds and roots of aquatic plants, their preferred food, in an environment that offers reasonable opportunities for escape from predators. A mallard my husband and I know quite well—she voluntarily spends spring and summer in the wild area near our home—recently had a successful nesting. Quite predictably, she soon left the nest, taking her ten ducklings to a nearby creek. All was well, until a flash flood turned the docile creek into a raging "riverlet" overflowing its banks. The female led all of her ducklings to high ground, returning only the next day when the creek was once again navigable by small feet. Only a few days later, hard rains returned. Once more, she took the ducklings to higher ground, where

The Argument from Marginal Cases

they were able to forage for food in shallow puddles. Frequently the mother duck would crane her neck and look carefully around the relatively open area. After a few hours, she returned with her ten offspring to the more protected creek. To our surprise, we found them all huddled together on the bank beside the creek instead of swimming in the still turbulent waters. She waited half an hour, facing the water, then took the ducklings back to the shallow puddles higher up. The next morning, all had returned to the quieted creek. "Blind instinct" alone cannot account for the evident deliberation the female mallard used in maximizing the safety of her ducklings. The common distinction between "instinct" and "intelligence," so often applied inconsistently to similar behavior of humans and nonhumans, appears to be a false dilemma.

One also finds the fallacy of false dilemma committed by some other critics of nonhuman autonomy. For example, Michael A. Fox has written that animals cannot *lead lives* or be autonomous because autonomy requires that one can "generate a life plan" to guide one's life as a whole.[202] Fox concluded that nonhuman animals can have no value in themselves.[203] R. G. Frey likewise claims that the ability to order and direct one's entire life, an ability restricted to humans so far as we know, is the only "autonomy" worth the name, the only sort that "confers value upon a life."[204] Implicit in their reasoning is the assumption that "autonomy" is tantamount to "full autonomy": one is either autonomous or, like a rock, incapable of leading a goal-seeking life, thus having a life devoid of value in itself. No distinction is made here between the purposeful being who acts with a life plan in view and the purposeful being who has shorter-range plans. One can plan for the next five minutes, for the next hour, for the next week, or for years in advance. As we discussed at the beginning of this chapter when canvassing the candidates for moral considerability, autonomy does not seem to be an "all or nothing" matter. Instead, we distinguish between *degrees* of autonomy, as animal rights critic Loren Lomasky does (for humans!). As Regan argues, it makes sense to say that some nonhumans (and humans!) have "preference autonomy." They may not be highly autonomous, but they give every indication of engaging in goal-directed behavior. It is not so easy to dismiss such lives as "valueless."[205] (This discussion has a rather unexpected postscript. Michael A. Fox, after years of writing against "animal liberation" and "animal rights" views, including a full-scale book defending animal experimentation, has made a stunning reversal. Publicly castigating the claims mentioned above in this paragraph as "arrogant" and "speciesist," Fox has become a vegetarian and abolitionist on the subject of animal experimentation.)[206]

No convincing case has been made, then, for the contention that intelligence, rationality, creativity, purposeful communication, and autonomy are exclusively human traits. Homocentrists must seek further arguments to support their claim to human superiority.

The Moral Agency Defense of Homocentrism

At this point, homocentrists might counter that creativity, intelligence, rationality, and autonomy are not really morally relevant anyway. They could argue that it does not matter if nonhumans share any measure of these capacities with humans: membership in the moral community requires the capacity for moral agency, a capacity lacking in nonhumans. H. J. McCloskey[207] and A. I. Melden[208] take this view. Although neither of these philosophers is a homocentrist in the strict sense, homocentrists might use their view to exclude nonhumans from significant moral consideration.

Is it really so clear, however, that the capacity for moral agency has no precedent in any other species? Certain other capacities are required for moral agency, including the capacities for emotion, memory, and goal-directed behavior. As we have seen, there is ample evidence for the presence of these capacities, if to a limited degree, in some nonhumans (again, just as evolution would lead us to expect). Not surprisingly, then, evidence has been gathered that indicates that nonhumans are capable of what we would call "moral" or "virtuous" behavior. James Rachels discusses published research done on rhesus monkeys at Northwestern University in which the authors conclude that a majority of the subjects prefer to go hungry rather than hurt other monkeys. (Pulling a chain to obtain food would also severely shock another monkey who had been placed in full view of the subject.)[209] It is depressing to realize that we humans have not done comparably well in similar experiments. The infamous Milgram experiments showed that the overwhelming majority

The Argument from Marginal Cases

of human subjects, normal people, were willing to deliver severe, even fatal, shocks to other humans, just because the experimenter told them to do so. The "shocked" humans were just acting, unlike the rhesus monkey victims, but they were very convincing. Unlike the monkeys, the human subjects were not even tempted with food, but still were willing to fry another human, a fifty-year-old moaning, gasping man who claimed to have a heart condition![210]

Significantly, the monkeys were not related, so their behavior cannot be explained merely as an evolutionary "strategy" to perpetuate the actor's genes. This typical "sociobiological" explanation also fails to apply to the behavior of a female rhesus monkey in another captive colony who repeatedly rushed to the defense of a weak, unrelated female when that female became embroiled in fights.[211] (Note too that the stronger female did not act for the "selfish" reason of having the protected monkey return the favor under like circumstances.) Rats exhibit the same apparently altruistic behavior, keeping other rats from drinking salty water after they themselves had a drink, as was reported in a 1975 study.[212] In another psychological study, rats were faced with dangling blocks of plastic and other rats dangling in a harness. The rat subjects could lower whatever was dangling by pressing a bar. Consistently rat subjects lowered the harnessed rats far more often than the plastic blocks, especially when the other rats squeaked.[213] One is tempted to conclude that the nonhuman subjects in the experiments described above exhibit far more compassion than their manipulators.

These are just a few examples of many cases that have been documented of apparently virtuous behavior on the part of nonhumans. No one pretends that rats, dogs, cats, monkeys, and so on, act consistently or even largely "morally," of course. Our own companion cats, so loving to us and even sometimes to each other, have no discernibly charitable feelings toward baby birds, moles, rabbits, and all the other sundry examples of life forms weaker than they are. (I am told that some cats will adopt mice if they have grown up with that species, but it is too late to try this in our household. The no-contact policy is our only resort.) Reason suggests that the feelings they have toward creatures stronger than they are also have precious little to do with moral concern. Even the kindliest of dogs, and I have known several, cannot be described as chock-full of moral concern. Interestingly, A. I. Melden, who is on the

The Argument from Marginal Cases

whole quite opposed to the view that nonhumans can have moral rights, is willing to consider extending some sort of minimal rights to "canine 'members of the family,'" "conceptually truncated" though any rights attributions would allegedly be, on the grounds that the dog seems to "demand its rights" at times, and can show what appears to be shame or a sense of guilt.[214] One might say it "dogs" moral agency, and hence deserves a little consideration. (It is no wonder that Melden does not include cats here. They are notoriously shameless, although they do seem to demand their rights!) Nevertheless, as Sapontzis has pointed out, such nonhumans are not moral agents, or "moral beings," although they can behave virtuously.[215] It is not necessary to claim more, since the point of our discussion of apparently moral behavior by dogs and others is that "moral agency" has primitive nonhuman counterparts. We found the same to be true of human intelligence, creativity, autonomy, and rationality. No characteristic has yet been found that is *wholly* lacking in nonhumans and wholly present in humans.

Defenders of human superiority have but one reply remaining. They can argue, with justification, that only humans are capable of having the mental development sufficient for *autonomous* moral agency. Nonhumans may have lesser degrees of the relevant characteristics, but, so far as we know, none can match the capacities of the mature, normal human being. In short, only humans appear to be full-fledged persons. The moral community, they can hold, is restricted above all to such beings, for only they are capable of recognizing and claiming moral status. Do we finally have a good argument for homocentrism? No, for as we shall shortly see, despite the continued focus on humanity, acceptance of such a view actually requires the rejection of homocentrism.

FREQUENTLY HELD VIEWS ON WHO COUNTS MORALLY: THE FULL-PERSONHOOD VIEW

Let us identify those who locate the source of maximum moral significance in the capacity for fully developed personhood as followers of the *full-personhood view*. Immanuel Kant, whose concept of "rational being" includes the capacity for moral agency, gives a classic statement

The Argument from Marginal Cases

of this view: "Now I say that man, and in general every rational being, exists as an end in himself and not merely as a means to be arbitrarily used by this or that will . . . Beings whose existence depends not on our will but on nature have, nevertheless, if they are not rational beings, only a relative value as means and are therefore called things. On the other hand, rational beings are called persons inasmuch as their nature already marks them out as ends in themselves, i.e., as something which is not to be used merely as means and hence there is imposed thereby a limit on all arbitrary use of such beings, which are thus objects of respect."[216] Carl Cohen provides us with an example of a modern statement of the full-personhood view: "[Rights] are in every case claims, or potential claims, within a community of moral agents. Rights arise, and can be intelligibly defended, only among beings who actually do, or can, make moral claims against one another. Whatever else rights may be, therefore, they are necessarily human; their possessors are persons, human beings."[217] According to both authors, full moral status and respect are restricted to "persons" who are moral agents. While followers of the full-personhood view emphasize different morally relevant aspects of fully developed personhood, from moral agency and social interaction (e.g., Cohen, Melden, McCloskey) to full autonomy (e.g., Frey and Narveson),[218] they fundamentally agree on the sorts of beings who can have maximum moral significance.

Normative Ethical Positions Compatible with the Full-Personhood View

Followers of the full-personhood view can be found among those who take otherwise radically different stances in normative ethics. Normative ethics is concerned with identifying acceptable principles about (1) right and wrong conduct and (2) values.[219] Thus, it is standardly divided into theories of obligation and theories of value. Theories of obligation attempt to establish criteria for the rightness, or obligatory nature, of an action. Ethical theories of value aim to provide criteria for goodness. Values may be *moral* or *nonmoral*. *Moral* values pertain to persons' characters, motives, or intentions (e.g., we may judge Mohandas Gandhi's commitment to nonviolence to be morally good).

The Argument from Marginal Cases

Nonmoral values pertain to things, states of affairs, experiences, institutions, and the like (e.g., happiness and pain are plausible examples of nonmoral goodness and badness, respectively).

Since our basic question is what obligations we moral agents have to other beings, let us very briefly look at normative ethical theories of obligation. A *consequentialist* (or *teleologist*) holds that the obligatoriness of actions is determined solely by their consequences, that is, by the balance of (nonmoral) good over bad produced. (The consequentialist cannot make the rightness or obligatoriness of an action depend on the *moral* goodness it produces, for example, upon the virtues reinforced by performance of the act. According to such a view, good character is judged in relation to one's inclination to do what is right, not conversely. As Frankena points out, it would be circular for the consequentialist to explicate morally good character in terms of one's inclination to bring about morally good consequences.)[220] Consequentialists take as basic one of two principles: According to the principle of utility, roughly, we ought to maximize nonmoral good ("utility") *in general;* according to the egoistic principle, one ought to maximize *one's own* nonmoral good. (There are many variations on the utilitarian and egoistic themes, but the characterizations above capture the thrusts of both types of teleologism.) *Deontologists,* or *nonconsequentialists,* hold that consequences are not the determinant, or the sole determinant, of obligatoriness in actions: they believe that an action (e.g., keeping one's promise) may be right *apart* from or even despite the consequences it has. Deontologists may take just one principle to be basic in ethics. For example, Kant takes the "categorical imperative" to be the principle from which all others can be derived: "Act in such a way that you treat humanity, whether in your own person or in the person of another, always at the same time as an end and never simply as a means."[221] Alan Gewirth's "Principle of Generic Consistency," which enjoins us to "act in accord with the generic rights of your recipients as well as of yourself,"[222] is also presented as a basic deontological principle.

Alternatively, a deontologist might take a number of ethical principles (e.g., "Act justly," "Do not lie," etc.) to be equally basic, that is, not derivable from other principles or one another. W. D. Ross took this view.[223] A deontologist might even incorporate a *consequentialist* principle into a set of allegedly basic principles, as William Frankena

The Argument from Marginal Cases

does: he suggests that we ought to maximize good in this world and act justly.[224]

Deontologists, egoists, and utilitarians can each take the full-personhood view. Kant, McCloskey, and Melden are all deontologists who take full persons or moral agents to be the recipients of our moral obligations. Deontologists of this ilk can attribute basic moral rights to full persons. As Regan has said, a basic moral right is not a *consequence* of a moral obligation, but its ground. If anything has a basic moral right, it has it *because of the sort of being that it is,* not because of the consequences that result from attributing and respecting rights.[225] Turning to teleological views, we see that Frey, a utilitarian, believes that we ought to maximize nonmoral good (value). He also believes that fully autonomous lives contain more nonmoral good, more richness, than other lives do. While he prefers not to say that full persons have "rights," he holds that there is a much stronger presumption against killing them than there is against killing others: the amount of value destroyed by the death of a fully autonomous being far outweighs, he thinks, the "disutility" produced by the death of a less well-endowed being.[226] Even egoists can take the full-personhood view, as the example of Jan Narveson shows. He holds that it is in the moral agent's best interests to forge mutual bonds of respect and concern with those who can make commitments and enforce their claims. The moral agent is "better off" extending basic rights to fully rational, communicating individuals: this is, he believes, the basis of the moral community.[227] Thus, we see that the full-personhood view is an umbrella covering quite a diverse collection of ethical views.

There is another respect in which followers of the full-personhood view may differ. They might hold that all and only full persons are morally considerable, or they might hold the less stringent view that all and only full persons are *maximally* morally significant. Putting the last alternative in "rights" terms, one would say that all and only full persons have *full* moral rights, including a right to life. These two views have significantly different implications. Although any being with a right to life must be morally considerable, the converse need not hold at all. A morally considerable being is a being to whom moral agents have moral obligations. Just what those obligations are depends on that being's characteristics. For example, persons unable to work might have a right

The Argument from Marginal Cases

to life but not a right to equal employment opportunity. It is also possible that moral agents are obligated not to wantonly inflict suffering on a sentient being who fails to be a full person, but that they have no obligation to refrain from taking his or her life, especially if doing so furthers their own interests. As mentioned earlier, not all morally considerable beings need be equally morally significant. Thus, if one were able to establish that all sentient beings are morally considerable by virtue of their sentience, it would not follow that sentient beings should not be "harvested" for food or subjected to experimentation. It would seem to follow, however, that one should inflict minimum suffering during the "harvesting" procedure. Followers of the full-personhood view who claim only maximum moral significance for full persons can agree with this, but those who go beyond this to tie moral considerability to full personhood cannot. Unless it makes a difference, I will characterize the full-personhood view as the view that all and only full persons are maximally morally significant, since this is a claim all the view's followers would accept.

The Incompatibility of the Full-Personhood View and Homocentrism

Let us conclude this characterization of the full-personhood view and its normative variations by underlining its incompatibility with homocentrism. Although the full-personhood view can arise out of the homocentric concern to find a morally relevant trait that is exclusively human, it is not at all a homocentric view. First of all, "full personhood," not "humanity," is claimed to be the source of maximum moral significance. Kant was certainly aware of this when he spoke of "rational beings in general" being ends in themselves. It is entirely conceivable that God, extraterrestrials, or even other animals are full persons. It must be admitted that we do not know enough to judge whether any of these possibilities are realized, but the view certainly leaves room for nonhuman membership in the moral community. However, the view remains "human centered" in as much as, to the best of our knowledge, only humans can be *full* persons.

The second respect in which the full-personhood view is not homocentric is far more disturbing to homocentrists than the first. If basic moral rights, or maximum moral significance, are reserved for full persons, what of *humans* who fail to be full persons? Examples are fetuses, children, the brain-damaged or congenitally retarded, those who suffer from insanity, and the senile. Some of these humans are "persons" in the same sense as dogs, cats, and apes, but they are not full persons, and some of them never will be. Some of them cannot even be called "persons" in the most minimal sense. Depending on the severity of the case, they may be self-conscious but lacking in autonomy, or even just "merely" conscious. Some of them, for example, the irreversibly comatose, may not even be conscious at all. The full-personhood view must, it seems, exclude all who fall short from full moral consideration. We have just seen that proponents of the full-personhood view are not committed to the claim that "only" humans can be maximally morally significant. Now we see that, apparently, "all humans" cannot be said to have that status either.

This is an extremely disturbing implication. Humans have routinely eradicated, hunted, trapped, skinned, eaten, done toxicity testing upon, and experimented with nonhuman animals because it was assumed that they had little or no moral significance. Humans have reserved paramount moral status for themselves, so much so that even the desire for barbecued ribs is thought to outweigh the suffering and death of a factory-farmed pig. If the source of our alleged moral preeminence is our fully autonomous, richly complex kind of life, then it seems that it would be permissible to barbecue a few other folks.

Now, most of us, one hopes, are horrified by the thought of treating any humans as we typically treat nonhuman animals. Although much biomedical research of value to normal humans could be done using "defective" humans, rather more, in fact, than that done with nonhumans, few of us would support such experimentation. Fewer still would smile at the sight of penned humans being fattened up for the butcher. However, if it is wrong to spray a severely retarded human with an entire can of oven cleaner in order to test its toxicity, is it not also wrong to do this to a nonhuman animal with equivalent or even higher mental capacities? If full personhood truly is necessary for a right to life, or maximum moral significance, it seems that we are playing favorites by persisting in our differential treatment of nonhuman animals and

The Argument from Marginal Cases

certain humans. On the other hand, perhaps something is amiss with the full-personhood view! This brings us, of course, to the challenge to the full-personhood view that has changed more than a few minds: the argument from marginal cases.

THE ARGUMENT FROM MARGINAL CASES: TWO VERSIONS

Peter Singer, Bernard Rollin, and Tom Regan have all employed the argument from marginal cases to show that our differential treatment of "marginal" (impaired or undeveloped) humans and nonhuman animals is morally suspect.[228] (Note that the term 'marginal' simply means 'not paradigmatic': it in no way implies that "marginal humans" fail to be human beings.)[229] Upon close inspection, one sees that there are two different versions of the argument. Tom Regan gives both in one passage: "Proponents of the type of argument I have in mind may argue *either* that (1) certain animals have certain rights because these [marginal] humans *have* these rights *or* that (2) *if* these [marginal] humans have certain rights, *then* certain animals have these rights also. The former alternative represents what might be termed the stronger argument for animal rights; the latter, the weaker."[230] One can see why Regan gives them these names. Only the first, "stronger," argument implies that some nonhuman animals have rights, whereas the second has only a conditional conclusion. Let us now sketch each argument in full, as Regan has given us abbreviated versions.

The Categorical Version

As stated, Regan's "certain animals have certain rights because these [marginal] humans have these rights" is an enthymeme. Moreover, it is couched in terms that would be rejected by those utilitarians or egoists who object to rights attributions. In order to make the argument directly applicable to consequentialist as well as deontological holders of the full-personhood view, I will replace the "rights" reference to the more neutral "maximum moral significance." It is understood that "maximum moral significance" implies either basic moral rights, including the right to life, or a strong presumption against killing. The argument can now be completed by the addition of two premises:

[1. Beings who are similar in all important morally relevant respects are equally morally significant.]
[2. Nonhumans exist who are similar in all important morally relevant respects to marginal humans.]
3. Marginal humans are maximally morally significant.
4. *Therefore,* the nonhumans who are similar in all important morally relevant respects to marginal humans are also maximally morally significant.

Taking our cue from the logical form of the third premise and conclusion, let us call this "stronger" argument for nonhuman animal moral significance *the categorical argument from marginal cases.* This categorical version is implicit in Bernard Rollin's attack on what I have called the full-personhood view: "If indeed, as the Kantian argument [for the nonmoral status of animals] suggests, only rational and linguistic beings fall within the scope of moral concern, it is once again difficult to see how we can allow infants, children, the mentally retarded, the insane, the senile, the brain-damaged, the autistic, the comatose, etc., to be considered legitimate objects of moral concern. We do consider them such objects; yet they lack rationality and/or language. This shows that rationality and language do not represent a necessary condition for moral concern."[231] If the categorical argument from marginal cases is sound, the full-personhood view is plainly false. Shortly, we will see how followers of that view try to counter it.

The Biconditional Version

Let us now consider Regan's "weaker" form of the argument from marginal cases, which he states as "*if* these [marginal] humans have certain rights, *then* certain animals have these rights also." Since no conditional statement can be an *argument,* we are clearly faced once more with an enthymeme. In this instance, only the conclusion is stated. The unstated premises are the same first two premises of the categorical argument sketched above. Implicitly, it is claimed that beings who are morally relevantly similar in all important respects are equally morally significant, and that certain nonhumans and marginal humans are comparable in this way. It would then follow that if marginal humans have certain rights, then nonhumans who are morally relevantly similar to them in all important respects also have those rights. Moreover, the converse would also follow: If some nonhuman animals have certain rights, then marginal humans who are morally relevantly similar to them in all important respects also have those rights. Regan's statement is really the more controversial half of a biconditional conclusion. If we change from his "rights" terminology to more inclusive "moral significance" language, we can reconstruct the argument as follows:

[1. Beings who are similar in all important morally relevant respects are equally morally significant.]
[2. Nonhumans exist who are similar in all important morally relevant respects to marginal humans.]
3. *Therefore,* those nonhumans who are similar in all important morally relevant respects to marginal humans are maximally morally significant if and only if marginal humans are maximally morally significant.

Again taking our cue from the logical form of the conclusion, let us call this argument *the biconditional version of the argument from marginal cases.*

Peter Singer adds a twist to this version of the argument by noting that some nonhumans may have higher degrees of some morally relevant characteristics than some marginal humans do:

[W]e must allow that beings who are similar in all relevant respects have a similar right to life . . . we may legitimately hold that there are some features of certain beings that make their lives more valuable than those of other beings; but there will surely be some nonhuman animals whose lives, by any standards, are more valuable than the lives of some humans. A chimpanzee, dog, or pig, for instance, will have a higher degree of self-awareness and a greater capacity for meaningful relations with others than a severely retarded infant or someone in a state of advanced senility. So if we base the right to life on these characteristics we must grant these animals a right to life as good as, or better than, such retarded or senile humans.[232]

The Argument from Marginal Cases

The biconditional argument from marginal cases is profoundly disquieting. Our version, which concludes that "Those nonhumans who are similar in all important morally relevant respects to marginal humans are maximally morally significant if and only if marginal humans are maximally morally significant," is logically equivalent to a very ominous disjunction: "Either *both* marginal humans and any nonhumans who are similar to them in all important morally relevant respects are maximally morally significant, or *neither* are." As Singer says, "This argument cuts both ways."[233] Clearly, it is an appeal to moral consistency, and as such it leaves room for an unwelcome response. This argument, in fact, unlike the categorical argument from marginal cases, is entirely compatible with the full-personhood view. It could conceivably even be used to *support* that view! One might argue as follows: The suggestion that marginal humans do not have a right to life, or maximum moral significance, seems shocking. On the other hand, if we grant them full moral status, consistency requires us to do the same for the nonhumans we currently use and kill. This is plainly an unacceptable consequence, so we must restrict full moral status to paradigmatic, "nonmarginal" beings. (One is reminded of Victorian philosopher Thomas Taylor's dubious argument *against* women's rights. If women had rights, he reflected, surely cats and dogs would too!)[234] The biconditional form of the argument from marginal cases is intended to make full-personhood-view followers reconsider their beliefs, and it has had that effect in a number of cases known to me, but it has the limits of any appeal to consistency. Nothing prevents followers of that view from accepting the argument and holding that marginal humans lack full moral status.

What do followers of the full-personhood view have to say in reply to either version of the argument from marginal cases? Let us turn to the next chapter for some interesting responses.

2

RESPONSES TO THE ARGUMENT

FROM MARGINAL CASES

As discussed in the previous chapter, those who hold that persons with highly complex, autonomous lives are the paradigms of moral significance readily exclude nonhuman animals from the moral community on the grounds that they lack the necessary qualifications. Few, however, have openly argued that humans who lack those qualifications should also be excluded. Both versions of the argument from marginal cases, the categorical and the biconditional, challenge these attitudes. The view that only normally developed persons can be maximally morally significant, and that "lesser" beings—so long as they are not human—may be sacrificed for the former's benefit, stands accused of inconsistency and bias. How have the charges been answered?

FAILURE TO ADDRESS THE ISSUE

Some have chosen to say almost nothing at all about this fundamental challenge to the full-personhood view. For example, Ernest Partridge has endorsed the view that only linguistically articulate, psychologically complex beings can have a right to life.[1] He draws the conclusion that nonhuman animals can have no such right. What about humans who do not meet this high standard? They are mentioned in just one paragraph: "What, then, of so-called 'marginal cases' of human beings with only partial or potential person-traits? As with animals, they might be accorded such rights as they have the capacity to exercise."[2] Might they be accorded the right to life? That would not be consistent with Partridge's expressed view. May they then be sacrificed to further the interests of full persons, as nonhuman animals are? Is it permissible to test potentially dangerous drugs on the severely retarded before the drugs are offered to normal humans? May we "harvest" their hearts for transplantation into ailing full persons? We are simply not told.

Similarly, Charlie Blatz, who (unlike Partridge) goes so far as to restrict moral *considerability* to moral agents, buries the only mention of a problem case in a footnote. There he says that "the matter of the ethical significance of children is a complex one. Still, something must be said here."[3] He argues that moral agents would not be conscientious if they did not "nurture" children as future moral agents. The same applies, he says, to the "socially or intellectually retarded" who are capable of very imperfect moral agency. But what of those humans who cannot develop into even the least perfect of moral agents? What implications does his view have for *their* treatment? Blatz argues at length for the view that it is permissible to raise and slaughter nonhumans for food if doing so benefits moral agents. According to the title of his article, "Why (Most) Humans Are More Important Than Other Animals," humans who cannot ever be moral agents should be in the same nonmoral pen with food animals. Of course, moral agents can become attached to marginal humans, just as they can become attached to cats, dogs, or prize lambs. We would harm these morally considerable persons by eating those they care about. However, suppose no moral agent cares about a marginal human? May we then use or abuse that being with impunity? Not only does Blatz not answer any such questions: he does not even raise them.

Quite understandably, it seems that the prospect of accepting the permissibility of killing marginal humans for the benefit of normal humans is too upsetting, too distasteful, for many to acknowledge. Consequently, the argument from marginal cases is swept under the argumentative rug with as little comment as possible. Some recent followers of the full-personhood view do not even comment at all. In a defense of sport hunting, philosopher Theodore Vitali argues that we do not violate the rights of those who essentially lack the capacity for (full) personhood when we hunt or kill them for pleasure, because moral rights are restricted to those who have that capacity (even if it is undeveloped, as in normal babies, or inactive, as is the case for senile adults). As far as we know, he says, no nonhumans can be persons, so killing them for sport is justifiable.[4] May we then declare open season on humans who have never been and can never be (full) persons? Some might even enjoy this. In Texas, some law enforcement officials invite their friends to participate in "the ultimate hunt," as they proudly call it: in this permutation of an antebellum "slave sport," the men and their dogs chase two temporarily released prison inmates across the plains.[5] The inmates are always caught. Oh, they do volunteer (their sentences will be reduced), they are given a few hours' head start, and they have gotten to wear protective clothing since 1983 (this requirement was added after an unprotected inmate was badly lacerated by dog bites). This puts them ahead of the nonhumans whose bodies decorate walls and car hoods, all without their consent. "Only one" inmate has been seriously bitten in the last three years. Now, if the inmates were incapable of ever being full persons, by Vitali's reasoning we could have unrestricted hunts! Why bother with getting consent or issuing protective clothing? A more "natural" hunt might give more pleasure to some hunters.

Unfortunately, the above possibility is not particularly unrealistic, at least in my own country. In the United States, many severely mentally retarded convicted criminals are imprisoned and even executed. For example, as recently as 1990, 10 percent of the inmates on Georgia's death row were extremely retarded. Fully 14 percent of those Georgia death row inmates recently executed fit this description as well.[6] Large numbers of people are at best indifferent to these prisoners' fates: expressions of glee after their executions are not uncommon. Some sample comments I have heard from college students during discussion of the killing of severely mentally retarded prisoners are: "They can't be cured anyway"; "Why waste money on a mad dog?"; and "We don't need garbage like this alive." One such convicted murderer, Johnny Paul Penry, with an IQ of 50–63 and a mental age of *seven* (facts undisputed by the prosecutors), was targeted for execution in Texas immediately after the 1989 U.S. Supreme Court ruling (*Penry vs. Lynaugh*) explicitly sanctioning the common practice of killing such prisoners.[7] The fact that Penry committed an especially ghastly crime—raping, then murdering a young woman with a pair of scissors—is, in the opinion of many, sufficient to warrant his death, even though he is no more morally responsible for what he has done than a small child or a nonhuman animal. In fact, quite a few people think that "humane" execution is far too painless for people like Penry. I have students who claim that morality requires a death at least as horrifying as the death of the victim: relatively decent conditions for such prisoners while they are alive especially incenses these proponents of "cruel and unusual" treatment. Why not just turn the dogs loose on him and the many others like him? ("Dangerous" pris-

Responses to the Argument

oners could be hunted on islands if we fear their escape, or we could restrict the "hunt" to fairly harmless human nonpersons, so long as it doesn't upset anyone too much.) I hasten to add that while some might relish this scenario—I know some people who would find it to be grand "sport"—I doubt that Vitali would support such a hunt, even though his position permits it. However, one waits in vain for him to address the issue of permanent human nonpersons, who must lack all moral rights if his view is correct. It does not even rate a footnote in his article.

C. E. Harris provides another interesting example of total failure to address the issue in his *Applying Moral Theories*. His explication of the Kantian "ethics of respect for persons" embodies a contradiction. After linking "personhood" to moral agency (" 'Treating a person as an end' means respecting the conditions necessary for his or her effective functioning as a moral agent"),[8] he remarks that "The ethics of respect for persons takes as its central theme the equal dignity of *all human beings*."[9] Nowhere in Harris's book do we see the realization that there is a problem here. If only moral agents have moral rights, all human beings are not due equal respect and dignity. It is fascinating to see how often homocentrism, although incompatible with the full-personhood view, is held in conjunction with it.

Little better is this "response" to the biconditional version of the argument from marginal cases, made by the anonymous author of chapter 4 of *Alternatives to Animal Use in Research, Testing, and Education,* a report done for the U.S. Congress and published in 1988. The author suggests that "the consistency argument" ignores the fact that "most" humans have the qualities that characterize (full) personhood, whereas no nonhumans do: "If most humans have these characteristics, it might be appropriate (or at least convenient) to treat humans as a homogeneous group, even though some members lack these characteristics. If all animals lack certain characteristics, it may be similarly appropriate to treat them as a group, regardless of whether some humans also lack these characteristics."[10] This is hardly a serious response to the charge of inconsistency. It is frequently "convenient" to behave inconsistently, particularly when it preserves an institution persons perceive as highly beneficial to themselves (in this case, the nonhuman experimentation institution). Whether it is "appropriate" to continue the differential treatment of humans and nonhumans with the same capacities is the very question at issue.

Responses to the Argument

It is a bit surprising to see a prominent philosopher give the same extremely short shrift to the argument from marginal cases as the anonymous author of a congressional study. This is precisely what Robert Nozick, chair of the philosophy department at Harvard University, does in a review of Tom Regan's *The Case for Animal Rights*. Nozick rightly identifies the argument from marginal cases as central to Regan's case, and he is fully aware of its challenge to the now orthodox full-personhood view: "[I]t is not easy to explain why membership in the human species does and should have moral weight with us. Shouldn't only an organism's own individual characteristics matter?"[11] One waits for Nozick's explanation, but none is forthcoming. Although he acknowledges that "this does present a puzzle,"[12] he ends by simply dismissing the argument: "Nothing much (certainly not the large institutional changes Mr. Regan favors) should be inferred from our not presently having a theory of the moral importance of species membership that no one has spent much time trying to formulate because the issue hasn't seemed pressing."[13] Going on to muse that "perhaps" individuals are morally entitled to favor members of their own species over members of other species, Nozick leaves us with no justification whatever for such an entitlement. Suggesting that the matter is all too complex to sort out (and having the grace to express some uneasiness about making such a reply),[14] he does not even attempt to make a start at solving the "puzzle." One can hardly construe this as a serious response to the argument from marginal cases. It is a refusal to discuss the matter, not a rebuttal.

Followers of the full-personhood view, one and all, are going to have to do better than ignoring, evading, and dismissing the argument from marginal cases. To use Nozick's language, the issue is very pressing indeed.

UNSUCCESSFUL ATTACKS ON THE ARGUMENT FROM MARGINAL CASES

Others have realized that a genuine response to the argument is mandatory but have failed to construct successful rebuttals. An examination of their replies will prove instructive. I have divided them into two categories: attempts to show the argument to be internally flawed, and attempts to show that the argument lacks import even if it is sound.

Responses to the Argument

Alleged Internal Flaws

I will consider several attempts to attack the argument head on. It stands accused of being weak, unnecessary, and inconsistent. Some have charged that it grossly underestimates the capacities of marginal humans; others—very different critics, to be sure—have accused it of underestimating nonhuman animals instead. Each of these attacks will be taken up in turn.

Reversibility and "Redundancy"

Philosopher Alan Holland has criticized the argument on the following two grounds. First, he holds that the "reversible" character of the argument constitutes a serious "weakness": it could be used to sanction the treating of marginal humans as we now treat many nonhuman animals.[15] To avoid this result, proponents of the argument from marginal cases need to establish the high moral significance of both marginal humans and nonhumans similar to them. But if they do this, Holland believes the argument becomes vulnerable to his second charge: "redundancy."[16] If there is a positive case to be made for the rights of certain nonhumans and deficient humans, the appeal to marginal cases is superfluous. So, the argument is either unnecessary or—if no positive case can be made—it is dangerous.

Neither of Holland's criticisms refutes the argument from marginal cases. The "reversibility" charge, revealing the usual lack of concern for exploited nonhumans, applies only to the *biconditional* version of the argument from marginal cases. As developed in the previous chapter, that version says:

1. Beings who are similar in all important morally relevant respects are equally morally significant.
2. Nonhumans exist who are similar in all important morally relevant respects to marginal humans.
3. *Therefore,* those nonhumans who are similar in all important morally relevant respects to marginal humans are maximally morally significant if and only if marginal humans are maximally morally significant.

However, Holland's criticism does not show the argument to be unsound. It is in the nature of a biconditional conclusion to be "reversible."

Calling this a "weakness" in the argument is akin to objecting to it for being deductive. This version of the argument from marginal cases is not intended to do more than it says. Naturally, those who firmly believe that both nonhumans and humans who lack full personhood can be maximally morally significant will not rest their case after giving this argument.

This brings us to Holland's "redundancy" charge. Technically speaking, he is quite right to point out that a positive case for the high moral standing of beings who are not full persons, perhaps not even persons at all, makes the appeal to marginal cases unnecessary. Let us remember the *categorical* version of the argument:

1. Beings who are similar in all important morally relevant respects are equally morally significant.
2. Nonhumans exist who are similar in all important morally relevant respects to marginal humans.
3. Marginal humans are maximally morally significant.
4. *Therefore,* those nonhumans who are similar in the important morally relevant respects to marginal humans are also maximally morally significant.

Clearly, without a supplementary argument to establish the third premise, this version of the argument from marginal cases simply begs the question against the full-personhood view. But if such an argument is given, and if it is clear that there are nonhumans who are similar in the important morally relevant respects to marginal humans, why not rest the entire case here? Why bother with an obviously incomplete argument?

As Roger Crisp has retorted in a reply to Holland, the argument from marginal cases would never have been necessary if so many did not believe that full personhood is the foundation of membership in the moral community.[17] The entire point of the biconditional version of the argument is to show us exactly where the full-personhood view leads. It is a challenge to that view. Holland is trying to shift the burden to opponents of the full-personhood view by demanding a positive argument from them. The burden is accepted, by Tom Regan among others, when the categorical version of the argument from marginal cases comes into play. However, this does not make either version of the argument unnecessary. The full-personhood-view proponent *also* owes us a response

Responses to the Argument

to the original challenge, that is, to the argument from marginal cases. Without that challenge, it is doubtful that the philosophically orthodox full-personhood view would have come into question. Thus, while the appeal to marginal cases is *technically* unnecessary once a positive case is made for the high moral standing of those who lack full personhood, it remains *dialectically* necessary. That dialectic is being followed in this very book. My strategy is to explore every response a follower of the full-personhood view can make to the challenge of the argument from marginal cases. After it becomes abundantly, painfully clear that the moral status of marginal humans cannot be salvaged given that view, or given related views giving moral primacy to full persons, I will move to positive cases for the basic moral rights of sentient beings.

We will return to the views of Alan Holland when we later consider his own positive case for the moral superiority of marginal humans over nonhumans. For now, it is enough to note that he has not exposed any obviously fatal flaws in either version of the argument from marginal cases.

Alleged Inconsistency

Earlier in this chapter, we looked at a very poor response to the argument from marginal cases by the Office of Technology Assessment. In the report's attempt to defend continuation of medical research on nonhumans, it was suggested that it "might be convenient" to, in effect, simply ignore the argument. At the time, I noted that we would later consider a far better attempt by the author of that report to come to grips with the issue. We have now reached that point. The author attacks the argument from marginal cases, called "the consistency argument" in the report, as follows: "Ironically, the consistency argument contains a basic inconsistency. On the one hand, the argument asserts that humans are not superior to animals; animals should therefore be treated like humans. On the other hand, the very nature of the moral argument is promotion of morally superior behavior: Humans should refuse to exploit other species, even though the other species exploit each other." [18] Humans cannot both be morally superior to animals and not morally superior to animals. Hence, so the reasoning goes, we really ought to call the argument from marginal cases "the inconsistency argument."

Although the report only gives a hypothetical version of the argument from marginal cases (properly speaking, the *biconditional* version, although this is not said),[19] this criticism really applies to the *categorical* version. Only that version asserts that nonhumans comparable to marginal humans *have* maximum moral significance. Given the undisputed assumption that normal humans, as full persons, are also maximally morally significant, it follows that normal humans are no more morally significant than certain nonhumans. In that respect, humans would not be "morally superior" to the latter. This version, moreover, does indeed imply that we humans ought not to exploit such nonhumans, any more than we ought to exploit each other or marginal humans. No comparable moral obligation is imposed on chimps, dogs, cats, rats, and so on, since they are not moral agents. They are not held to the same high standard of moral behavior humans require (sometimes!) of each other. In this respect, normal humans, at least, might be said to be "morally superior" to such nonhumans. Is the argument from marginal cases, then, actually committed to the claim that (normal) humans both are and are not "morally superior" to many of the nonhumans we routinely exploit? Is it guilty of the charge of inconsistency?

No: the argument is quite free of inconsistency. First, while it makes sense to say that one moral agent can be "morally superior" to another moral agent (e.g., Gandhi was morally superior to Hitler), it is far from clear that a moral agent can sensibly be said to be "morally superior" to a being who is *incapable* of exhibiting moral agency. Is the number one tennis player in the world "superior" as a tennis player to people with no arms? Humans who refuse to exploit beings with basic moral rights are "morally superior" to humans who deliberately, knowingly, choose to violate the rights of others, but are they really "morally superior" to caribou-eating wolves? Second, even if we were to grant that human moral agents can be said to be "morally superior" to those incapable of moral agency, it does not follow that the argument from marginal cases also *denies* that humans are "morally superior" *in the same respect*. Plainly, the 'moral superiority' in question has two quite different meanings. A human who is morally superior to another being might be *more significant* morally, having a claim to greater protection or consideration than that other, *or* he or she might exhibit, or be able to exhibit, more exemplary moral behavior. Although moral meritori-

Responses to the Argument

ans might hold that such a moral agent *deserves* to be more morally significant than another, they would have to argue for the connection: it is not a matter of definition. It makes perfectly good sense to say that Mohandas Gandhi was a better moral agent ('morally superior' in one sense) than 99 percent of the remaining human population, but no more morally significant (the other sense of 'morally superior') than most of them. Both Gandhi and an income tax evader have equal "rights," or claims, to life: it would surely be wrong, as Gandhi would be the first to say, to do toxicity testing on the tax evader in order to ensure the safety of the Indian leader! Similarly, a nonhuman (or marginal human!) might be morally "inferior" to a normal human in lacking the capacity for moral agency, or in behaving "less" morally, but not necessarily inferior in the sense that he or she has no claim to life equal to the normal human's. So, the inconsistency charge dissolves, replaced by the justified countercharge of equivocation.

Another issue deserves comment before we move on. Although the inconsistency charge is couched in terms of "human" moral superiority or its lack, it is plain that "full persons" is the relevant group. Consider a second formulation of the inconsistency charge in the report: "Yet it would be inconsistent to assert that humans are not superior to animals while suggesting that humans should refuse to exploit other species, even though other species exploit each other."[20] Now substitute "full persons" for "humans," and "retarded children" for "animals" and "species." The charge is essentially unchanged, although most full-personhood-view followers, including the author of this report, evidently find it much more disturbing. Consistency, however, requires acceptance—or rejection—of both formulations.

The author of this article, despite various attempts to skirt the issue of marginal humans' moral status, at least shows signs of uneasiness about the matter. Despite all I have said in criticism of the report, it is in many ways remarkably fair. The author does not succumb to the temptation of caricaturing antivivisectionism in *Reader's Digest* style,[21] attempting instead to deal even-handedly with the arguments of Tom Regan and Peter Singer. The author even admits that "it may be arbitrary" to experiment on nonhumans but not on marginal humans,[22] tacitly conceding the point of the (biconditional) argument from marginal cases! He or she appears to be aware of the inadequacy of the case against non-

Responses to the Argument

human moral standing, for the very last sentence in the article is startling in its modesty: "Animals are morally entitled to be treated humanely; whether they are entitled to more than that is unclear."[23] Those Congress members who actually read the report they commissioned must have found it to be rather a shock.

"Underestimation" of Marginal Humans

According to the second premise of either version of the argument from marginal cases, there are nonhumans who are similar in the important morally relevant respects to marginal humans. It has been held that this is highly insulting to such humans. Some vehemently deny that any nonhuman on this planet could be as mentally or emotionally developed as even the most limited of humans. Thus, they accuse the argument (either version) of having an offensively false premise. Philosopher Carl Cohen appears to lodge this very criticism against the argument from marginal cases, as we shall soon see.

A staunch advocate of the full-personhood view, Cohen holds that only moral agents can have basic moral rights: "Rights arise, and can be intelligibly defended, only among beings who actually do, or can, make moral claims against one another. Whatever else rights may be, therefore, they are necessarily human; their possessors are persons, human beings."[24] Let us not quarrel here with Cohen's assumption that only humans can be persons. Let us instead focus on the obvious objection such a view inspires: the argument from marginal cases. There are plenty of humans, after all, who are not persons, or whose personhood is so limited that they fail to be moral agents. Are they to be excluded from the "community of moral agents" along with pigs, cats, rats, and apes? Cohen raises the objection himself, paraphrasing the argument as follows: "If having rights requires being able to make moral claims, to grasp and apply moral laws, then many humans—the brain-damaged, the comatose, the senile—who plainly lack those capacities must be without rights. But that is absurd. This proves [the critic concludes] that rights do not depend on the presence of moral capacities."[25]

As we have seen, Cohen is here paraphrasing the *categorical* version of the argument from marginal cases. How does Cohen reply to that argument?

Responses to the Argument

This objection fails; it mistakenly treats an essential feature of humanity as though it were a screen for sorting humans. The capacity for moral judgment that distinguishes humans from animals is not a test to be administered to human beings one by one. Persons who are unable, because of some disability, to perform the full moral functions natural to human beings are certainly not for that reason ejected from the moral community. The issue is one of kind. Humans are of such a kind that they may be the subject of experiments only with their voluntary consent. The choices they make freely must be respected. Animals are of such a kind that it is impossible for them, in principle, to give or with[h]old voluntary consent or to make a moral choice. What humans retain when disabled, animals have never had.[26]

I have quoted Cohen's reply in full because it lends itself to two interpretations. Neither holds up as a refutation of the argument from marginal cases, as we shall now see.

According to the first interpretation, Cohen is asserting that marginal humans are moral agents *with reduced capacities*. While they cannot "perform the *full* moral functions natural to human beings" (emphasis mine), they nevertheless are capable of "freely" giving or denying consent to be experimental subjects. Presumably, this is a moral (as opposed to nonmoral) choice inasmuch as one decides to participate or not participate in procedures that could benefit rights holders. Nonhuman animals, Cohen believes, are incapable of ever making such a choice. Thus, it would follow that even marginal humans qualify as rights holders, unlike nonhumans: "What humans retain when disabled, animals have never had." If this is the case, the argument from marginal cases obviously errs in implying that any nonhuman could have morally relevant capacities equivalent to those of marginal humans.

However, if Cohen is claiming that any marginal human has the capacity to consent freely to be an experimental subject in a sense in which a nonhuman cannot, his claim is patently false. The permanently "comatose" and some of the "senile," to use his own terms, lack any such capacity. Although many such humans *earlier* had such a capacity, and perhaps even were able to express their wishes in writing, they do not *now* possess it. Moreover, there are some unfortunate humans, the "merely conscious," who have never had and never will have the capacity for even diminished agency. If Cohen replies that these humans (apart from the irreversibly comatose!) *can* be regarded as marginal agents, inasmuch as they would be able to accept or reject their roles as experimental subjects by submitting to or resisting procedures, he will have to agree that nonhumans can do the same! As S. F. Sapontzis has pointed out, nonhumans can consent or deny consent to experimentation in this very straightforward sense.[27] If a thrashing, screaming, severely senile individual is "denying consent" to the injection of an experimental drug in his arm, a hissing, yowling, struggling cat likewise "denies consent" to injection. Of course, it is doubtful that either human or cat can be seen as exhibiting *moral* agency in such circumstances, qualifying neither for rights (given Cohen's view). For these reasons, such a reply would be inadvisable on his part. On the other hand, his alternative appears to be insistence on the obviously false claim that every marginal human is capable of free, informed, moral choice.

Perhaps Cohen's response to the argument from marginal cases will fare better on a second interpretation of his remarks. According to this interpretation, Cohen does not really mean to suggest that every marginal human is capable of giving free, informed, rational consent to experimentation. Rather, he is claiming that even humans who lack such a capacity nevertheless differ from nonhumans in being the *kind* of beings who can do this sort of thing. That is, humans *normally* have the capacity in question, although some may lack it altogether. "What humans retain when disabled, [and what] animals have never had" would, in this reading, be membership in the kind of species whose normal adult members are moral agents (full persons). Simply comparing the capacities of individuals without regard for the "kind" of beings they are would be "underestimating" marginal humans with respect to nonhumans, according to this second interpretation of Cohen.

Is Cohen's reply to the argument from marginal cases tantamount to an endorsement of "speciesism"? Although I shall not discuss that view in detail until the next chapter, this much can be said: Anyone who believes that species membership can itself, independently of the capacities of the individual, be a morally relevant characteristic, is a speciesist. There can be no doubt that Cohen accepts this view: he entitles a later section of his paper "In Defense of 'Speciesism.' " Although the language used in his reply to the argument from marginal cases suggests that he also believes that marginal humans have the capacity, moral agency, he believes to be the basis of rights, we need not read him in this way. In that case, however, Cohen owes us an argument in support of the view that species membership can be a morally relevant characteristic.

We do not find a convincing argument in Cohen's "Defense of 'Speciesism.'" He begins by claiming that there is a vast gulf between the morally relevant characteristics of human and nonhuman species: "Humans engage in moral reflection; humans are morally autonomous; humans are members of moral communities, recognizing just claims against their own interest."[28] The trouble here is that all humans clearly are not described by Cohen's passage. The point of the argument from marginal cases is that full personhood is not a universal human characteristic. The following addition by Cohen is hardly helpful: "Speciesism is not merely plausible; it is essential for right conduct, because those who will not make the morally relevant distinctions among species are almost certain, in consequence, to misapprehend their true obligations."[29] This argument will hardly impress anyone who is searching for a reason to believe that species membership can be a morally relevant characteristic. Converts are seldom won by begged questions.

Perhaps others will succeed in providing a successful defense of speciesism. If they do, they will indeed have defeated the argument from marginal cases, for they will have shown that there is a crucially important morally relevant difference between otherwise similar humans and nonhumans. Various efforts to defend speciesism will be explored in the next chapter. However, *this move is not open to followers of the full-personhood view,* including Cohen. Those who claim that "[t]he holders of rights must have the capacity to comprehend rules of duty, governing all including themselves"[30] cannot also assert that beings lacking in moral autonomy are rights holders. One cannot have it both ways.

Thus, given the first interpretation of Cohen's criticism of the argument from marginal cases, he either makes the obviously false claim that all humans are moral agents, or he must include some nonhumans in the moral community—just as the very argument he criticizes concludes. According to the second interpretation, he tries to undercut the argument by espousing speciesism, a view incompatible with his own claim that only morally autonomous full persons can have rights. (Cohen is guilty of this inconsistency even if the first interpretation is correct, since he clearly does espouse speciesism later in his paper.) In any case, especially considering the absence of a convincing defense of speciesism, Cohen has given us no reason to reject the argument from marginal cases.

He tries to supply a "practical" sort of reason at the end of his article. Cohen concludes with an admittedly ad hominem appeal.[31] He warns us that it is inconsistent to reject the killing of nonhuman animals for human benefit in some contexts but not in others. Extending the rights enjoyed by marginal humans to nonhuman animals would require us to cease eating them, making furs and shoes out of them, and otherwise killing them for our own convenience. He is quite right in noting these implications. He is mistaken, however, in claiming that this poses "an inescapable difficulty" for those who believe that invasive nonhuman experimentation is wrong. On the contrary, this is exactly what advocates of the categorical version of the argument from marginal cases have said all along! (In fact, his appeal here is oddly inverted. Many who are inclined to include some nonhumans in the moral community have a far easier time rejecting the killing of animals for fur, hides, and food than they do in forgoing the apparent benefits of nonhuman experimentation.) Of course, as Cohen no doubt realizes, such considerations have no bearing on the soundness of the argument from marginal cases. According to any interpretation of his attacks, even the most sympathetic, that argument remains unscathed.

"Underestimation" of Many Nonhuman Animals

One final attack on the soundness of the argument from marginal cases remains to be discussed. It is a very different sort of attack from the others we have been considering, for it does not come from the full-personhood-view camp at all. Unlike Cohen, who charges the argument from marginal cases with greatly underestimating marginal humans, those who raise this objection believe that the argument denigrates the abilities of many nonhumans. Also unlike Cohen, those who raise this objection are already convinced that these nonhumans are highly morally significant. Steve Sapontzis, strong supporter of the moral considerability of any being possessing interests, as well as opponent of the argument from marginal cases, provides us with a good example of this attack: "[I]t is similarly insulting, even paradoxical, to attempt to enhance the moral status of animals by drawing analogies between them and severely incompetent humans, humans who are so defective they must be institutionalized."[32] As we have seen, the second premise in both versions of the argument from marginal cases posits the morally relevant similarity between certain nonhumans and marginal humans. Sapontzis joins Cohen (from a very different perspective, to be sure) in rejecting this assumption. Let us see if this attack on the argument fares any better than Cohen's.

Unquestionably, there are differences in the capacities of marginal humans and nonhuman animals. First of all, most animals are able to lead independent lives. Wolves may not be able to solve differential equations, but they have complex social relationships and can sustain themselves quite well (when humans do not war against them). By contrast, as Sapontzis suggests, severely mentally handicapped humans require a great deal of assistance from the rest of us in order to survive, and may have very impoverished social lives. Even many domestic animals, whom humans have bred to be dependent, will revert to ancestral independent traits when released from human "care." Abandoned domestic dogs will team up in packs to sustain themselves. Animals that have been altered far more drastically than the dog, like present-day domestic factory-farmed chickens and pigs, start to exhibit the traits of their self-sustaining wild precursors some time after being freed from confinement (they need some initial help before they can make the adjustment).[33] On the other hand, marginal humans with mental abilities comparable to some nonhumans fare very poorly when released from institutions and left to their own devices, as recent disgraceful mass releases of institutionalized patients in the United States during the 1980s have shown us.

Secondly, many sentient nonhumans appear to be better equipped mentally than many marginal humans. As mentioned earlier, the chimpanzee Kanzi was able to learn a human-constructed language without any instruction. Sue and Duane Rumbaugh, research directors at the Georgia State University Language Research Center, report that Kanzi has begun to converse about past events, and can recognize individuals in photographs and videotapes.[34] (His favorite videotape at the time of their report features his mother, Matata, who had temporarily been

Responses to the Argument

taken from the lab. Kanzi, who had been asking "Matata hide?" after looking again and again in Matata's former hiding spots in the lab, hooted excitedly when shown the videotape, and requested that it be shown repeatedly.) At the same lab, chimps Sherman and Austin are apparently able to grasp the concepts of numbers and addition, if at a primitive level: they are able to count to four and add numbers to make four.[35] Chimps in the wild have been observed eating leaves of certain plants when they are sick.[36] They consistently choose leaves from the right plants, using, for example, only three of the four species of Aspilia. Native humans living in the same area of Africa use the same three species to dose stomach ailments and wounds. (Manuel Aregullin, University of Arizona botanical chemist, recently discovered that these species of Aspilia contain a natural antibiotic.)

How many severely mentally handicapped humans would be able to treat themselves in this way without instruction? Even primates considerably less well-endowed mentally than chimps have demonstrated capacities, both inside and outside the laboratory, beyond the abilities of some humans. Abel and Baker, rhesus monkeys at Georgia State, can distinguish and order numerals up to nine.[37] Baboons in the wild, even very young ones, have been repeatedly observed by different researchers engaging in what appear to be acts of deception. For instance, a young baboon, whenever he spied another baboon enjoying a delicious morsel of food, would emit the particular piercing scream young baboons give when they are being threatened. His mother would come rushing to his aid, scolding and driving away the hapless and innocent baboon. The youngster, of course, always got the treat. The little baboon never went through this routine when his mother was nearby and able to observe what was really happening.[38] Birds can also carry out acts that appear to require considerable planning, cooperation with others, and coordination, as we saw in the case of the milk-loving English blue tits described in chapter 1. Unfortunately, there are many humans who could never equal any of these feats.

Nevertheless, this evidence of (sometimes) greater nonhuman independence and ingenuity does not indicate that the argument from marginal cases is based on a faulty comparison. Both marginal humans and sentient nonhumans, however different they otherwise may be, do not appear to differ in ways that would affect their basic moral status.

Responses to the Argument

This is the case regardless of one's acceptance or rejection of the full-personhood view, the target of the argument from marginal cases. (Of course, according to that view, marginal humans and comparably mentally equipped nonhumans are overwhelmingly morally similar. They lack the very quality allegedly essential for moral significance: the capacity for full personhood.) The point of either version of the argument is not to get us to treat marginal humans and sentient nonhumans in identical ways (e.g., institutionalization or round-the-clock care): it is to make us realize that these beings have similar moral status, whatever that status may be. Marginal humans differ at least as much in their abilities as individual marginal humans differ from individual nonhumans, but we do not conclude that an adult with a mental age of four is less morally significant than an adult who has attained the mental age of eight. We do not normally think that mentally handicapped humans who can manage to add up to four are more morally significant than those who cannot count to two. The argument challenges us to admit that a chimpanzee who can add up to four is no different in this respect. In recognition of the psychological and intellectual similarities between chimps and some marginal humans, the Rumbaughs' studies of Kanzi's language abilities are being applied to the teaching of severely mentally retarded human children. The argument from marginal cases requires us to explain why we do not believe Kanzi and the human children to be morally analogous as well, if that is indeed our view.

We must not be misled by the greater independence of most nonhumans in comparison to most marginal humans. Those who cannot achieve full personhood differ in their competence to live without assistance. The specific obligations we would have to these "non(full) persons," if we have any obligations to them at all, would differ accordingly, but this would not signal a difference in *moral status*. The same holds for full persons. Mentally competent quadriplegics require a lot more assistance to live and thrive than other full persons do, but this does not make them either more or less deserving of basic moral consideration.

Thus, the differences in marginal human and nonhuman abilities that opponents of the full-personhood view point out in this last attack on the argument from marginal cases are irrelevant to the issue of moral status, whether or not one subscribes to the full-personhood view. One would think that these critics, of all people, would be reluctant to give

Responses to the Argument

the impression that greater independence or intelligence translates into greater moral significance! Nevertheless, despite its failure, this last internal criticism of the argument from marginal cases provides us with a valuable reminder: We are simply not justified in making the common assumption that *any* human must necessarily be mentally superior to *any* nonhuman. Nonhumans can have a very impressive array of intelligence-related qualities, contrary to the view of philosophers such as C. A. J. Coady, who remarks that "the wildest claims on behalf of Washoe, the talking chimpanzee, do not really establish him [*sic*] as an even moderately boring dinner guest."[39] As the erroneous pronoun suggests, the author of this remark has very probably read none of the accounts of the linguistic research on chimpanzees. (If he had, he would have realized that his choice of adjectives is questionable. Lucy, a chimpanzee contemporary of Washoe brought up to use signs [not to talk] in a psychologist's household in which she was treated as a family member, regularly ate dinner with her human family, enthusiastically downing glass after glass of their expensive wine. When her "parents" decided to economize by giving her Boone's Farm apple wine while they continued imbibing their choice of fine Chablis, she sipped from her glass, paused, then reached across the table for first one, then the other glass of Chablis, draining both. Whatever one might say about Lucy's manners, they are clearly beyond "boring.")[40] There is no longer any excuse for maintaining that the abilities of any human far eclipse those of any nonhuman. Critics like Sapontzis are surely correct in underscoring this fact, even if it does not defeat the argument from marginal cases.

We have now considered the various attempts that have been made to show either version of the argument from marginal cases to be unsound. Each has failed: the charges of weakness, redundancy, inconsistency, and underestimation of marginal humans or of nonhumans have not withstood scrutiny. Proponents of the full-personhood view (and an opponent of that view) have not yet succeeded in exposing any internal flaws in the argument.

However, they can point out quite correctly that the categorical version of the argument cries out for an additional argument to establish its premise that marginal humans are maximally morally significant. Such an argument is indeed owed to us, and it will be given in chapter 5. As for the biconditional form of the argument, the situation is different: full-personhood-view advocates have found no logical means of escaping its acceptance.

Let us see where this leaves them. Readers will recall that the biconditional version of the argument asserts the following:

1. Beings who are similar in all important morally relevant respects are equally morally significant.
2. Nonhumans exist who are similar in all important morally relevant respects to marginal humans.
3. *Therefore,* those nonhumans who are similar in the important morally relevant respects to marginal humans are maximally morally significant if and only if marginal humans are maximally morally significant.

The conclusion is logically equivalent to the following disjunctive statement: "Either *both* marginal humans and those nonhumans who are similar to them in the important morally relevant respects are maximally morally significant, or *neither* is." Followers of the full-personhood view, like it or not, are forced to accept the latter disjunct. They are, in short, committed to this additional argument:

1. Those nonhumans who are similar in the important morally relevant respects to marginal humans (humans who are not full persons) are maximally morally significant if and only if marginal humans are maximally morally significant.
2. Only full persons are maximally morally significant.
3. *Therefore,* neither marginal humans nor the nonhumans who are similar to them in the important morally relevant respects are maximally morally significant.

Readers will remember that "maximum moral significance" implies a right to life, or a strong presumptive claim to life. Therefore, given the failure of attacks on the soundness of the biconditional version of the argument from marginal cases, the proponent of the full-personhood view must accept the justifiability of exploiting marginal humans. If it is morally permissible to hunt, trap, confine, slaughter, eat, do toxicity testing on, and vivisect nonhuman animals, as the full-personhood view holds, then it is equally morally permissible to do this to marginal humans. These immodest proposals are quite sufficient to drive many away from the full-personhood view. Given the failure of homo-

Responses to the Argument

centrism, the obvious choice seems to be recognition of the maximum moral significance of both marginal humans and many nonhumans.

Does this leave advocates of the full-personhood view in the unenviable position of either rejecting their view or accepting practices such as of marginal-human vivisection? Not necessarily. One option remains to them. They could try to show that although the biconditional version of the argument from marginal cases appears to be sound, warranting the further conclusion that marginal humans have no right or strong presumptive claim to life, no actually devastating consequences need be faced, because there are *other* excellent reasons for refusing to exploit marginal humans as we do so many nonhumans. They must show that those with a capacity for full personhood would somehow be wronged by such treatment of marginal humans. This is precisely what a number of philosophers who support the full-personhood view have tried to do, as we shall now see. If these philosophers succeed, they will have managed to deflate the significance of the argument from marginal cases. In effect, their response to its challenge is "So what?"

Attempts to Deflate the Argument from Marginal Cases

I will consider four such attempts: the charge that the rights of full persons would be endangered by the "devaluation" of marginal humans; arguments that attempt to justify the differential treatment of marginal humans and nonhumans on egoistic grounds; the attempt to do the same on utilitarian grounds; and the charge that the number of human problem cases can easily be reduced and readily protected. I will argue that each of these efforts to deflate the argument from marginal cases is unsuccessful.

The "Endangerment of Full Persons' Rights" Argument

A. V. Townsend, an adherent of the full-personhood view, provides us with a clear example of the first argument. Townsend fully accepts the implication that marginal humans can have no basic moral rights. Nevertheless, he argues, if we do not treat them *as if* they have rights, our own rights would be jeopardized. When distinctions among humans

Responses to the Argument

are blurred, normal humans risk having their own rights threatened.[41] All human life is devalued if we begin to regard some human lives as inferior and expendable. Thus, for the sake of full persons, we must treat all such lives with respect, even if they do not merit it for their own sakes.

Peter Carruthers, another full-personhood-view advocate, offers us another example of fundamentally the same argument. According to him, while we would be *theoretically* justified in excluding humans who fail to be moral agents from the moral community, we would be very ill-advised to *act* on such a principle: "For one of the facts that rational agents will know is that most people are not very deeply theoretical. They [rational agents] should therefore select moral principles that will provide a stable and easily understood framework within which ordinary people can debate questions of right and wrong. Seen in these terms, a rule that accorded rights in proportion to degree of rational agency *would* be wide open to creeping abuse . . . So I conclude that our . . . argument is indeed successful in according rights to all human beings."[42] In short, typical moral agents are, in Carruthers's view, not sophisticated enough to draw the essential distinction between humans who are capable of moral agency (and thus due full moral rights) and humans who are not. Although Carruthers speaks of the advisability of moral agents' "according" rights to marginal humans instead of urging that we treat these humans "as if" they have such rights, he is in essential agreement with Townsend. Moral rights that are "given" are, after all, not to be confused with rights that are due one regardless of the views of others: the latter sort of basic moral rights, not the former, is at issue in the argument from marginal cases.

As can be seen, Townsend and Carruthers accept the argument from marginal cases in its biconditional form, reject the categorical form (as they must, given their commitment to the full-personhood view), but deny that we should treat marginal humans as we do the nonhumans whom we routinely "harvest" for our own purposes. The argument they use could be employed by any deontologist, egoist, or utilitarian who believes that maximum moral significance is limited to full persons (including oneself). In fact, the argument is also sometimes used by homocentrists *against* those whom they believe to hold the full-personhood view: opponents of abortion and any form of euthanasia frequently use this very appeal to buttress their positions.

Responses to the Argument

Philosopher Jane English concedes the force of such an appeal in the abortion debate.[43] Her version of the "endangerment of full persons' rights" argument, a version that precedes Townsend's and Carruthers's, focuses upon that issue rather than upon the argument from marginal cases. Although she warns that the concept of (full) personhood is imprecise, she regards it as obvious that unborn members of the human species have not achieved that status. English then poses a question: "But how do we decide what you may or may not do to nonpersons?"[44] Her answer reveals her to be a proponent of the full-personhood view *and of* the endangerment argument: "It is crucial that psychological facts play a role here. Our psychological constitution makes it the case that for our ethical theory to work, it must prohibit certain treatment of nonpersons which are significantly personlike. If our moral rules allowed people to treat some personlike nonpersons in ways we do not want people to be treated, this would undermine the system of sympathies and attitudes that make our ethical system work."[45]

Thus, nonpersons who *resemble* (full) persons, physically and (to a limited extent) psychologically, are to have protection extended to them for the sake of "the ethical system." That system, of course, has "people" as its primary beneficiaries. English notes that antiabortion forces who show pictures of late abortions and use the term 'baby' to describe aborted fetuses are actually making "their strongest arguments":[46] they are underlining the *similarities* of these nonpersons to ourselves. English then turns this double-edged argument against abortion foes, by pointing out that embryos and early fetuses do *not* much resemble (full) persons: "Remember, however, that in the early weeks after conception, a fetus is very much unlike a person. It is hard to develop these feelings for a set of genes which doesn't yet have a head, hands, beating heart, response to touch or the ability to move by itself. Thus it seems to me that the 'slippery slope' between conception and birth is not so very slippery. In the early stages of pregnancy, abortion can hardly be compared to murder for psychological reasons, but in the latest stages it is *psychologically akin* to murder."[47]

English's meaning could not be plainer. Nonpersons whom we kill are not "murdered": the death of those who are most *like* us *reminds* us of murder. Nonpersons who are not fortunate enough to resemble us much should be extended no protection; killing them should not be considered murder (wrongful death). The same applies to nonpersons

Responses to the Argument

of other species: "Thus it makes sense that it is those animals whose appearance and behavior are most like those of people that get the most consideration in our moral scheme."[48] Although English does not address the argument from marginal cases, we can infer what she would say: clearly, human nonpersons (from the late stages of pregnancy on) resemble us more than cats, dogs, or birds. None have inherent moral rights, but killing these human nonpersons is much more likely to undermine the ethical system that protects genuine rights holders. Thus she, Townsend, and Carruthers would agree in rejecting the categorical form of the argument from marginal cases.

The endangerment argument is fallacious, however. Those who urge that the exploitation of marginal humans for their medical usefulness, for example, would lead us, helplessly, to generalize such treatment and prey upon normal humans, are in fact guilty of the notorious slippery slope fallacy. Ironically, Carruthers anticipates his opponents by admitting that the endangerment argument is "a version of slippery slope argument."[49] He even grants that the argument is open to a specific instance of the standard objection raised against all such arguments: "If the argument has a weakness, however, it lies in its empirical assumption—namely, that a rule according direct rights only to rational agents would be likely to be abused in such a way as to undermine itself."[50] (He nonetheless thinks that it can be defended, as we shall see shortly.) What reason do we have to believe that such a disastrous erosion of moral rights would occur? Alas, normal humans are perfectly capable of being highly discriminating in their treatment of other beings, even when the latter do *not* differ from them in any significant way, as Carruthers concedes.[51] Any who live in bigoted societies can testify that there is very little tendency to generalize good and bad treatment beyond designated boundaries. It is doubtful that normal humans would have difficulty distinguishing between themselves and those who *do* differ profoundly from themselves.

It is instructive to realize that this very fact undermines a famous slippery slope argument parallel to the one currently under discussion. St. Thomas Aquinas and, half a millennium later, Immanuel Kant each denied moral standing to nonhuman beings. Each also warned that wanton cruelty toward these morally inconsequential beings might well encourage the ill treatment of rational beings; thus, we are well advised to

Responses to the Argument

avoid such cruelty, even though it cannot wrong its victims.[52] Peter Carruthers endorses a very limited version of this argument in his attempt to reconcile the denial of all moral standing to nonhumans with the "commonsense" view that cruelty to nonhuman animals is wrong. It is pretty plain, however, that Carruthers himself is aware of the weakness of this argument: he gives us example after example of humans who cause dogs, cats, rabbits, calves, and others great suffering in the course of their jobs as detergent testers, butchers, or farmhands, noting in each case that their brutality is very unlikely to be generalized to other humans.[53] While an unrepentant sadist who enjoys torturing nonhuman animals has a very unlovely character, and is not to be trusted around helpless humans, most individuals who hurt nonhumans are not motivated in this way. (Note that even in this case, it is implausible to hold that sadism toward nonhumans *causes* similar treatment of humans: the individual described is probably a sadist who chooses weak victims whom others are least likely to avenge.) Carruthers holds that almost everyone who causes suffering to nonhumans does so for "nontrivial" reasons, such as earning a profit or a livelihood; desensitization to the screams and howls of those sacrificed for these purposes is unlikely to make us try the same thing on the neighbor's little daughter. "I think that human beings are more discriminating" than that, Carruthers rightly notes.[54]

That is precisely the problem with both slippery slope arguments, warning us as they do that humans (at least the "rational" ones) are threatened by abuse of nonhumans or of nonrational humans. We humans are outstanding "discriminators." White supremacists who have no difficulty being kind to those of their own ilk while blowing up black churches during services are also not likely to confuse chickens with their fellow cross-burners.

Carruthers nonetheless proposes that "psychological separability" allows us to treat normal humans and nonhuman animals very differently: in view of this, he believes that mistreatment of nonrational humans would be very inadvisable. These humans are simply too much like *us* in physical appearance and behavior: If we mistreat them, we will soon find it difficult not to mistreat rational moral agents.[55] Lamentably, all the varieties of carefully compartmentalized bigotry we see practiced on our planet undermine this psychological thesis. However, there is a far more directly relevant reply to Carruthers's psychological claim.

Responses to the Argument

That reply appears fatal to the endangerment argument, as we shall now see.

To his credit, Carruthers raises the reply himself.[56] It appears that various quite stable human cultures have systematically excluded some "nonrational" members from the moral community without endangering the status of normal members. In fact, as Peter Singer points out in his brief response to another supporter of the endangerment argument, Townsend, historical and anthropological evidence suggests that societies with no particular concern for newborn or handicapped humans tend to be *less* likely to disregard the rights of normal adult humans than members of allegedly enlightened societies![57] It seems, then, that the endangerment argument is a resounding failure as an attempt to deflate the argument from marginal cases.

Carruthers's Defense of the Endangerment Argument

Carruthers tries to convince us otherwise, setting out to reinterpret the anthropological data. He holds that the cross-cultural data indicating that we could ensure the safety of rational humans while according no rights to humans without a capacity for rational agency can be explained away as follows. First, societies condoning infanticide, killing of the handicapped or aged, and so on are unified by religious traditions. Let us suppose that these societies genuinely exclude those humans from moral considerability (Carruthers actually doubts this, as we shall see below). Allegedly, *we* cannot seek stability from such a source: "In our modern world, moral rules have to be defensible in the face of free and open discussion, without appeal to religious sanction."[58] Without such a source of stability, those of us in "modern" societies would not be safe in adopting rules reserving moral standing to rational agents. Second, a closer look at societies condoning or participating in the killing of humans who fall short of full personhood indicates, according to Carruthers, that these disadvantaged individuals are probably not regarded as having no basic moral rights. He proposes that these societies have addressed the problem of seriously limited resources by taking actions that will promote the survival of most of their members, even at the cost of some deaths. One may act in this way while acknowledging that those who are killed or allowed to die have as much moral signifi-

Responses to the Argument

cance as those who live: it is simply a matter of self-preservation on the part of those able to act for themselves. If one individual is dependent upon another for survival, as is the case for the very young, very old, and severely handicapped, but both individuals will die unless the weak one is sacrificed, the "sacrifice" is permissible.[59] Moreover, Carruthers thinks that no dependent rights holder is *entitled* to have his or her existence continued. Benevolent sustaining of weak life is not required, particularly if it would cost other lives.[60] Thus, he strongly suspects that the anthropological data are not contrary to the rights endangerment argument: we are, after all, not given clear cases of moral rights being denied to human nonagents and accorded only to agents. If we truly did deny that rights apply to some humans but not to others, he is convinced that we would be inviting the infringement of rights for full persons whom the majority finds distasteful or inconvenient. For these two major reasons, Carruthers holds that the slippery slope endangerment of full persons' rights argument is shown to be not fallacious.

Carruthers's defense of the endangerment argument's attack on the argument from marginal cases is unsuccessful, however. Let us consider the first prong of that defense. Our "modern" society, he says, could never bring off the refusal to ascribe rights to humans lacking a capacity for rational agency because "religious sanctions" would have no force in ensuring societal stability and the noninfringement of genuine rights. Societies that *appear* to have "succeeded" in making such a distinction had centuries of religious tradition to ensure cohesion and reinforce boundaries, tradition that would have no force in our times (he thinks). It is ironic that Carruthers, of all people, should be making such a point. As we have seen, in making the case for the endangerment argument he reasons that "ordinary people" are too simple-minded to make the supposedly justified moral distinction between human agents and human nonagents; this *lack* of sophistication would thus result in "creeping abuse" imperiling real rights holders if we tried to adopt such a rule. *Now,* in defending his argument against purported counterexamples of societies that may very well have made the distinction in question, he replies that we are *too* sophisticated, too unlikely to be taken in by appeals to tradition and religion, to adopt such a rule without endangering ourselves. Which is it to be? Either most of us are not theoretically minded, open to the blandishments of religion and custom, or we are capable of reasoning out justifiable moral actions and policies. If we primarily fall into the first category, nothing would prevent us from excluding certain humans from the moral community; we should be at least as successful in not endangering ourselves as was ancient Greek society. Already, alas, many folk in "modern" society see humans falling short of full personhood as less morally significant than themselves, actually loathing the mentally handicapped as "unnatural" (see my discussion of "normalism" in chapter 3). It is not the case that such a rule would be utterly alien and uncustomary: it jibes with the "gut feelings" of surprisingly many. If, on the other hand, we are above all open to rational persuasion, why should we not be convinced by advocates of the full-personhood view that we rational agents alone have basic moral rights? If we adopted such a rule on the basis of reasoning rather than mere "gut" feelings, we would be unlikely to generalize it beyond its intelligible boundaries. In attempting to have it both ways, Carruthers doubly discredits his own defense.

Now let us turn to the second prong of that defense. He proposes that the societies cited by the anthropological appeal were really engaged in "triage" rather than the refusal to attribute rights to human nonagents. Unfortunately for him, the evidence does not support his interpretation. First of all, in at least one intensively studied society, the Japanese village of Nakahara in the eighteenth and nineteenth centuries, infanticide was routinely practiced by affluent couples in stable relationships, primarily for convenience's sake.[61] Wealthy citizens of Greece have acted similarly, particularly when the child was born handicapped or was not the desired sex.[62] No dire necessity motivated *these* killings, although limited resources unquestionably play a role in many other acts of infanticide. Secondly, there is every reason to believe that societies with the custom of killing certain human nonagents have indeed refused to attribute rights to them. In these societies, *a general proscription of killing members of the community* held; thus infants slated for death were killed *before* being named or otherwise ceremoniously included in the group.[63] The inadequacy of the slippery slope endangerment argument, as Carruthers himself characterizes it, is particularly evident here. Moreover, societies now exist in which even those human nonagents who are given some membership in the community are regarded as having little moral significance in contrast to others. For cultural and economic reasons,

Responses to the Argument

female infanticide is common in many parts of the world, much to the dismay of those governing these countries. In certain rural Indian villages, the practice is defended as follows: "Even a useless male buffalo calf fetches 100 rupees. A girl child means nothing but expense." [64] If the child is allowed to live, chances are that she will be denied the nourishment, education, and care routinely extended to her brothers. Can anyone doubt that such children are seen as *at best* marginal members of the moral community? Those accorded full membership are in no danger of "creeping abuse," contrary to the endangerment argument.

The slippery slope endangerment argument has now been thoroughly discredited. We shall see if the next attack on the argument from marginal cases, superficially similar to this one, fares any better.

Appeals to Self-Interest

Another "deflationary" attack avoids the blatant fallaciousness of the previous one by appealing to a *direct* connection between ourselves and humans who are not or who are no longer full persons. C. A. J. Coady, an unabashed full-personhood-view advocate, makes such an appeal in his dismissal of the argument from marginal cases: "[I]t is of course true that there are immature, senile, and defective members of the species, but only an inordinately individualistic ideology can hold that such members should be given treatment that takes no account of their species membership. We have a vital interest in the immature, the retarded, and the defective of our kind since, apart from anything else, we normal adults have been immature and may become damaged or handicapped." [65]

Although marginal humans allegedly lack the "cluster of qualities" Coady believes to be constitutive of "human superiority," such as rationality, intelligence, creativity, the capacity for love, and "moral goodness," [66] he suggests that it would be contrary to the self-interest of those of us who are blessed with these qualities to exclude such humans from the moral community. Coady does not spell out his suggestion in his brief article, so let us turn to another philosopher who has had quite a bit to say in taking this line of argument: Jan Narveson.

Narveson is an ethical egoist. He has long been opposed to the inclusion of nonhumans, at least in any serious way, in the moral community, for the simple reason that it does not serve one's interests to include them. The test of a principle of morality, he tells us explicitly, is whether "there is good reason to think that moral agents will be better off having such a principle than they would not having one."[67] He has written that his version of egoism is inspired by Jesse Kalin, who holds that "a person ought, all things considered, to do an action if and only if that action is in his overall self-interest."[68] According to this view, rational individuals (full persons) living in proximity to other rational individuals find it mutually beneficial to forge bonds of trust and respect with each other, to form a moral community. Moral agents are the creators and beneficiaries of this contractarian community, alone entitled to moral consideration. Nonhuman animals have no moral status given such a view, since they are unable to make commitments, claim rights, or seriously threaten those who harm them. Beloved pets may be granted protection from those who do not care for them, but only because moral agents happen to hold them dear.[69] Nonhumans who are hunted, trapped, or farmed for their fur or food, or used for research that interests moral agents, or gassed to test the latest hair sprays are fair game, so long as rational humans have an interest in these practices. Plainly, according to this egoistic view, nonhumans "certainly can be used for human purposes in ways that will undoubtedly be uncomfortable or fatal to them."[70]

What is the status of marginal humans, according to such a view? They are also incapable of contracting with rational humans. May we also make them "uncomfortable" or even kill them if it serves our interests? Narveson grants, as he must, that such humans "are not inherently qualified for basic rights."[71] Nevertheless, he holds that it is not in our interests to treat marginal humans as we prefer to treat many nonhumans: "The question of how to treat such cases is to be answered by reference to two strongly supporting sets of considerations. First, that essentially every subnormal or infant human individual is the offspring, and often the sibling, of persons who take a close sympathetic interest in its welfare; and second, that there simply is no appreciable general interest in treating such individuals adversely."[72] In addition, as Narveson earlier pointed out, and as we saw Coady state, "we shall want the feeble-minded generally respected because we ourselves might become so . . ."[73] In reverse order of presentation, the rational agent has three reasons for not exploiting marginal humans: (1) one might oneself become disabled; (2) some rational agent (perhaps oneself) very probably cares deeply about every such human, and it is not in one's interests to destroy those in whom others have a compelling interest; and (3) rational agents in general have no interest in exploiting marginal humans. None of these reasons applies to the nonhumans we use and destroy for our own purposes.

Narveson concludes that marginal humans, unlike nonhumans, should be "given" moral status: " 'Given' is the crucial term here. Marginals are not, so to speak, charter members of the moral club; normal adults are." [74] Marginal humans and many nonhumans thus both fail to qualify for basic rights, but should nevertheless be treated in very different ways. The soundness of the argument from marginal cases in its biconditional form is conceded, but, as Narveson has long believed, it has been effectively disarmed by egoism: "Egoism seems to give a coherent and quite theoretically smooth account of our moral intuitions and of our attitudes about animals which preserves the latter rather than rejecting them." [75] Does it, indeed? Has Narveson really defanged the argument from marginal cases?

No, he has not. First of all, it is highly doubtful that his explanation of how marginal humans may be accorded protection really does "give a coherent and quite theoretically smooth account of our moral intuitions." While it is true that many normal humans are quite unconcerned about the sacrifice of billions of nonhumans annually for food, research, and recreational purposes, the hesitation many have about treating humans with comparable abilities similarly is not captured very well by Narveson's account. If you, a rational agent, decide *not* to kill, cook, and eat a succulent mentally handicapped baby who has crawled into your yard, is your decision justified *because* it is in your self-interest? After all, the baby's parents might get angry with you, and it is probably also true that you would not want to take an action that might result in a mentally handicapped baby of yours becoming someone else's supper in the future! Readers, ask yourselves how "smooth" an account egoism gives of your moral intuitions in this regard. The innocence of the child, the suffering and death that would be inflicted upon it purely to satisfy a gustatory interest, receive no weight in Narveson's account. Of course, the same reasoning applies to veal calves, as well as to all the other nonhumans with whom some of us fill our bellies.

Secondly, as Tom Regan has pointed out in a partial reply to Narveson's earlier article,[76] it is easy to provide an egoistic justification for extremely callous treatment of many marginal humans. We could, for example, agree to a rule that rational humans who *become* mentally enfeebled or irredeemably insane in the future will be accorded protection. Thus, the rational agent need not worry about his or her own fate, and one of Narveson's reasons for sparing the marginal humans who never achieve rationality falls by the egoistic wayside. Furthermore, we can solve the problem of harming those rational agents who have sentimental attachments to marginal humans (thus weakening the bonds of trust and respect that are to one's advantage to preserve) by restricting exploitation to those nonrational beings whom no one cares about.[77] Although Narveson claims that "essentially every subnormal or infant human individual is the offspring, and often the sibling, of persons who take a close sympathetic interest in its welfare," this is sadly not the case. It is not uncommon for parents to feel horror rather than affection for their severely handicapped children. These days, increasing numbers of drug-addicted and permanently brain-damaged babies are born to parents unable or unwilling to care about them. This also holds for many babies who are infected by the AIDS virus. Even undamaged infants are sometimes abandoned or abused by their relatives. Some of these children are so impaired emotionally by their treatment that they are unable to bond with new caregivers. Shunted from foster home to foster home, they may inspire little affection from those closest to them. The rational agent would have quite a number of marginal humans to consider exploiting without fear of hurting other rational agents. Thus, the second of Narveson's three reasons for refraining from treating marginal humans as we treat many nonhumans collapses along with the first one.

Narveson's third and final reason can also be shown to be insufficient to ensure the protection of marginal humans in a society devoted to rational egoism. As we saw, he holds that "there simply is no appreciable general interest in treating such individuals adversely." This may be the case now, in certain societies, but it has not always been so, nor can we be confident that it will remain so. Narveson himself points out, a few sentences before the sentence quoted above, that good treatment of marginal humans is not a cultural universal: "Why, then, should we be as concerned for their well-being as we mostly are? Why not allow people to hunt *them*? Or what about infants? All of these are important

Responses to the Argument

cases—though it is well to remember that they are also cases concerning which there has been tremendous variation in approved treatment in the *de facto* moralities of different ages and cultures. Exposure of unpromising infants, for instance, was routine in many cultures."[78] The interests of rational agents can and do vary. These interests also change, especially when changing them is to one's advantage. It is true that there is little general interest in cannibalism outside of emergency situations, despite the fact that "the long pig" is reputed to be the best tasting of all meat. It is also the case that, apart from Nazi horrors, human skin is not readily sought for warmth or decoration. One may hope that this will remain so, although there is no guarantee. Many humans have such interests in nonhumans, although neither these humans' survival nor their health depends upon it. However, there is another area in which the exploitation of marginal humans might be of considerable interest. *As Narveson himself says*, "Apart from the special case of medical experimentation, there is no comparable interest in marginal humans."[79] He leaves the topic immediately, without pointing out just how useful marginal humans would be to other humans in this regard.

For example, fetal tissue and organs are highly suitable, medically speaking, for transplantation because they are "immunologically naive"; that is, they do not stimulate rejection responses from the transplant recipient. Such transplants appear to be useful in the alleviation of Parkinson's disease, diabetes, kidney disease, leukemia, damage from severe burns, and radiation sickness (a number of Chernobyl victims had fetal cells transplanted into their bone marrow in order to reinitiate the formation of blood cells).[80] Already, some cases have been reported of women deliberately conceiving in order to abort the fetus and harvest its organs for family members in need of a transplant.[81] Abortions of this kind must be rather late; otherwise, the organs will not be developed sufficiently. By then, the fetus has in all probability achieved sentience. By thirteen weeks after conception, all the major neural components of the brain have differentiated.[82] It begins to have REM sleep ("rapid-eye-movement" sleep occurs when we dream and at no other time, at least for those of us who have been born) by twenty-three weeks,[83] and is able to hear by the sixth month of gestation. Shortly after that time, by the twenty-fifth and twenty-sixth weeks, all the neural pathways necessary and sufficient for pain perception are being forged.[84] Despite its

Responses to the Argument

sentience, however, the fetus has not achieved anything like full personhood.[85] Therefore, on Narveson's principles, it is a marginal human with no claim to moral rights. (Narveson thinks normal children are "a special case," deserving of special protection even though they have no moral rights, because they are "our only source of future adults."[86] Presumably, rational agents have an interest in the perpetuation of their society. However, he would have to agree that the interests of rational agents would have to take precedence over the interests of those who have no claim to rights given his view, like fetuses.) To be sure, there is as yet no general clamor for "fetus farms": a June 1991 poll of U.S. adults done by Yankelovich Clancy Shulman indicates that 71 percent of the respondents believe that it is morally unacceptable to "conceive and intentionally abort a fetus so the tissue can be used to save another life" (18 percent thought this was morally acceptable, and 11 percent were "not sure").[87] However, opinions can shift, especially if the general populace were to be persuaded by the theory of rational egoism!

Imagine the benefits if not just fetuses but also unwanted infants and those who will never achieve full personhood (provided that no person has ever loved them) could be used for medical research and procedures. They are far more similar to human persons than any rat, cat, dog, rabbit, or chimpanzee. Stephen Suomi, who, with Harry Harlow, has conducted deprivation experiments on rhesus monkeys over several decades, has said: "An animal model is almost never the 'real thing'; it is, instead, only a model of the real thing . . . the primary rationale for creating most animal models lies not so much in any obvious and impressive strengths of such models as it lies in the problems inherent in conducting research with humans as subjects."[88] Narveson's theory would remove any constraints we might have about the use of marginal human models, so long as they are not former full persons and they are unloved. Already, scientists recognize that brain-dead humans whose bodies are sustained by life support could be a valuable resource for medical education, toxicity testing, drug testing, disease induction and cure, transfusions, and so on.[89] They are already very valuable sources of organs for transplant, which are in very short supply. The number of humans that could be used for such purposes would be greatly increased by "rational egoistic" considerations: Why limit ourselves to the brain-dead? In short, Narveson is on very shaky ground when he

Responses to the Argument

asserts that "there is no appreciable general interest in treating such individuals adversely." Rational agents may make any decisions they please about suitable subjects for exploitation, so long as the subjects' future selves and those who have a sentimental interest in them are protected. They may even decide to spare nonhumans rather than marginal humans! The fate of all who can never achieve full personhood would be entirely contingent on the "sentimental" interests of full persons, as I have pointed out elsewhere,[90] and so—as Dale Jamieson independently concluded—it is now painfully clear that "the moral framework that emerges from rational egoism is inherently unstable."[91] The attempt to deflate the argument from marginal cases by appeal to egoism has failed.

The Appeal to Utilitarian Side Effects

Utilitarianism, while it is more plausible than egoism as a consequentialist normative theory, succeeds no more than egoism in deflating the argument from marginal cases. I will discuss utilitarianism and its implications for the treatment of humans and nonhumans in much more detail later in this book (see chapter 4). For now, I will confine myself to a brief sketch of the utilitarian side effects argument in the context of the argument from marginal cases. Its major problems will then, I think, be obvious.

Normal humans ought not to exploit marginal humans, a utilitarian can say, because the practice is bound to generate massive disutility (nonmoral evil). Even if we treat these marginal humans with utmost "humanity" (as we signally fail to do in the case of exploited nonhumans), sparing them all the pain and fear that we can, allowing them to enjoy the lives we allot to them to the limits of their abilities, and replacing them after their deaths with other marginal humans whom we treat in the same way, the benefits they would provide normal humans would be far outweighed by the following: Any who love marginal humans will be devastated by their loss; there would be fear that one's own loved ones might become disabled and subject to exploitation; and (last but far from least) there would be great concern about one's own future fate (no one wishes to contemplate an old-age home that is actually a charnel house). In short, it is argued that the practice of killing marginal humans for the benefit of full persons would cause so

Responses to the Argument

much fear, anxiety, insecurity, and anger among full persons as to outweigh the benefits of human experimentation, organ transplants, superb toxicity-testing "models," and the like.[92]

All these concerns, however, can easily be circumvented, just as their egoistic counterparts have been. As we have just seen in the case of the appeal to egoistic concerns, all normal humans need do to avoid the scenario sketched above is adhere to rules that would protect their future selves and their loved ones. Continuing to exploit (humanely, of course) other marginal humans would then maximize utility. If utilitarians reply that we must factor in the outrage many humans would feel at the "harvesting" of marginal humans, even if this does not threaten themselves or their loved ones, it can be answered that (1) we can do our exploitation secretly, and (2) any such outrage is decidedly irrational given the utilitarian view, and calls for utilitarian "reeducation." (For a more detailed reply along these lines, see my chapter 4.) Moreover, as pointed out in the preceding section, societies that would not require such "reeducation," that fully accept the practice of killing marginal humans, have existed and could exist in the future. The fear, horror, and anguish predicted by the utilitarian side effects argument does not come into play in these instances. Agents in such societies appear to accept even their own eventual disposal should they become disabled. Societies of dedicated eugenicists, opposed to the "purposeless" maintenance of "useless eaters," to use the notorious Nazi designation, would regard the use of such humans for the benefit of the "racially pure" as supremely justified. As we all well know, this is no mere science fiction scenario, and the side effects argument is powerless to combat it. If the maximization of nonmoral good (utility) is to be our primary guiding principle, marginal humans are due no more protection than nonhumans. (It must be said, however, that life and death for nonhumans would be greatly improved if we humans took utilitarianism seriously. Nevertheless, that view would still entitle us to exploit them for our own benefit. My point here is that it would also entitle us to exploit marginal humans.) Therefore, an appeal to utilitarian considerations also fails to blunt the impact of the argument from marginal cases.

Responses to the Argument

The Alleged Inconsequentiality of the Argument from Marginal Cases

A final attempt to defuse the argument from marginal cases will now be considered. After the foregoing discussion of egoistic and utilitarian attempts to do the same, it should become clear why the following attempt also does not work.

As we have seen, Steve Sapontzis rejects *both* the full-personhood view and the argument from marginal cases. Earlier, we considered an attack he made on the argument on behalf of nonhuman animals; namely, the charge that the argument underestimates their capacities. Now we turn to an attack he makes on behalf of the full-personhood view.[93] Although he rejects that view, he believes it can easily counter the horrific implications of the argument. In his discussion of the view that moral rights are restricted to those who are able to recognize and respect the rights claims of others, a view that identifies the moral community with the community of moral agents or full persons, Sapontzis raises the argument from marginal cases as an obvious response. According to the (categorical version of that) argument, moral rights cannot be restricted to moral agents, because this would disenfranchise beings with moral rights: marginal humans. Sapontzis then dismisses the argument as "neither particularly insightful nor telling" against the full-personhood view, because all that view need do is modify its requirement for moral rights as follows: "Only those who will be able to, are at least a threshold degree able to, may again be able to, or did respect the moral rights of others are entitled to moral rights."[94] Making this adjustment leaves only a few problematic marginal cases, and these too can easily be handled, he says: "The remaining marginal cases, namely, the severely, incurably retarded or psychopathic from birth, constitute a very small, sequestered group. This small, isolated group can plausibly be treated as 'honorary rights-holders' out of deference to the feelings of species affinity most all of us share."[95] Thus, he holds that the full-personhood view is unthreatened by the argument from marginal cases. Sapontzis contends that moral theories are formulated for "ordinary" or "common" experience: they are not refuted by isolated problem cases. If the full-personhood view fails, as he believes it does, he thinks it must be for some other reason.

While I agree with Sapontzis that the full-personhood view fails for other reasons (see my chapter 5), I do not think that he has succeeded in rescuing it from the implications of the argument from marginal cases. First of all, even if it were true that only a "small, isolated group" of marginal humans pose a problem for the full-personhood view—and I will soon argue that this is not the case—such "uncommon," exceptional cases cannot be dismissed as inconsequential. The claims made by any normative moral theory, be it the full-personhood view, homocentrism, utilitarianism, egoism, or any other normative view, are necessarily *general:* they tell us who is deserving of moral considerability, provide criteria for moral significance, and specify what the basis of our duties is. They are not restricted to the context of "ordinary experience," whatever that may be for a person or culture. As Socrates knew, views that seem beyond the pale in ordinary situations wither and die when exposed to the counterexample. If the full-personhood view restricts moral rights to moral agents, but we are convinced that beings who cannot be moral agents nevertheless have moral rights, then we must reject the full-personhood view as false. The *number* of problem cases faced by a theory of moral value and obligation is not the issue: the fact that there *are* problem cases is.

There is a legitimate concern behind Sapontzis's rejection of the counterexample technique in moral arguments. He thinks that attention to exceptional cases distorts the content of moral views. He uses the old lifeboat precept—"Women and children first!"—as an example: those who hold this view do not really believe that women and children are more morally significant than men. They believe that all are equally entitled to rights, other things being equal. When other things are not equal, we decide otherwise. Thus: "Morally special cases are cases in which our common moral principles must be superceded; consequently, we cannot infer from our practice in such special cases to what our common moral principles are." [96]

However, Sapontzis's concern is misplaced. A moral theory is not just about ordinary life. It includes principles that help one to determine the appropriate actions in special cases. Utilitarianism is an obvious example of such a theory: taking the simplest version of the theory, we are to maximize utility (nonmoral good) as best we can in every situation. A deontological rights theory worth its salt will also have something to say about adjudication of conflicts of rights. Perhaps our "ordinary" moral experience will be "superseded" in extraordinary situations, but

Responses to the Argument

our moral *principles* will not be. To return to Sapontzis's lifeboat example, a homocentric theory that holds that every human has a right to life can also hold that, in case of conflicts, the very young, who have not yet had a chance to fulfill their lives, should be given precedence over those who have had such a chance. Since they would perish without their caretakers, one could conclude that the latter should also be given precedence. If one accepts a utilitarian view, one could reach the same conclusion for different reasons: utility would be maximized if the young life is extended rather than the older life. We might also reach this conclusion on the basis of false assumptions about who is most weak, helpless, or nurturing, or by adhering to a stereotypical heroic macho ideal: our ethical basis or our factual beliefs may not be particularly defensible or unprejudiced. The point is, however, that uncommon cases do not distort normative moral theories: they test them. Nothing reveals more about our moral commitments than an emergency!

Of course, Sapontzis is correct in pointing out that we cannot simply infer the content of a normative moral theory from actions taken in an emergency situation. Different theories might have the same implications for right conduct for very different reasons, as we just saw. It would also be a mistake to interpret the principle governing the action too simplistically, as we would if we inferred that "Women and children first!" must mean that women and children are more morally significant than men. But it does not follow from this that theories have no implications in unusual situations, or that theories should not be rejected because of their implications in those situations.

Sapontzis is also on shaky ground, sadly, when he estimates that very few humans can never become even minimally competent moral agents. Their numbers are growing all over the world in these times when AIDS is becoming a leading cause of death in women of childbearing age, and in which drugs permanently impair developing fetuses. He is on shakier ground still when he asserts that this "isolated group" can be made " 'honorary rights-holders' out of deference to the feelings of species affinity most all of us share." Do "most" of us share this? What of those who don't? In some past and present cultures, "most" did not or do not share this. As we saw in the discussions of appeals to the egoistic concerns of moral agents and to utilitarian side effects, the "giving" of rights to those who allegedly do not merit them is a very contingent

Responses to the Argument

affair indeed. Any theory that leaves the welfare of sentient beings who cannot become moral agents or full persons to the whims of those who have achieved this high status is worth a long, hard, skeptical glance.

Finally, it is far from clear that the full-personhood view can restrict the numbers of marginal human problem cases in all the ways that Sapontzis suggests. He holds that it would be easy for proponents of that view to declare that those who (1) *will* be moral agents, or (2) who are only minimally qualified moral agents, or (3) who are perhaps only temporarily unable to be moral agents, or (4) who *have* been moral agents are full rights holders (not merely "honorary" ones). The second and third of these categories are indeed unproblematic for the full-personhood view. Those who are minimally qualified moral agents (should we call them "full-enough persons"?) are still moral agents, and those who are temporarily disabled still have the *capacity* for full personhood. (If we are not sure if they can recover, we ought to give them the benefit of the doubt whenever possible.) But on what basis would the first and last of these rights attributions be made? Large numbers of humans are included in these two categories. Every one of us has been in category 1, and many of us are destined by accident, aging, or disease to be in category 4. If only those with the capacity for moral agency are maximally morally significant, as the view holds, how can any who do not yet have or who no longer have this capacity qualify for moral rights? Neither egoistic nor utilitarian principles can ground such rights attributions, as we have seen: at most, such principles would sanction an "honorary" rights-holder status for such humans. Not only is this highly chancy status insufficient for these humans' protection: it is also far from being the unqualified, warranted moral status Sapontzis claims the full-personhood view can extend to such cases.

Therefore, contrary to Sapontzis's contention, the full-personhood view does not at all have an easy time circumventing the impact of the argument from marginal cases. Let us check more closely, however, to see if the full-personhood view could find some basis for justifying the ascription—not the gift—of moral rights or full moral significance to future and to past full persons. Not only do we need to address this issue in order to determine the scope of the argument from marginal cases: it is of great importance in its own right. Even so, whatever we may discover in this regard, however many humans cannot be shown to pose a

Responses to the Argument

problem for the full-personhood view, those cases that do remain show the argument from marginal cases to be anything but inconsequential.

THE SCOPE OF THE ARGUMENT FROM MARGINAL CASES

First, we will consider potential full persons, then we will turn to living beings who have permanently lost the capacity for full personhood.

Potential Full Persons

Normal humans do not develop a capacity for full personhood until adolescence, but they have the potential to become full persons from the moment of their conception. Can this potential support the ascription of maximum moral significance to them, from the perspective of the full-personhood view? Many philosophers would answer this question in the negative. For example, Joel Feinberg has argued, in agreement with others, that any attempt to assign moral significance on the basis of potential is infected by a fatal logical flaw. He dismisses the view that all and only actual *and potential* persons are due full moral rights as follows: "It is a logical error, some have charged, to deduce *actual* rights from merely *potential* (but not yet actual) qualification for those rights. What follows from potential qualification, it is said, is potential, not actual, rights; what entails actual rights is actual, not potential, qualification. As the Australian philosopher Stanley Benn puts it, 'A potential president of the United States is not on that account Commander-in-Chief [of the U.S. Army and Navy].' This simple point can be called 'the logical point about potentiality.' Taken on its own terms, I don't see how it can be answered as an objection to the strict potentiality criterion." [97]

Now, it is true that any view whose criterion of moral significance is the possession of some attribute or network of attributes cannot also claim that those who only *potentially* possess the relevant attribute(s) are thereby morally significant. The same holds for views that tie moral significance to possession of a capacity: Having the potential for full personhood is not to be confused with having the capacity for full personhood. Proponents of the pure, unadulterated full-personhood view

Responses to the Argument

cannot simply graft potential full personhood onto their criterion of moral significance. To this extent, Feinberg and Benn's charge of logical error is fully warranted. However, if a morally relevant link between the potential for full personhood and the capacity for full personhood could be discovered, full-personhood-view advocates could legitimately modify their criterion. They could then propose that potential as well as actual possession of the capacity for full personhood is sufficient for maximum moral significance. In that case, they would not be subject to "the logical point about potentiality," since they would not be confusing potential rights bearers (to return to Feinberg's "rights" terminology) with actual rights bearers. According to their view, potential full persons would be actual rights bearers. Feinberg's dismissal of a potentiality criterion for moral rights is far too sweeping.

Nevertheless, advocates of the full-personhood view have their work cut out for them if they wish to make a case for the moral relevance of potential. If they retreat to homocentrism, arguing that as far as we know only humans can be full persons, and that potential full persons are deserving of moral consideration on the grounds of their humanity, they contradict their own view. In any case, homocentrism's indefensibility, to which the full-personhood view is after all a response, makes it a poor candidate for assistance. On what other grounds can a case be made for the moral significance of potential full personhood?

A. I. Melden takes an interesting approach to this problem. He suggests that the infant is one stage or "segment" of the life of a person. The very concept of "infant," he claims, entails that the being so named will develop into a moral agent. Melden goes so far as to say that severely defective babies who cannot ever achieve this are "deviant beings brought out of the womb . . . for which special terms are employed in order to make clear how far they deviate from the paradigm cases to which we apply the term 'infant.' "[98] I find Melden's definitional move rather implausible, not to mention distressing: mentally handicapped infants appear to be "infants" in the full sense. (Interestingly, the term 'infant' is derived from the Latin *infans,* which simply means 'incapable of speech.') However, he would be on solid ground in claiming that the concept of *normal* human infancy implies potential moral agency, and this is all he need claim for his purposes. For Melden, full moral status extends forward and backward to include the entire life of the individual

Responses to the Argument

who is a (full) person during only part of that time. It is the prospect of development in the future that invests the infant with moral significance. Although Melden is reluctant to even use the word 'potentiality,' given all the problems it causes,[99] it is plain that an infant's moral status is entirely determined by its potential for future moral agency.

But why should an advocate of the full-personhood view regard such an infant as fully deserving of moral consideration? Why should the fact that the infant probably *will have* the capacity for full personhood, that she or he is in some sense the same individual as the individual who probably will exist as a full person fifteen years in the future, translate into maximum moral significance? Melden is well aware that an argument is needed here. He begins by pointing out that many moral concepts, such as the key concept of moral agency, include an essential reference to the future.[100] It would be impossible for us to proceed as moral agents, or even to speak of moral agency, if we literally confined ourselves to the present. All talk of goals, motives, and plans would be nonsense. From this very reasonable contention, he moves to the next premise: *infants* (i.e., normal human infants) are, by definition, immature moral agents. Their future moral agency is an essential, not merely accidental, part of their nature. He concludes that:

> The conception of an infant connects, therefore, as essentially with the life of a human being, with respect to which infancy is only one segment, as much so as present phenomena of human life such as purpose, intention and prudence, etc., connect essentially with the future phases and conditions of human beings . . . In ascertaining, therefore, the moral status of an infant we need to take account not only of its condition in the infant segment of its life, but in those subsequent segments in which, as a result of the ministrations of its parents or of any others who substitute for them, the development in some substantial measure of the agency and understanding of persons takes place.[101]

This will not do. Unfortunately for the potentiality view, Melden's argument simply does not establish the conclusion that the (normal) human infant, *when she or he is still an infant,* has the same high moral status the full-personhood view accords to the moral agent the infant will become. If reference to future moral agency is essential to the concept of infancy, and moral agents are maximally morally significant, it

Responses to the Argument

does not follow that the infant qua infant is therefore also maximally morally significant. We certainly cannot apply other predicates appropriate to descriptions of moral agents with equal abandon to infants. A hibiscus plant first had to be a seed, but the seed does not require sunlight, trimming, or protection from spider mites. Just as a seed is not a hibiscus plant, an infant is not a moral agent. Melden's argument is simply a non sequitur: he has not begun to show that potential moral agents are inherently morally significant.

Perhaps someone else will be able to establish this conclusion, thus allowing full-personhood-view proponents to modify their position in favor of potential full persons (moral agents). As yet, no convincing case along these lines has been made, but it would be unwarranted to assume that none could be constructed. It must be admitted, however, that many full-personhood-view proponents believe that this would not be a fruitful line of inquiry. R. G. Frey, for example, a utilitarian who supports the full-personhood view, points out that many moral rights theorists would deny that infants have rights: they count *actual* autonomy (full personhood), not potential autonomy.[102] If there is little hope for a case being made for the moral significance of potential full personhood, must we continue to include human infants among the desperately problematic marginal cases challenging the full-personhood view?

There is one other possible way out for those who cede maximum moral significance to full persons while still believing that unqualified protection is warranted for potential full persons. We could argue on behalf of the full-personhood view that, although the potential full person has no high moral status, the individual it will *become,* in the course of time if all goes well, does. Therefore, we should treat such an infant with care and respect, not because it is directly deserving of moral consideration, but because the being who will exist would be directly wronged by earlier mistreatment. H. J. McCloskey, another follower of the full-personhood view, has apparently made something like this suggestion, although he did not there work it out: "I suggest that it is meaningful to ascribe rights here [to infants] on the basis of what would be/will be the moral will of the being who is now an infant."[103] Following this suggestion, infants would receive the full protection of the moral community even though they would have no moral claim to it. Their future selves would be the morally considerable beneficiaries, and

Responses to the Argument

on their behalf, moral agents would be making (as it were) retroactive claims. Thus, although normal human infants would in the strict sense be marginal humans, they would not be counted among the problem cases that threaten the acceptability of the full-personhood view.

It is important to see that the above suggestion differs essentially from other, seemingly similar proposals about the inclusion of normal human infants in the moral community. It differs from Melden's proposal in its denial of moral rights to the infant qua infant: only the moral agent who will exist has that status. If we value the hibiscus plant, we will plant and water the seed, but we do not do this for the seed's sake. It differs from Narveson's proposal—that human infants be given the "gift" of rights out of deference to the moral agents who value them— by extending no gift and by regarding other moral agents' sentiments as beside the point. For this reason, it also must be distinguished from the proposal that normal human infants should be given protection because of concern for the allegedly inevitable "side effects" (e.g., fear, insecurity, anguish) present moral agents would experience if such protection were to be withheld. It is the moral agent (the full person) the infant will become who sets the moral agenda, not any other moral agent, and not the infant as such.

Now, it is plausible to suggest that future rights holders impose moral constraints on our present actions. Although some deny this, as we shall see in the discussion of utilitarianism in chapter 4, most of us think that it would be wrong to poison the water and land that will be used by beings yet unborn. These unborn beings have no moral status at present, but they will exist as rights holders, and our present actions could violate those rights. Nevertheless, the proposal that normal human infants be accorded full protection on behalf of the full persons they will eventually be fails just as thoroughly as all the proposals above with which it has just been contrasted. The difficulty is that infant protection is based upon the hypothetical existence of future rights holders into which these infants have turned. *But if we decide to exploit any of these infants in ways that would prevent them from ever achieving the status of rights holders,* no wrong would be done! If we significantly impair them mentally, or *kill them,* no future rights holders can have any claims on us. Future rights holders constrain our present actions just in case they will exist regardless of what we now decide. For example, if we poison land

Responses to the Argument

and water that will be needed by those who will exist in the future, they will have been wronged as soon as they exist, but if we blow up our planet instead, we only wrong those who now exist. There would be no one to point the accusatory finger of a wronged moral agent after an event of that kind!

If one replies that these beings would have existed had we not decided as we did, and that we have counterfactually, as it were, violated their right to life, the reply is obvious. If we violate future beings' right to life by preventing them from coming to be, every act of contraception, every act of abstinence, is equivalent to murder. Even the most militant opponent of contraception is unlikely to condemn popes, nuns, or twelve-year-old girls who "just say no." By analogy, if one genuinely believes that only full persons have basic moral rights or maximum moral significance, one cannot maintain that a future rights holder's right to existence would be violated if an infant is killed when its organs are "harvested." Rights holders can have a right to life: non-rights-holders do not. Therefore, not only does the present proposal fail to accord full protection to normal human infants: it actually requires any who would seriously harm them to be sure to prevent them from ever achieving full personhood! Full-personhood-view advocates with tender feelings for infants cannot take much heart in this "solution."

Before consigning this proposal to oblivion, I must make a further comment. There seems to be something very misguided about any view that locates the wrongness of maiming an infant in the fact that the moral agent the infant will become would be impaired by the experience. Surely our repugnance concerning the mistreatment of infants has little to do with their future moral agenthood! We should not simply let our feelings be the criterion of moral rightness, of course: we could be mistaken in thinking that the infants, right now, are being wronged. I do not think we are wrong, and I will argue for this in the course of chapter 5, but let us concede the possibility. Those humans who are not similarly distressed by the mistreatment of nonhumans just as sensitive as human infants may also want to recognize the possibility that their feelings are not good moral guides.

Thus, we have found no good arguments that would allow full-personhood-view proponents to extend unqualified protection to potential full persons. All these humans join the already disenfranchised men-

Responses to the Argument

tally handicapped infants, children, and adults as marginal cases with no claim to life or respectful treatment. Those who are convinced that any of these beings are due such treatment might do well to consider alternatives to the full-personhood view. One such alternative, to which we will later return at length, is the view that sentient beings are maximally morally significant. If this is the case, infants, children, and handicapped but conscious adults would all be morally considerable. So would fetuses after some point in the second trimester. So would large numbers of nonhuman animals.

For now, we need to continue our exploration of the implications of the full-personhood view. Let us turn to its view of the moral status of those who once were full persons. Can these beings, at least, somehow be included in the moral community?

Former Full Persons

This is an extraordinarily important question for all of us, but especially for those whose criterion of moral significance is full personhood. Any of us, as well as those we hold most dear, could permanently lose the capacity for personhood. Of course, the full-personhood view does allow for some protection in these cases. Self-interested and other-regarding moral agents committed to the full-personhood view can stipulate that those who suffer this fate are to be treated with benevolent respect, even though they have allegedly lost their high moral status. As we saw in our earlier discussions of egoism and utilitarianism, this could be done in deference to full persons who do not want themselves or their loved ones to be exploited for the benefit of others if they should lose their full personhood. As we also saw, this leaves the fate of former full persons entirely contingent on the concerns and sentiments of members of the moral community. Any culture (e.g., one devoted to the priority of "the best" in all cases) in which the mature inhabitants agree to family members' and even their own extermination or exploitation for the good of others upon the loss of mental competence would be doing no wrong if the full-personhood view is to be believed—unless we can discover a firmer basis on its behalf for different treatment.

A. I. Melden tries to provide such a basis, just as he has tried to show that potential full persons or moral agents are full members of the moral community. He holds that the former full person is a "segment" in the entire life of the moral agent, just as the infant is. As we saw, he tries to show that infants are essentially moral-agents-to-be, reasoning that this warrants ascribing the same basic moral rights to the infant as to the mature moral agent. He cannot use the same line of reasoning (which is just as well, since it does not work) to warrant rights ascriptions for former moral agents, because the loss of moral agency is purely contingent on disease, accident, or age. Instead, he argues that the denial of moral rights to a former full person would require us to deny rights to those who are asleep or temporarily unconscious.

He asks us to imagine a sleeping man. Surely such a being has full moral rights, even though he is unconscious. Were he to die without ever regaining consciousness (and moral agency), we would still not revise our view that he had rights while asleep.[104] All the network of social and personal relationships he has established by virtue of his past personhood is intact while he sleeps, Melden argues; this is what makes him a full member of the moral community. Now Melden asks us to imagine the same man after an accident, lying in a hospital bed in a terminal coma. Even if we are positive that he will never again regain consciousness and moral agency, we accord him full rights, including the right to life: "All we can do . . . is to accord him the right that he has to life itself by continuing to give him medical attention."[105] Again, the source of these rights is the past moral agency that ensconced the patient firmly in the moral community. Melden asks us to contrast the care professionals and family members would give to this man, lying permanently and terminally comatose in his hospital bed, with the treatment a nonhuman animal (fully conscious?) would receive: "some animal whose demise they might hasten without any moral compunction."[106] Melden fully approves of such differential treatment: "Devoid as he [the terminal coma patient] may now be of all capacity for agency or understanding of his own moral status or medical condition, he remains, so long as he lives, a human being who as the possessor of rights merits treatment quite different from that which we owe animals with whom no moral relations of any kind may be possible."[107]

Why should we accept Melden's conclusion that the irreversibly comatose former person described remains a full member of the moral

Responses to the Argument

community, unlike a (perhaps conscious) nonhuman animal? Melden now returns to his sleeping person analogy: If we do not make past moral agency the basis of full moral rights, "any moral claim we make about anyone with whom we are presently concerned is subject to defeat by the momentary flickering out of his consciousness."[108] None of us believes that the dreamlessly sleeping or freshly fainted individual has lost all claim to rights; therefore, the same holds for those who have been rendered permanently non compos mentis.

Melden's argument does not succeed in showing that former full persons remain members of the full-personhood moral community. There is a fundamental disanalogy between a temporarily unconscious person and a permanent nonperson. Smith, while asleep, retains his capacity for full personhood: that capacity has been irretrievably lost when he lies in a terminal coma. The full-personhood view can easily accommodate a sleeping or knocked-out Smith, since its criterion for moral standing is the capacity for full personhood; it cannot accept the terminally comatose Smith on the same basis. Excluding such cases from the moral community does not threaten the rest of us, all of whom are subject to the "momentary flickering out" of consciousness. Melden might reply that the sleeping person *is* a moral agent, because of the network of relationships he has established in the past, and that it is this fact, not Smith's capacity for full personhood, that warrants rights ascriptions. The same, by this argument, would hold for those who can no longer be full persons.[109] But what does it mean to *be* a moral agent? It means that one is *capable* of understanding moral principles and of recognizing the rightful claims of others. One's past behavior provides evidence for one's moral agency. The sleeping Smith is indeed a moral agent, just as he is a full person: both these concepts (like the concept of concert pianist) imply capacities for certain attitudes, beliefs, skills, and other behaviors. Sadly, the irreversibly comatose Smith is no longer capable of any of these things.[110]

Besides being based on a disanalogy, Melden's argument also has implications that many would reject. This is a serious problem for him, since he takes himself to be explicating *our* concepts of person and moral rights. According to him, a brain-dead former full person whose body is sustained by life support technology has a right to continued medical treatment. It is far from clear that this should be so. Although the law is surely not a reliable guide to reality, let alone morality, "brain-death statutes," stipulating as they do that persons cease to exist when their brains irreversibly cease to function, seem to be on the mark. Without rehashing the lengthy philosophical debate on criteria of personal identity, I will merely point out that bodily continuity alone is an insufficient basis for survival of the self. Smith's body, removed from "life support" and interred in the grave, is not Smith: many, myself included, believe the same about his brain-dead, mechanically sustained body. We continue to refer to both the mechanically sustained and the interred body by Smith's name, it is true, but we do know the difference painfully well. Contrary to Melden's assertion that "we" labor to keep loved ones alive *even when we know they can never regain consciousness,* family members are much more likely to accept the cessation of life support in those circumstances. Those who do not are hoping that somehow some measure of recovery is possible, or they are unconvinced that their relatives are really unconscious. I have frequently heard students (some of whom hoped to become nurses) say that brain-dead individuals might be aware of being disconnected from life-sustaining machinery. When these misconceptions are dispelled and it is clear that consciousness is forever more impossible for such a human, most agree that death has already occurred. I do not think that Melden plausibly captures our common moral judgments here, although he claims to be doing so.

Finally, I ask readers to reflect on Melden's comparisons between humans and nonhumans. Do we owe an irreversibly comatose, terminally ill human every medical effort needed to sustain such "life" as remains for him or her, while a nonhuman animal is due no special consideration whatever, as Melden suggests? Should we make heroic efforts for brain-dead humans but, "without any moral compunction," give lethal injections to blind dogs? Or cause calves suffering and death because we like their tender, "milk-fed" flesh? No doubt some would agree with Melden in finding nothing wrong with this and other common practices, but others should ask themselves how justified such differential treatment can really be.

We will return to the above question again and again, but for now it is sufficient to say that Melden has not been successful in making a case for the high moral status of humans who were formerly full persons. However, I believe that he is correct in assigning moral relevance to *the*

Responses to the Argument

past in his analysis of the status of those who lose their personhood. The past does not warrant the ascription of rights to such individuals (according to the full-personhood view), as he thinks, but, as we shall see below, it can warrant their respectful treatment.

We turn now to a suggestion that is parallel to one we took up in our consideration of the moral status of potential full persons. There it was argued that the full person who *will* exist should not be harmed by our treatment of her as an infant. While this is highly plausible, we found that it sanctions treatment of infants that would prevent them from developing into full persons. We can now argue, with more success, that at least those who *have* been maximally morally significant, as the full-personhood view interprets this, have the right to stipulate that they be treated with respect and consideration if they lose all or part of their personhood.

Joel Feinberg has plausibly argued that living persons can have interests and claims that should be respected after their deaths.[111] In general, most agree that wills should be respected and promises kept, unless, perhaps, doing so would cause considerable unjustified harm to innocent living beings. According to the full-personhood view, a former full person is similar to someone who has died: the being who was maximally morally significant is now no more and cannot be restored. Just as it would be wrong to abuse the body of a dead human contrary to the wishes of the person when living, one can argue that it would be wrong to use a senile human for medical experimentation and toxicity testing—provided that the person who once existed did not want this to be done. If the individual never expressed any views on this subject when a full person, we do what is standardly done in cases of mental incompetence: we ask what the person probably would have wanted to be done, or what the rational wishes of the person would have been. Thus, on this suggestion, the full-personhood view would accord protection to those who have become permanent nonpersons out of consideration for the beings they once were. The beings they now are would have no moral status in themselves, as they would under Melden's proposal: the beings they once were would set the moral agenda. Former full persons would not be included within the scope of marginal cases that threaten the full-personhood view.

This suggestion definitely has its merits. First, it is not subject to the fatal flaw that destroys the parallel argument for the protection of infants. The latter argument sanctions any treatment of infants that would not harm any future moral agents these infants might turn out to be, *including* mistreatment that would prevent them from ever developing into moral agents. No similar drawback holds for the former full-person proposal, since no amount of chicanery can alter the fact that someone once had all the attributes of a full person. The individual *after* the loss of full personhood is far safer than the individual *before* the advent of full personhood. Second, it is intuitively plausible that full persons should have the prerogative to request respectful treatment for what remains of themselves if they should be deprived of all or part of their personhood. Even if they should request destruction of themselves for the good of others in those circumstances, as would likely be the case in cultures where such treatment is the norm, we believe that their wishes should be given considerable weight. There is an excellent philosophical case to be made for rational suicide, after all, and this would be a special case of it, provided the person is not subject to physical or emotional coercion, and not deluded by false ideals (e.g., "I must end my worthless life when I can no longer carry out the Fatherland's glorious purposes").

The proposal is implausible in one very important respect, however. It implies that the sentient senile or otherwise brain-damaged individual has no *inherent* claim to life or respectful treatment: according to this view, if we refrain from tossing them on the scrap heap or sending them off to the glue factory, this is only because the morally significant beings they once were would not have wanted this to happen. Mistreatment of former full persons would be on a par with desecration of dead bodies. Under this proposal, we have no such duties to former full persons, just as we have no duties to dead bodies. Our duties are restricted to full persons, even if they no longer exist.

Now, I have no quarrel with this proposal if the former full person has become brain-dead or is in a permanent "vegetative" state: the person who once existed is really dead, metaphysically if not legally, in those cases. The concept of the living will, which allows persons to specify in advance the treatment they want when their minds might be destroyed while their bodies still live, is based on respect for personal autonomy; the proposal is in line with the soundness of this approach. The problem arises when we consider former full persons who are *still conscious,* have wants, needs, and emotions. Do we really have no significant duties to them? I believe that most of us think that we have strong duties to them, *not merely to the persons they once were*. Of course, we may be wrong in this assumption, although I do not believe that we are. It would be question begging to dismiss the proposal on the grounds that it does not accord significant moral status to former full persons. It behooves us, though, to be aware of the implications of any view that we are considering adopting. If any go rather thoroughly against our grain, the view deserves very careful examination indeed.

Yet another implausibility bears mentioning. Imagine two humans: one has become senile, the other has been brain-damaged from birth. Each is sentient; each cares about the treatment given him or her. Each is capable of suffering and happiness. According to the proposal we are now considering, although we have no significant duties to either, we should treat the senile human respectfully, as an end in herself rather than a commodity for our use, because the person she once was had a strong interest in respectful treatment continuing after the onset of senility. The other, provided we don't upset any moral agents who might be attached to him, may be subjected to medical research or toxicity testing. Such differential treatment is a fully expectable consequence of the full-personhood view, of course, but that does not make us like it any better.

To conclude our discussion in this section, the full-personhood view can make a case, although that case grates against our common moral assumptions, for protection for former full persons even while denying that they have any claim to life or respectful treatment. It cannot make room for the protection of potential full persons. We have been able to reduce the types of marginal cases that plague the full-personhood view by only one (to be sure, large) category: former full persons who, when they were still full persons, requested or would have wanted respectful treatment in their reduced state. Remaining fully within the scope of the argument from marginal cases are very young potential full persons as well as all those humans who can never and have never achieved full personhood. Contrary to what Sapontzis has suggested on behalf of the full-personhood view, there is no way to duck these serious problem cases.

We seem to have exhausted all the attempts advocates of the full-personhood view can make to defeat the argument from marginal cases. We considered attempts to show either version of the argument unsound; these all failed. At most, one can argue that the categorical version of the argument has a key, unestablished premise: its claim that marginal humans are maximally morally significant. (Attempts to justify this premise will be explored in chapter 5.) But this is not the sort of criticism to push if one wants one's view to be acceptable to others who are not already convinced. We then looked at attacks that conceded the soundness of the biconditional version of the argument but tried to deflate its importance: these also were unsuccessful. How, then, must those convinced of the correctness of the full-personhood view respond to the argument from marginal cases?

THE FINAL RESPONSE

They must reject one version of the argument and accept the other, with all its unpalatable consequences. They cannot accept the categorical version of the argument, because that version asserts that marginal humans are maximally morally significant. They cannot reject the biconditional version of the argument, because according to their view those who are not full persons, be they humans or nonhumans, are in the same moral (or to be more exact, nonmoral) boat. Either both are highly morally significant or neither are. As the argument spelled out earlier in this chapter makes explicit, the latter alternative is the one that a full-personhood-view advocate must embrace:

1. Those nonhumans who are similar in all important morally relevant respects to marginal humans (those humans who are not full persons) are maximally morally significant if and only if marginal humans are maximally morally significant (*conclusion* of the biconditional version of the argument from marginal cases).
2. Only full persons are maximally morally significant.
3. *Therefore,* neither marginal humans nor nonhumans similar to them in the important morally relevant respects are maximally morally significant.

As we have just seen, the lack of maximum moral significance for marginal humans is not merely theoretical: the full-personhood view can provide them no real protection, apart from some cases of former full persons. An advocate of the full-personhood view has a very tough, oversized bullet to bite.

Some full-personhood-view advocates understandably find such a "meal" most unappealing. For example, David DeGrazia, who defends the view that "normal adult humans" have greater moral status than nonhumans because the former have richer lives,[112] has been challenged by commentator Kathy Squadrito[113] to spell out the implications of his view for less well-endowed human beings. He forthrightly admits that "differences among humans are sometimes very pronounced, bringing us to another area where I am unsure what to argue: the problem of marginal cases. I do not think anyone has provided a truly adequate solution to this problem."[114] DeGrazia recognizes the seriousness of the problem. According to him, if it is deemed necessary to do medical research that will harm or kill nonconsenting subjects, the dog is to be preferred as a research subject to a normal adult human.[115] By the same token, it seems that the retarded child should be sacrificed instead of the normal adult. Although DeGrazia suggests that the problem *might* be solved by an appeal to the side effects of accepting exploitation of marginal humans, or by an attempt to confer rights on marginal humans in order to protect them, he does not express confidence in the likely success of these moves.[116] (Rightly so, for as we have seen, both these attempts to do an "end run" around the biconditional version of the argument from marginal cases are failures.) DeGrazia is clearly troubled, but he does not take the further step of simply accepting the equivalence of certain humans and nonhumans.

Not so in the case of R. G. Frey, whose views on moral status DeGrazia explicitly shares.[117] In a discussion of the benefits of vivisection, he unflinchingly faces the implications of the full-personhood view for human marginal cases:

> I remain a vivisectionist, therefore, because of the benefits medical/scientific research can bestow. Support for vivisection, however, exacts a cost: it forces us to envisage the use of defective humans in such research . . . The fact that not even all human life has the same value explains why some [*sic*] argument from marginal cases, one of the most common arguments in support of an equal value thesis, comes unstuck. Such an argument would only be possible if human life of a much lower quality were ceded

Responses to the Argument

equal value with normal (adult) human life. In that case the same conces-
sion could be requested for animal life, and an argument from marginal
or defective humans could get underway.[118]

The version of the argument from marginal cases that "comes unstuck"
is the categorical one, for it alone asserts that marginal humans have the
same high moral status as normal adult humans. Clearly, Frey accepts
the biconditional version of the argument, quite consistently drawing
the further conclusion that marginal humans and mentally comparable
nonhumans can be vivisected with equal justification. He is aware, of
course, that a great many humans would regard human vivisection with
horror. He actually draws the conclusion that, in all fairness, those who
react in this way are obliged to reconsider their acceptance of nonhuman
vivisection: "Paradoxically, then, to the extent that one cannot bring
oneself to envisage and consent to their [defective humans'] use, to that
extent, in my view, the case for anti-vivisectionism becomes stronger."[119]
Of course, this is exactly what the marginal cases challenge has main-
tained all along. I doubt that one could ever find a plainer acceptance of
the biconditional form of the argument from marginal cases than this
proponent of the full-personhood view has given us.

Frey himself is not enthusiastic about the prospect of marginal human
vivisection, although he, as a utilitarian, is willing to accept it under
utility-maximizing conditions: "Always in the background, of course,
are the benefits that medical/scientific research confers: if we desire to
continue to obtain these benefits, are we prepared to pay the price of
the use of defective humans? The answer, I think, must be positive, at
least until the time comes when we no longer have to use either humans
or animals for research purposes."[120] All who are truly committed to
the full-personhood view must see that this is where logic leads them,
given the failure of their attacks on the argument from marginal cases
and its significance. But how many will wish to remain committed to a
view with such implications? DeGrazia, for example, after stating that
no one has succeeded in defeating the (biconditional) argument from
marginal cases, says that one option is to accept Regan's view (i.e., that
harmful experimentation violates the moral rights of *any* nonconsenting
subject):[121] taking this option is tantamount to accepting the categorical
version of the argument and rejecting the biconditional version, thereby
abandoning the full-personhood position.

Responses to the Argument

While some will have qualms, others clearly will affirm the full-personhood position despite its implications, with more enthusiasm than Frey. Bernard Rollin tells the story of a medical researcher he knows who thought there was no moral issue involved with the use of nonhuman animals in research. It was purely a question of science, the man held, not ethics: nonhumans happen to be excellent "models" for humans. When Rollin asked him why he did not just use human children in that case, since they are yet better "models," the scientist responded in frustration: "Because they won't let us!" [122] Those "dedicated" U.S. researchers who let a "control group" of black men, without their consent, suffer and die from untreated syphilis for decades, until 1972, would go even further. If these researchers could miraculously be cured of their bigotry, they would still be left with many genuinely marginal humans to manipulate. To people such as these, the sacrifice of other humans poses no problems.

For the rest of us, however, such consequences are unacceptable. Some of us, turning to take a long, and we hope less prejudiced, look at the treatment of nonhuman animals who are at least as sensitive and life-loving as a child or a retarded adult, have come to regard such treatment as equally unacceptable. Full-personhood-view advocates who remain convinced that their view is fundamentally correct will reject this enhancement of the status of nonhuman animals. However, I believe that most of them will also find themselves unable to support the exploitation of marginal humans.

They must abandon their view in that case, but they can do this in a way that leaves its core almost intact. They can try to show that membership in a *species* characterized by full personhood is sufficient for maximum moral significance. Marginal humans, unlike any nonhumans we know of, belong to such a species. In short, full-personhood-view advocates who resist the exploitation of marginal humans but see nothing wrong with the continued exploitation of nonhumans must become *speciesists* instead. We will now turn to their attempts to show speciesism morally justified.

3

SPECIESISM AND FULL PERSONHOOD

Many people believe that exploitation of nonhumans by humans for a myriad of motives, from the culinary to the scientific, is justifiable because of the gap in intelligence between the "exploitees" and typical mature members of the human species. As we have seen, this line of reasoning has an implication that distresses many who find themselves unmoved by the exploitation of nonhumans. If one genuinely believes that only moral agents, beings capable of highly autonomous, richly complex lives, can have full moral status, consistency forces one to deny that status to many humans: the very young and those who can never achieve full personhood.[1] Basic moral rights, including most prominently a right to life, would not be owed to them by moral agents. (Consequentialists uncomfortable with 'rights' terminology may substitute "strong presumptions against" killing and the like instead. This will not affect the argumentation in this chapter.) As has been shown in chapter 2, supporters of the full-personhood view are fully subject to the biconditional version of the argument from marginal cases:

1. Beings who are similar in all important morally relevant respects are equally morally significant.
2. Nonhumans exist who are similar in all important morally relevant respects to "marginal" humans (i.e., to the very young and to those humans who will never achieve full personhood).
3. *Therefore,* those nonhumans who are similar in all important morally relevant respects to marginal humans are maximally morally significant if and only if marginal humans are maximally morally significant.

If maximum moral significance is reserved for full persons, marginal humans and many nonhumans, including those whom we eat, skin, test cosmetics on, and divest of organs, are lacking in the necessary moral qualifications. Even the less stringent supporters of the full-personhood view, who accord a right to humane treatment to the nonhumans whom we exploit, would have to accept the "humane" exploitation of marginal humans as well. The right to be treated as "an end in oneself" (rather than as a mere means, however humanely one may be treated) is restricted to those who are maximally moral significant.

Supporters of the full-personhood view cannot escape this consequence. They can, however, try to replace their view with a position that accords maximum moral significance to full persons *and* to marginal humans, but not to the nonhumans we exploit. I am not suggesting a retreat to homocentrism; we have already seen that this view cannot be justified. Instead, they could attempt to show that *membership in a species characterized by full personhood* is sufficient for maximum moral significance. They could, in short, become *speciesists*. This is exactly what a number of former full-personhood-view advocates have recently chosen to do, as we shall soon see.

THE SPECIESISM DEBATE: A BRIEF HISTORY

Some will question the wisdom of substituting speciesism for the unadulterated full-personhood view. After all, the term 'speciesism,' made famous by Peter Singer after first being coined by Richard Ryder, has been used as an epithet for some time now.[2] Singer initially characterizes speciesism as "a prejudice or bias in favor of the interests of members of one's own species and against those of members of other species."[3] He then asserts that speciesists believe even their most "trivial" interests are important enough to outweigh the vital interests of members of other species.[4] When speciesists are asked why they would favor members of their own species under all circumstances, they reply that human life is innately superior, more valuable because more self-aware and autonomous. Here again we see the inconsistent alliance of homocentrism and the full-personhood view. Singer exposes this inconsistency when he points out that: "The only position that is irredeemably speciesist is the one that tries to make the boundary of the right to life run exactly parallel to the boundary of our own species. Those who hold the sanctity of life do this, because while distinguishing sharply between human beings and other animals they allow no distinctions to be made within

Speciesism and Full Personhood

our own species, objecting to the killing of the severely retarded and the hopelessly senile as strongly as they object to the killing of normal adults."[5] He then raises his (biconditional) version of the argument from marginal cases. Thus, speciesism as characterized is a most unattractive view: it is biased in the most extreme way and egregiously inconsistent into the bargain. It is no accident that the word 'speciesism,' coined and made familiar by its very opponents, reminds one of racism and sexism. Singer wastes no time in pointing out the obvious comparison.[6] One can see how an unreflective homocentric attitude, allied with the assumption of human superiority, could give rise to such a view. But why would anyone make a clear-eyed, *considered* choice to embrace speciesism, especially if one wishes to avoid the argument from marginal cases? Is this not tantamount to deliberately choosing to be a bigot? Let us see what supporters of speciesism have to say about bigotry.

Speciesism, Racism, and Sexism

Some speciesists, that is, believers in the justifiability of favoring members of one sentient species over another, reject the very term 'speciesism,' with its unwholesome associations, because they do not see *their* view as bigoted.[7] Others defiantly proclaim that they are speciesists and feel no cause for shame.[8] Both types of speciesists, whatever they call themselves, agree in believing their view to be untainted by prejudice. They indignantly reject the analogy drawn between their view and obviously bigoted attitudes such as racism and sexism. (Many are the forms of bigotry, but these two have been singled out in the speciesism debate.) For example, Leslie Francis and Richard Norman were among the first to find the comparison highly insulting to racial minorities and women. They argue that Singer's analogy between nonhuman animal liberation and the black and women's liberation movements, the inverse of the speciesism/racism/sexism analogy, "trivializes" those "real" movements: "Liberation movements have a character and a degree of moral importance which cannot be possessed by a movement to prevent cruelty to animals."[9] Carl Cohen later agreed with their assessment. After quoting Singer's drawing of the analogy between speciesism, racism, and sexism, he replies that: "This argument is worse than unsound; it is

Speciesism and Full Personhood

atrocious. It draws an offensive moral conclusion [i.e., that speciesism is as objectionable as racism and sexism] from a deliberately devised verbal parallelism that is utterly specious."[10] Cohen notes that racism and sexism are plainly irrational because they do not discriminate on the basis of morally relevant differences. All humans have basic moral rights as autonomous moral agents, he claims, whereas no nonhuman can warrant such status. Thus, speciesism is held to be justified, quite unlike racism and sexism. Michael A. Fox once made much the same objection to the analogy. He argued at that time that racial minorities and women, as autonomous beings, have basic moral rights that are violated by racists and sexists; nonhumans cannot be said to have any such rights in the first place.[11]

These objections at least tacitly concede that protesters against the exploitation of nonhuman animals also find racism and sexism to be thoroughly reprehensible. This is a change from the stereotypical view that "animal lovers" are all misanthropes. (In fact, a 1991 survey of subscribers to *The Animals' Agenda* by sociologists at the University of Utah shows the opposite. Eight hundred fifty-three randomly selected participants [84 percent of the sample] were overwhelmingly supportive of the civil rights movement, feminism, the struggle against apartheid, pacifism, and gay rights.[12] These results are compatible with a 1989 survey of Congress members: those with the most favorable "pro animal" voting records also had the strongest records of support for social justice causes. The converse held as well: those who had the least favorable records on such causes were also the least likely to support legislation with positive implications for nonhumans.)[13] However, Francis and Norman, Cohen, and (the earlier) Fox agree in charging that supporters of nonhuman moral significance vastly exaggerate the importance of nonhuman interests in comparison to human interests. Exploitation of nonhumans, as they see it, is incomparably less significant than exploitation of humans.

The objectors to the speciesism/racism/sexism analogy rightly reject bigotry directed against other humans, but they have not defeated the bigotry charge against speciesism. Their arguments both beg the question and miss the point of the argument from marginal cases, raised by Singer after he draws his analogy. The claims by the earlier Fox and Cohen that only autonomous moral agents can have basic moral rights, from which it follows that racists and sexists, but not speciesists, violate rights, clearly beg the very question at issue. (In all fairness, it must be noted that Cohen does try to offer some support for his view of rights: he attributes the same contention to Sts. Augustine and Aquinas, as well as to Hegel, Bradley, Pritchard, and Kant.[14] Regardless of how eminent some of the supporters of this position on rights may be, however, the fact remains that their view is the very one in question. Appealing to these philosophers as authorities can hardly count as support for Cohen's claim that rights are restricted to moral agents.) Indeed, as I pointed out in chapter 2, Cohen follows his already question-begging rights view with the claim that "[s]peciesism is not merely plausible; it is essential for right conduct" given that there are "morally relevant distinctions among species."[15] Pro-speciesist arguments of this kind are less than logically compelling.

Francis and Norman also beg the question by claiming that supporters of nonhuman animal rights "trivialize" genuine liberation movements by comparing issues altogether incommensurate in their levels of moral importance. As Steve Sapontzis has pointed out, these claims are redolent of "human chauvinism."[16] If such assumptions of human superiority could be justified, well and good, but the speciesist cannot convince anyone who is currently unconvinced by assuming what must be shown. One of these very objectors decided that he could no longer convince *himself* in this regard. Michael A. Fox, who completely changed his mind only months after the publication of his book supporting nonhuman animal experimentation, has dropped his claim of human superiority. He now rejects his earlier view as arrogant and prejudiced: "With some trepidation, but also not a little smugness, I took on the mantle of speciesism . . . [b]ut I could not yet see that this kind of thinking, as well as the hierarchical view of humans as superior to all else in nature, to which I still adhered, were indeed analogous to those specious and loathsome arguments used to promote racism and sexism."[17] Who is correct, the earlier or the present Fox? Argumentation free of fallacies must decide this issue.

In addition to begging the question, the insistence that a high degree of autonomy is a necessary condition for the possession of basic moral rights is actually incompatible with speciesism. Many humans would not qualify for rights in this view, as the argument from marginal cases has revealed to us. With the possible exceptions of whales and dolphins, there certainly does appear to be a large gap between the mental capacities of normal adult humans and other animals. However, the very same gap is present between the abilities of normal adult humans and very mentally impaired or undeveloped humans. The reader may recall that Singer calls "irredeemably speciesist" the view that *only* humans, even humans no more mentally developed than some nonhumans, are deserving of a right to life. As we discussed in chapter 2, the mental capacities of some nonhumans appear to be greater than those of some humans. Reflection about the comparable cases of marginal humans and sentient nonhumans reinforces the claim that speciesism, racism, and sexism are analogous: all three views imply that two individuals who do not otherwise differ in morally relevant respects may not receive equal consideration because of their species, race, or sex.

Steve Sapontzis objects to the above analogy between speciesism, racism, and sexism for quite a different reason and with a very different motive. He emphatically rejects speciesism, unlike Cohen et al., but he does not believe that relating that view to the argument from marginal cases yields a plausible analogy. Casting the debate about the prejudicial character of speciesism in this way is tantamount, in his view, to denigrating women, racial minorities, *and* nonhumans: "[W]hen people point to sexism and racism as prejudices, it is not because there are some women and blacks who are as intelligent as defective men and whites but are not being given rights or other considerations equal to those of the defective men and whites. Even suggesting that this is the sort of prejudice involved in sexism and racism would be insulting to women and blacks—and, I may add, it is similarly insulting, even paradoxical, to attempt to enhance the moral status of animals by drawing analogies between them and severely incompetent humans, humans who are so defective they must be institutionalized." [18]

Sapontzis's objection to Singer's (and my) linkage of the argument from marginal cases to speciesism [19] is based on his disdain for that argument. He holds that the argument is flawed, easily circumvented, and irrelevant to actual speciesism. Sapontzis's objections to the argument from marginal cases have already been considered and refuted in chapter 2, including his claim that nonhumans are grossly underestimated by that argument. The objections and refutations will not be repeated here.

Speciesism and Full Personhood

I add only that I join Sapontzis in scorning any view that directly compares women and racial minorities to defective white males. However, no one has ever suggested that this is the way in which the speciesism/racism/sexism analogy is intended to work. No nonspeciesist, to my knowledge, would ever draw such a comparison. The point of the analogy is that it is prejudicial to treat beings who are morally similar, be they marginal humans and nonhumans or women and men or blacks and whites, in morally dissimilar ways. Singer's "irredeemable speciesist," who inconsistently combines homocentrism and the full-personhood view, is directly targeted by the analogy *and* by the argument from marginal cases (the biconditional version). Contrary to Sapontzis's claims, speciesists apparently do not regard the problem of marginal cases as irrelevant to their view: Francis and Norman, Cohen, and the earlier Fox all address it, and, as we shall soon see, other recent speciesists do the same. The relevance of that issue is further underlined by the fact that the U.S. Congress, in a moderately speciesist 1988 Office of Technology Assessment report on human treatment of nonhumans, discusses the problem with great seriousness (and lack of success).[20] Thus, the issue of marginal humans does not derail the debate over speciesism, nor does it discredit the analogy between that view and other forms of bigotry.

Let us now turn to another philosopher's criticisms of the analogy. Like Sapontzis, Mary Midgley, a well-known ethical theorist who believes that nonhumans are morally considerable, questions the equation of speciesism with racism (as we shall see, Midgley thinks that sexism is more aptly compared to the former view). She holds that the analogy is faulty because, allegedly, (1) species membership is a marker for important differences among individuals, unlike racial identity, and (2) racism is an inherently confused concept.

In her first objection to the analogy, Midgley correctly points out that members of different species have different characteristics, characteristics that should be noted and respected rather than ignored.[21] While we ought to be "color-blind" in deciding about whom to rent an apartment to and whom to vote into political office, we endanger individuals if we are "species-blind." Infant baboons require different care and a different habitat from that required by human infants, wildebeest and chickens thrive on very different diets, and cats, unlike many young humans, do very poorly in college. Midgley argues that one's sex, age, and cultural background are similar to one's species in indicating important differences among individuals.[22] One's needs may vary at certain times because of these factors (e.g., to date, only women have been able to become pregnant and breast-feed infants). One ought to refrain, therefore, from castigating recognition of such differences as invidiously discriminatory.

This is true, but it is not to the point. Although Midgley is right to take note of the differences obtaining among individuals belonging to different species, this observation is irrelevant to the analogy between speciesism and racism. Both views are charged with implying that *morally similar* individuals may be treated in *morally different* ways, merely because of their species or race. Two individuals could be quite different without differing in morally relevant respects. The fact that some individuals like to have their ears scratched or prefer to spend time in trees or react to smiles with aggression, while others do not, indicates that their needs must be satisfied in different ways. It is hard to see how such differences could be morally relevant. Thus Midgley's first argument fails to discredit the analogy between speciesism and racism.

Midgley's second argument against the analogy hinges on the interesting claim that racism is an inherently confused concept. Critics of speciesism charge that it is always unjustified, and many of us likewise assume that racism is impermissible. But if we ask ourselves what the concept of racism actually entails, it is not clear what we ought to think. If the racist treats two individuals in morally different ways merely because of their different racial identities, must not so-called reverse discrimination be racist? Yet, many argue that it is justified to practice such a policy in a country where slavery and subsequent systematic denial of rights has had devastating effects upon current members of the disadvantaged race. But if racism is sometimes justified, is it really analogous to speciesism?[23] If we try to redraw the concept of racism so as to ensure its unjustifiability, we run into more problems. For example, if we stipulate that racists act to favor members of *their own* race, we get the white American employer off the racist hook when he hires a qualified African American rather than a qualified white. However, the African American employer who does the same would still be "racist." Far worse, as Midgley points out, is the implication that racial minorities who "buy into the system" by favoring the dominant group at every

Speciesism and Full Personhood

turn would *not* be guilty of racism.[24] She notes that if we stipulate instead that racists always act to favor the dominant race, thus garnering the politically correct designations for the African American employer and the collaborationist, we would prevent members of a race newly dominant after a revolution against their oppressors from temporarily giving qualified impoverished members of their own race preference in hiring over qualified rich members of the formerly dominant race.[25] I would add that such a move allows members of a dominated race to be viciously prejudiced on principle against innocent members of the dominant race without ever being "racist." Some Americans have recently defended this newly drawn concept of racism. For example, rap singer Sister Souljah angrily proclaims that "[t]here is no such thing as a black racist."[26] Blacks are the oppressed group in America, not whites. But surely the hate-filled African Americans who pulled a white driver from a stalled truck and beat him nearly to death, merely because he was the same race as the police officers who severely beat another African American, are also racist? The Ku Klux Klan has no monopoly on racism. Suppose, as seems increasingly likely, that apartheid is finally abolished in South Africa, and through democracy the country becomes largely governed by members of the black majority. I wonder if Sister Souljah (along with some white sociologists) would then say that a white South African who kidnaps and kills members of the now dominant race is not really racist. Defining 'racism' in this way enshrines a moral double standard that the oppressed group, of all people, should reject!

How, then, should we think of racism? Is the concept too confused to be compared to speciesism, as Midgley believes? I do not think so. We need to return to the initial concept of racism: the view that morally similar individuals may be treated morally differently simply because of their race. Midgley objects that this implies that justified "reverse discrimination" is racist, thus implying that racism *can* sometimes be justified. Many would reply to this by denying that "reverse discrimination" can ever be justified, any more than the original acts of discrimination the policy attempts to ameliorate; they are happy to call it "racist" in the most pejorative sense.[27] (The very name "reverse discrimination," as opponents gleefully point out, is highly suspect. Friends of this policy are apt to use a less negatively charged designation, like "affirmative action." I prefer the neutral "preferential consideration.")

Speciesism and Full Personhood

This way of addressing the issue preserves the analogy between racism and speciesism. I do not agree with this view, however.

Justified preferential consideration is not racist at all. When such action is justified, individuals belonging to disadvantaged racial minorities are given preferential treatment because they are victims of injustices done in the past and the present, whereas those who are edged in their favor are the (perhaps innocent) beneficiaries of those same injustices. This situation certainly obtains in the United States, where the African American population is disproportionately subject to poverty, unemployment, poor health, high infant mortality rates, and hopelessness. Those who succeed despite this have had to struggle mightily. Whites, whatever their other burdens, have not had this systematic handicap; in this respect, they are better off than their black counterparts.

Whites often forget this, especially when they think *they* are the losers. Even if prejudice magically ceased today, the burden of the past would remain. Former U.S. President Lyndon Johnson reportedly said that it will not do to shackle a man for three centuries, break his legs, then dump him among able-bodied runners at the starting line of a race with the words: "You see, we're giving you an equal chance!"[28] Although the persons in the race are not literally the same as the masters and slaves of three hundred years ago, the disadvantages and advantages of those times have indeed been bequeathed to succeeding generations. Thus, the "winners" and the "losers" in properly applied preferential consideration are *not* morally similar apart from race. Injustices of the past and present have led to a morally relevant difference between the parties; their race *as such* is not the issue. By contrast, it would be both racist and unjustified for a U.S. firm to give former Ugandan dictator Idi Amin job preference over a poor white from a New York slum on grounds of skin color. Preferential consideration should be *compensatory*. Such a policy properly applies to any member of an oppressed group, whether that group is a racial minority or not.[29] (I am not arguing that compensation requires, e.g., preferential hiring when a black competitor is unqualified for the position or is substantially less qualified than a white competitor. Preferential hiring in such situations creates far more problems than it solves: instead of helping to restore equal opportunity, it perpetuates the myth of racial inferiority.)

Midgley briefly considers a response such as mine, but she rejects

Speciesism and Full Personhood

it, saying that racists too claim to be motivated by historical considerations.[30] Regardless of what racists may say, however, it is quite plain that *in fact* they regard race as a characteristic that in itself warrants morally different behavior. If a black were to pop out of a visiting spaceship, Ku Klux Klan devotees would be no less prejudiced against her than they are against blacks who have lived here all their lives. (They would probably be even more prejudiced, since the new arrival would be "un-American"!) Thus Midgley has not discredited the concept of racism as the morally different treatment of morally similar individuals on grounds of race. Moreover, this is the very concept that is apparently analogous to speciesism. The analogy has survived both of Midgley's arguments against it.

Midgley's second argument attacked the concept of racism. By contrast, Bernard Rollin has raised doubts about the concept of species. His point is not to support speciesism or to attack the analogy between speciesism and other forms of bigotry: he is actually arguing against those critics of genetic engineering who warn us not to interfere with species as they now are.[31] However, his argument sheds new light on the analogy under discussion here. Rollin observes that there is some degree of arbitrariness in the way popular opinion and even science regard species. Taxonomic systems are neither wholly arbitrary nor wholly reflective of reality; they are a mixture of discovery and decision. Many schemes are possible. One way to see Rollin's point about competing classification schemes is to go one level up, as it were, to genus classifications. Traditionally, taxonomists group beings into genera and species on the basis of judgments about how important the functional differences between the various beings are. Humans are thought to be functionally different in very important ways from the great apes; they are therefore grouped in their own genus (*Homo*). According to the cladistic school of thought, however, biological classifications should be based on the genetic "distance" between beings. For example, chimpanzees (*Pan troglodyte* and *Pan paniscus*) and gorillas (*Gorilla gorilla*) are genetically more similar to humans (*Homo sapiens*) than they are to the gibbon. A cladistic classification scheme would put humans, chimpanzees, and gorillas into their own genus: the genus *Homo* (according to the conventions of classification, the oldest name is to be preferred when we decide that beings belong under the same genus: *Homo* predates both *Gorilla* and *Pan*).[32]

Speciesism and Full Personhood

What a difference it can make to our view of ourselves when we reconceive our relations to other beings! *Homo paniscus* but not *Homo sapiens* may be torn from their mothers, stuffed into cages, displayed in zoos or bombarded with AIDS virus injections. This new taxonomic suggestion has not been pushed, although it does seem more objective than the traditional system (it is no surprise that humans have decided they are so functionally distinct as to deserve their own genus). Yet, Rollin reminds us that the genetic school of thought offers us but one among many reasonable classification schemes.[33] Our choices are a function of our purposes and our biological theories. Appearance is one such factor. Some creatures who diverge enough genetically to be sorted into different species are still so close that they are almost indistinguishable by appearance, while other beings accounted to be in the same species appear incredibly different (Rollin's example here is the Chihuahua and the Great Dane).[34]

Speciesists would do well to bear in mind the conventional element in our species designations. Basing moral distinctions on partially conventional distinctions is a risky enterprise. In fact, Rollin's point underscores the similarity between speciesism and racism: the latter view is also based on questionable classifications. (To a lesser extent, this is also true of sexism. Some individuals who are genetically male or female are in appearance members of the opposite sex, and some apparently clear cases of males or females are anatomical mixtures of both sexes.) Appearances are our guide to race, but persons designated as belonging to different races are closely interrelated. White South Africans are sometimes horrified to discover that even the "purest" of them has Negroid blood. Some very light-skinned people are more Negroid than some dark-skinned people. Indeed, if recent genetic studies are correct, *all* living humans are descendants of one woman or several closely related women who lived in Africa roughly two hundred thousand years ago.[35] More fundamentally, all of us arose from a common ancestral bacterium some four billion years in the past. Biological distinctions certainly exist, but so does commonality. Racists and speciesists ignore this fact at their own peril.

At this point, the bigotry charge against speciesism remains unanswered. All the initial attempts we have explored to defeat the charge have only led to its reinforcement. If speciesists want to show their view disanalogous to racism, sexism, and other invidious forms of preju-

Speciesism and Full Personhood

dice, they will need to make a case for the justifiability of linking moral consideration to species membership. In order to succeed, they must reformulate their view. This is exactly what recent sophisticated defenders of speciesism have attempted to do.

Replacing Homocentric Speciesism with Full-Personhood-Related Speciesism

The rather primitive, albeit widespread, speciesist view that *humanity* as such is necessary for maximum moral significance does not stand up to rational scrutiny. This is the version of speciesism most obviously vulnerable to the bigotry charge. Why indeed should humanity warrant one's inclusion in the moral community, any more than one's race, sex, sexual orientation, age, or culture? Homocentrists who defend the humanity criterion by appealing to human intellectual superiority only get into worse trouble, as we have seen: they inconsistently ally speciesism with the full-personhood view. The problem is that species lines do not fall along full-personhood lines. The bigotry charge against this self-contradictory view takes on a new dimension, because now the speciesist stands accused of investing moral significance in human nonpersons while denying it to nonhumans who fall short of the mark. Full-personhood-view supporters are not speciesists and avoid this bigotry charge, but they face their own dilemma: they cannot defeat the biconditional argument from marginal cases, and most balk at accepting the low moral status of marginal humans.

The new speciesists, who are also former full-personhood-view advocates, try to do better. They hold that beings who have higher-order wants enabling them to live reflective, richly complex lives, including lives of moral agency, are the *primary* possessors of basic moral rights or maximum moral significance. But full moral status is not restricted to full persons: these speciesists believe that beings who cannot or who have not yet achieved full personhood are also due maximum moral significance—*provided that* they belong to species whose normal adults are full persons. Thus, full personhood is thought to set the parameters for full inclusion in the moral community.

One very economical way to state this view is provided, ironically, by

Michael A. Fox, who gives us this characterization of a view he has since rejected: "[A]ll and only those beings *which are members of a species of which it is true in general* (i.e., typically the case at maturity, assuming normal development) that members of the species in question can be considered autonomous agents are beings endowed with [basic] moral rights."[36] Simply belonging to a species whose normal adult members are autonomous moral agents is said to be necessary and sufficient for maximum moral significance, whether one achieves full personhood or not. Thus, nonhumans with mental capacities equivalent to marginal humans would be denied basic moral rights if typical members of their species can never attain moral agency. A similar suggestion has been made by Stanley Benn: "[W]e respect the interests of men and give them priority over dogs not *insofar* as they are rational, but because rationality is the human norm."[37]

This formulation of speciesism has several theoretical advantages. It avoids the inconsistency of the old homocentric–full-personhood view of speciesism; it is quite economical in offering but one necessary and sufficient condition for maximum moral significance; and it avoids simple-minded homocentrism: *Full personhood,* not *humanity,* is the focus of the species-norm view. It appropriately leaves open the possibility that nonhumans, from whatever planet, might be due full moral status because normal adult members of their species achieve moral agency. Nevertheless, this particular formulation of speciesism requires amendment. As it stands, it excludes from full moral consideration highly developed persons emerging from species whose typical members fall short of such qualities. Random mutations could lead to such a result—isn't that what happened to us?—as could deliberate genetic manipulation. As both Singer (in a partial reply to Benn)[38] and Rachels[39] point out, requiring individuals to be treated in accordance with the *norm* for their species rather than their own individual characteristics is outrageously unfair.

Michael Wreen has avoided this defect by admitting that there are two sufficient conditions for achieving basic moral rights: (full) personhood and belonging to a species typified by (full) personhood.[40] Although he does not offer us an inclusive definition, it is easy enough to formulate one: *Speciesism (in the new sense) is the view that those who possess maximum moral significance, including what we call a right to life, are*

Speciesism and Full Personhood

either (a) full persons (i.e., moral agents) or (b) members of a species characterized by full personhood. This definition sacrifices some economy for a gain in plausibility. From now on, unless otherwise specified, this is what I will mean by 'speciesism.'

Speciesists agree in denying maximum moral significance to nonhumans belonging to species uncharacterized by moral agency. It does not follow that they must deny *all* moral significance to these beings. James Rachels points out that speciesists may take a "mild" or a "radical" position. In case of a conflict of interests between members of full-personhood-characterized species and members of other species, they may opt for the former only if vital interests are served. This is the mild view. On the other hand, they may take the radical position that in case of conflict, the interests of the favored species' members should be served, even if those interests are trivial and call for the sacrifice of the other party's vital interests.[41]

Singer characterized speciesism in the radical way in *Animal Liberation*.[42] He was not fashioning a straw target when he did this. Countless numbers of humans subscribe to this view, including those who would trap and kill furbearers to feed human vanity, or engorge the liver of a duck by force-feeding and killing it to obtain paté de fois gras, or feast on the anemic flesh of calves whose short lives have been spent in two-foot-wide crates in isolation and darkness, to mention but three examples. "Kinder, gentler" speciesists are possible too. In fact, there is a whole spectrum of possible speciesist views, from mild to radical. Where a speciesist falls on this scale depends upon how much moral significance he or she attributes to nonpersons who are typical members of their species. One might hold that maximum moral significance, including a right to life or a strong presumption in favor of preserving life, is reserved for moral agents or members of moral-agency-characterized species, but that lesser moral significance accrues to some nonhuman nonpersons who are normal for their species. Most commonly, one might hold that sentient beings should not be made to suffer if this can be avoided, yet be in favor of their "humane" dispatch. Alternatively, one might hold that only humans (and moral agent mutants or members of other moral-agency-characterized species, if any) are morally considerable. In that case, zero significance would be assigned to those incapable of moral agency who conform to their species norm. As Rachels notes, Aquinas,

Speciesism and Full Personhood

Descartes, and Kant all took this view.[43] Depending on the degree of one's speciesism, one will support or oppose the common forms of non-human exploitation. Former advocates of the full-personhood view who do not accept the exploitation of marginal humans but who do wish to continue exploiting nonhumans, even if "humanely," will have to take a relatively stringent position.

Defending Speciesism: Two Strategies

Speciesists who have reformulated their view in a more plausible way are in a position to defend it against the charge of bigotry. They can show that speciesism is not morally equivalent to racism, sexism, and all the other depressing doctrines humans inflict upon each other if they succeed in doing one of two things: (a) establishing that membership in a species characterized by full personhood is a morally relevant characteristic, or (b) showing that *even if* marginal humans and sentient nonhumans are not *in themselves* different in morally relevant ways, moral agents are justified in continuing to exploit the second group but not the first.

These two strategies for defending speciesism are also two ways of trying to overcome the argument from marginal cases. If the first strategy succeeds, a key premise in both versions of the argument from marginal cases will have been shown false (i.e., "nonhumans exist who are similar in all important morally relevant respects to marginal humans"). If the second strategy succeeds, the argument will have been shown to have no practical import. In fact, these defenses run parallel to the two types of attack on the argument from marginal cases that were surveyed in chapter 2: (a) attempts to show the argument unsound, and (b) attempts to show the argument inconsequential. As we saw in that chapter, supporters of the full-personhood view have not been able to refute or even to undermine the argument. Speciesists will now try to succeed where the others have failed.

ATTEMPTS TO SHOW THAT MEMBERSHIP IN A SPECIES CHARACTERIZED BY FULL PERSONHOOD IS A MORALLY RELEVANT CHARACTERISTIC

These attempts will be addressed in ascending order of plausibility. The first defense of full-personhood-characterized species membership as a morally relevant characteristic focuses upon an alleged partially definitional link between being a member of such a species and being a subject of rights.

The Quasi-Definitional Defense

Alan White declares that according to the "full language" of rights only "persons"—highly autonomous moral agents capable of claiming and recognizing rights—are rights holders.[44] However, he believes that marginal humans are also rights bearers: "Nor does this, as some contend, exclude infants, children, the feeble-minded, the comatose, the dead, or generations yet unborn. Any of these may be for various reasons empirically unable to fulfill the full role of a right-holder. But so long as they are persons—and it is significant that we think and speak of them as young, feeble-minded, incapacitated, dead, unborn *persons*—they are logically possible subjects of rights to whom the full language of rights can significantly, however falsely, be used." [45] According to White's view, this does not hold for the nonhumans whom we exploit. They are said to be "tautologically" incapable of claiming and recognizing rights, having duties, and so on; thus, they are not logically possible bearers of rights.[46] In a species characterized by full personhood, individuals are capable of generating and using the language of rights, and of extending that language to those who are "empirically" incapable of doing this. According to White, extending such language to nonhumans who are typical members of their own species is literally inconceivable. This, then, is said to be the morally relevant difference between a severely retarded human and, for instance, a chimpanzee or a dog.

White is clearly defending the reformulated speciesist view we currently have under discussion. (He actually denies that his view is speciesist, but that is because he assumes that 'speciesism' is a pejorative term

Speciesism and Full Personhood

denoting an unreasoned, arbitrary form of prejudice.)[47] Is his defense successful? Hardly, for a number of reasons.

First of all, being a *logically possible* subject of rights does not make one a subject of rights. Secondly, White himself actually *denies* that these "logically possible subjects of rights" are rights bearers when he claims that the "language of rights" is used *falsely* when it is applied to them! Clearly, if it is false to say that marginal humans have basic moral rights, they have no basic moral rights. Thirdly, White trades on the fact that we allegedly "think and speak" of marginal humans as "persons." In the sense of 'person' relevant to the rights discussion, they are not persons, according to *his own* characterization of their inability to conceive of and act upon moral principles. They are sometimes called "persons" in quite another sense, of course: as we well know, "person" can simply mean "human being." White is guilty of equivocation.[48] Fourthly, White does not show that it would be *inconceivable* to ascribe basic moral rights to nonhumans. If it is logically possible for marginal humans to be rights bearers, why can this not also be the case for nonhumans? If it were impossible to conceive of nonhumans as being rights bearers, there could be no debate over nonhuman rights in the first place, just as there is no debate about whether circles can be four-sided. In fact, White once again gives an example that contradicts his own claim. After citing "the law" as evidence for the fact that we tie rights attributions to claims, duties, and responsibilities of rights holders, White himself points out that the law has sometimes treated nonhumans as persons, on whose behalf rights claims can be made.[49] He further adds that our conceptions can shift as we become more morally sensitive, giving the example of slavery: a being considered a "thing" with no legal rights would now be termed a "person" with rights-bearing status.[50] Obviously, the same can happen with nonhumans, and to some extent it already has—by his own admission.

Michael Wreen has given a similar linguistic argument. He holds that there is a definitional, not merely an empirical, link between *being human* and *being a person*, in the sense of 'personhood' relevant to basic moral rights (i.e., autonomy and moral agency). He claims that the following is an allegedly plausible "criteriological" assertion: "It is *necessarily* true that the statement 'X is a live human being' is good evidence for the statement 'X is a human person.' "[51] The connection Wreen claims to hold is not a *strict* definitional one: he does not maintain that it is necessarily true that all humans are persons. The connection is said to be looser than that while still not being merely empirical: it is allegedly a "criteriological" relationship, in the sense of 'criterion' explicated by philosopher Sidney Shoemaker.[52] If the two concepts of human being and human person are "criteriologically" related, this means we find it *inconceivable* (or necessarily false) that 'X is a live human being' would not be *good evidence* for the claim that 'X is a human person' (an autonomous moral agent).[53] If the two concepts were merely *empirically* related, we would have no difficulty imagining the second statement being false while the first statement is true. As Wreen puts it, he is claiming that there is a "quasi-metaphysical linkage" between (full) personhood and humanity.[54] Unlike White, Wreen does not think this is sufficient to show that marginal humans therefore also have basic moral rights (we shall soon examine the consideration he does believe to be sufficient), but he does believe this alleged linkage is weighty evidence in favor of such rights attributions.

Unfortunately for this defense of speciesism, the "linkage" dissolves upon reflection. As I have pointed out in a critique of Wreen's article,[55] all that one need do to defeat Wreen's criteriological assertion is conceive of circumstances in which it would be false to say that 'X is a live human being' is *good evidence* for 'X is a human person.' Alas, it is very easy to conceive of such circumstances. For example, a horrible new plague could sweep the earth, robbing all existing humans of their capacity for personhood and ensuring that human young born thereafter will never become persons. We can also imagine that humans might have evolved differently than they in fact have. In response, although Wreen agrees that the *sort* of test I am using is relevant to the defeat of a criteriological claim, he has, rather oddly, denied that my counterexample defeats that claim. He claims that my all-too-possible scenarios of worlds in which disease or random mutations have made all human beings nonpersons "doesn't show that being a live human being is not good evidence for being a human person in these worlds."[56] The evidence would still be *good,* he says, it just would not be "sufficient" evidence.[57] On the contrary, in the easily imagined worlds I have sketched, an individual's being a live human would not only be "insufficient" evidence for that individual's being a person, it would be *counterevidence* for that claim! Thus any link between humanity and (full) personhood is fully empirical. No quasi-metaphysical or quasi-definitional link distinguishes members of species characterized by full personhood from those not so characterized.

In general, attempts to settle debates by appealing to definitions are less than promising. If definitions do rule in a clear fashion, one's opponents must be hopelessly stupid or confused in refusing to see this fact. Although this degree of thick-headedness or ignorance can indeed occur, especially among those who have not quite mastered the language of the dispute, it is seldom found in debates involving mature, intelligent people. Definitions in such disputes are rarely so clear-cut. I will illustrate this by briefly returning to the full-personhood view. Full-personhood-view supporters who reject any attempt to ascribe basic moral rights to nonhumans have sometimes tried to argue that their view is simply true by definition. (Of course, their position also implies that marginal humans can have no basic moral rights, as we have seen.) For example, H. J. McCloskey has argued that only morally autonomous agents, and possibly also potentially morally autonomous agents, can coherently be said to possess basic moral rights.[58] More recently, Ann S. Causey, in a moral defense of sport hunting, has made the same claim:[59] No rights can be violated if nonhumans are slain if they are not even logically possible possessors of rights. She supports her contention by citing Paul Taylor's recent book, *Respect for Nature*,[60] claiming that Taylor has shown that it is logically impossible to attribute rights to nonhumans. In fact, however, Taylor himself exposes the error in making such a claim. Although he agrees that there is a traditional conception of moral rights which does indeed restrict such rights to moral agents, he points out that this is not the only conception of rights enjoying wide currency. A "modified" conception also exists, a conception that allows for the attribution of moral rights to marginal humans *and* nonhumans. If we insist upon using the traditional conception alone, as McCloskey does, we really gain nothing substantive by it, Taylor thinks. It would still be perfectly coherent (and correct, given Taylor's view) to argue that moral agents owe nonhumans (and marginal humans) the same kind of respectful treatment they would be due if we did ascribe moral rights to them.[61] Real skirmishes cannot be reduced to linguistic ones. Attempts to destroy opposition to the full-personhood view on verbal grounds are no more successful than the quasi-definitional arguments for the moral relevance of membership in species characterized by full personhood.

From now on, the defenses of speciesism we will discuss will be fully substantive. Let us turn next to the argument from charity or benevolence.

The Appeal to Benevolence

It is sometimes argued that moral agents should be benevolently inclined toward members of their species who are not and have never been moral agents. "Charity, benevolence, and humaneness" should keep one from exploiting such beings in the ways in which we exploit nonhumans.[62] This is an inherently limited defense of speciesism, because protection of marginal humans is construed as "charitable"—praiseworthy but not mandatory. Charity is not strictly owed to anyone, unlike respect for that individual's rights (if any). Still, if the defense succeeds, it would show that membership in a full-personhood-characterized species would be morally relevant. An attitude of "charity, benevolence, and humaneness" is morally virtuous, and the claim is that members of one's species who lack moral agency should have such an attitude extended to them.

However, the defense is not successful. Suppose the speciesist holds that anyone who is not, has never been, or will never be a full person is lacking in moral standing, *apart* from that individual's species membership. The speciesist could not then argue that moral agents should be benevolent, charitable, or humane toward marginal humans: we can only take such attitudes toward beings who are *already* morally considerable. The beneficiary of a benevolent disposition must be the sort of being for whom moral concern is appropriate, otherwise our virtuous inclinations are misplaced. Suppose, on the other hand, that the speciesist takes a less radical stance, holding that *apart* from species membership, those who are not, have not been, or never will be full persons are morally considerable but not maximally morally significant. Considerations of species membership aside, they would have some moral standing, but they could still be used and even killed if such treatment served important interests of full persons. In this case also, the appeal to benevolence will not establish the conclusion that members

Speciesism and Full Personhood

of full-personhood-characterized species should be spared such treatment, unlike others. For why should benevolence be extended toward one group of morally considerable beings—marginal humans—and not another? Why not heap the same benevolence on sentient nonhumans? This argument can give us no answer to this question. The appeal to benevolence is at best incomplete, as well as inherently weak. If there are good reasons for differential treatment of humans and nonhumans who fail to be full persons, we must continue to look for them.

The Appeal to Fairness

Stanley Benn goes beyond mere charity in an initially plausible argument for the moral relevance of membership in a species characterized by full personhood. He points out that: "We say it is *unfair* to exploit the deficiencies of the imbecile who falls short of the norm, just as it would be unfair, and not just ordinarily dishonest, to steal from a blind man."[63] The implication is that exploitation is an outstandingly unjust response to impairment. Thus, belonging to a species whose norm is full personhood would morally distinguish a severely mentally deficient human from a similarly endowed nonhuman. Michael Wreen extensively and independently develops this initially plausible suggestion. He notes that marginal humans are as they are, for the most part, through no fault of their own. *Fairness* requires that those of us who have been more fortunate *compensate* such individuals for their loss by ascribing basic moral rights to them, Wreen argues: "although in the primary case it is persons who are ascribed basic rights, equality of opportunity, or, better, fairness, requires us to ascribe basic rights to human non-persons as well."[64] If there were to be nonhuman species that are also characterized by full personhood, the same obligation would hold. This line of reasoning, of course, would not warrant the ascription of basic moral rights to any nonpersons who do not belong to such a species.

This argument also fails. The fundamental problem with his reasoning is that any appeal to fairness to support the ascription of basic moral rights to marginal humans is inherently circular. If moral agents are indeed *required* to extend fair, equitable treatment to marginal humans, as Wreen says, those humans must *already possess at least one basic*

Speciesism and Full Personhood

moral right: the right to equitable treatment or fairness! Speciesists are not entitled to assume the very conclusion they must establish.[65]

If we are to transcend this begged question, a morally relevant difference must be found between those who fail to be full persons but belong to species whose typical adult members are full persons, and those who are normal members of their species. Benn's and Wreen's appeals to fairness do not succeed, but they strike a sympathetic chord by reminding us that marginal humans are bereft of the moral agency we take for granted. Perhaps a closer look at the nature of their apparent "loss" in contrast to our own gifts will lead to a stronger defense of speciesism. The next argument I want to suggest, then, is in the spirit, if not the letter, of Benn's and Wreen's proposals. I call it "the appeal to thwarted potential."

The Appeal to Thwarted Potential

Suppose a case could be made for the moral relevance of a being's *potential* for full personhood. Now consider a being who has been deprived of this potential. There is a sense in which she has suffered a *loss:* she has been denied the kind of life she would have had if luck had been with her. A dog, by contrast, has no potential for full personhood. One's species determines one's possible potentialities; thus, those with rather limited intellects who are typical of their species have lost nothing, unlike the severely mentally handicapped human. If this argument succeeds, membership in a species characterized by full personhood would indeed be morally relevant. The speciesist could then argue that such a difference warrants our refusal to exploit marginal humans while we continue to use nonhumans for our own purposes.

Although I will make the best case for this argument that I can, it must be admitted that it faces severe difficulties. First of all, it must be shown that *potential* full personhood has moral weight. As discussed in chapter 2, many philosophers, for very good reason, doubt that this can be done. From the perspective of the full-personhood view, even future generations seem to have no rights *as potential full persons:* it is the fact that they *will* exist as *actual* full persons that morally constrains us from poisoning the planet they will inhabit. To give the speciesist every bene-

Speciesism and Full Personhood

fit of the doubt, however, suppose that we can somehow show the direct moral relevance of potential personhood. We would then have another extraordinarily high hurdle to clear: we would be required to show how the *loss* of potential full personhood could be morally relevant. It is very difficult to argue that a being *who no longer has* the characteristic that formerly gave him moral status nevertheless retains that moral status. *Perhaps* this could be done. Joel Feinberg has persuasively argued that it is possible to wrong (even harm) dead persons, although they no longer exist.[66] Possibly the case of a former potential full person is analogous to the case of a deceased full person: current exploitation of the impaired human could be construed as a lack of respect for the being she once was. Feinberg would certainly reject this extension of his argument, since he is convinced that potential personhood carries no moral weight in itself,[67] but we would be free to argue in this way if (as we are supposing) a case had been made for that potential's moral relevance. Suppose, then, that we are able to solve two problems that many believe are insoluble. How much moral weight could "thwarted potential full personhood" carry?

This would depend on how much moral weight has been assigned to the possession of potential full personhood. Feinberg distinguishes two possible potentialist positions: the *strict potentiality* view and the *gradualist potentiality* view.[68] The first view assigns full moral status to any potential full person. One well-known defender of this view is John T. Noonan.[69] The second is more complex: gradualists hold that any potential full person is morally *considerable,* but they believe that one's moral *significance* increases as one approaches actual full personhood. According to that view, one does not achieve maximum moral significance—that is, one does not gain a full moral right to life—until one attains full personhood. Until then, one has at most a strong claim to life, a claim whose strength increases as one comes closer to full personhood. Philosophers Daniel Callahan[70] and L. W. Sumner[71] have each defended gradualist views. Supposing, as we are, that potential full personhood has moral weight, as does its loss. Which of the two views ought one to adopt?

The strict potentiality view has the merit of straightforward simplicity. Potential full personhood is assigned exactly the same weight as actual full personhood: the maximum obtainable. Given the thwarted-

Speciesism and Full Personhood

potential argument, individuals who have been deprived of their potential full personhood would retain all basic moral rights. Exploitation of them in any way would be morally countermanded. However, although this very lack of ambiguity and simplicity attracts some adherents, it drives even more away. The strict potentiality view implies that a just-fertilized ovum has the same moral status due to full persons. This seems extremely implausible. Is taking a "morning-after pill" that causes the egg to be flushed away long before implantation in the uterus could occur morally equivalent to murdering a woman in her sleep? Are the two beings killed really equally wronged? Potentialists who see a vast difference between these two acts retreat to gradualism in short order.

Gradualism seems to be more acceptable, although it is far more "messy." In denying that all potential full persons are equal, it accords with the common view that it is far worse (other things being equal) to kill a third-trimester baby than to use the morning-after pill. As the unborn grows and develops, many of us have increasing qualms about destroying it. *If* potential full personhood has moral weight, the gradualist position appears to be more reasonable than the strict position.

Now, *if*, as we are supposing for the sake of argument, potential full personhood's *loss* also has moral weight, we can integrate gradualism with the thwarted-potential view. Alas for the speciesist, grave difficulties develop. If one's moral significance increases as one approaches full personhood, the moral weight of one's *loss* of potential would seem to depend on how close one is to full personhood before disaster strikes. According to this view, a human damaged as a three-month fetus has less moral significance than a child whose brain is damaged after birth, *even if they have equivalent mental capacities.* This seems extraordinarily implausible. Moreover, gradualism falls quite short of protecting marginal humans from exploitation. Gradualists hold that those who are deprived of their potential for full personhood before actualization of that potential do not have a moral right to life. Depending upon *when* the loss of potential occurs, one would have a weaker or a stronger claim to life, but never a claim equal in strength to a full person's right to life. This means that marginal humans may be sacrificed if such a sacrifice is required to save the life of a full person.

Radical speciesists should, then, not be attracted by the gradualist version of the thwarted-potential argument. Such an argument would

Speciesism and Full Personhood

not proscribe the use of marginal humans for medical research, organ supplies, or food if no alternatives were available. Mild speciesists might find the argument a bit more acceptable, since it does imply that human nonpersons would be due more consideration than nonhuman animals. This would mean that we ought to kill the nonhuman for food, organs, and so on rather than the human—*if we have the choice!* If there were to be no suitable nonhuman donor, gradualism would dictate the sacrifice of the mentally deficient human. Moreover, the gradualist thwarted-potential argument would also imply that a marginal human afflicted as a three-month-old fetus ought to be used *before* one deprived of potential at four months of gestation. Few speciesists, however mild, can find comfort in such implications.

Considerations of this sort drive the potentialist speciesist back to the strict version of the thwarted-potential argument. Unlike the gradualist version, it does provide the theoretical underpinning needed for the view that unfortunate humans all have the same right to life, regardless of the point at which loss of potential occurs. It is also compatible with radical speciesism, the position that must be taken by the speciesist who defends the exploitation of nonhumans but condemns the exploitation of mentally comparable humans. True, it does imply that a fertilized human ovum has the same moral status as a fully cognizant human, but the speciesist may think this a small price to pay. Even if one accepts this implication, however, the thwarted-potential argument has another implication that is far too nasty to swallow.

Imagine the following all-too-realistic situation. A normal adult human has contracted hepatitis B (let us assume through no fault of her own). She will die unless she receives a new liver. Imagine further that the only feasible organ donors are three healthy individuals, none of whom are full persons. The first is a human who has lacked the potential for full personhood from the moment of conception. The second is a human who was normal at conception but developed severe brain damage at six months of gestation when his mother was hurt in a car accident. The third is a baboon who is quite normal for her species. Suppose that a new drug to prevent organ rejection (e.g., FK-506) makes each of the three equally suitable donors.[72] Suppose too that all three are orphans, and that no other individual would be devastated by any of their deaths. If one believes, in accordance with the strict thwarted-potential view, that the right to life is restricted to full persons, potential persons, and those who have lost their potential for full personhood, the choice one should make in such a case is clear. The second human who lost the potential for full personhood through a car accident should be spared. A coin can be flipped to decide whether the baboon or the first human, *who never had any potential full personhood to lose in the first place,* should be the donor. One cannot be robbed of what one has never possessed. (The same implication would hold for the gradualist thwarted-potential view: those who never had the potential for full personhood would not even have a weak claim to life.)

We find this to be a totally unacceptable consequence. After all, neither of the two humans chose to be as he is. The time that one has been alive without the potential for full personhood—from conception or from six months of gestation—seems to be morally irrelevant. This very reflection, in fact, leads us even further from speciesism, for what we have said about the first human also holds for the baboon. *She, too, was conceived without the potential for full personhood!* She had no more to say about her mental abilities than either of the other two potential donors.

Thus, even if a case for the moral relevance of potential full personhood could be made, as well as a case for the moral relevance of its loss, the thwarted-potential argument fails to support speciesism. The failure of this argument suggests that we have to dig yet more deeply in search of a morally relevant difference between humans and nonhumans who have never had the potential for full personhood.

The Appeal to Harmful Life

Suppose it could be shown that humans without the potential for full personhood, but not nonhumans, are in a *harmed* or *impaired* condition? Might this be a morally relevant difference that would justify differential treatment?

Let us take care, however, not to exclude from the scope of this argument humans who have been *conceived* without the potential for full personhood. Strictly speaking, they have not been "harmed" or "impaired": both these concepts imply that one had a prior condition preferable to the present one.[73] Those who were once potential full persons or actual full persons may indeed be impaired by events that render them permanently incapable of full personhood, but this cannot be said of those who were conceived in that condition. If we take the view that all marginal humans, regardless of the source of their incapacity, have similar moral status—as we have just seen, the denial of this seems outrageously arbitrary—we must recast this argument.

To set the stage for this recasting, let us turn to the concept of "wrongful life" (i.e., wrongfully given life). For example, suppose that a severely mentally and physically handicapped human child has been intentionally or negligently conceived by parents who had excellent reason to believe that such a child would probably result. Joel Feinberg argues that a child whose life quality is so poor that nonexistence would be preferable has a "wrongful life."[74] In fact, we can say that the child has been wrongfully conceived. The spate of law suits in recent years on behalf of such children suggests that the concept of wrongful life is gaining common acceptance. Indeed, some have pressed such suits on their own behalf, or had such suits pressed by their estates after their deaths: a man in Ohio who was revived in a hospital contrary to his own instructions claimed that medical personnel gave him a wrongful life.[75] The common element in such cases is the fact that nonexistence can be preferable to life.

Now, when an individual has been wronged, a right of hers has been violated; that is, a justified claim that individual has against others (whether the being is capable of making the claim or not) has not been upheld.[76] In the case of wrongful conception, Feinberg argues, the parents have violated the child's right to *a life worth living*. Normal humans have "basic" interests in health, intelligence, absence of debilitating suffering, freedom, and a minimally decent environment, as well as all the "ulterior" interests (e.g., in a career, loving relationships, art, scholarship, etc.) that satisfaction of their basic interests makes possible. The child we are considering can never satisfy even those basic interests required for a minimally worthwhile existence.[77] She has not been *harmed,* because no previous condition of hers has deteriorated, but she is, Feinberg suggests, in a condition which is *harmful* to herself.[78] Her life is full of harm for her in the sense that misery is inescapable. Following Feinberg's terminological suggestion, let's stipulate that she has a "harmful life," in the sense that her life is detrimental to her well-being, as well as a "wrongful life."

Now let us alter the case in one respect. Suppose the severely handicapped child was not deliberately or negligently conceived: no one could have foreseen her condition and no one is at fault. We cannot now say that she has a *wrongful* life, for no one has wronged her. Her right to a life worth living has been *violated* by no one. Bad luck rather than malice or negligence is the source of her miserable existence. She suffers because of *nonmoral* evil. Let us mark this distinction by saying that the accidentally conceived child has had her right to a worthwhile life *defeated* by circumstance, whereas the wrongfully conceived child's right has been *violated*. Both have *harmful* lives, but only the second has a *wrongful* life. A parallel distinction would hold for individuals who were potential or actual full persons and then became severely damaged and permanently incapable of full personhood through accident or intention. They would all have *harmed* lives, as well as *harmful* lives, but only those who were intentionally harmed (perhaps by themselves) would have been wronged. All of these individuals—those who were conceived without the potential for full personhood and those who lost that potential, whether through accident or intention—seem to be on a similar moral footing. All have harmful lives.

Let us next consider a human child, conceived with a genetic makeup that precludes his ever becoming a full person, but who has a very happy life. All his basic needs are satisfied. However, he will never have more than rudimentary interests, unlike his normal counterparts. Isn't there a sense in which he too has a *harmful* life? The desperately miserable child we considered above cannot even have her basic interests met, so she is surely worse off than the happy child we are now considering. Nevertheless, from our point of view, this happy child also leads an intrinsically "interest-impoverished" life. In this respect, *any* human with no potential for full personhood who belongs to a species characterized by full personhood, no matter how happy he or she is, could be said to have a harmful life (although some will surely have a life more harmful than others). A normal baboon, on the other hand, who also lacks the potential for full personhood, cannot be said to have a harmful life in this sense, because she does not have an intrinsically interest-impoverished life in comparison to other baboons.

Speciesism and Full Personhood

Let us now return to our organ donor dilemma. Two humans and a baboon are the possible suitable donors for a full person who will die without a new liver; all three are incapable of full personhood. The first human has never had any potential for full personhood, the second lost that potential through accident, and the baboon is a normal member of her species. According to the argument from harmful life as we have developed it, the two humans have harmful lives *given their species membership,* but the baboon does not (yet!). Doesn't this argument show that species membership can have a morally relevant consequence? If there is a morally relevant distinction between the two humans, on the one hand, and the baboon, on the other, does this justify the sacrifice of the baboon? In general, does the harmful-life argument show that it is correct to use nonhumans for our own benefit while refusing to use marginal humans?

Note, however, that one type of speciesist cannot make use of this argument. Speciesists holding that marginal humans would be morally inconsiderable were it not for *their species membership* are barred from using the appeal to harmful life to show how species membership can be morally relevant. Clearly, one must already be morally considerable in order to be *wronged* or to suffer nonmoral *evil.* On the other hand, it appears that speciesists taking the milder position that moral considerability, if not *maximum* moral significance, accrues to sentient beings who fail to be full persons is in a position to use the harmful-life appeal. They could argue that all sentient beings who fail to be full persons are due some moral concern, *regardless of their species membership.* They could then appeal to harmful life to try to show that marginal members of full-personhood-characterized species are due *additional, maximum concern.* This position does not license the all-out exploitation of sentient nonhumans now occurring, but it does permit "humane" exploitation of such beings, just as it forbids the same treatment for marginal humans. As we shall soon see, though, the appeal to harmful life does not succeed in establishing even mild speciesism. Upon closer examination, this new argument collapses just as resoundingly as the appeals to fairness and thwarted potential.

As we saw, the appeal to harmful life implies that even a very happy, accidentally conceived marginal human has had a right defeated. But what is that right? Surely not the right to a worthwhile existence: such

Speciesism and Full Personhood

an individual obviously does have a life worth living, unlike some other extremely unfortunate handicapped humans. Those who nevertheless insist that his life is not worth living are guilty of unempathetic arrogance. Perhaps, on the other hand, it would be correct to say that such a human's right to a worthwhile existence *as a human being* has been at least partially defeated. He is, as indicated above, "interest impoverished" in comparison to a normal human. In this sense, he is not a well-functioning member of his species.

Suppose there were such a right. The speciesist cannot very well hold that such a right is restricted to members of species characterized by full personhood, since this would obviously beg the very question at issue. The speciesist must show, not assume, that marginal members of full-personhood-characterized species have basic moral rights not possessed by similarly endowed but normal members of other species. It is very unlikely that the speciesist could avoid the begged question charge by making a case for such a restricted right. If there is a right to be a well-functioning member of one's species, why should humans or members of other full-personhood-characterized species, if any, be the only creatures in the universe with such a claim on moral agents? Such a restriction seems quite arbitrary.

On the other hand, we might be able to make a case for a more generalized right to be a well-functioning member of one's species. Updating Aristotle's concept of telos, Bernard Rollin has argued that every sentient being has a specific nature, set by genetic parameters. That being's nature or telos, defined in terms of its functions, should be respected, Rollin argues: beings should not be prevented from living the sorts of lives appropriate to their kind.[79] This is the theoretical basis of Rollin's defense of nonhuman sentient animal rights. Biocentric environmental ethicists, who regard *all* life as morally considerable, would go even further. Now, following this reasoning, we could say that a being, human or nonhuman, whose telos is unfulfilled is in a "harmful state." If her condition is due to malice or negligence, her right to be a well-functioning member of her species has been violated; if no moral agent was at fault, her right has been defeated.

Let us see how this line of thought affects the organ donor dilemma. Since it does not now matter whether the possible human donor was conceived without the potential for full personhood or somehow lost that potential, let's simplify the dilemma. We now have just two suitable donors: a baboon and a human, each permanently incapable of full personhood. If our liver-diseased full person is to live, one of these potential donors must die. The human has had her right to be a well-functioning member of her species defeated or violated, but the baboon has not. Should the baboon, a normal member of his species, then be sacrificed instead of the human?

According to the line of reasoning we have been considering, the answer is "no!" Neither should be sacrificed. First of all, if at least every sentient being has the right to live the kind of life that is worthwhile for members of his or her species, we would be violating that being's right by taking his or her life. One cannot have the right to live as a well-functioning member of one's species without having the right to life itself. Second, the fact that the human's right to be a well-functioning member of her species, but not the baboon's, has *already* been violated or defeated does not warrant the deliberate violation of the baboon's right on this occasion. We cannot appeal to such a right in order to justify its violation! The speciesist might reply that we would violate the fully developed human's right to be a well-functioning member of his species by refusing to kill a donor. But why should the full person's telos-right justify the violation of the baboon's telos-right? Any attempt to show the full person's life to be more valuable than the baboon's will have the implication that marginal humans' rights are also canceled by the needs of the full person. This is exactly the implication that speciesist are attempting to avoid.

Thus, the right to a worthwhile existence as a member of one's species, far from supporting the continuation of nonhuman exploitation, reveals the routine captivity and slaughter in laboratories and on farms to be unnatural crimes. Appealing to the concept of such a right in order to explicate the concept of *harmful life* has backfired utterly for the speciesist. We have still found no morally relevant difference between marginal humans and the nonhumans whose lives we so freely sacrifice.

The Appeal to Misfortune

The appeals to fairness, thwarted potential, and harmful life have all failed to support speciesism, but they point toward another argument which may succeed. Alan Holland argues that moral agents are, prima

facie, the only morally considerable beings, but adds that other characteristics can "make moral consideration appropriate."[80] As far as he is
concerned, chickens lack any of these redeeming characteristics: their
lives are due no respect whatever.[81] Severely mentally defective, "marginal," humans are another matter: "They have status by virtue of what
they, as the individuals they are, might have been but by misfortune are
not."[82]

The key word here is "misfortune." Surely it is morally relevant if
individuals have been victims of circumstance, especially if they have
had no say in the outcome. The fact that these humans belong to a
species whose normal members are full persons *makes* them "unfortunate," unlike their nonhuman mental equivalents. If Holland is correct,
then, marginal humans' membership in a full-personhood-characterized
species would be morally relevant in the sense that it makes a morally
relevant category applicable to them. Holland may have something here,
although he does not give a good argument to support his contention
that "misfortune" can warrant moral considerability. He merely points
out that moral agents consider it appropriate to send disaster relief to
stricken human communities.[83] The trouble with this rationale is that
most humans in such communities *already have* moral status according
to Holland's view. Why should the misfortune of beings who *otherwise*
have no moral status at all be sufficient to warrant such status? Let us
see how other speciesists try to defend the appeal to misfortune.

A. I. Melden approaches the argument by focusing on the feelings a
moral agent should have toward severely defective humans: "[T]here
are other matters that may determine the moral stance we take towards
them: compassion . . . and pity for them as they now are. For the human
being who is so far different from the rest of us that he must be placed
in an institution, is an object of sorrow and pity, and all the more so
the more his state is like that of an animal; yet we do not pity animals
because they are animals."[84] James Nelson pushes the argument further
by appealing to the concept of tragedy: "The marginal humans have
suffered a tragedy in becoming the psychological equals of animals—a
tragedy that animals have escaped. The sentiments evoked by the recognition of such a tragedy—pity and compassion—speak strongly against
further injury to someone already so afflicted."[85] Despite the eloquence
of Nelson's appeal, it is best to leave *tragedy* out of this discussion.

'Tragedy,' unlike 'misfortune,' suggests a worsening of one's prior condition, and this does not apply to the human who is conceived without the potential for full personhood (although it may well apply to her parents). Nonetheless, with this emendation, we have the gist of a plausible argument for speciesism.

One can argue that the marginal human—even if he has all his basic needs satisfied, is very happy, and would not have existed at all had he not been conceived as he was—is *less fortunate* than a normal sentient nonhuman. The nonhuman has received a full complement of normal genetic material at conception; the human, by contrast, has genetic defects. Marginal humans who were once normal but who have lost their potential for full personhood through mishap are also less fortunate than the normal sentient nonhuman. Returning to the organ donor dilemma, if we choose to sacrifice a marginal human rather than a baboon in order to save a moral agent, we make the marginal human even *more* unfortunate than she already was. This seems very unjust. One is reminded of Stanley Benn's claim that exploiting a marginal human is analogous to stealing from a blind man.[86] Can speciesists successfully appeal to this misfortune attendant upon abnormality to justify the differential treatment of marginal humans and sentient nonhumans?

No, they cannot. Although they are unquestionably right to remind us that mere luck—the roll of the dice at or after conception—separates us from marginal humans, they cannot show, *given their own assumptions,* that this fact endows marginal humans with moral standing or maximum moral significance. Both radical and mild speciesists fail in this attempt, as we shall now see.

Although he calls himself a "moderate" speciesist, Holland subscribes to the radical thesis that moral considerability is, prima facie, restricted to moral agents. Apart from their species membership, those incapable of moral agency are held to lack moral standing altogether. Given this view, if the present argument is to succeed in showing that membership in a species characterized by full personhood leads to a characteristic—misfortune—that is sufficient to bestow moral standing upon marginal humans, it cannot presuppose that those humans are *already* morally considerable. Yet this is precisely what the argument from misfortune does. It implicitly appeals to the principle of distributive justice. This principle enjoins moral agents to distribute benefits *and burdens*

Speciesism and Full Personhood

in an equitable manner. Inflicting further misfortune on an already unfortunate being instead of on a more fortunate being exacerbates the
inequality between the two. Clearly, however, the assumption that the
principle of distributive justice applies to marginal humans entails that
they have a basic moral right: the right to be treated equitably. Thus,
they are *already assumed* to be morally considerable. Like the appeal
to fairness considered earlier in this chapter, the appeal to misfortune,
in the hands of a radical speciesist, begs the question. We cannot show
that marginal humans have basic moral rights by assuming that they
have a basic moral right. It is even more embarrassing to note that the
distributive justice principle is clearly taken to apply to sentient *nonhumans:* otherwise, the misfortune of marginal humans could not be
weighed against the "fortune" of normal nonhumans. This contradicts
radical speciesism's denial of moral standing to these nonhumans.

Mild speciesists, who accord moral considerability to all sentient
beings but reserve maximum moral significance for full persons and
members of full-personhood-characterized species, run into their own
difficulties when they use the appeal to misfortune. As we saw, the argument implies that normal sentient nonhumans are also subject to the
principle of distributive justice: their relatively good fortune is weighed
against the marginal human's misfortune to yield recommendations for
action. This line of argument is all too likely to backfire. The typical
marginal human is more fortunate in many respects than the typical
laboratory or farm nonhuman. Unlike the latter, the human is allowed
to fulfill her basic interests in a happy, comfortable life. Her initial
misfortune in comparison to the nonhuman has weight, but so do subsequent misfortunes, for *both* parties. A baboon who has spent fifteen
years confined to a small cage has had his own share of misfortune,
even before he is killed for his liver. All things considered, the argument from misfortune may well yield the result that the happy marginal
human's liver should be "harvested" instead! The distributive justice
principle also leads to another difficulty. If the principle applies to sentient nonhumans, how can sacrificing them to benefit a moral agent be
"equitable?" Offhand, killing them for their organs (or flesh, for that
matter) seems to be an inequitable distribution of burdens and benefits.
If speciesists retreat to the claim that a full person's life is simply more
valuable than a baboon's, adding a surcharge, as it were, to the burdens

Speciesism and Full Personhood

and benefits of the full person in comparison to those of the baboon, they are in great difficulty. This move would also devalue the burdens and benefits of marginal humans, the very result speciesists try to avoid. *At best,* they could then argue that a normal sentient nonhuman should be sacrificed instead of a marginal human *if* the nonhuman has had an overall more fortunate life than the marginal human. If this is not the case, or if human organs are required to save our normal human, they would have to sanction the sacrifice of the marginal human. Speciesists can hardly regard this as a happy result.

Even this extraordinarily limited "success" is not to be theirs, however. Speciesists, mild or otherwise, who adopt the argument from misfortune face a fatal objection. By hypothesis, the marginal human and the sentient nonhuman we are considering are mentally and emotionally matched. *The* difference between them is the fact that the first falls short of his species norm of full personhood, whereas the second is a normal member of her species. The first is claimed to be unfortunate, unlike the second, for *no other reason* than his abnormality. Regardless of how content he is, even if from the moment of conception he could be no other than he is, we pity him because he will never be a normal human: a full person. When we attach moral significance to this fact, however, granting a moral status to the human that we deny to the nonhuman, *we are attaching moral weight to membership in a full-personhood-characterized species.* Alas for the speciesist, this begs the very question at issue. Speciesism cannot be supported by the assumption that marginal members of a species where full personhood is the norm are *thereby* due more moral consideration than those incapable of full personhood who are normal members of their species. To make that assumption is to assume the thesis of speciesism itself, according to which membership in a full-personhood-characterized species, that is, a species in which full personhood is *normal,* has moral weight. Thus, the appeal to misfortune is a circular argument.

"Disadvantage," Independence, and Moral Considerability

The more one reflects upon the individual characteristics of a marginal human and a sentient nonhuman, the more inclined one is to doubt the speciesist thesis. Why should the moral status of a being incapable of full personhood depend upon the purely contingent question of what *most* members of his or her species are like? If we humans manage to poison our planet so thoroughly that, one hundred years from now, 90 percent of all humans would be genetically incapable of full personhood, it would no longer be true that humanity is a species characterized by full personhood. Depending on the century one lives in, a human incapable of full personhood would have or lack basic moral rights. To say the least, this seems incredibly arbitrary.

Speciesists might at this point reply that they are not really interested in statistical frequencies. In our hypothetical (we hope) planet-poisoning scenario, they could say that the vast majority of humans would be *disadvantaged* through no fault of their own even though they would be statistically normal humans at that time. Why disadvantaged? Because they would lack the full range of interests moral agents enjoy. This alone, it might be said, would entitle them to moral consideration (from the few moral agents remaining). By extension, the same would hold for present marginal humans.

However, it would follow from this line of reasoning that many sentient nonhumans are equally "disadvantaged"! They too, through no fault of their own, lack the ability to be autonomous moral agents. Speciesists cannot protest at this stage that the nonhumans are not disadvantaged, since they, unlike marginal humans, are normal for their species. Not only does this return us to the statistical frequency account of normality, it leads us directly back to the very circular reasoning that has just been exposed. Speciesists cannot attach moral weight to membership in full-personhood-characterized species in the attempt to show that this very characteristic has moral weight.

Speciesists could now try to argue that beings incapable of full personhood are disadvantaged only if at least one member of their species could become a full person. That species need not be *characterized* by full personhood for the individual to be considered deprived. This is a better reply, but it still seems very arbitrary. Imagine a world, Planet X, that is populated by the same species as our own, with one exception: dogs are full persons there. Suppose Earth sends Beauregard, a normal Labrador retriever, to Planet X, where he is harmlessly retrieved from his space capsule. After noninvasive testing, the dogs of Planet X determine that Beauregard is indeed a dog. However, he is indistinguishable from the retarded dogs they care for in the more civilized areas of their planet. Beauregard would not be disadvantaged on Earth by his lack of full personhood and would be due no right to life, by speciesist lights, but he would be classified very differently by speciesists on Planet X. Is it believable that a right to life, not just recognition of a right to life, could depend upon a mere accident of location? Why should one's own moral status depend upon the endowments—or lack of endowments—of anyone else?

The unsuccessful appeal to disadvantage, combined with further reflection upon the individual characteristics of marginal humans and sentient nonhumans, does reveal a morally relevant difference, however. One is very reluctant to classify wolves, for example, as "disadvantaged" simply because they cannot be full-fledged persons with extensive "ulterior" interests. This reluctance need have nothing to do with the fact that full personhood is not a "norm" for their species; instead, it focuses on wolves' ability to lead lives relatively independently of human assistance. Marginal humans, on the other hand, frequently are far less able to satisfy their basic interests. They tend to depend much more on the good will of moral agents than nonhumans in the wild do. (Many *domestic* nonhuman animals rely far more upon us, given the concrete, automobile-infested, high-rise-apartment environments we place them in.)

The greater helplessness of marginal humans quite rightly inspires our compassion. As moral agents, we have a greater obligation to assist such individuals than we do to assist those capable of more independent lives. Thus, there *is* a morally relevant difference between a very mentally limited human and a wolf. However, this difference inspires no speciesist conclusions: it is *not* morally relevant to the ascription of basic moral rights. Our greater positive obligations (obligations of assistance) to the helpless in no way entail a lack of obligations to the more independent, nor do they show the helpless to have superior moral status. For example, we have more positive obligations to a quadriplegic than we do to a track star, but this does not mean the quadriplegic is more morally significant. The more independent individuals become, the more important our *negative* obligation of noninterference in their lives becomes, but they do not diminish as fit objects of moral concern.

Speciesism and Full Personhood

Thus, the greater helplessness of marginal humans is not sufficient to warrant their moral elevation at the expense of others. The same holds for domestic nonhuman animals. As we look at the characteristics of individuals, their species—as opposed to their need for assistance—seems increasingly irrelevant.

The Appeal to Kinship

Perhaps, however, the exclusive focus on individual characteristics is a major mistake. Several speciesists have argued exactly this. Individuals exist in a web of relations, they hold, and this web is allegedly sufficient for the conferral of moral considerability or maximum moral significance on marginal humans. In his 1986 book, M. A. Fox held that: "Just as our untutored moral sense tells us that we have very strong obligations to members of our immediate families, so it seems that preferential treatment should, under certain circumstances, accordingly be granted to members of the human family."[87] Mary Midgley has made the same suggestion, claiming that no case has been made for the moral irrelevance of kinship, "nor for denying that closeness imposes special duties."[88] Alan Holland has also appealed to kinship, arguing that "defective human beings" have relationships to the rest of us that are barred to nonhumans: "no other animal at least could be daughter or cousin, mother or child."[89] Leslie Francis and Richard Norman have argued that biological barriers prevent the kind of morally relevant closeness we have to other humans, including marginal ones.[90] From a different perspective, that of environmental ethics, J. Baird Callicott contends that we belong to "nested communities" or "moral spheres," with obligations that on the whole become diluted in strength as one progresses from family to neighbor to fellow citizen to more remote humans, then to nonhumans in general.[91] He is certainly not a typical speciesist; for example, he believes that we incur special obligations to the nonhumans we *domesticate,* but he also sees no problem in our raising and killing them for food, provided that we avoid factory-farming techniques. He does not approve such treatment of other humans. Holding as he does that our strongest obligations are to family, and asserting that "I have obligations to human beings in general which I do not have to animals

Speciesism and Full Personhood

in general," Callicott joins the more typical speciesists above in giving kinship moral weight.

If our kinship to one of two otherwise relevantly similar beings does indeed constitute a morally relevant difference between the two, the argument holds, we are justified in awarding preferential treatment to our "kin." Speciesists who are unwilling to eat or "harvest" the organs of marginal humans but have no qualms about doing the same to non-humans use this argument to defend themselves against the charge of prejudice. In doing so, they are appealing to *relational* rather than *intrinsic* characteristics of the beings in question.

There is a kernel of truth in this argument, but careful examination will show that this attempt to justify speciesism also collapses. At the core of the appeal to kinship is an analogy between our obligations to our "kin" and our obligations to mentally impaired humans. But how are we to interpret "kinship" here?

The kind of kinship most relevant to speciesism is *genetic* relatedness. Nonhumans *are* cousins to us, but we are more distantly related to them than we are to any human. Life on earth originated some four billion years ago. The lines culminating in chimpanzees (our closest "cousins") and humans diverged from common ancestors some five million years ago, according to genetic analyses. Humans alive today, by contrast, may be able to trace their mitochondrial DNA back to a woman or small group of women living only two hundred thousand years ago. If genetic relatedness imposes special obligations, we have more of those obligations to any human than we do to nonhumans. But it is far from clear that we have obligations to certain beings *because* we are genetically related to them, let alone obligations to discount others' needs in relation to theirs. We have just as many obligations to our adopted children as we have to our biological children, and we have stronger obligations to our (probably unrelated) life mates than to our siblings. Some, of course, deny this, even some philosophers, holding that we ought to prefer our brothers, biological parents, or cousins to unrelated individuals, regardless of the fact that we had nothing to do with the existence of our kin. When asked why this should be, however, we are told that this is what "most people think," or that to hold otherwise is "fatal to family morality."[92] Of course, anyone who seriously questions the existence of genetically based obligations is not going to be convinced by these

Speciesism and Full Personhood

rejoinders. (We do indeed have special obligations to offspring whom we have brought into the world, but we have the same special obligations to any being we have undertaken to nurture and protect, regardless of genetic closeness. Parents who give their biological children up for adoption have no further obligations beyond doing their best to place the children in good care; parents who choose to raise their biological children rather than give them up remain as obligated as adoptive parents do.) Yes, many people do believe that we should prefer our kin to others; many also believe that we should prefer members of our own race to members of others. After all, we are genetically closer to members of our own racial group, even if racial purity is a myth. Questioning this may be "fatal to race morality," but so much the better.

Thus, speciesists trying to avoid the charge that their view is analogous to racism are well advised to interpret kinship in terms other than genetic relatedness. Close relationships do impose special obligations, but those relationships are not confined to our relatives. If we construe kinship more broadly, such that adoptive relationships and commitments to our mates are encompassed, we undercut speciesism even more. We may well be closer to an adopted nonhuman than to a cousin or to an indifferent parent. Francis and Norman argue that nonhumans are too limited in their intellectual capacities to enter into the rich relations that language makes possible with other members of our own species,[93] but this need have no bearing on the closeness of a relationship. If one maintains that more evenly matched capacities, or the potential for such capacities, are essential to the sorts of relationships that impose special obligations, this surely disqualifies severely mentally impaired humans along with nonhumans. Moreover, a closer look at the source of the special obligations we have to significant individuals in our lives further undermines the speciesist position, as we shall now see.

John Rawls distinguishes between *acquired* and *unacquired*, or "natural," duties.[94] Our duty to respect the basic moral rights of others is unacquired: it holds regardless of our actions and our relationships to them. We acquire other duties as a result of our voluntary actions or the voluntary actions of others. For example, we are obligated to provide food and shelter to minor children we have not given up for adoption, we are obligated to honor contracts, and so on. Tom Regan has also plausibly argued that our close relationships impose special obligations.[95]

Speciesism and Full Personhood

Duties of this kind do not hold independently of our actions. Our relations with children, mates, and friends all generate new duties. This does *not* imply, however, that we should prefer our loved ones in all circumstances to others or that we are entitled to violate the basic rights of others for the sake of our loved ones. For example, you would be obligated to use your limited funds to shelter and feed your child rather than the neighbor's, but you would not be entitled to confiscate your neighbor's house to gain a better domicile for your child. Now suppose that your neighbor's child and your child have both fallen into water with a dangerous current, and that you are the only one in a position to help. Suppose further that you cannot save both. Since you owe your child special protection, you should save her rather than the unfortunate other child. However, you would not be entitled to *kill* another child to save yours (e.g., by "harvesting" his liver). Now let us see what these reflections do to the appeal to kinship.

First of all, treating humanity in general as a "family" in contrast to nonhumans does not give us a good model for condoning the kind of treatment that deprives innocent nonhuman animals of life and well-being. While we may be justified in providing for and protecting children and mates instead of using those same resources to benefit those more remotely related to us, the special obligations we have do not seem to include harming innocent others for the sake of our "kin." The standard ways in which nonhumans are exploited, and marginal humans are not, do not fit the model of appropriate treatment for family as opposed to strangers. Speciesists would have to agree that the appeal to kinship breaks down at this point, particularly given their own views about the moral status (or nonstatus) of nonhumans. The best reply they can make, I believe, is to assert that innocent full persons (normal humans, so far as we know) can indeed not be sacrificed for the sake of our mates or children because this would be a violation of their basic moral rights. Nonhumans, on the other hand, are in a different moral sphere altogether, since they fall short of full personhood, and thus are not to be compared to our neighbor's children. However, this admission not only undercuts the analogy at the basis of the appeal to kinship: it makes the argument unusable by speciesists.

The problem is that speciesists agree that *primary* rights holders are full persons. Speciesists must *establish* that marginal humans can be

Speciesism and Full Personhood

included in the moral community as rights holders too, in a way that does not apply to nonhumans. The kinship argument cannot be used to make this case. Consider those speciesists who believe that prima facie only full persons are *morally considerable,* but that those without this capacity belonging to a species characterized by full personhood *can be shown* to be morally considerable as well. Kinship, broadly construed, warrants preferential treatment of one being in comparison to another because we have *acquired duties* to one and not the other. However, one can only have duties, acquired or unacquired, to beings who are *already morally considerable.* To be morally considerable is to be the sort of being to whom others can have duties. Kinship interpreted in terms of closeness can be used to justify the favoring of one morally considerable being over another, without violating the other's basic rights, but it cannot be used to show that a being *is* morally considerable.

Now let us consider speciesists whose views are not so strict. They believe that sentient nonhumans as well as humans without the capacity for full personhood are *morally considerable.* They hold that, prima facie, only full persons have *maximum* moral significance, including a right to life, but believe that marginal humans can also be shown to have a right to life because of their species membership. Are these more moderate speciesists in a better position to use the appeal to kinship to make their case? No, they are not. Unless we have entered into close relationships with marginal humans, our duties to them are *unacquired.* Any such duties (e.g., the duty not to torture them) would have to be commensurate with their degree of moral significance and could not *already* include according them a right to life. We cannot presuppose what must be shown. By the same token, we would have these unacquired duties to morally considerable nonhumans. If we try to construe the extension of a right to life as an *acquired* duty instead, we would run into the same begged question, as well as giving a most implausible turn to the concept of a right to life. We construe our duty to respect others' lives as a "natural" or *unacquired* duty, holding regardless of our relation to those others.

Therefore, the acquired obligations stemming from close relationships cannot be used to show why marginal members of a species characterized by full personhood must have a right to life. The appeal to kinship fails to support speciesism.

Speciesism and Full Personhood

The Appeal to Opportunities for Interaction

Peter Wenz makes an apparently similar but crucially different proposal to justify preferential treatment of humans over nonhumans. Like Callicott, he is far from being a typical speciesist. He objects to the confinement, testing, and routine killing of nonhumans.[96] However, he also believes that humans have moral precedence over nonhumans, and he supports subsistence hunting by humans.[97] He has tried to avoid being called a speciesist, apparently construing the view as inherently arbitrary and unjustified, but these views nevertheless mark him as one.[98] As we shall see, he has recently explicitly defended a speciesist view. In any case, his argument could be used by far stricter speciesists, so I shall turn to it as the next proposed defense of that view.

Wenz proposes a "concentric circle theory" to explain our obligations to other morally considerable beings. He begins by making the plausible assumption that we have a greater number of *positive* obligations to individuals with whom we are more likely to interact. After all, we cannot assist them if we are not in contact with them. Roughly, he holds that individuals with whom we have a greater opportunity, or potential opportunity, to interact occupy morally "closer concentric circles" to us (we are in the center) than those more removed from us. He makes clear that he does not interpret "closeness" in terms of emotional attachment or even physical proximity. Although those who are physically far from us are less able to interact with us directly, modern technology has made it possible for us to affect them by "remote control." Thus, we incur obligations to them (e.g., the obligation to help them detoxify environments fouled by the chemicals we have sold them).[99] He also, very importantly, does not interpret closeness in terms of *biological proximity*. This clearly distinguishes his view from the appeal to kinship above. He asserts that *mere* biological relatedness does not impose any obligations, thus avoiding, he claims, views such as racism and (unjustified) speciesism.[100]

Yet, Wenz's argument continues, as a matter of fact we simply do have more opportunities for interaction with other humans than we do with nonhumans. Thus, we have positive obligations (obligations of assistance) to them that supersede our obligations to others. Of course, opportunities for interaction do not affect any *negative* rights (i.e., rights to noninterference) others may have: if we do come in contact with them, we ought not to violate any such rights. Nonhumans, except for those we have domesticated, are like citizens of remote countries who have *not* been affected by our actions. We ought to leave them alone, if possible (according to Wenz we do have negative obligations to them), but they are less important to moral agents than humans: we have no positive obligations at all to these remote nonhumans.[101] Domesticated nonhumans are also allegedly less important, because the kind of interactions they can offer us is necessarily limited. (This also holds for marginal humans. We shall see how Wenz deals with this problem shortly.)

Speciesists with far stricter views than Wenz's could accept his model, with one significant modification: they would deny that we have serious negative obligations to nonhumans as well as positive ones. Thus, they could use the modified concentric circle view to justify continued exploitation of nonhumans. As we look more closely at Wenz's argument, however, we shall see that it fails to support speciesism.

As an illustration of the implications of his concentric circle view, Wenz gives us a classic dilemma: A little girl and a troop of chimpanzees, all strangers to us, are running down the road where we are driving. The only way to avoid hitting the girl is to run over the chimpanzees, and the contrary action would be called for if we are to avoid hitting the chimpanzees (assume we can't just pull over on the shoulder!). Wenz says that his theory requires us to save the girl. He runs into serious difficulty, however, in explaining why this should be so. He first argues that one should save the child just as one would save one's own father rather than a stranger.[102] This clearly won't do. By hypothesis, all the "road runners" are strangers to us. Bringing in the father-stranger analogy can only mean one thing: the girl is like one's father in being a member of the human family, unlike the chimpanzees. This move is not open to Wenz, given that he has explicitly rejected the view that biological relatedness is in itself morally relevant. Perhaps realizing this will not work, Wenz then offers a different explanation: "Because moral considerations are generally tied to actual or potential interaction, and the possibilities for interaction between human beings are generally greater than the possibilities for interaction between human beings and animals, more moral considerations compete with the negative rights of animals than with the negative rights of human beings . . . Thus, when a direct choice must

Speciesism and Full Personhood

be made, and all other things are equal, the negative right of a human [i.e., the right not to be killed] overrides the negative right of a non-human animal."[103] Nonhumans are like citizens of a remote country, presumably relatively unaffected by our actions; humans, by contrast, are at least as close as "neighbors" in Wenz's car dilemma.

This reply by Wenz also will not do. If we ought to favor those with whom we have more opportunities for interaction, Baptists should favor Baptists, Penn State faculty should favor other Penn State faculty, Nazis should favor other Nazis, and whites should favor whites. Our opportunities for interaction are clearly a function of our predispositions. This implication is particularly unwelcome to one who is utterly opposed to racism, as Wenz is.[104] Moreover, the remote country analogy backfires. Wenz has argued that we do have positive obligations to humans living far away whose lives have been affected by our actions. The same holds for wild nonhumans, whose habitats have often been devastated by the consequences of human decisions. (This particularly holds for chimpanzees. A troop of these nonhumans wandering down a road in North America has either escaped from a laboratory or from a zoo. Wenz should perhaps have picked another species for his dilemma!) Indeed, we may have caused far more serious harm to many nonhumans than to a given human child. It would seem, then, that we might well owe the nonhumans more in a particular case. This is certainly not a desirable outcome for Wenz or for speciesists in general.

Perhaps Wenz became troubled by considerations such as these. He has recently modified his view. He now holds that moral significance is correlated with "capacities."[105] As he now puts it, beings do not possess the same negative rights after all. Although he does not specify *which* capacities, he must mean intelligence-related ones, for otherwise it would not be true to say that human needs trump all others. What, then, of the mentally deficient human? She has the same negative (and positive) rights as a normal adult human, Wenz holds, because "I now think negative rights obtain in different degrees of strength, varying with the inherent capacities of different *species*."[106]

Thus, Wenz now endorses an *explicitly* speciesist view. Unfortunately for speciesism, he offers no justification for his moral worth/intellectual-capacity-of-species correlation claim. What is the moral relevance of such capacities? As Paul Taylor has said in discussion of a similar view

Speciesism and Full Personhood

held by Louis Lombardi, no one has given an adequate argument for the contention that the existence and number of such capacities translate into increased moral significance.[107] Even if such an argument could be made, we are left with our original question: Why should the mere fact of species membership confer maximum moral significance on those without such capacities? As we have seen, the original concentric circle view either collapses into the already discredited kinship argument or into racism (to mention but one type of bigotry). The amended concentric circle view also does not result in an argument that justifies speciesism, since it presupposes speciesism's truth. We still have no plausible argument supporting the favoring of humans, especially mentally limited ones, over sentient nonhumans.

Speciesists must try a different reply altogether. Reflection on the chimpanzee-girl dilemma can lead them to make the following rejoinder: "Let's be honest. The real reason for the fact that we would choose to save the girl instead of the chimpanzees is the *emotional tie* we feel to another human being. While we do not object to using certain nonhuman animals for food and research purposes, we cannot stomach the notion of doing the same to defective humans. Even if they have no right to life—even if, technically, they are not even morally considerable—our feelings will not permit us to treat them in these ways. This is what makes, and should make, the difference."

Those who would argue in this way are not holding that membership in a species characterized by full personhood can warrant moral considerability or maximum moral significance. This is just as well, since all attempts to show this have so far failed. Up to now, we have looked at arguments that try to justify speciesism by specifying morally relevant differences between marginal humans and sentient nonhuman animals. The differences pointed to were either intrinsic characteristics, such as having one's potential for full personhood thwarted, or relational ones, such as biological kinship or the potential for interaction with moral agents. The entire argument for speciesism has now been redirected: emphasis is placed on the emotional attachment one feels to certain beings rather than on the morally relevant characteristics these beings might have. One is arguing that speciesism can be justified *even if* no morally relevant difference exists between humans who fail to be full persons and sentient nonhumans. If this line of attack works, the argument from

Speciesism and Full Personhood

marginal cases will be discredited as *irrelevant* although sound, and speciesism will be morally vindicated. Let us then turn to the first of two such arguments in this new line of attack: the appeal to emotion.

ATTEMPTS TO SHOW THAT SPECIESISM IS JUSTIFIED EVEN IF SPECIES MEMBERSHIP IS NOT A MORALLY RELEVANT CHARACTERISTIC

The Appeal to Emotion

Mary Midgley claims that a preference for members of one's own species is due "considerable respect" because it is a "natural, emotional preference." [108] The earlier Fox made the same point when he asserted that "natural emotional responses" should have weight in our moral judgments about marginal humans. [109] Instead of arguing that "we prefer individual A to individual B because it is right to do so," one is claiming that "our preferring A to B makes it right to do so." Let us now consider this very different kind of attempt to justify speciesism.

Certainly, emotions play a role in our moral decision making. Those humans who, for whatever reason, are unable to empathize with others tend to have little regard for those others. If they nonetheless behave correctly, they are probably conforming to societal mores rather than displaying virtuous behavior. As I shall argue in chapter 5, although one can make a purely logical case for the respect of others' rights claims, logic alone is often not psychologically compelling. These considerations notwithstanding, however, the appeal to emotion above is dangerously faulty.

The lives and well-being of nonhumans and humans falling short of full personhood are said to be contingent on the emotional ties one may or may not have to these beings. Alas, the most obvious kinds of prejudices are sanctioned by such a view. For example, many people who happily consume pork chops wax apoplectic at the notion of eating a beagle; some who are horrified by the agony of rabbits used for cosmetics testing are unconcerned if rats are the rodents involved; and many who would never wear a coat fashioned from skinned Persian cats don shoes or belts made from skinned foxes, minks, and alligators.

Speciesism and Full Personhood

Speciesists unconcerned by such attitudes should consider the fact that some humans have far stronger emotional ties to their companion animals than they do to other humans, including mentally impaired ones. Although sociobiologist E. O. Wilson claims that altruism is a function of the degree of biological relatedness one has to another,[110] the facts do not bear this out. The earlier Fox indignantly reported the true story of a man in a small lifeboat who refused to throw his dog overboard to make room for two drowning men.[111] If those two men had been seriously mentally handicapped, they (as well as the dog) would be lacking in basic moral rights, given the earlier Fox's full-personhood view. Unhappily for speciesists, the argument from emotional attachment would tell us that the man in the lifeboat acted correctly in saving the individual with whom he felt the strongest bond.

Similar problems arise when the appeal to emotion is generalized. Most humans, it is often argued, would feel threatened and upset by the practice of treating marginal humans as harvestable natural resources, realizing that accident might deal them or their loved ones the same hand. Allegedly, the damaging "side effects" of the practice, from terror to anger, would outweigh any resulting benefits. This appeal to *aggregate* emotion (for oneself as well as for others) also fails, as was argued in chapter 2. It would be easy to institute rules protecting humans who lose their capacity for full personhood through mishap or age. Similarly, marginal humans whose families care for them could also be protected from exploitation. Congenitally marginal humans who have never been loved would be out in the cold. Moreover, societies in which the abnormal are shunned and scorned even by their own families, and in which persons accept the prospect of death should they lose their personhood, would simply not encounter the "side effects" a more compassionate society might experience. Neither self-love nor sentiment can be relied upon to provide the results speciesists desire.

The appeal to emotion dissolves into an appeal to bigotry. No support for speciesism can be found from this quarter.

The Appeal to Rational Preferences

In order to avoid the bankruptcy of an unadorned appeal to emotional preferences, speciesists must appeal to *rational* preferences instead. They can argue that well-informed, clearly thinking persons simply would not want marginal members of their own species to be "harvested," but would have no aversion to the "humane" use and disposal of other beings allegedly lacking in basic moral rights. Thomas Young has made precisely this argument.[112] He holds that beings who are incapable of being troubled by the fact that society regards their lives as expendable have no moral right to life as such, although they may have an "other-based" right to life if someone cares a great deal about them.[113] (As Young makes clear, the "other-based" right to life is purely reducible to respect for the preferences of moral agents who care about these other humans.) What of the many very young and seriously mentally limited humans who are not loved by those close to them? He contends that we have a (probably innate) tendency to prefer members of our own species, even if they lack an inherent right to life and we feel no personal attachment to them.[114] Citing Richard B. Brandt's theory of rational preferences,[115] Young then argues that tendencies of this kind are fully defensible.

Before we examine Brandt's theory and Young's application of it, let us pause to note that Young is clearly offering us a defense of speciesism. He himself denies that he is doing any such thing, but this is because he takes 'speciesism' to denote an unjustified view, defining it as "ignoring the interests of members of other species for no other reason than that they are members of other species."[116] This is the view that James Rachels calls "radical speciesism." Young certainly does not adopt such a view; he believes that the nonhumans whom we raise and kill for our own purposes should be treated humanely. He is, however, a "moderate speciesist," granting some but not maximum moral significance to sentient beings who are not full persons, yet extending protection along lines of species preferences. Of course, he takes his view to be justified, unlike speciesism as he has construed it. Let us see if it is.

According to Richard Brandt, *irrational* preferences are preferences that would be extinguished by an individual's repeated, vivid reflection on relevant information, including logic. Any preference that would not be extinguished by such a procedure is, he says, *rational*.[117] Young believes that no amount of logic and informed, vivid reflection will alter one's preference for members of one's own species. Thus, speciesists are "rational" persons. Young uses this line of argument to support an "ideal" version of the utilitarian side-effects argument for speciesism:

Speciesism and Full Personhood

If only *rational* preferences are counted, the side effects of harvesting marginal humans would create massive nonmoral badness or disutility (anger, indignation, fear, etc.) compared to the humane use and disposal of sentient nonhumans.[118] However, one need not be a utilitarian to use the Young-Brandt line of argument. As we saw, Mary Midgley holds that preference for members of one's own species is due respect because it is a "natural" preference. Despite the fact that she characterizes this preference as "an emotional, rather than a rational preference,"[119] it is "rational" in Brandt's sense if logical, informed reflection would not extinguish it. What better justification could speciesism have than a demonstration of its rationality?

Nevertheless, despite its potentially broad appeal to consequentialists and nonconsequentialists, this final attempt to justify speciesism fails. The reason is as simple as it is devastating: Given Brandt's view, it is impossible to distinguish "rationality" from *extreme bigotry.* Brandt himself points out that his view has this "surprising" implication: Preferences and aversions that are so firmly ingrained that no amount of vivid, informed, logical reflection on the part of the individual who has them are "rational."[120] Unfortunately, as we all know, die-hard bigots are notoriously undisturbed by facts and logic. They are unmoved by considerations that change other minds. I have had lengthy full-scale discussions, including evaluation of writing and reading assignments, with confirmed homophobes. Every argument they put forward is shown faulty, the latest data on the factors shaping sexual orientation are fully displayed, and they are asked to vividly imagine what it must be like to have one's natural inclinations despised. None of this has any effect. As one quite intelligent "A" student wrote in her follow-up paper summarizing the arguments and counterarguments, "The evidence is overwhelmingly against the anti-homosexual point of view, but I still say homosexuality is wrong. The very idea of it is an offense to me." Now, we have always considered views that are immune to rational persuasion quintessentially *irrational,* but according to Brandt's theory, the opposite is the case.

Thus, the "rational preference" line of argument would "justify" deep-seated racial, sexual, and cultural prejudice. The human tendency to prefer those most similar to oneself often takes such forms. Midgley notes that this is the case, but dismisses such attitudes as mere "pseudo-speciation," that is, as the confusion of race, sex or sexual orientation, culture, and so on with species.[121] This reply could hardly be used to distinguish speciesism from these bigoted views, however, since it would clearly beg the question. The very term 'pseudo-speciation' in this context implies that preferences along species lines are legitimate while the others are not. Speciesists must *show* that their view is not merely another form of deep-seated prejudice. The appeal to rational preferences hardly helps them to do this.

Worst of all, from the speciesist point of view, is the fact that yet another type of bigotry would be sanctioned by Brandt's rational preference theory. It may be true that humans, like many nonhumans,[122] tend to favor members of their own species. Species survival may be generally enhanced by such preferences, although we must remember that altruism is not confined to conspecifics. Unfortunately, there is evidence that *normal* members of species are the ones that are favored, whereas the *abnormal* are often shunned, despised, and even attacked. These attitudes, abhorrent though they are, also may contribute to species survival. Most humans do indeed have tender feelings for very young humans, but there is often little tolerance for physical or mental deformity. Young does not consider the likelihood that dislike or even hatred of many marginal humans may count as "rational" if his Brandt-inspired view is correct.

The very fact of species *resemblance* seems to fuel the aversion some who are normal feel for those who are not: the latter are perceived as caricatures rather than as individuals with interests and needs. This nasty fact undermines the view held by philosopher Peter Carruthers, among others, that "sharing human form" and "many human patterns of behavior" with mentally defective humans naturally impels us to be far more sympathetic to them than to nonhumans who, he admits, may be higher in intelligence.[123] I call this preference for normal or typical members of one's species *normalism*. Lamentably, many humans have such attitudes. In 1986, syndicated newspaper advice columnist Ann Landers printed several letters from readers who protested that handicapped people should not be seen in public. One found the sight so offensive that she claimed it violated her rights: "I believe my rights should be respected as much as the rights of the person in the wheelchair . . . maybe even more so, because I am normal and she is not."[124] Die-hard "normalists" want no part of those who live "worthless lives,"

Speciesism and Full Personhood

even when their own family members are involved. Some abandon their handicapped children or refuse them life-saving surgery despite the fact that the children could live contented lives. When asked if this is how *they* would wish to be treated if they become mentally impaired, normalists say they hope that someone will have the sense to lock them away or even shoot them. Vivid reflection about the abnormal seems to *increase* rather than to extinguish their horror and disgust. As Ann Landers wrote, "[p]lease forgive me if I do not answer these folks. They are too far gone for me to reach." It is ironic indeed that their very unreachability should be interpreted as "rationality" by Brandt's view.

To say the least, the existence of such attitudes casts grave doubt on Young's assertion that rational persons in Brandt's sense would always be horrified by the exploitation of marginal humans for the benefit of others. Not only have experiments on the retarded and senile taken place in the past [125]—including the U.S. Willowbrook study, in which retarded children were given hepatitis *with the consent of their parents* [126]—they continue to occur now. The British Medical Association has documented worldwide reports of experimentation and organ "harvesting" in mental institutions and prisons. [127] A less extreme but no less revealing study was conducted as late as 1986 by the University of Maryland School of Medicine. [128] Fully one-third of surveyed family members who believed that their hospitalized mentally incompetent elderly relatives (168 in all) *would not have wanted to participate* in an experiment on the adverse effects of urinary catheters nevertheless gave their permission. Of those family members who said they would *themselves* not have wanted to volunteer, nearly 25 percent "volunteered" their incarcerated elders. Why? Because *others* would "possibly benefit" from the experiment. "Normal" humans are also sometimes targeted unethically for experimentation or even death, particularly when they are regarded as "subhuman" or as having forfeited any right to life. Reuters' news service reports that prisoners in China are being executed and their organs sold in Hong Kong. [129] It was in the United States, not Nazi Germany, that the notorious Tuskegee study on syphilis was done: Hundreds of black men with syphilis were allowed to go untreated for forty years (1932–1972) in order for the U.S. Public Health Service to determine the long-term effects of the disease. These men died in agony decades after a simple cure for the disease—penicillin—had been found. Marginal

Speciesism and Full Personhood

humans, who often cannot speak for themselves and who are regarded as legally incompetent, are the most vulnerable group of all. Although he believes otherwise, Young's reasoning does nothing to protect them.

In short, the "appeal to rational preference" defense of speciesism has eviscerated itself.

I can conceive of only one response to my charge that this last defense "justifies" ingrained bigotry. Some people (quite a few, one hopes) are able to overcome racist, sexist, homophobic, ethnocentric, and "normalist" attitudes. Perhaps preferences and aversions that some, if not all, persons can overcome by vivid, informed, logical reflection should be deemed "irrational." Speciesists could claim that this modification of Brandt's "individualistic" theory of rational preferences defeats the bigotry charge.

Indeed it would—but at the cost of defeating speciesism itself. Some humans, if not all humans, have altered their belief that any member of their own species should be favored over any sentient member of another species. Thunderstruck by the argument from marginal cases, they have racked their brains to find a morally relevant difference between marginal humans and routinely exploited sentient nonhumans. Finding none relevant to a right to life, as we have seen in this chapter, they have rejected speciesism. The burden is on speciesists to show this rejection to be confused, illogical, or misinformed. So far they have failed. It is speciesism—not its denial—that appears to be irrational.

IMPLICATIONS OF THE FAILURE TO JUSTIFY SPECIESISM

The most plausible version of speciesism remains unsupported. No morally relevant difference between marginal humans and sentient nonhumans has been found to legitimize the very different ways in which these beings are standardly treated. Nor has speciesism been shown to be correct *despite* the lack of a morally relevant difference. Followers of the full-personhood view attempting to preserve the core of their position by retreating to speciesism are left without defense. We are once again left with the dilemma posed at the end of chapter 2: One must either give up the belief that autonomous moral agents are the *primary* subjects of moral concern and respect, or one must accept the full, ghastly (for marginal humans and sentient nonhumans alike) implications of that view.

The failure to justify speciesism leaves intact the biconditional or equivalence version of the argument from marginal cases: Either both sentient nonhumans and marginal humans are maximally morally considerable or neither is. Unless it can be shown that the first half of this disjunction is true (thus supporting the *categorical* version of the argument), this leaves open the possible justifiability of "species-blind" exploitation for the benefit of full persons. Many who reject speciesism become logically and emotionally committed to the high moral status of *any* sentient being, especially after vivid reflection upon the extent of our use and disposal of beings who have the same *basic* interests that we do. Others, as we saw at the end of the previous chapter, opt for the other half of the disjunction. In the next chapter, we will focus on a major form that rejection of speciesism has taken among followers of the *first* half of the disjunction. Many erstwhile speciesists, after becoming convinced of the moral bankruptcy of their position, believe that *utilitarianism,* correctly construed, mandates the impartial consideration of interests of all sentient beings. I will argue that utilitarianism falls quite short of warranting the protection that many believe sentient beings of all species deserve. I will then offer and defend a view that does provide such protection. Those who have opted for the *second* half of the disjunction, advocating with varying degrees of reluctance the "species-blind" exploitation policy, will then be answered.

Speciesism and Full Personhood

4

UTILITARIANISM AND THE PROTECTION
OF INNOCENT LIFE

The view that moral agents (full persons) alone are due maximum moral consideration has now been stripped of all its humanitarian pretensions. The intellectual "superiority" that allegedly justifies the sacrifice of sentient nonhumans for our purposes also sanctions the sacrifice of many humans. In chapter 2, we explored every reasonable way to avoid this conclusion: it could not be avoided. In chapter 3, we sought to extend the moral umbrella to humans incapable of moral agency by replacing the full-personhood view with the most plausible version of speciesism, the view that membership in a species characterized by full personhood entitles one to maximum moral significance even if one can never achieve full personhood. After considering the best defenses of speciesism that could be mustered, we saw that it cannot be justified. The choice is clear: The linkage of moral significance and intellectual superiority must either be accepted, with all its grisly implications for humans and nonhumans alike, or it must be abandoned.

Peter Singer was one of the first to make a strong philosophical case for abandoning a restrictive view of moral significance. In his 1975 classic, *Animal Liberation,* he posed the argument from marginal cases, pilloried speciesism, and offered an alternative: the equal consideration of interests. Although he did not stress this at the time, he was arguing from a *utilitarian* perspective. In subsequent works he allowed his argumentation to take a more sophisticated form than he wished it to have in his popular call for radical change. Unquestionably, Singer's work has had a worldwide impact on public awareness of the abuses we humans have heaped on sentient nonhumans, as well as on the members of our own species. He has sacrificed much time and, undoubtedly, material comfort to fight for the discontinuation of these abuses. Anyone who has seen Singer speak, a lean vegetarian in his denim jeans and canvas shoes, has seen a man putting his moral convictions into action. It is not an exaggeration to say that many sentient beings—including humans—owe a great deal to Peter Singer.

In this chapter, I will explore the philosophical basis of Singer's alternative to the full-personhood view and speciesism. Unfortunately, as we shall see, his utilitarian views fail to provide the protection for innocent life that many of us require for a morally acceptable view. We are forced to look elsewhere for an alternative to the dangerously restrictive focus on autonomous moral agency. Despite these problems, however, Singer's contribution to the debate about the boundaries of moral concern remains enormous. Nothing I have to say is meant to belittle it.

UTILITARIANISM AND THE FULL-PERSONHOOD VIEW

Utilitarianism is a normative ethical theory that, in its *classic* form, does not tie moral considerability or moral significance to autonomous moral agency (full personhood). Instead, it bids us to maximize overall nonmoral goodness ("utility"). Not surprisingly, utilitarians sometimes differ on what they count as utility. The theory as originally proposed and developed by Jeremy Bentham[1] identifies utility with *pleasure* and disutility with *pain,* but a utilitarian need not embrace a hedonistic or even a monistic theory of value. Some contemporary utilitarians, such as L. W. Sumner,[2] allow for a pluralistic theory of value and prefer to speak of maximizing "welfare." With some notable exceptions, however, utilitarians tend to agree that utility in general, not primarily utility for "intellectually superior" individuals, should be one's focus. Any being with a welfare, be he or she Albert Einstein, Sojourner Truth, Conan the Barbarian, Baby Jane Doe, Lassie, or Henrietta the chicken, is said to count morally.

As discussed in chapter 1, however, a utilitarian can also be a follower of the full-personhood view. R. G. Frey takes this position, holding as he does that highly complex autonomous lives contain more nonmoral value than other lives. He thus reserves maximum moral significance for such lives, and does not flinch from the conclusion that "infants, defective humans, and animals" may be killed in circumstances that would not warrant the killing of "normal adult humans."[3] As we have seen, Frey accepts the biconditional argument from marginal cases, finding marginal humans and many nonhumans to be equivalent in *their lack of high moral significance*. Singer and Sumner, at least on the face of it, *seem* to be defending a utilitarian view with rather different implications. As we shall see, however, Singer's and Frey's views are remarkably close in key respects.

Initially, Singer's position seemed to pose a clear contrast to the full-personhood view. His appeal to "the equal consideration of interests" of all sentient beings[4] follows consistently from the classical utilitarian tradition. Much of classical utilitarianism's moral force is due to its scrupulous impartiality: there is no room here for the disregarding of interests on the grounds of race, sex, species, or intellect. Thus understood, utilitarianism is said to be "no respecter of persons." Persons and sentient nonpersons alike, human and nonhuman, are to be due equal consideration in relevantly similar circumstances. Singer has eloquently argued that we humans are morally obligated to forgo the advantages that accrue from the exploitation of nonhumans. He attacks the modern practice of raising and killing nonhumans for their flesh as the sacrifice of nonhuman well-being and life to trivial gustatory preferences. (R. G. Frey, by contrast, has written an entire book devoted to the defense of meat eating.[5]) Moreover, unlike the full-personhood view, the equal consideration of interests principle implies that very young or seriously mentally disabled humans are due moral consideration *in their own right*.

Some followers of the full-personhood view are truly horrified by Singer's view. Peter Carruthers goes so far as to proclaim that it would be preferable to do "without any theory of morality at all" than to accept Singer's equality of interests position.[6] He finds Singer's view "far too extreme to be taken seriously" because "we find it intuitively abhorrent that the lives or suffering of animals should be weighed against the lives or suffering of human beings."[7] Singer's utilitarianism is rejected as being "at odds with apparently fundamental features of our moral thought."[8] Quite consistently, Carruthers defends commercial exploitation of nonhuman animals, even if they are caused great suffering[9] and the purpose of the exploitation is to satisfy a relatively trivial concern (e.g., developing a new perfume). It is far from clear, however, that "we" all have the same attitude as Carruthers. "Our" moral thought cannot be all that univocal; there would hardly be a debate about the moral status of nonhumans if that were the case. One cannot help but observe that quite a few people do not find it "intuitively abhorrent" to weigh the sufferings and lives of *all* sentient beings, contrary to Carruthers's claim. Still, numbers of people taking one view or the other are not the point: the question is what view can be best defended. Readers of Carruthers and my chapter 1 might remember that Carruthers's sole defense for his own moral theory, contractualism, is the splendid way in which it coheres with his intuition that nonhuman animals are worthy of no moral concern. Nazi ethics, which Carruthers certainly does not support, could be "defended" by its followers in much the same way. Singer, by contrast, argues that alternatives to his view are vulnerable to the charge of unjustifiable discrimination. There is nothing wrong with bringing our deeply held convictions about rightness to the evaluation of competing ethical theories, so long as we are willing to scrutinize— and, if necessary, drop—those convictions in turn. In the rest of this chapter, we will be examining the implications of Singer's theory and asking ourselves if we can accept those implications. If the answer is "no," we must ask if our response is justified, not simply terminate the discussion.

Singer's utilitarianism, then, like classical utilitarianism in general, seems to imply that the lives and welfare of *all* sentient beings are due protection. But is this really the case? Is his theory as egalitarian as Carruthers fears it to be?

UTILITARIANISM AND THE CHARGE OF INADEQUATE INDIVIDUAL PROTECTION

The Killing of Innocents Argument

Classical utilitarianism's impartiality has not been doubted, but its ability to warrant adequate protection for individual life and well-being has been strenuously challenged. Since *total* utility is to be maximized, innocent individuals' lives and welfare should be sacrificed whenever doing so would achieve that goal. This would hold even if the gain would be quite small! If it were the case, on the other hand, that sacrificing an innocent person and pursuing another course of action would create an equal balance of utility over disutility, both courses of action would be equally permissible. Ought one, then, to flip a coin? The problem seems to be that classical utilitarianism appears to make no room for what we would term significant rights. Rights act as *constraints* on the pursuit of goals; hence, rights in any serious sense would seem to be inconsistent with the pursuit of maximum utility.[10] It is no small wonder that many find unacceptable a moral theory that would sanction the serious harming or killing of innocents for the purpose of increasing overall utility. (Some people profess to be untroubled by this. On several occasions, students have told me that if a heinous crime has been committed and the person convicted of the crime and sentenced to death is actually innocent, that person should still be executed. Why? Because it would soothe the outrage of the population, not to mention those close to the original victim, and be an example to other potential criminals. The loss of the executed person and the anguish of those close to that person would be outbalanced by these other considerations, they say. However, they often retract this view after imagining themselves in the prisoner's situation.)

Utilitarians have gone to great lengths to overcome this fundamental objection. For example, as we have already seen in the context of the argument from marginal cases, they have argued that we must take "side effects" of utility-maximizing actions into account, and that when we do, killing or seriously harming innocents would not be routinely justified. A society that treats its members so unjustly would create massive disutility, for example, fear, insecurity, anger, distress for the relatives and loved ones of those who are sacrificed, and so on. Critics reply that *secret* killings, particularly of beings for whom no one has deep feelings, would still be justified by utilitarianism, provided that no alternative course of action would create at least an equal amount of utility. Admittedly, such cases would not be commonplace, but they could still occur.

Some utilitarians respond to this by accepting the implication. Singer himself, as we shall see when we discuss his "preference utilitarianism," has accepted it with regard to very young and severely mentally disabled humans[11] as well as with regard to many sentient nonhumans. As we shall also see, consistency requires him to accept it for normal adult humans as well, deny it though he may. Other utilitarians recoil from the

Utilitarianism and the Protection of Life

implication, at least as far as humans are concerned, and propose that, instead of acting to simply maximize utility, we should follow the moral code that, if generally *accepted,* would maximize utility.[12] Proponents of "acceptance utilitarianism" reason that most humans would abhor any moral code that sanctioned the secret (or public, for that matter) sacrifice of innocents, even of innocents who are loved by no one. Hence, they argue that their form of utilitarianism is immune to the standard criticism.

Acceptance utilitarianism seems much more palatable than the bullet-biting approach that the classical utilitarian would take. Unfortunately for utilitarians, however, the theory is not particularly successful. It has been contrived specifically for the purpose of avoiding implications that many of us find morally repugnant, and the contrivance seems contrary to the very spirit of utilitarianism. Acceptance utilitarianism concedes that most of us are *not* utilitarians: We do not believe that the welfare and lives of innocents should simply be factored into overall utility, to be overridden when utility would thus be maximized. Building our anti-utilitarian sentiments into a revamped utilitarian theory has an unmistakably ad hoc air. As the criticism is so often put, acceptance utilitarianism gets the right answer for the wrong reason. The committed utilitarian with the courage of his or her convictions should instead, it would seem, work for public enlightenment. R. G. Frey takes this approach in defending the vivisection and killing of defective humans in order to greatly benefit others: "There are, of course, the likely side-effects of such experiments. Massive numbers of people would be outraged, society would be in an uproar . . . It must be noted, however, that it is an utterly contingent affair whether such side-effects occur, and their occurrence is not immune to attempts—by education, by explaining in detail and repeatedly why such experiments are being undertaken, by going through yet again our inability to show that human life is always more valuable than animal life, etc.—to eliminate them."[13]

This approach lacks the hypocritical, contrived air of acceptance utilitarianism. While it accepts implications that many find deeply repugnant, it can at least avoid acceptance utilitarianism's flaws.[14] Nevertheless, many of us, pending reeducation, will remain anti-utilitarian in our sentiments.

The Replaceability Argument

Utilitarians can always reply that the above sentiments are prejudicial. They might add that, *often,* given that so many cannot fully subscribe to the utilitarian credo, utility would not be maximized by the sacrifice of innocent life. Even if this is the case, however, it does not lessen the ugliness of the theory's consequences. Moreover, their view has still other implications that even the most dedicated utilitarians are loathe to embrace. Not only does classical utilitarianism sanction the practice of raising and killing sentient nonhumans for our own purposes: the same reasoning supports parallel treatment of humans.

According to utilitarianism in its classic form, it would be right to raise, use, and kill a sentient nonhuman if:

1. the nonhuman would not otherwise have existed;
2. the nonhuman has had a pleasurable life;
3. the death of the nonhuman causes it no pain, fear, or other disutility;
4. those close to the nonhuman (e.g., mothers, mates) are not allowed to suffer as a result of its use and killing; and
5. the nonhuman is replaced at death by another nonhuman for whom conditions 1–4 hold.[15]

Before considering the extension of this argument to humans, let us have a look at its implications for the treatment of nonhumans. Although the replaceability argument sanctions the breeding, use, and killing of nonhumans for purposes of food, research, fur garments, and even recreation (for example, so-called hunting "preserves" where semi-tame "game" animals are given food and shelter so that they can be killed by "sports"-men or -women who fancy severed heads on their walls), it is obvious that it would by no means justify most of these practices as they currently exist. Life on the factory farm, the fur farm, and in most research labs is no bowl of bananas. If the replaceability argument were taken seriously, these conditions would have to be radically improved. This is the thrust behind the "humane" movement to improve conditions for nonhumans on farms and in research laboratories.

For example, recently amended U.S. law requires that primates (nonhuman primates, that is) who are research subjects must be provided with living conditions that promote their psychological well-being.

Moreover, dogs are to be provided with exercise, and anesthetics and analgesics are to be used whenever possible. None of these requirements existed before the mid-1980s.[16] Unfortunately, most nonhumans used in laboratories are not covered by the regulations, even the minimal stipulations regarding control of physical pain: rats, mice, and birds are not defined as "animals" in U.S. laws![17] (Former President George Bush apparently saw no problem with these bizarre exemptions. Every Christmas season, he celebrates by shooting birds raised in captivity at a Texas ranch. When asked in 1989 if he were not engaging in cruelty to animals, he responded that birds are not "animals."[18]) Humans, too, are erroneously not classified as "animals" under the law, giving an indication of how far our civic convictions lag behind science (not to mention ethics). Utilitarian education regarding the need for impartial equal consideration of interests would have yielded very different results. Perhaps we may expect some change for rodents and birds in laboratories, at least: The Animal Legal Defense Fund has sued the U.S. Department of Agriculture (the government agency entrusted with enforcement of the Animal Welfare Act) to contest this biologically questionable exclusion, and a U.S. district court judge has agreed with them.[19] If appeals do not alter the judgment, some animals in research laboratories are legally entitled to equal treatment in some contexts. (Human animals, of course, would find these assurances of equality very wanting were they applied to human research subjects.)

Even if the vast majority of nonhumans used in U.S. laboratories are no longer exempted from humane legislation, however, this means little if the law is not enforced. The U.S. Department of Agriculture's own regulations for the care of nonhuman laboratory animals offer far less protection to subjects than do the recent amendments to the Animal Welfare Act. Challenged by yet another lawsuit brought by the Animal Legal Defense Fund, the U.S.D.A., joined by lobbyists for the biomedical research industry, argued that enforcement of the amendments would require institutions to make overly costly adjustments. From a utilitarian perspective, monetary costs should indeed be figured into the utility equation, but so should the costs exacted of sentient beings forced to participate in biomedical research. Once again, a U.S. district court judge has tilted in the direction of the interests of sentient beings, ruling in 1993 that the U.S.D.A. must comply with the Animal Welfare Act.

This decision has been appealed; we shall see if any improvements in the lives of U.S. nonhuman research animals eventually result.[20] Countries such as Great Britain and Canada have gone a good deal further than the United States in trying to minimize the suffering of nonhuman research subjects. Even if all of these measures were to be scrupulously followed, however, including in the United States, a classical utilitarian would judge that they do not go nearly far enough to alleviate suffering and make life pleasurable for those subjects. Nevertheless, legislation of this kind does take a step in the utilitarian direction, and could obviously be extended along the lines suggested by the replaceability argument.

The lot of nonhumans raised for food could also be considerably improved, if classical utilitarianism were taken seriously. Most of the nonhuman animal protein consumed now results from intense confinement on factory farms. In terms of nonhuman animal suffering, the price of supermarket eggs and nonhuman flesh is very high indeed. It is no accident that one of the best exposés of these conditions has been coauthored by Peter Singer himself. His and Jim Mason's *Animal Factories,* now in its second edition, carefully documents, in text and photographs, "life" for layer hens, "broilers," turkeys, pigs, veal calves, dairy cows, and beef cattle.[21] Even "animal husbandry" experts at major agricultural universities and institutions, who have promoted factory farming methods to farmers in the Western world and a number of developing nations, are now beginning to publicly concede that these methods compromise "animal welfare." I witnessed this firsthand as a discussant at the first International Conference on Farm Animal Welfare, held in Maryland in June 1991. Although there were representatives of traditional nonhuman welfare groups, as well as a small number of philosophers, most of the participants were "animal husbandry" experts and industry representatives. Some U.S.D.A. officials also spoke. The major sponsors, significantly, were the University of Maryland animal husbandry department and the National Science Foundation. I heard plenty of resistance to changes that would lessen confinement, but there were also many admissions that factory-farmed nonhumans have a poor quality of life. Utilitarian principles would mandate reforms.

Some European countries have already taken steps to ameliorate some conditions. Switzerland has passed laws to phase out the battery cage system for hens, as has the Netherlands. In England, publicity about so-called "milk-fed" veal calves has so upset consumers that the largest English veal producer has moved his calves into group pens with straw bedding. Free-range eggs are widely available in Western Europe and in Australia.[22] Switzerland has outlawed the tethering of breeding sows.[23] The country of Sweden, however, has gone further than any other in rejecting factory farming. In July 1988, a law was passed to phase out factory farming within the next several years.[24] According to the Swedish government (which is indeed enforcing the law), the purpose of the action is to ensure that "animal rearing in the future will be geared towards keeping animals healthy and happy." In terms of this law, cattle are given the right (the law actually uses that term!) to graze, pigs the right to be untethered, and both are given the right to straw, litter, and (for pigs) food areas separate from their sleeping areas. Chickens are to be released from their cramped cages and allowed to enjoy the life a chicken has evolved to enjoy. Nonhuman animals on farms are to be subjected to antibiotics and other drugs only if these are necessary to treat disease, not to accelerate growth. Slaughtering procedures are also to be reformed in such a way as to minimize terror and pain. Swedes are sharing the knowledge needed to accomplish the alteration of conditions for nonhumans in agriculture. At the first International Conference on Farm Animal Welfare, mentioned above, I attended a lecture by a Swedish expert on animal husbandry on the research used in his country to phase out battery hen operations.[25] Alternative housing methods are being tried, and the chickens are selecting the ones they prefer! The scientist was constantly referring to the "chickens' preferences." If Sweden succeeds in its "rights program," it will have created a model of utilitarian legislation.[26]

If more humans took the replaceability argument to heart, the increased well-being of the nonhumans who are routinely exploited on farms and in labs would add considerably to the sum of utility in the world. "Humane exploitation" adds utility-generating beings to the world who would not otherwise have existed, then replaces them with other such beings, while simultaneously generating utility for the humans who benefit from these practices (assuming for the moment that the world is big enough for all of us). Many would welcome this implication: nonhuman animal welfare groups typically push for just such reforms (advocates of *moral rights* for nonhuman animals, by contrast, would reject it utterly, since no right to life is respected by exploitation, however humane). Would the implication still be welcomed if it were realized that the replaceability argument applies to humans too?

Human Replaceability

Quite simply, the replaceability argument applies to any individual with a welfare, including human beings. To be more precise, it applies to *the welfare* of those individuals. Classical utilitarianism implies that individuals are of secondary moral importance: their *experiences*, not they themselves, count as intrinsically valuable. As Singer has put it, classical utilitarianism "regards sentient beings as valuable only in so far as they make possible the existence of intrinsically valuable experiences like pleasure. It is as if sentient beings are receptacles of something valuable and it does not matter if a receptacle gets broken, so long as there is another receptacle to which the contents can be transferred without any getting spilt."[27] In this sense, individuals, human or otherwise, are interchangeable, provided that their capacities for various experiences are commensurable.

More recently, Singer has regretted the "receptacle" terminology as misleading, because it suggests that experiences and individuals can be separated in the way that wine may be emptied from one bottle and poured into another. He reasons that *while* an individual is having an experience, the two are not separable. In this sense, the *experiencing individual,* not just the experience, can be said to be intrinsically valuable. However, the *continued* existence of that individual is not morally mandated by classical utilitarianism if another similar individual can be created to take his or her place, picking up where the other life stops.[28] Hence the interchangeability of like individuals remains, and experiences—not individuals—are clearly assumed to be of primary moral value.

The prospect of human replaceability distresses even those utilitarians who accept the justifiability of killing *without* replacement when utility would be maximized. The notion of breeding, using, and killing humans, then promptly replacing them, is rather unsavory. It would also be permissible to kill humans who have not been bred for the purpose, provided that we do so without causing them or their loved ones pain or fear, and that we replace them by beings who are similar. Indeed, *it would be obligatory to do so* if the replacement would have a better life than the replacee!

Perhaps we need intensive utilitarian reeducation so that we may find all of this acceptable. Alternatively, we could try to show that utilitarianism can be plausibly reconstrued in such a way that the replaceability argument can be rejected, in part or in its entirety. If this approach fails, we must choose between utilitarianism with its upsetting implications[29] and a nonutilitarian view.

UTILITARIAN ATTEMPTS TO REJECT THE REPLACEABILITY ARGUMENT

Replacing Total-View Utilitarianism with Prior-Existence-View Utilitarianism

Peter Singer has wrestled with the replaceability argument for years. Trying first one approach and then another, he has, by his own admission, found no entirely satisfactory way of resolving the problem.[30] The evolution of his thinking on this issue gives us an instructive look at the dilemmas utilitarians face in attempting to render their view more plausible. Consideration of utilitarian responses to the replaceability argument also raises perplexing questions about the moral considerability of those yet unborn. Few of us, utilitarian or otherwise, can claim to have obviously justified answers to these questions, as we shall see.

In the first edition of *Animal Liberation*, Singer rejected the replaceability argument in its entirety.[31] He agreed with Henry Salt, who in 1892 dismissed an early version of the argument with this diagnosis of an allegedly fatal flaw: "The fallacy lies in the confusion of thought which attempts to compare existence with non-existence. A person who is already in existence may feel that he would rather have lived than not, but he must first have the *terra firma* of existence to argue from: the moment he begins to argue as if from the abyss of the non-existent, he talks nonsense, by predicating good or evil, happiness or unhappiness, of that of which we can predicate nothing."[32] The replaceability argument is held to have an absurd consequence: by counting the utility the non-existent life would have, then weighing that hypothetical utility against the utility generated by existing beings, it allegedly makes a nonsensical comparison. If this is correct, classical utilitarianism errs in including future beings in its utility calculations. Singer calls the classical utility-calculating approach "the total view." If we only count the utility that can be generated by *existing* beings, thereby adopting what Singer calls "the prior existence view," the replaceability argument is obviously defeated. The utility lost by killing an existent being could not be equaled or outweighed by the utility a nonexistent replacement would bring into the world.

As Singer later recognized, however, this way of trying to defeat the replaceability argument loses its appeal on closer inspection. In the second edition of *Animal Liberation,* he goes so far as to declare that "[m]y unequivocal rejection of this [Salt's] view is, in fact, the only philosophical point made in the earlier edition on which I have changed my mind." [33] In what follows, the reasons for his change of mind will be explored. To put those reasons in context, I will first raise an objection to Salt's charge of absurdity that Singer does not mention. Salt's objection would imply that we speak nonsense whenever we discuss that which, strictly speaking, does not exist. When we speak of the future, are we babbling "of that of which we can predicate nothing"? Polluters who object to environmental regulations intended to unfoul the air on some glorious future day might find this argument appealing, but no one else will. Salt's prior-existence view also makes a hash of the moral obligations we believe we have to future generations. If it makes no sense to talk about future beings, we can certainly have no duties to them.

It is worth pausing a moment to consider the ethical implications of Salt's prior-existence view. If I secretly bury toxic wastes in the sandbox my neighbors have installed for the child they will have in a year's time, the only moral wrong I am committing is against my present neighbors! Unfortunately, this is not an unrealistic example. Are all those who have knowingly dumped toxic wastes around and even on residential areas morally innocent of any crime against the unborn children of the unwitting inhabitants? Moreover, to mention another horrifyingly realistic example, if we knowingly deposit highly toxic waste products in containers sure to crack after one hundred and fifty years, poisoning millions of human and nonhuman animals but endangering no one living now, we would do no wrong at all!

Extending the Prior-Existence View

Although Singer has not raised this objection, he seems to have anticipated it at the very time he accepted Salt's dismissal of the replaceability argument. After saying in his 1975 book that the very phrase "non-existent being" is self-contradictory, and that consequently we can neither harm nor benefit "it," he adds in parentheses: "The only qualification required is that we can benefit or harm beings who will exist in the future, which is why it is wrong to damage the environment, even when the effects of the damage will not be apparent for fifty years."[34] If Salt (and the early Singer!) had been correct, this qualification could make no sense. If we can talk about "beings who will exist," we *are* talking about "non-existent beings," and we appear to be making perfectly good sense when we do so. Singer reasons inconsistently here, but the qualification he suggests points to another possible way of circumventing the replaceability argument.

Unlike Singer, S. F. Sapontzis, who supports the prior-existence view, has argued that there would be no problem in accepting the implication that we have no obligations to future generations.[35] However, fully aware of many individuals' reluctance to do this, he notes that "it would not be inappropriate to require that prior existence utilitarians include among their moral deliberations a concern with the likely effects of their actions on the enjoyment or fulfillment of future generations. Since those generations are (*ceteris paribus*) definitely going to exist, it could reasonably be claimed that, for utilitarian purposes, they already do have a sort of existence and must be included in our moral deliberations."[36] There is warrant for doing this, but it requires that we reject the highly restrictive version of the prior-existence view following from Salt's objection to the replaceability argument. In his 1979 book *Practical Ethics*, after writing that he can no longer accept Salt's position, Singer recasts the prior-existence view as follows: "The second approach is to count only beings who already exist, prior to the decision we are taking, *or at least will exist independently of that decision*."[37] This "extended prior existence view," as Sapontzis has called it, distinguishes between beings who will exist *regardless* of the particular action we are now contemplating (including our own future children, as long as we are not now deciding about whether to conceive them) and those beings whom we are now considering creating. L. W. Sumner terms them "independent" and "dependent" beings, respectively.[38]

The extended prior-existence view is certainly an improvement over its predecessor. It nullifies the replaceability argument, since as-yet-nonexistent replacements for already existing beings are "dependent" upon our current decisions. Any utility they would generate once in existence does not yet count in the extended prior-existence view, unlike the utility now generated by independent beings; thus, decisions to kill and replace those beings would not maximize utility. The extended prior-existence view also avoids Salt's and (early) Singer's Parmenidean perplexities about "non-existent" beings and allows for obligations to future generations. The distinction between beings who will exist no matter what we decide and those whose existence depends on our decisions does not appear to be contrived. Surely it is less arbitrary to include independent beings in our moral deliberations than to leave them out. It seems that we would do well to modify classical utilitarianism by replacing its total view with the extended prior-existence view. The old problems about harming or killing innocents when utility would thus be maximized would remain, but at least the utilitarian would no longer be required to accept the replaceability of sentient individuals, human as well as nonhuman.

Despite all the advantages the extended prior-existence view offers the beleaguered utilitarian, Singer later found himself forced to reject it. It has an implication just as unpalatable as replaceability itself.

REJECTION OF THE EXTENDED PRIOR-EXISTENCE VIEW

The Case of the Wretched Child

The very feature of the extended prior-existence view that allows it to circumvent the replaceability argument leads to a deeply distressing consequence. As we have seen, balancing the utilitarian equation by replacing an existing being whom we plan to kill for the laboratory or dinner table with a newly created substitute, with the same pleasant existence as the "replacee" before slaughter, is impossible in that view: "dependent" beings-to-be (as it were), whose existence depends upon our own decisions, cannot be included in our deliberations. The killing and replacement involved in perpetuating "humane" exploitation would thus constitute a utility drain. Unfortunately, however, if the future happiness of a "dependent" does not count, neither does its future misery. It follows that it would not be wrong for a couple to conceive a child whose life would be wholly wretched. Although Singer often warns us to be suspicious of our deep-seated moral aversions, he finds this implication abhorrent.[39] Both Derek Parfit[40] and L. W. Sumner[41] have been driven back to the total view for the same reason. Sumner puts the objection especially well, after noting that the non-total view would make it wrong for the couple not to kill the child once it has begun to suffer: "But what plausibility is there in a theory that gives a woman no moral reason to avoid creating a child whose life will be intolerable but does give her a reason to kill such a child once it has been created?"[42] Sumner reasons that the case of the wretched child brings out the arbitrariness of the extended prior-existence view, making it obvious that the theory violates a principle rightly sacred to utilitarianism: impartiality.[43] He seems to be quite correct. Why should the utilities of dependent beings who do not yet exist count for less (for nothing, in fact!) than the utilities of *independent* beings who do not yet exist? Why is it wrong for me to bury toxic wastes in my neighbors' sandbox in order to poison *their* future child, but not wrong for me knowingly to conceive *my own* wretched child?

The best reply an advocate of the extended prior-existence view could give, Singer believes, is that the prospective parents wrong themselves in initiating such a project. Once the suffering child exists, it should mercifully be put to death in order to decrease total disutility. However, mercy killing is very traumatic. The parents would have spared themselves this trauma if they had forgone the conception in the first place. Whatever disutility might be created by the frustration of their wish to have such a child would perhaps be outweighed by their pain as child-killers. If this is the case, it would be wrong to conceive a child one knows will be wretched.[44]

Utilitarianism and the Protection of Life

This is not a good reply, as Singer himself is the first to say.[45] Although he does not explain his assessment, we can readily see why such a response utterly fails. Parents who would not be particularly troubled by the act of killing their child are very easy to imagine: we know that such people exist. Whatever pleasure they derive from conceiving a wretched child would certainly outweigh any transitory "unpleasantness" mercy killing might bring (let us assume that they have no reason to fear any legal sanctions). Alas, they might even enjoy killing the child; this would further improve the utility count. These "monster parents" would be maximizing utility by carrying through their project, in the extended prior-existence view: far from being wrong, they are entirely justified! On the other hand, parents who would suffer great anguish in carrying out the mercy killing of their suffering offspring would be creating more disutility for themselves by deliberately conceiving such a child. Thus, the more sensitive, concerned parents would act *wrongly* in initiating the pregnancy, whereas the "monster parents"—and the happier they are about killing a wretched child, the better!—would be acting *rightly*. Far from saving the extended prior-existence view, the suggested reply starkly underscores its unacceptability.

Back to the Total View?

Singer wastes no time clinging to this obviously inadequate response. Without further ado, he rejects the extended prior-existence view. But the total view, which counts the future happiness and misery of all those who could exist as well as all those who do and will exist, also has extremely disturbing implications. We have already seen that it cannot circumvent the replaceability argument: Innocents, human or nonhuman, may be raised, killed, and replaced so long as utility is not diminished. Here is yet another problem. Singer rightly notes that if the future misery of a child-to-be is a reason for *not* bringing it into existence, its future happiness seems to be a reason *for* bringing it into existence. If this sounds innocuous, reflect that this kind of utilitarian thinking obligates us to bring *as many happy beings into the world as we can*[46] (one's own significant diminution in welfare would easily be outweighed by the addition of these happy folk to the population). The most efficient way of generating utility seems to be to create utility generators. If so, those who practice contraception when they would be able to produce happy children act wrongly. *Moreover, they act just as wrongly as those who secretly kill a happy child in its sleep!* Even the not inconsiderable number of people who might very well accept such a massive procreative obligation are unlikely to condemn contraception as harshly as infanticide.

In fairness, I must point out that not everyone finds the total view's equation of possible and actual life to be absurd. For example, Joseph Scheidler, speaking for a U.S. antiabortion group called the Pro-Life Action League, rejects both "the contraceptive mentality" and "the abortion mentality" as "anti-child."[47] Randall Terry, the founder of Operation Rescue, a movement devoted to disrupting the operations of clinics where abortions are performed, made the same point when asked by an interviewer why he opposes contraception as well as abortion. Terry asserts that couples who flout their alleged obligation to "leave the number of children they have in the hands of God" are following "Satan's agenda" to "destroy children."[48] Those of us who find such a view grotesque, making as we do a distinction between *preventing* and *destroying* life, are thoroughly at odds with the total view. Singer, on the other hand, tilts toward acceptance of the procreative imperative and the impartial consideration of actual and possible children. Unlike Scheidler and Terry, he is not enthusiastic about any of this: it simply appears to be less objectionable than the extended prior-existence view's sanctioning of the creation of wretched children.

It only gets worse. People who do not quail at the notion that they have a duty to create the maximum number of happy progeny might well be unsettled by an even more shocking implication of the total view. As Derek Parfit has pointed out,[49] for any population of happy, utility-rich beings, there is another possible world containing many more beings whose lives are just barely worth living. Due to their large numbers, despite their relatively very low quality of life, they generate more overall utility than is to be found in the world of many fewer yet much happier individuals. According to total-view utilitarianism, the world full of miserable people is to be preferred! Thus, individuals enjoying a high quality of life ought to overpopulate their planet, filling it with lives that are virtually not worth living. Those with a lower quality of life would be obligated to do the same, of course. This scenario, which Parfit calls "the repugnant conclusion,"[50] surely lives up to its name. We have come full circle: The *total view* enjoins us to populate the planet with wretched children (and adults)! (To be sure, these lives can only be "99 percent wretched"; otherwise they would constitute a utility drain.) Of course, all the sentient nonhumans that would be displaced and destroyed by such a policy must also be considered; but this simply means that we must count all potential utility generators. If one quite miserable human generates more total utility in a lifetime than many exceedingly miserable chickens, our utilitarian duty is clear. (I will have more to say about the implications of the total view for sentient nonhumans shortly.)

Considerations such as these drive many of us to reject utilitarianism altogether, not just one version of it. We are forced, it seems, to choose between the bad and the ugly. Singer, on the other hand, actually accepts the "repugnant conclusion," as does Parfit, remaining convinced that total-view utilitarianism is the better of the two alternatives. Singer tries to show that the conclusion is not all *that* repugnant by pointing out that the lives we have *now* are probably not that much better than those of a larger population who are *almost* better off dead: "If we take a more pessimistic view of our own lives, the average life in Z [the hypothetical alternative population] might be only a little worse than our own lives— and what is so repugnant about believing that a large number of lives a little worse than our own could be better than a small number of lives much better than our own?"[51]

Singer is inclined to believe that such a pessimistic view of our lives is warranted, believing as he does that most normal human lives are geared toward the attainment of deferred goals, containing relatively modest overall value. (I will have more to say about this view of Singer's in another context later in this chapter.) We need not quarrel with this pessimism just now. Even if he is correct in thinking that our lives are only a bit better than the lives of those who *almost* should be dead, "the repugnant conclusion" remains as repugnant as ever. All one need do is take the perspective of a smaller population of persons whose lives are very well worth living. The implication that *these persons* ought to procreate to the point of generating a much larger population who are only a hair away from being justifiable suicide or mercy-killing candidates still stares us in the face. This is the thoroughly unpalatable price of the total view.

One's depression over the price is augmented by the fact that "the repugnant conclusion" would sanction a world almost indistinguishable from our own. We humans have acted as if we were converts to the total view: we have increased our numbers exponentially so that, even now—to speak of but one factor necessary for a life worth living—the food we produce on earth is insufficient for our numbers. The Allan Shawn Feinstein World Hunger Program at Brown University has calculated that, *if food were equally distributed,* and at present levels of food production, a population of *5.5 billion people* (the earth's population at the end of 1992) could receive adequate nutrition, *provided that a lacto-vegetarian diet is followed.*[52] This estimate takes into account the fact that millions of tons of grains and legumes now fed to nonhuman animals we eat would be diverted to humans, giving us more total protein than is now available for our species:[53] still there would barely be enough! The World Hunger Program's projection tells us that this number of humans could be sustained nutritionally only if equal distribution of primary food resources were magically instituted and diet, particularly in affluent countries, were radically altered. Heaven help us if our numbers increase, as they will, barring an asteroid impact or a rather more likely massive die-off from disease and famine. Even under ideal distribution conditions, the researchers at Brown concluded that an omnivorous diet in which only 25 percent of calories were obtained from nonhuman animal sources would sustain no more than 2.8 billion humans; 3.7 billion humans getting 15 percent of their calories from nonhuman animals could manage under the same circumstances. We humans are well past an optimum population. A larger population could be sustained if present levels of food production could be significantly increased, but doing so without further despoiling the planet and ultimately causing yet more misery is extraordinarily difficult. Singer's pessimistic view of our current lives is an accurate description of much of the world's population, although not, I suspect, because we defer so many of our pleasures in planning for the future!

What are the implications for nonhuman sentient animals? Singer has pointed out that if we are indeed obligated to create as many humans as possible (up to but not including the point of *total* wretchedness), we must also be obligated to become vegetarians:[54] more humans, as the Brown researchers have also told us, can be sustained on such a diet. Billions of domestic nonhuman animals killed every year would no longer be bred. Considering the fact that most of these animals are on factory farms, the elimination of so many wretched lives would result in a net gain in utility. But what would happen to sentient wildlife? *If* one assumes that most human lives contain more utility than most nonhuman animal lives, as most humans and Singer himself do assume, then human habitats and human needs should have precedence over those of wildlife. Present levels of food production could be boosted if as much land as possible could be conditioned for food production,[55] greatly reducing wildlife habitats. A much smaller human population would be compatible with flourishing, coexisting wildlife, and would make possible a higher quality of life for all sentient beings, but this would be *contrary to our duty*—according to total-view utilitarianism. Many humans already routinely assume that any sacrifice of other sentient beings for human purposes is fully justified, while simultaneously holding that unlimited reproduction—human reproduction, that is—is an inherent right. It is sad enough to contemplate the world resulting from such attitudes; it is more distressing still to see that result sanctioned by an ethical theory.

Classical total-view utilitarianism has the even more outrageous implication that any sentient individual can, in principle, be killed and replaced by another. Singer's initial efforts to escape the replaceability argument threaten to drive him even more firmly into its clutches. Although Singer reluctantly accepts, as we have seen, some extraordinarily upsetting implications of the classical view, he refuses to have any part of this one. Instead of defeating the replaceability argument by wholly rejecting the total view, as he had earlier attempted, Singer chooses to amend classical utilitarianism in a different manner.

PREFERENCE UTILITARIANISM AND REPLACEABILITY

Self-Conscious and Non-Self-Conscious Life

Singer's proposed new theory, preference utilitarianism, at best allows for only partial escape from the replaceability argument. Nevertheless, the solution he offers is, if successful, sufficient for any persons who are convinced that creatures *like themselves* should not be killed and replaced. Singer holds that classical utilitarianism is correct in identi-

Utilitarianism and the Protection of Life

fying the utility generated by *merely conscious* beings with pleasurable experiences. On the other hand, the utility generated by *self-conscious* beings should not be construed in this simple hedonistic way, according to Singer's current view. Self-conscious beings are not merely blobs of experiencing protoplasm: as beings who are aware of themselves as existing over time, they have *preferences,* including (in most cases) a preference for continued existence. Singer believes that classical utilitarianism ignores this dimension of self-conscious life. Utility in the case of self-conscious beings is a matter of bringing about what they prefer to happen, whether or not this results in pleasurable experiences. Although classical utilitarianism is justified in the case of sentient beings who merely float from one experience to the next with no awareness of doing so, preference utilitarianism is, Singer holds, the theory of choice in the case of self-conscious individuals.[56]

Singer attempts to employ this bifurcated utilitarian approach to exempt self-conscious beings from the replaceability argument. The argument is admitted to hold for merely conscious beings. Perhaps a cinema analogy will help to explain his view. When we kill and replace a *merely* conscious being by another such being, we are simply removing one disjointed, incoherent film from the projector and replacing it by another jumbled creation. One unintegrated stream of consciousness has stopped and another has begun. It makes not the slightest difference to anyone, including the replacee, since he or she is incapable of desiring to live: the same holds for the merely conscious replacement. All we need to do as utilitarian "movie projectionists" is see to it that the total number of pleasurable experiences contained in each film is maximized. By contrast, when we kill a *self-conscious* being and replace that being with another, we are not just changing films: we are destroying the last reel of one coherent film in order to bring on an entirely different cinematic sequence. It is as if we lopped off the ending of *Gone with the Wind* in order to show the first half of *Tarzan of the Apes,* going on to interrupt the latter film with two-thirds of *Jurassic Park,* and so on. The lives of self-conscious beings are coherent wholes, like plotted films, unlike the lives of merely conscious beings. Why, according to Singer, do we generate extra disutility when we kill and replace a complex being underpinned by a coherent thread of consciousness?

According to preference utilitarianism, Singer thinks, instead of maximizing the fulfillment of preferences by killing and replacing a self-conscious being, we are frustrating that being's preference to continue living. Indeed, *all* preferences that presuppose continued life would also be frustrated. This would be so even if the individual killed were to die in a state of blissful ignorance about our actions. This is not the case for merely conscious life, innocent as it is of a preference for continued life. Singer explains it this way: "To this extent, with non-self-conscious life, birth and death cancel each other out; whereas with self-conscious beings the fact that once self-conscious one may desire to continue living means that death inflicts a loss for which the birth of another is insufficient compensation."[57]

Thus, Singer rejects neither the replaceability argument nor classical utilitarianism: they are simply *restricted* to those sentient beings who are incapable of caring whether they live or die. In this way, Singer believes that he has avoided the implication that many humans mind the most: the idea that persons *like themselves* may justifiably be killed and replaced.

Candidates for Replaceability in Singer's View

As discussed in chapter 1, "self-consciousness" can be highly implicit and relatively uncomplicated, or it may be clearly explicit and articulable. One need not realize that one's mental life is a relatively continuous flow of experiences in order to be self-conscious. Child-development researchers now have evidence that children under seven are not normally able to consistently remember what they had just been thinking. Studies indicate that very young humans apparently believe that experiences are interspersed with large "blanks" of nonawareness; only in their eighth year do they see themselves and others as having a fairly continuous stream of consciousness.[58] Yet, all these young humans can tell you who they are and what they want—often in great detail; they can make plans; and they do not suffer from any inability to distinguish themselves from others. It would be outrageous to claim that they are not self-conscious. Are they sufficiently self-conscious to be protected from killing and replacement? Yes, according to Singer. In his view, any awareness that one is a distinct being, however primitive and inarticulate that awareness may be, is sufficient to render one irreplaceable. Those who have no self-awareness of any kind do not realize that they have a past, present, and future; thus, they are "incapable of having desires for the future," as Singer puts it in the second edition of *Animal Liberation*.[59]

It is, of course, not always an easy matter to determine the presence of self-consciousness in other beings. One must make the best inferences one can from their behavior, in light of the similarity of their nervous systems to one's own. One rough measure of self-awareness in humans, used by developmental psychologists, is the ability to recognize one's own reflection in a mirror. Normal human babies over the age of roughly eighteen months can do this. As Donald Griffin points out, captive chimpanzees and orangutans have responded in the same way during controlled studies, scrubbing at marks that had been placed on their faces while they were anesthetized as soon as a mirror is placed in front of them.[60] Although Griffin notes that no other species has demonstrated such an ability, there is evidence that gorillas can also recognize their reflections. Koko the gorilla, who has been taught the rudiments of American Sign Language, has been videotaped while giving every indication that she recognizes her image. (Koko also takes photographs of herself as she appears in the mirror, and seems to have no problem identifying the subject of the snapshots developed from her 35 mm camera. When asked if she was an "animal or a person," Koko is reported to have signed "fine animal gorilla.")[61] However, it is conceivable that one might have a basic concept of self without yet being able to identify one's reflection. Moreover, one might be able to make the connection but regard it as too unimportant to acknowledge. Self-referential language—"Koko want banana"—is also a sufficient condition of self-consciousness, but none have shown it to be necessary. Other behaviors that we humans recognize as signs of our own self-awareness (e.g., deception of another for our own benefit) can be seen in many nonhuman animals.[62]

Singer himself is fairly generous in identifying the likely class of self-aware beings. He is inclined to attribute self-consciousness to normal humans past infancy and to adult mammals: after all, these beings do not appear to confuse their body parts with those of their fellow creatures. (The felines living in our house are crystal clear on the difference between washing their own and each others' faces. They enthusiastically engage in the former and disdain to perform the latter.) He suspects that reptiles, fish, and birds lack self-consciousness, along with infant mammals of any species.[63] Humans (and other mammals) with severe enough mental deficiencies also fail to be self-conscious. Singer thus joins Regan in holding that normal mammals over one year of age are *clear cases* of beings with superior moral status. In contrast to Regan, however, Singer holds that sentient beings—*human and nonhuman*—who lack self-consciousness are in principle replaceable.

As discussed earlier in this book, the class of beings who count as "merely conscious" may be much smaller than Singer and others assume. The reader may recall Bernard Rollin's neo-Kantian argument for self-awareness in all beings capable of learning:[64] *experiences,* as opposed to disconnected sensations, seem to require the "glue" of a sense of self, however rudimentary that sense may be. Griffin argues that "perceptually conscious" beings of any species must have aspects of their own bodies and their own behaviors open to "view," along with other physical objects and living things. But does the animal know that she is observing *her own* body, that *she* is lapping up water? Griffin responds that the animal gives every behavioral indication of recognizing that *other* animals are drinking, eating, and so on; why should she not realize the same about herself?[65] One need not look to humans past infancy and adult mammals for behavior suggestive of self-consciousness. Most birds, for example, appear to be far too adept at learning and altering their behavior in changing circumstances to be accused of being *merely* conscious. I have never observed the renowned English blue tit, but their American cousins the chickadees are quite impressive also, as are other birds. Consider a very humble example. Seed-eating parent birds will spend most of their time at summer feeders stuffing their begging fledglings. By late summer, the offspring are often fatter than their exhausted parents and are perfectly able to feed themselves, yet they still beg for seeds. The parents will still pop in the occasional seed, but for the most part, they consistently turn away from their giant progeny, seemingly so as not to see the begging motions. Then a sort of hopscotch ensues: the youngster will hop in front of a parent to beg, the parent again turns away, the "kid" tries again, and so on. None of the parties involved in this "dance" seems to be unaware of their separate identi-

Utilitarianism and the Protection of Life

ties; certainly they do not behave as if they "can have no desires for the future"! Alarm cries specific to certain dangers have been identified among birds, even the supposedly mentally challenged domestic chicken (calls vary depending upon the threat's airborne or earthbound status).[66] This is impressive enough, but consider the fact that cognitive ethologists have documented the use of *false* alarm cries among birds during times of food scarcity! The apparently deceitful birds take advantage of their competition's precipitous departure by gorging on available food. Mature birds do not do this during times of plenty.[67] The hypothesis of intentional deception neatly explains this behavior, and that hypothesis in turn leads us to postulate self-awareness on the part of the "lying" bird. Surely one must have a firm grasp of the difference between oneself and others in order to deceive. Ethologists have related examples of apparently nonmechanical behavior in many other nonmammalian species.

It is *possible,* however, that extremely young or severely mentally underendowed sentient beings might not yet have a sense of self. Their sensations might be disjointed and unidentified, awareness of their own bodily states undifferentiated from the sensations of other things and beings. Such a being would not be likely to survive without the protection of others. If we fulfill the restrictions imposed on us by the replaceability argument, we are entitled to kill and replace such beings instead of continuing to protect them.

Humans who are fond of eating flesh or who support vivisection may find this result agreeable. It would seem that, if Singer is right, one need have little compunction about raising, killing, and eating *some* animals, provided that we allow them pleasant lives and painless, fearless deaths, which assuredly does not happen now on factory farms, then replacing them with their own kind. Singer does *not* advocate raising, killing, and replacing animals for food purposes, but he realizes that his current arguments lend support to that position. Although he fears that humans who regard *any* animals as mere objects of gustatory satisfaction are apt to begin treating self-conscious animals in the same manner, he seems to realize that this is a slippery slope argument. If the abuse prediction turns out not to be correct, he writes, humane and limited use of merely conscious animals for food would indeed be permissible.[68] We would have to take care to slaughter them before they mature or exhibit behavior suggestive of self-consciousness. Infant mammals (e.g., calves, lambs) would also be fair "game," although adults would not be. To be sure—if we assume that human lives are more utility rich than nonhuman lives—raising such animals for food would have to be very limited, unless the human population is reduced: the chosen animals could not be fed plant proteins humans could eat or take up land that would produce more food for humans if it were directly planted with grains, legumes, and vegetables. We could, however, use unlimited numbers of such animals for research and even vivisection if we could somehow manage to keep their lives and the lives of their replacements pleasant.

Of course, it would also follow that we could do the same with severely mentally deficient humans. Singer bravely draws this conclusion: "The position applies equally to members of our own species who lack the relevant capacity [i.e., self-consciousness]."[69] R. G. Frey agrees, as we saw earlier. From a purely clinical point of view, normal humans would on the whole be benefited more by experimentation on members of their own species than by experimentation on nonhumans. Would not utility be maximized by the practice of vivisecting non-self-conscious humans? Many humans do not find this to be an agreeable result at all, but as Frey has argued, intensive education and explanation may well change these attitudes.[70]

We can see that Singer's preference utilitarianism is surprisingly close to R. G. Frey's full-personhood version of utilitarianism. Each ascribes superior moral status to more mentally complex lives; each is willing in principle to accept the raising and killing of simpler sentient beings; neither is speciesist in drawing these moral distinctions.[71] Important differences remain, however. Singer's "self-consciousness" criterion sets a much lower standard for moral superiority than does Frey's "autonomy" requirement and Singer, unlike Frey, suspects that eating "lesser" animals will encourage us to feast upon their betters. Thus Singer advocates vegetarianism while Frey strongly supports extensive use of sentient nonhumans for food.

Neither Frey nor Singer discusses raising non-self-conscious *humans* for food, but the same principles permitting vivisection of such humans apply in this case. Cannibals reportedly have said that, of all the meats they have feasted upon, "the long pig" (guess who?) is the most deli-

Utilitarianism and the Protection of Life

cious. Of course, we would have to confine ourselves to very mentally undeveloped humans if we are to adhere to preference utilitarianism. Jonathan Swift's savage satire, "A Modest Proposal for Preventing the Children of Poor People from Being a Burthen to their Parents or Country, and for Making Them Beneficial to the Publick," puts forth the suggestion that poor eighteenth-century Irish babies be bred, farmed, and sold for food: "I have been assured by a very knowing American of my acquaintance in London, that a young, healthy child well nursed is at a year old a most delicious, nourishing, and wholesome food, whether stewed, roasted, baked, or boiled . . . when the family dines alone, the fore or hind quarter will make a reasonable dish, and seasoned with a little pepper or salt will be very good boiled on the fourth day, especially in winter."[72] One wonders how many of Swift's readers thought he had made an excellent proposal. Perhaps the numbers of folk partial to the notion of "milk-fed biped" could be increased by extra-diligent exposure to the replaceability argument and preference utilitarianism. (In these health-conscious times, we could add to the appeal by feeding the stock only organic food and by keeping them lean, so that they would not be loaded with pesticides or saturated fat.)

One may desire to kill and replace a human infant for other than gustatory reasons. In preference utilitarian terms, it matters not if the infant is normal or severely mentally damaged. H. L. A. Hart has pointed out that Singer's view would imply that the parents of an infant would be justified in killing it, provided that no one else wanted to adopt it into a good home and they undertook to replace it by conceiving another infant who would have a marginally happier life. More shocking yet, parents who kill a normal infant and do not replace it because they do not want the burden of parenthood are *no more wrong* in preference utilitarian terms than a couple with the same motive who refuse to conceive a child in the first place.[73] In his reply to Hart, Singer fully accepts these implications about human infants, including the equivalence of killing and failing to conceive a child.[74]

Is Self-Conscious Life Irreplaceable?

One might argue that these implications are the price one must pay for the preference-utilitarian exemption of self-conscious life—the sort of life we have—from the replaceability argument. However, as we shall now see, this is not the case. Singer does not show that self-conscious life would be irreplaceable.

H. L. A. Hart was one of the first to say this,[75] and others, myself among them, independently came to the same conclusion.[76] Granted, a self-conscious replacee's preference for continued life would be frustrated by killing. Nevertheless, a new self-conscious being who would not otherwise have existed, *with his or her own preference for continued life*, would take the place of the original. On what grounds could preference utilitarianism disallow such an action?

Singer's Prior-Existence Defense of Irreplaceability

Singer tries to provide such grounds, but his efforts in this regard are truly perplexing. He sometimes argues that the preference for continued life which the replacement *will* have does not count so long as the replacement does not yet exist. The living replacee's preference to go on living does count; hence, we reduce utility by killing him or her. Singer puts the point this way in his reply to Hart: "There is a difference between killing living, self-conscious beings who desire to go on living, and failing to bring into existence a being which, since it is unborn, can have no desire to come into existence."[77] According to this line of argument, only the preference of *existing beings* are to be included in utility calculations. Future preferences simply do not count. As readers will have noticed, the prior-existence view, the very view Singer found himself forced to reject earlier on, has been resurrected.

Singer says so explicitly, offering a "compromise" between the total and prior-existence views: "We might grant that the total view applies when we are dealing with beings that do not exist as individuals living their own lives . . . When we switch our attention to self-conscious beings, however, . . . we are justified in concerning ourselves first and foremost with the quality of life of people who exist now or, independently of our decisions, will exist at some future time, rather than with the creation of possible extra people."[78] To be precise, Singer is endorsing a limited application of the extended prior-existence view. Although he found the joining of the prior-existence view to classical hedonistic utilitarianism unacceptable, he now puts that view in the service of preference utilitarianism. Can construing utility and disutility in terms of happiness and unhappiness, on the one hand, or preferences fulfilled and unfulfilled, on the other, change the way we regard not-yet-existent beings?

Let us remind ourselves of Singer's reasons for rejecting the hedonistic version of the extended prior-existence view. He noted that it would not be directly wrong, given that view, for a couple to deliberately conceive a child who would have a wretched life. Singer shares the widespread assumption that the future misery of the child should be taken into account before—especially before!—the child exists. Singer has not retracted this objection at all; indeed, he reiterates it in the 1990 edition of *Animal Liberation*.[79] If we do count future misery, however, it certainly seems that we should also count future unsatisfied *preferences*. According to the extended prior-existence view, it would not be wrong to conceive a being whose preferences will be systematically thwarted by a life of suffering. If these future unsatisfied preferences should be counted after all (and surely anyone who thinks future *misery* ought to count would hold this), the extended prior-existence view is wrong. Therefore, Singer, of all people, cannot appeal to this view to support the irreplaceability of self-conscious life.[80]

Singer's Total-View Defenses of the Irreplaceability of Self-Conscious Life

More promisingly, if inconsistently, Singer also uses the total view to support his irreplaceability thesis. In the first such argument, instead of dismissing a hypothetical replacement's preference for continuing to live on the grounds that the replacement does not yet exist, he has argued that creating a new preference is like going into debt. The debt is allegedly erased when the preference is satisfied. Hence, creating a new being with a preference for going on living, then allowing that being to live, would add up to zero. By contrast, thwarting the *replacee's* existing preference to live by killing him or her puts one into the minus (disutility) range. So, it seems that replacing an existing self-conscious being, with preferences about the future, cannot maximize utility.[81]

Singer has since rejected this particular irreplaceability defense. For example, it implies that it would be wrong to bring any children into the world if they would have even *one* unsatisfied preference in their lives! Suppose all but one of their preferences would be satisfied: their lives would still have a minus utility value.[82] Normal lives would be far more deeply in hock. Singer is surely correct in finding this defense to be implausible.

A second total-view defense by Singer of the irreplaceability thesis for self-conscious life seems less open to objection. He suggests that the killing of a self-conscious being introduces an *extra* disutility that cannot be counterbalanced or outweighed by the creation of a replacement utility generator whose satisfied preferences receive positive values. The extra disutility is the frustrated preference for continued life. He expresses the point this way in a recent article: "Killing an individual who prefers to go on living is not justified by creating a new individual with a preference to go on living. Even if the preference of the new individual will be satisfied, the negative aspect of the unsatisfied preference of the previous individual has not been made up by the creation of the new preference plus its satisfaction."[83]

This approach has the merit of being consistent with Singer's rejection of the extended prior-existence view. According to this total-view reasoning, we may regard satisfaction of the replacement's preference for continued life as equal in value to satisfaction of the replacee's preference, but the disutility created by *thwarting* the replacee's preference gives a negative value to the exchange.

However, this defense of the irreplaceability of self-conscious life will not do as it stands. Unless a being has ceased to have a preference for continued life, death is guaranteed to thwart that preference eventually. The resulting disutility implied by preference utilitarianism will be created *in any case*, whether the being dies "naturally" or is killed without distress to the being or loved ones. Killing merely alters the timing of the unavoidable disutility. Assuming that preference utilitarianism is correct, so long as the replacement being would have satisfied preferences comparable to those the replacee had and would have had, the killing and replacement is justified. If one could create a being that would have *more* preferences satisfied than the predecessor, the exchange would be obligatory!

Singer does not mention this refutation of his argument, but he clearly came to recognize that more must be said. He has most recently supplemented the above total-view-style defense of the irreplaceability thesis by sketching a very interesting account of preference satisfaction in self-conscious life.[84] As we mature, he argues, we develop a set of long-range preferences to guide our actions. Typically, we endure some hardship for a number of years in order to satisfy these preferences (e.g., getting a terminal degree, writing a book, becoming a poet, solving the riddles of the universe, alleviating world hunger, ameliorating human and non-human suffering, building a house, raising good-hearted and successful children, etc.). If we were to be killed prematurely, before "the big pay-off," a futile mockery would have been made of our lives. The fact that new lives, with new long-range preferences, would replace ours would not outweigh the huge loss imposed upon us. Suppose one individual is killed prematurely and replaced by another one who in turn develops long-range preferences he or she struggles to satisfy. If the replacement is allowed to live long enough to satisfy these preferences, utility is created, but there is still a *net loss* in utility. As Singer puts it: "[T]here will be the hardships of two journeys [struggles], and the rewards of only one."[85] On the other hand, if the replacement, like the replacee, is *not* allowed to reap the rewards, the net loss is even greater.[86] By this reasoning, the point at which death occurs matters very much indeed. If we view self-conscious life as Singer does, the premature death of a self-conscious being is not counterbalanced by the birth of another.

Has Singer finally shown that the killing and replacement of self-conscious beings cannot be justified? I am afraid that he has not. First of all, according to the reasoning above, we would be justified in killing and replacing an individual *after* "the big pay-off" has arrived. The individual would die enormously satisfied, would not have anticipated or experienced the killing (if we do the job correctly), and would never suffer from post-pay-off disappointments. The individual who has "peaked" may not wish to go gently into that good night, but he or she can nonetheless be assisted gently thither, never to suffer the indignity of sliding downhill. The years of decline would be traded for the hope and promise of the young replacement life. The policy of systematically replacing older, post–pay-off people with youngsters may in fact maximize (preference) utility, as Sapontzis has pointed out in a related context.[87] (Some leaders of countries have actually thought that such a practice is desirable. The former dictator of Romania, Nicolae Ceauşescu, demanded that elderly people—other than himself and his wife Elena, of course—

be refused medical treatment. Simultaneously, he boosted the birthrate by outlawing both contraceptives and abortions, in order to create a more youthful population.[88] To be sure, his methods fell short of the humaneness decreed by utilitarianism, but replacement was undeniably his goal. For his efforts, he and his wife were in turn "replaced" by a somewhat more democratic leadership in a firing squad finale.)

My second and more fundamental objection to Singer's "hardship/pay-off" model of self-conscious life is that it simply does not apply to many self-conscious beings. Children, some mentally deficient humans, and many adult nonhuman mammals do not fit this mold at all. Are they then replaceable at any time, contrary to Singer's thesis? Paradoxically, their lives may be filled with far more satisfied preferences than the lives of those devoted to the work ethic. Those of us who have companion nonhuman animals might ask how we compare with them in this regard! Moreover, why assume that the *typical* adult human life consists of years of struggle, ideally capped by one major pay-off? This is not true of many humans, nor is it at all clear that it *ought* to be true, especially from the perspective of preference utilitarianism. It seems that a life in which struggle is rewarded by frequent pay-offs, rather than one that is primarily devoted to hardship in the service of a distant goal, would contain more utility. Interrupting a life like this, then replacing it with a similar one, does not turn a lifetime of hardship into an exercise in futility. Singer's reasoning, ingenious as it is, shows at most that we should not replace a workaholic with another workaholic!

None of Singer's various strategies has defeated the replaceability argument for self-conscious beings. What are utilitarians to think at this point? Whether they are preference utilitarians or hedonistic utilitarians, if they accept the total view, they are apparently committed to holding that present and future individuals are interchangeable in the right circumstances. The extended prior-existence view would avoid this implication by not counting the utility or disutility that would be generated by beings who would not exist independently of our decision to create them (dependent beings). But have we not seen that the case of the wretched child bars utilitarians from accepting the extended prior-existence view? Must we not reject any view that finds no direct wrong in deliberately conceiving a miserable life?

Utilitarianism and the Protection of Life

RETURN TO THE CASE OF THE WRETCHED CHILD

Perhaps a closer look at the wretched-child argument will rescue utilitarians from the dilemma sketched above. S. F. Sapontzis has argued that the wretched-child case does not, after all, refute the extended prior-existence view.[89] If he is correct, Singer and other like-minded utilitarians can avoid all of the serious difficulties posed by the total view. It would follow that no sentient beings, human or nonhuman, are replaceable, be it on the farm, in the laboratory, or in their own lairs.

On the Alleged Implausibility of the Case of the Wretched Child

Sapontzis begins by observing that it is difficult to take the wretched-child argument very seriously. He finds it almost inconceivable that an actual couple would deliberately conceive a child who could have only a brief, agonizing life. He believes that an ethical view's acceptability should not hinge on such an outrageously far-fetched counterexample.[90]

I wish that the counterexample were far-fetched, but unfortunately it is not. News reports are filled with accounts of "monster parents" who systematically, brutally abuse a child, then go on to procreate more victims, perhaps because they were themselves brutally abused as children. Child after child is maimed or even killed. The creation of these children is at best negligent and at worst premeditated. It hardly stretches the imagination to picture such parents deliberately, knowingly conceiving children who will have brief, horrible lives. Children in many cultures have been conceived in order to be sold to abusers. In parts of countries where female child prostitution brings "sex tourists" from many lands, girl children are "prized" and male infants not uncommonly killed. These wretched children fare little better than the wretched chickens or dogs raised to kill each other in staged combat.

One need not even be a "monstrous" or venal parent to deliberately conceive a child one knows will be wretched. Many people believe that they were meant to procreate, no matter what lethal genes they may carry and regardless of ghastly environments sure to maim even normal children after birth. Deeply opposed to abortion *and* contraception, these people sincerely believe that such miserable children are part of

"God's plan." A churchgoer and antiabortion activist in Hannibal, Missouri, was asked if he truly believed that a severely deformed fetus ought to be brought to term, only to be sentenced to a brief life of suffering. He replied without hesitation that "God makes no mistakes, no errors." [91] It is very hard for others of us to avoid the conclusion that *something* has gone terribly wrong, most likely in human decision making, when such pain is knowingly visited on innocents. We may be inclined to partially *excuse* such parents, since they do not intend to do wrong. Any such inclination on our part, of course, implies that we believe wrong has been done, even if unwittingly: otherwise, we would cite no *mitigating* circumstances. Alas, the case of the wretched child is not unrealistic in the least. If the extended prior-existence view sanctions any such procreative plans, not even allowing us to *excuse* some of the parents, one is strongly inclined to reject it.

The Bad-Character Argument

Despite his doubts about the wretched-child argument's plausibility, Sapontzis takes it seriously enough to try to refute it. He argues that, upon reflection, we can see that the objectionable nature of the wretched-child case leaves the extended prior-existence view untouched. He holds that we need not count the disutility that would be generated by a not-yet-existing wretched being in order to understand why it would be wrong to plan having such a child. When such a plan is scrutinized, one discovers that it has three stages: (1) intending to have the child, (2) conceiving the child, and (3) keeping the child until it dies "naturally." Grievous wrong, argues Sapontzis, occurs only at stage 3, when an innocent being is greatly harmed. However, at that stage the child exists, and the disutility generated by its life is fully countable by followers of the extended prior-existence view. Those of us who are inclined to say that wrong is also done at stages 1 and 2 are not really counting the nonexistent child's misery, Sapontzis says; we are making a *character judgment* instead: "But if such people did exist, they would have a perverted idea of reproducing and parenting and would show, by keeping the child alive for its two miserable years, their willingness to use others merely as a means to their own satisfaction. Consequently, this whole project of parenting would express a kind of demented character that would give the project a strong immoral value . . . Prior existence utilitarianism can account for this intuition, since this is an evaluation of character, and prior existence utilitarianism no more precludes making character evaluations than does the total population view."[92] At all stages, then, even before the birth of the unfortunate child, the extended prior-existence view can allegedly account for our revulsion. No child is wronged before its birth, but the parents-to-be can be said to act wrongly by displaying bad character.

Refutation of the Bad-Character Argument

Unfortunately, Sapontzis's ingenious argument does not succeed. First of all, let us return to the example of parents who deliberately conceive a child who they know will have a brief, agonizing life because of their sincere but confused belief that "God makes no mistakes." Well before the child is born, we shake our heads at what they have done, finding it *wrong* if not entirely blameworthy. Sapontzis's strategy will not even allow us to excuse them. *"Bad character" is not the problem here.* Until the child is born, by Sapontzis's account there can be no wrong to excuse. He can make no sense of our moral judgment before the birth.

Sapontzis could reply here that we may well be confused in such a case. He need not claim to offer an account that comports with our moral inclinations in every instance. The lack of fit here between argument and moral inclination does, however, cause one to take a closer look at that argument. This further look leads to a much more fundamental objection: Sapontzis's argument will not work *even if the parents are willfully, inexcusably monstrous,* as I shall now argue.

Sapontzis is correct in saying that any form of utilitarianism can license the making of character judgments. However, the grounds for a bad character evaluation are not the Kantian ones he suggests. Utilitarians can judge character traits to be good or bad *solely by reference to their consequences.* Specifically, one must ask how much harm (disutility) such traits are apt to cause. As L. W. Sumner, himself a utilitarian, says: "For utilitarians the future matters; indeed it is all that matters."[93] For a utilitarian, the bad characters of the parents do not "give the project a strong immoral value": it is the project that makes their characters bad. As we shall now see, extended prior-existence view utilitarianism cannot make the character judgment Sapontzis describes.

The evaluation of bad character is based upon the enormous disutility that the life of the wretched child will generate, a disutility that far outweighs the satisfaction of the parents' desire to create the child. A *total-view* utilitarian has no problem making such a judgment. *However, an extended prior-existence-view utilitarian cannot make such a character evaluation before the project is completed!* To do so would be to count the disutility generated by the as-yet-nonexistent child. (One might try to argue instead that a couple that gets enormous satisfaction from setting such a project in motion would probably be a menace to independent beings, and can be judged to have bad character for that reason, but this would be a very weak response. Cases of individuals with one obsession in otherwise unremarkable lives are not uncommon. Our couple might easily fall into this camp. Indeed, the planning and execution of their dearly wished project might make them even more pleasant to those around them!)

Given the extended prior-existence view, then, there are no grounds for saying that a couple initiating the project of creating a wretched child are deficient in good character *until the wretched child exists*. We are barred from saying that what they have done *prior* to that point is wrong in any way, even in Sapontzis's indirect sense.

Returning to the case of the wretched child has given us even more grounds for doubting utilitarianism. Readers may agree with me in finding correct Sapontzis's Kantian character assessment of the selfish would-be parents of a wretched child. Their willingness to sacrifice the interests of an innocent child in order to please themselves is odious: they are treating the planned child as a mere means for their own gratification rather than as an end in itself. The accidental stillbirth of the child would not change our judgment in the least, although it would cause us to heave a sigh of relief. This seems to be a decidedly *non*utilitarian character assessment.

I say this despite the fact that there *is* a sense in which utilitarians can agree that individuals should be treated as "ends" and not merely as means. Singer has argued that sentient beings are not to be regarded as *mere* instruments for our satisfaction, since their lives generate intrinsic value (utility).[94] This is true, but only in a narrow sense that fails to capture what seems to be wrong in planning to have a wretched child. Singer is saying that utilitarians are required (according to the *total view* only) to count the utility and disutility a wretched child would bring into the world. Ignoring this and concentrating only on one's own satisfaction would be wrong. But what if the couple does *not* ignore their duty in this regard? Suppose they plan to kill it after it is born, so that it will not suffer. They may then take pride in their fecundity, potency, *and* their compassion. In a narrow sense, they are not regarding the child *merely* as a means, but in another sense that is exactly what they are doing: the child's very existence is intended only to satisfy their overwhelming procreative urge. They cannot be faulted on *utilitarian* grounds for anything that they have done. Their characters cannot even be attacked, since the project, including its termination, maximizes utility. Are they not actually *morally praiseworthy?* Such an assessment seems dreadfully wrong. Even though the child's misery (disutility) is being counted in the total, they are still using the child. Either those of us who find this morally objectionable are wrong, or utilitarianism, as it has so far been understood, is wrong.

Should preference utilitarians like Singer modify their view such that (to use Sapontzis's word) "demented" preferences are not counted? Our couple would not be maximizing utility by satisfying their procreative preference, regardless of how irresistible it is and how great their fulfillment would be, if their preference is demented or irrational. The trouble here is that it is hard to imagine a utilitarian account of what counts as "demented" *apart from consequences.* How can a view whose basic principle is the maximization of utility do this? The couple's views may be unusual (one hopes), but no utilitarian would discount them for *that* reason. The best attempt at an account has been made by utilitarian Richard Brandt, who has suggested that an *irrational* preference is one that would be extinguished by repeated, vivid reflection on relevant information, in accordance with logic.[95] Unfortunately, however, the parents we are imagining are all too vividly aware of the ramifications of what they are doing, and they make no formal errors in reasoning. Actually, their reasoning appears to be flawless in utilitarian terms.

Therefore, the extended prior-existence view has not been rescued from the case of the wretched child. If we cannot accept that view's sanctioning of such an act, then we cannot accept the way out of the replaceability argument which that view offers. There seems to be no utilitarian escape from replaceability, for self-conscious as well as merely conscious life. We are left with total-view utilitarianism and all of its own apparently morally repugnant implications.

TOTAL-VIEW UTILITARIANISM AND MORAL RIGHTS

Frey and "Shadow Rights"

Let us now consider one final attempt to rescue utilitarianism from the charge that it has implications most persons find to be morally unacceptable. We could show that sentient beings, or at least self-conscious beings, are not replaceable, and that innocent beings in general should not be sacrificed whenever utility would be thus maximized, if room could be found in utilitarian theory for *rights*. Utilitarian theory has traditionally been hostile to rights, but some utilitarians believe that this is based upon a misunderstanding. If concern for the overall maximization of goodness could be *combined* with a commitment to individual (and possibly collective) rights, it seems that utilitarianism's moral plausibility would be beyond reproach.

Making a place in utilitarian theory for rights is no easy matter, however. Utilitarian R. G. Frey is decidedly unenchanted by the prospect, but suggests a way in which it might be done. Humans tend to be disturbed by the notion that one is justified in killing innocent individuals whenever this would create more good than alternative actions. A code of rights that would protect babies, retarded or otherwise very mentally deficient people, and normal adults of our species would have, as Frey puts it, "high acceptance- and observance-utility." [96] Thus, maybe people would be happier and more secure (i.e., maybe more utility would result) with such a code of rights. Utilitarians could *increase* the utility that observance of the code would generate by fashioning *extra sanctions* against those who violate it. [97] In this way, a utilitarian case for rights can be made.

It is not a very satisfactory case, however. Paradoxically, as we saw in our discussion of acceptance utilitarianism earlier, it builds people's *anti*-utilitarian sentiments into the calculation of overall utility. Surely reeducating the people would be better than acceding to their "prejudices." Building in extra sanctions to increase the disutility of violating a code of rights is highly artificial and questionable in utilitarian terms. Why would a utilitarian be interested in buttressing biases?

There is no question that biases (not just anti-utilitarian sentiments) would be buttressed by such a scheme. It is doubtful that members of other species would gain protection, for example, since humans typically have much less concern for them than for members of their own species. Many societies, as Helga Kuhse and Peter Singer have pointed out, have also had no compunctions about killing newborns.[98] The same holds for defective humans. It would not maximize utility to extend the special protection of rights to them in those societies (although under utilitarianism, they would have to be treated "humanely"). All of this clearly undercuts utilitarian impartiality.

Finally, the secret killing of individuals in order to maximize utility (recall Singer's case of parents secretly killing their normal child in order to conceive a child who would have an even happier life) would still be the right thing to do, given this scheme. As James Nelson has argued, a society in which people generally observe rights (in accordance with their nonconsequentialist leanings) *and* in which intelligent utilitarians secretly violate those rights when utility dictates it might actually maximize utility.[99] Frey's scheme will not convince skeptics that utilitarianism is compatible with genuine rights.

Frey himself is entirely aware of this. He doubts that any attempt to incorporate "full-blooded" rights into utilitarian theory can be successful,[100] simply because the principle of utility must be *basic* in such a theory. Thus, utility ultimately "trumps" rights. Frey warns that "rights" in a utilitarian theory can only be "mere shadows of the rights of rights theorists."[101] As such, these "rights" have no real force: "The real point is this: this combination of the above factors makes moral rules and rights *at best* mere appendages to a theory of right and wrong. If moral rules and rights are not basic in the theory, and so do not form part of the theory's account of what makes right acts right, they are dispensable. All that prevents this happening are the practicalities of our human situation, which can and often do alter."[102]

Are all attempts to find a place for genuine "full-blooded" rights in utilitarianism doomed, as Frey suggests?

Utilitarianism and the Protection of Life

Sumner's Utilitarian Case for Rights

L. W. Sumner disagrees with Frey's contention. I believe that he has made the best case that can be made for genuine rights within a utilitarian framework. In his earlier book, *Abortion and Moral Theory,* Sumner made an embryonic attempt, as it were, to reconcile his utilitarianism with his defense of a right to life for sentient beings.[103] Dissatisfied with the result, he has since devoted another book to the topic. In *The Moral Foundation of Rights,* he argues that in an ideal world, in which all moral agents were omniscient, scrupulously impartial, and flawlessly logical, all talk of rights would indeed be superfluous.[104] In such a world, he holds, we would always follow the *direct* utilitarian strategy of acting so as to maximize utility. However, as anyone can plainly see, we live in no such world. We make too many mistakes when we pursue the direct strategy, making case-by-case decisions. He argues that we will have a better chance of achieving the goal of maximizing utility if we above all pursue the *indirect* strategy, which calls for us to constrain our goal-directed behavior by extending prima facie rights to certain individuals.[105]

The purpose of these rights is to *constrain* actions done in pursuit of utility maximization: they are to be genuine checks, not mere "shadow rights." For example, researchers testing a new drug on human volunteers may be very tempted not to inform their subjects of certain possible side effects. Suppose the side effects would be extremely serious, but the chance of their occurring is judged to be extremely low. Suppose that the drug, if it works, would save many lives. A direct strategist, fearing that no one will volunteer if given full information, might resort to deception in order to maximize utility. An indirect strategist would reflect that she might be wrong in her estimate of the risk-benefit ratio. Although deception might work out best in this case, we are apt to cause much more harm than good by acting this way each time we believe we are justified. Overall, the goal of utility maximization might be better served by extending and observing the right of informed consent to subjects.

Presumably, a similar case can be made for all the other standard rights. In accordance with utilitarian impartiality, Sumner thinks that the theory, when worked out, will show that all beings with interests, *including many nonhuman animals, sentient fetuses, infants, and severely mentally deficient sentient beings,* would be extended the prima facie rights appropriate for them.[106]

Sumner's case for rights within a utilitarian framework has a number of merits. The rationale for extending rights does not depend on the prejudices moral agents happen to have, nor does it depend upon their having anti-utilitarian sentiments, in contrast to Frey's rationale. It does not require artificial, disutility-generating sanctions to stack the deck against violating rights for the sake of a marginal utility gain. According to his theory, innocent individuals would be protected against utility-maximizing killing or replacement. As a version of total-view utilitarianism, however, Sumner's view is still subject to some questionable reproductive implications.

The first such implication, discussed earlier, is that we have a *duty* to have children, as many as is compatible with maximizing utility. Sumner accepts this implication, but he tries to make it more palatable by pointing out that utility would be maximized by making extra children only in some circumstances. For example, if we had sufficient resources for a larger population, we would have the obligation to augment that population. In a world hugely burdened by overpopulation, filled with lives *not* worth living, utility would be maximized by *refraining* from having children for a period of time.[107] This seems reasonable, surely, but Sumner does not succeed in making the reproductive implication fully palatable. Suppose, for example, that our efforts (with or without the assistance of famine and disease) were to reduce the population so considerably that utility would be maximized by creating more "utility generators." Sumner, quite consistently, holds that sanctions against the willfully childless would be appropriate, although he doubts that they would need to be invoked very often. Some readers may join me in finding the notion of such sanctions repellent. This was former Romanian dictator Nicolae Ceauşescu's justification for jailing women who, denied contraceptives and legal abortions, terminated their pregnancies illegally at a time when Romania's birthrate was considered dangerously low. Sumner, no doubt, would proceed far more humanely than Ceauşescu ever did, stressing incentives over punitive measures. Nonetheless, any sanctions against persons who do not want to reproduce stick in the craw.

It also seems to follow from any version of total-view utilitarianism that we cannot favor a sentient fetus (or child, or adult!) over a fertilized human egg. It appears that the latter's future interests must be given the same weight as the former's present interests.[108] Yet, it seems that there is an important moral difference between preventing the implantation of an egg and killing a nine-month fetus (or a woman who will die if her pregnancy comes to term). I find the logical extension of this implication even more disturbing: Total-view utilitarianism, as we have already seen, equates contraception with killing. Sumner himself is not happy with this implication: he continues to favor the view that *sentience* (not "possible sentience") marks the point at which a right to life should be accorded to an individual. He knows it would not be easy to defeat the implication and support his own suggestion, but he hopes that an *indirect* strategy would have the desired result.[109]

Even if Sumner is right about this last problem, we are still asked to accept the reproductive imperative first mentioned. The number of such unwelcome implications has, however, been sharply reduced for utilitarianism—if Sumner has made his case for the protection of innocent life.

Utility Still Trumps Rights

Unfortunately, a good part of this promised protection dissolves upon closer examination. This is because, despite all that has been said, Sumner's view implies that utility still ultimately trumps rights.

First, consider how society is to decide *which* rights to extend, according to Sumner: "a conventional right is (strongly) justified just in case the policy of recognizing it in the appropriate rule system will better promote some favoured consequentialist goal [i.e., the maximization of utility] than will any alternative social policy."[110] Sumner is very open in saying that it will be an extremely difficult matter to calculate this. He does not attempt to make a case for a specific set of rights.[111] We are entitled to wonder whether the right central to our discussion of killing and replaceability, the right to life, would really make the list.

Second, once the hard work of determining a set of specific rights has been done, the *distribution* of that right must also be decided by a utility calculation. For example, suppose we do decide that a right to life can be justified. We must then determine who should have it (e.g., a pre-sentient conceptus). The answer depends on which extension scheme would maximize utility: "In a consequentialist framework the distribution of a right is a policy question." [112] Once again, Sumner fully admits that the task of determining distribution is extraordinarily difficult, choosing only to guess about what the results might be. Whatever is decided depends on *overall* utility: *there is no built-in constraint here to protect individuals.*

Third, once we have finally determined which rights to extend and to whom they should be extended, violation of these rights would still be permissible. Traditional rights theories also imply that rights may be overridden at times (e.g., allowing killing in self-defense), but rights would be violated more readily if Sumner's theory were accepted. He does not propose that we pursue the "indirect strategy," which lets rights trump utility in particular cases, *instead* of the "direct strategy": he realizes that utility would be maximized if we pursued a "mixed strategy." [113] Although we error-prone moral agents should not leap to do this, sometimes we should let utility trump rights. Once again, the decision to respect or violate the rights of an innocent individual depends on a calculation of overall utility. For example, even if we have decided that sentient nonhuman animals have a right to have their interests respected, a case could be made in these terms for painful, fatal experimentation on them if overall utility would be maximized. (For those who are not perturbed by this, remember that the same would apply to humans.) But why should the benefit *for others* count for so much? How much protection does an individual really have, according to this view? Not enough, as we shall see below.

Sumner believes it likely that at least one right (assuming it has been shown justified by a utilitarian judgment procedure), the right not to be tortured, cannot be overridden. This would be good news for every sentient being, but note the reasoning used to support his belief. He thinks that the cases in which utility truly would be maximized by torture are probably so exceedingly rare, so very exceptional, that we would run the risk of torturing mistakenly (i.e., *not* maximizing utility) if we regarded the right not to be tortured as defeasible. [114] In short, *normally* we probably would cause much more harm than good if we did this. However, in times of war, particularly when many lives are at stake and the weapons to hand are exceptionably horrible, cases where torturing an innocent person maximizes overall utility may not be rare at all. It seems that we would be justified in pursuing the direct strategy here (although maybe we should return to the indirect strategy during peacetime). Once again, benefit to others all too readily trumps rights.

The failure of Sumner's strong attempt to make a case for genuine rights within a utilitarian framework indicates that Frey is correct in holding that "utilitarian rights" must be at best "shadow rights." Utility *must* trump rights—*if* utilitarianism is the correct moral theory.

Utilitarians, then, must accept the fact that their view, despite its considerable merits, has highly dubious implications concerning the harming and killing of innocents. As we have seen, the view that full persons are the primary possessors of moral rights has even more objectionable consequences. We must look to another moral theory if we are dissatisfied. But how may we justifiably choose among moral theories? Is it a simple matter of following our intuitions about moral acceptability? Not at all, as we shall now see.

5

JUSTIFICATION AND JUDGMENT: CLAIMING

AND RESPECTING BASIC MORAL RIGHTS

For some of us, becoming vividly informed about the horrors routinely visited on nonhuman animals, be they in battery hen cages or in leghold traps, is itself sufficient to alter our ethical presuppositions. However, we need more than printed descriptions, pictures, or even firsthand experience of nonhumans in these conditions if we are to clarify our fundamental moral beliefs. Is it permissible to kill nonhumans for our own benefit if we have treated them "humanely"? How should human and nonhuman needs be weighed against each other? Careful ethical deliberation and argumentation is required if one is to address these issues. Part of this deliberation involves reflection about perceived wrongful treatment of other humans. Many of us experience an instant sensation of clarification when we ask ourselves: "Would it be right to do this to another *human*? If not, what morally relevant difference would permit us to do this to a *nonhuman*?" Others, convinced that the moral community has only human citizens, may be little moved by the suffering and deaths of nonhumans, but they too must pause when the consequences of their beliefs *for other humans* are revealed to them. One hopes that most moral agents would be repelled by views implying that innocent humans may justifiably have their bodies confiscated for the greater glory of medical research or even for the discriminating palate. Moral positions that deny moral significance to sentient nonhumans have surpassingly ugly implications for all manner of innocents, including human innocents. We have examined a multitude of ingenious attempts to include all humans in the moral community, regardless of their intellectual prowess, while excluding nonhumans from serious moral consideration. Every one of these attempts has failed. As we have seen, those believing that maximum moral significance is reserved for autonomous, highly developed persons like themselves are unable to escape these implications for humans with fewer intellectual capacities. The philosophers who have recently tried to rescue so-called "marginal humans" by defending a sophisticated version of speciesism have also come a cropper. Utilitarians, who by contrast do extend moral considerability to some nonhumans, are nevertheless also unable to escape foul implications regarding the treatment of innocents, including innocent moral agents.

One would think that anyone realizing that even the finest, sharpest arguments cannot save the above views from hideous consequences would reconsider allegiance to those views. In fact, a number of persons who had been homocentrists, speciesists, advocates of the full-personhood view, or unreconstructed utilitarians have done precisely that. As mentioned earlier in this book, philosopher Michael A. Fox's life provides an outstanding example of this. After spending years philosophically attacking arguments for "animal liberation," and writing a full-length book defending even the most agonizing experiments done upon nonhuman animals, Fox came to regard his earlier views as "smug" and "arrogant." As he describes it, he finally began to scrutinize the assumptions he "had lacked the courage to examine fully."[1] He decided that his moral position lacked justification: "There is no nonarbitrary ground on which to argue that the differences between humans and animals, morally relevant though some of them may be, make humans morally superior and animals inferior or valueless forms of life."[2] Regardless of one's position on animal experimentation, one must acknowledge the enormous courage Fox's change of mind required of him. Those of us who have had the experience of rejecting very basic, treasured beliefs know how painful it is, but not that many of us have publicly announced our reversals to hostile audiences. Fox did so, incurring the fully expectable disgusted scorn of the very scientists who had been lionizing him. Bernard Rollin, Tom Regan, Peter Singer, and Steve Sapontzis have also incorporated their views into their lives, expending enormous energy and resources and enduring considerable antagonism in order to rationally change people's perceptions of nonhuman animals. They have had no small measure of success, but this has probably come at a substantial personal price. Ethical deliberation is no abstract exercise when it has such consequences.

However, one must also respect the courage of a philosopher like R. G. Frey. He has become fully cognizant of the consequences that his ethical position, full-personhood-view utilitarianism, has for mentally limited humans. As we have seen, he has chosen, very reluctantly indeed, to accept those consequences. Frey is certainly no monster; he is a philosopher willing to go wherever his argument logically takes him. Can those of us who disagree with him *justify* that disagreement, or are we limited to cries of horror?

Bernard Rollin has argued, I think quite rightly, that many of us have "consensus morality" that accords moral significance to humans because of those humans' interests rather than their rational capacities. He believes that those of us having such ethical presuppositions adhere to an ideal of conduct, an ideal that does not sanction ill-treatment of any innocent human for the sake of another. He then proceeds to show that, *given* this ideal, there can be no justification for denying significant moral status to nonhuman animals: "[I]t has been our concern to raise the problem of whether it makes any sense to raise moral questions about animals in themselves at all . . . We have attempted to answer this question by arguing that there are no defensible grounds for excluding animals from moral concern and the treatment of animals from moral discussion *if we grant, as do most people,* that *people* are legitimate objects of moral concern."[3] Rollin does exactly what he sets out to do. He does not pretend to offer arguments that would persuade those who do *not* grant that all sentient humans are morally significant. Can such arguments be supplied?

Let us hope so. People who continue to deny that nonhuman animals are due serious moral consideration, even at the cost of many humans, deserve logical argumentation in response. By the same token, those of us who think that sentient innocents of any species are morally considerable would like to say that our position is justified. It is no easy matter to accomplish this task, as will soon become evident. First, let us consider an argument that is intended to shift the burden of justification.

ATTEMPTS TO PROVIDE JUSTIFICATION FOR THE MORAL CONSIDERABILITY AND SIGNIFICANCE OF BEINGS WHO ARE NOT FULL PERSONS

Character, Happiness, and Fairness

Steve Sapontzis proposes an argument that would slam the ball into the other court. He believes that, in the final analysis, *opponents* of the position that nonhuman animals are morally significant beings are the ones who must scramble for justification, not supporters of that position. His *Morals, Reason, and Animals,* an excellent defense of the "animal liberation" position against objections and a skillful discussion of the implications of that position for everyday action, also contains an ingenious positive argument for his view. He argues that "three everyday moral goals"—developing moral character, increasing the sum of happiness in the world, and behaving fairly—are furthered when nonhuman animals are included in the moral sphere.[4] (The same, of course, could be said with respect to mentally limited humans, although Sapontzis, who rejects the argument from marginal cases, certainly does not argue this.) He challenges his opponents to show otherwise: "[T]he best a general moral argument for animal liberation can do is to show that it is the exploiting of animals, not the liberating of them, that should be regarded as morally deviant and in need of justification."[5]

Sapontzis has correctly identified three common moral goals. We do consider fostering virtue, increasing happiness (or at least reducing suffering), and furthering fair treatment to be highly worthy moral enterprises. Opponents of the moral status of nonhuman animals are not known to object to such goals. Nevertheless, the tables cannot be turned quite so easily on these opponents.

The Character Premise

Sapontzis's appeal to character is not to be confused with the argument posed by Aquinas and Kant (discussed in my chapter 2): as he himself points out, his point is clearly not to warn us that normal humans' rights will be endangered if we do not behave virtuously toward sentient nonhumans. Instead, he argues plausibly that extending virtuous activity to these nonhumans can be seen as instantiating *intrinsically valuable* traits like sympathy, kindness, honesty, and so on.[6] Moreover, if we include some nonhumans as recipients of our virtuous acts, we make behaving virtuously a more central, coherent part of our lives. If it is good for one to be virtuous, and if more instances of virtue add to the sum of intrinsically valuable goods in this world, then, Sapontzis holds, it is good to broaden one's sphere of moral concern. If one values this moral goal, how can one object to its promotion?

Unfortunately, the appeal to character development falls short. We can best see this by reminding ourselves of the arguments of an adamant opponent of nonhuman animal moral considerability, Peter Carruthers. Like Kant and Aquinas, who also deny any moral status to nonhumans, Carruthers believes that wanton cruelty toward nonhuman animals (supposing they can feel anything, contrary to Carruthers's own belief) is wrong *because it indicates a character deficiency.* Compassionate individuals will ordinarily respond sympathetically to apparent nonhuman animal suffering. Anyone who delights in using her living cat as a dartboard has got, to put it mildly, a character kink.[7] (We must assume that Carruthers's dart artist has not already been convinced by the arguments in the last chapter of his book: if she has, she has merely intentionally substituted an insentient furry target for a cork one! As he puts it, "[I]t ought to be strictly impossible to feel sympathy for animals, once the true nature of their mental lives is properly understood.")[8] Thus, we appear to have an opponent of nonhuman animal moral considerability who concedes, at least in the case of ordinary people unacquainted with his own arguments, that good character is exemplified in compassionate treatment of these morally inconsiderable beings. Nevertheless, Carruthers has no problem resisting an argument such as Sapontzis's, as we shall now see.

While conceding the value of character traits like sympathy and sensitivity, Carruthers would emphatically deny that extending virtuous behavior to the point of integrating nonhuman animals into the moral community increases morally good behavior. "Animal lovers," as he calls them, may have *inherently* laudable character traits, but from his perspective their goals are *fundamentally misguided,* detracting from right moral behavior: "Concern with animal welfare, while expressive of states of character that are admirable, is an irrelevance to be opposed rather than encouraged."[9] Why? Because "animal lovers" object to enterprises like factory farming that serve legitimate human interests in making profits and earning livelihoods. Sympathy is a valuable character trait, but *misdirected* sympathy *is not admirable:* If nonhuman animals have no moral significance whatever, action on their behalf that undermines the interests of morally significant beings (i.e., normal humans) is reprehensible.[10] It is not only a waste of energy: it is wrong. Imagine a group of "dartboard liberators," filled with anguish for the "suffering" cork targets, who channel enormous energy and resources

Justification and Judgment

into destroying companies that make dartboards, wreaking havoc for all those engaged in the business and depriving dartboard enthusiasts of legitimate enjoyment. This is how Carruthers sees "animal liberators." *Given* his view that only rational moral agents can be morally considerable,[11] this is how he *ought* to see them. Another philosopher who shares Carruthers's view, Carl Cohen, makes the same point when he warns that we "misapprehend" our "true obligations" when we regard nonhumans as having moral status.[12]

Unluckily, this dispute over the legitimate boundaries of moral concern cannot be adjudicated without addressing the basic issue: Are sentient nonhuman animals (and mentally comparable humans!) morally significant beings or are they not? The same difficulty hobbles Sapontzis's appeals to two other commonly accepted moral goals: increasing happiness and promotion of fair treatment.

The Happiness and Fairness Premises

Sapontzis argues that ceasing the exploitation of nonhuman animals would "make the world a happier place."[13] His arguments here are well taken: certainly, overall suffering in the world—nonhuman *and* human—would be reduced if we no longer factory-farmed billions of nonhuman animals every year. (See my discussion of vegetarianism in chapter 4 for more on this topic.) However, people who deny moral status or significance to nonhuman animals would regard *their* reduced suffering as *morally inconsequential*. In cases where nonhuman unhappiness is an inevitable consequence of activities that could enhance human happiness, these people would say, we should obviously engage in those activities. *Some* cases of nonhuman animal experimentation would be justified, according to such a view. (Charles Fink has argued quite cogently that much nonhuman animal experimentation causes more human suffering than it alleviates because it diverts resources that could have been used for direct humanitarian assistance to research projects with questionable human benefit. However, experimentation that would likely produce more benefit than an alternative use of funds would, as he agrees, be mandatory from a strictly anthropocentric point of view.)[14] Anyone rejecting the supposition that nonhumans have moral status or significance will not agree with Sapontzis's claim that we further a worthy moral goal—increasing overall happiness or reducing overall suffering—by ceasing to harm nonhuman animals. They, of course, believe that *human* happiness ought to be our concern; nonhuman well-being is tolerable so long as it cannot hurt "us."

By the same token, appealing to "fairness" or justice will not begin to move people who doubt that nonhumans are morally considerable or significant. They would furiously deny that we promote "fairness" by distributing burdens and benefits more equitably across species lines. As Carruthers puts it, expressing what he takes to be "our" intuitive moral conviction: "[T]here can be no question of weighing animal suffering against the suffering of a human being. Since animals are still denied direct moral standing, on this contractualist account, they make no direct moral claims upon us. There is therefore nothing *to* be weighed against the claims of a human being."[15] Given such a view, fairness—a moral category applicable only to morally considerable beings—is decreased rather than promoted when nonhuman animals are factored into our moral equations.

Thus, appeals to character, happiness, and fairness cannot faze anyone who does not already cede moral significance to some nonhumans. However, Sapontzis is correct in noting that opponents of "animal liberation" have no successful counterarguments on their side to buttress their own moral assumptions. For example, Carruthers's "contractualist" argument for a purely moral-agent-centered ethic rests on circular reasoning, as Sapontzis has pointed out elsewhere.[16] As I too have discussed, arguments advanced in support of homocentrism, the full-personhood view, and speciesism are all resounding failures. Where does this leave us? Our "common morality," if such there be, contains fodder for both sides of this debate. Carruthers believes that his exclusionary contractarianism reflects "our" moral intuitions that nonhuman animal "suffering" counts for nothing in relation to that of moral agents; Sapontzis, while agreeing that "anti-animal" sentiments are part of ordinary morality, argues that other elements in that morality pull us in the other direction.[17] Yet his attempt to put the burden of proof on the other side does not accomplish the desired "pulling." It can indeed be shown that anyone granting full moral significance to all sentient humans must grant that some nonhumans qualify for the same moral status. But what can be said to moral agents who retract their concern for mentally limited humans? Moreover, what reply is possible to utilitarians who hew to their view despite its failure to sufficiently protect *any* innocent sentient life? Somehow, we must get beyond the opposed moral convictions remaining after so much of the argumentative dust has settled.

Let us now turn to Tom Regan's classic attempt to settle this issue. We will find that it too falls short of providing the ultimate justification we seek.

Regan's Case for the Equal Moral Significance of All Subjects-of-Lives

Regan's *The Case for Animal Rights* [18] is an extremely impressive, richly argued defense of nonhuman animal moral significance. It is filled with excellent attacks on homocentric and speciesist positions. Most importantly for our purposes here, Regan also argues that his position meets fundamental criteria for adequacy in moral theorizing; alternative moral theories are said to be disqualified by those same criteria. First, let us briefly identify these opposing moral theories.

Regan's Rights View and Its Alternatives

Regan is a moral rights theorist. He adopts philosopher Joel Feinberg's sense of 'rights,' according to which rights are "valid claims" against other moral agents.[19] At issue here are *basic* moral rights such as the rights to life, liberty, and well-being. As I explained in the previous chapter, despite L. W. Sumner's admirable attempt to show that a consequentialist can espouse a full-blooded rights theory, it is plain that rights theorists must deny that consequences are all that matter morally. Regan does not deny that consequences have moral weight, but he clearly defends a nonconsequentialist or deontologist theory of obligation. According to rights theorists, morally considerable beings are due treatment that is commensurate with their moral significance. Traditional rights theories typically assume that humans, or the much narrower class of moral agents, are rights holders. Regan's theory, of course, is different. Being a "subject of a life" is at least sufficient, in Regan's view, for maximum moral significance. Let us repeat Regan's definition of "subjects-of-lives": "Individuals are subjects-of-a-life if they have beliefs and desires; perception, memory, and a sense of the future, including their own future; an emotional life together with feelings of pleasure and pain; preference- and welfare-interests; the ability to initiate action in pursuit of their desires and goals; a psychophysical identity over time; and an individual welfare in the sense that their experient[i]al [lives] fare well or ill for them, logically independently of their utility for others and logically independently of their being the object[s] of anyone else's interests." [20] Normally developed mammals over one year in age are *clear* cases of "subjects-of-lives," Regan holds.[21] Beings (e.g., birds) who may not meet all the specifications above should be given the benefit of the doubt, in his view (Peter Singer makes the same distinction in preference utilitarianism terms, as we saw in the previous chapter). Regan does not argue that being a "subject-of-a-life" is a necessary condition for having basic moral rights, but he seriously doubts that any who are not subjects-of-lives could be as morally significant as those who are.[22] He holds that subjects-of-lives, regardless of their very different mental capacities, are all equally morally significant (as he puts it, they have "equal inherent value").

Regan distinguishes his view from other consequentialist and non-consequentialist moral theories. These include Jan Narveson's "rational egoism" (I discussed and rejected Narveson's attempts to skirt the argument from marginal cases in my chapter 2), John Rawls's contractarian theory, and Kant's deontological moral theory: each of these views denies moral considerability to human or nonhuman beings incapable of moral agency.[23] Alternative views that allow at least some moral significance to be attributed to sentient beings who are not moral agents (or *full persons,* to use my terminology) are utilitarianism and perfectionism. Utilitarianism, a far more plausible consequentialist theory than egoism, has already been discussed at length in my chapter 4. I will add here that in an important sense, utilitarianism denies that one has direct duties to any *individuals:* one's duty is to promote (directly if one is an act utilitarian or indirectly if one is a rule utilitarian) happiness, interests, or preferences as such. According to perfectionism, the moral significance of beings increases in proportion to the degree to which they possess certain capacities or virtues: morally considerable beings are by no means equally morally significant in such a view. Although Regan does not say so, the above classifications are not mutually exclusive.

Perfectionists may be nonconsequentialist (and nonegalitarian!) rights theorists, or they may be utilitarians holding, as does R. G. Frey, that richer experiential lives instantiate more goodness than others do, warranting higher moral status. Perfectionists may be egoists, as Friedrich Nietzsche was, and Rawls holds that his view has strong affinities with Kant's.[24] Clearly, however, each of the five views above are incompatible with Regan's rights position. Let us now focus on Regan's strategy for rejecting these alternatives.

How does one evaluate alternative views on moral considerability and significance? Regan argues that we require such a view to display consistency, adequacy of scope, precision, simplicity, and conformity with our *reflective* intuitions about rightness and wrongness.[25] The conformity with reflective intuitions test is, as Regan fully admits, by far the most controversial. Unfortunately, it is also the key test. Regan explains that reflective intuitions are not "gut reactions": we are required to gather as much relevant information as we can; then we are to judge a moral view or principle calmly, rationally, clearly, and impartially.[26] Regan refers to impartiality as "the formal principle of justice": we are to treat similar cases similarly and dissimilar cases dissimilarly.[27] How, according to Regan, do alternatives to his own theory fall short?

I will attempt no comprehensive account of Regan's arguments here; readers should go directly to his book for that. They will find sophisticated, beautifully developed, cogent criticisms, but they will also find appeals to reflective intuitions that at least some of Regan's opponents can challenge. Although almost all the moral theorists whose arguments I have examined and rebutted in the remainder of my book themselves take reflective intuitions—especially the common moral belief that it is wrong to harm babies and mentally impaired humans—very seriously, going through amazing contortions in their attempts to reconcile their positions with these intuitions, theorists who *accept* the discrepancy between their views and commonly held moral beliefs are untouched by such appeals.

It will be instructive for us to first consider an ethical theory that Regan is wholly successful in arguing against. Then we will turn to his attacks on the remaining four alternatives.

Justification and Judgment

Attacks on Rawls's Contractarianism

One can interpret John Rawls's contractarian position, developed in his classic *A Theory of Justice,* as an egalitarian version of egoism. Imagine that you, a self-interested rational agent, know only that you will be a member of a given society. What rules would you select for that society? Rawls proposes that *justice* be identified with the rules chosen, or contracted to, by such imaginary agents in an imaginary "original position." They choose behind a "veil of ignorance" regarding their identities, though they are given all other relevant information needed to reach their normative conclusions. The "veil of ignorance" device proposed for "the original position" of choice makes it unlikely that principles would be chosen that would favor only a few: a rational self-interested agent, one hopes, would not choose a nonegalitarian society because she or he might wind up on the short end of the stick. Rawls's egalitarianism does not extend beyond human boundaries, however: he takes for granted that any hypothetical self-interested rational agent would not choose principles of justice applicable to nonhumans.[28] The veil of ignorance does not include ignorance about one's species membership in the hypothetical society to be: one would be guaranteed a human incarnation, and one is to choose for oneself. (Perhaps readers will already have begun to smell a rat, if I may be forgiven such a metaphor.)

Rawls's view has inspired many criticisms over the past decades. I believe that the most fundamental of these criticisms concerns the inherent circularity of the view. L. W. Sumner points out that principles of justice are identified with the choices made in the "original position." However, the "veil of ignorance" constraint imposed on the original position clearly presupposes an egalitarian principle of justice (at least with respect to humans!).[29] Obviously, the point of stipulating that agents cannot know which members of society they will be is to influence agents to choose principles that do not discriminate against *anyone* in an ideally just human society. Given Rawls's theory of justice, it is impossible to justify this fundamental presupposition of equality: if it is just, this must entail that it has been chosen in the original position; but the egalitarian principle is itself embedded in the very choice mechanism of the so-called original position. Alan Gewirth puts the criticism very elegantly: "Insofar, however, as this doctrine is viewed as giving a justificatory answer to the question whether humans have equal moral rights, it may be convicted of circularity. For the argument attains its egalitarian conclusion only by putting into its premises the egalitarianism of persons' universal equal ignorance of all their particular qualities . . . Hence, apart from an initial egalitarian moral outlook, why should any actual rational informed persons accept the principle about equal moral rights that stems from such ignorance?"[30]

L. W. Sumner extends this criticism, which he has also made, by posing a pernicious dilemma for *any* contractarian position, egalitarian or nonegalitarian, that purports to justify certain moral principles by claiming that rational agents would choose them. If the conditions under which these choices are to be made are wholly unspecified, there is no reason to grant moral force to the choices made. (We have noted the depressing fact that some of the most egregious bigots on earth can pass the narrow test of rationality: see my discussion of R. B. Brandt's view in my chapter 3.) On the other hand, if conditions are specified to constrain choices, prior moral principles are being presupposed, principles that cannot be justified in contractarian terms.[31] Thus, we have strong logical grounds for rejecting any such view.

Regan's critique of Rawls's view also turns largely on appeals to logic.[32] Regan argues that, although consistency requires Rawls to deny that we can have direct duties to any beings other than moral agents (i.e., Rawls must hold that only moral agents can be morally considerable), this denial precludes Rawls's egalitarianism. Regan argues very successfully that Rawls arbitrarily limits the imaginary positions in a given society to positions for *human moral agents*. Ruling out the moral considerability of nonhumans *and* humans who cannot be moral agents on the basis of such a theory is surely question begging; yet, this is exactly what Rawls does.

Regan also argues that Rawls's theory is not in accordance with our "reflective intuitions," implying as it does that only moral agents can be morally considerable.[33] However, this criticism is logically independent of his others, sketched above. Regan's earlier arguments against Rawls (as well as Gewirth's and Sumner's criticisms) are so successful because they turn on issues of consistency and logical adequacy. These matters are not so easily disputable as claims about our intuitions, however carefully thought out those intuitions may be.

Attacks on Egoism and Utilitarianism

Now let us turn to an unabashedly nonegalitarian theory. Regan decisively rejects egoism, which holds that agents ought to act to maximize their own interests, because of its "unacceptable implications" for the treatment of moral agents as well as people who cannot be moral agents.[34] Now, my reflective intuitions agree with Regan's in finding these implications unacceptable. The problem is: How is one to proceed if egoists do *not* find themselves in agreement with this judgment? Regan notes that philosopher Jan Narveson, whose egoistic position Regan attacks, cannot simply reject the appeal to reflective intuitions since Narveson himself accepts this as a test. Be that as it may, a rational egoist need not at all accept such a test. Moreover, even if he or she does, one suspects that an egoist's "reflective intuitions" might turn out to be radically different from a rights theorist's reflective intuitions!

Regan also rejects the varieties of utilitarianism because of their "counterintuitive" implications.[35] Act utilitarianism, which enjoins agents to maximize nonmoral good (utility), cannot adequately ground our belief that individuals ought not to be harmed, and rule utilitarianism, which (roughly) tells us to act in accordance with rules that would maximize utility, does not properly account for our belief that we have direct duties to the very young and mentally restricted.[36] Regan is correct in holding that utilitarian views have these implications. But what could he say to a utilitarian like R. G. Frey? How does one respond to "So what?" (Note that I did not follow Regan's strategy in my own discussion of utilitarianism in the previous chapter. I discussed the many attempts that have been made to show that utilitarian views do *not* have counterintuitive implications. None of these attempts succeed. As I point out at the end of that chapter, although this fact is enough to send many moral agents as far from a utilitarian perspective as they can get, I do not take this to settle the question of utilitarianism's correctness as a moral theory.)

Attacks on Perfectionism and Kantianism

Perfectionist theories of morality award greater moral significance to individuals exhibiting higher degrees of certain favored qualities, qualities that are typically related to intelligence. Regan finds such a view to embody an intuitively objectionable theory of justice. Again, many of us share his intuitions here, but people who, upon reflection, reject an egalitarian concept of justice in favor of a meritorian concept will conclude otherwise. Regan tries to sway such people by offering an additional argument that he regards as even more fundamental. He maintains that perfectionism must be rejected because it bases moral significance upon the presence or absence of abilities over whose acquisition one has no control. Whether, and to what degree, one is intelligent, rational, creative, and so on, depends upon the "natural lottery," not upon one's own efforts. Beings, human or nonhuman, who come up short do not deserve to have lesser moral significance any more than those at the other end of the ability scale deserve higher moral status.[37] Is it not obvious that such a view is patently unjust?

One is sympathetic to Regan's argument. Anyone who has waded through Friedrich Nietzsche's simultaneously brilliant and obnoxious paeans to "excellence" and sneers at "mediocrity," culminating in this claim—"[T]o a being such as 'we,' other beings must naturally be in subjection, and have to sacrifice themselves. The noble soul accepts the fact of his egoism without question, and also without consciousness of harshness, constraint, or arbitrariness therein, but rather as something that may have its basis in the primary law of things:—if he sought a designation for it he would say: 'It is justice itself' . . . [H]e looks either *forward,* horizontally and deliberately, or downwards—*he knows that he is on a height*"[38]—is indeed inclined to wonder what bearing such a view has on actual justice. Following cool, rational reflection one is unbearably tempted to reward such pronouncements with a giant raspberry. Still, are we not simply affirming our reflective intuitions instead of his? Nietzsche's rhetorical raspberries at conventional morality are at least as violent and deeply felt as one's own reaction to the "master morality."

Moreover, Regan's "nature's lottery" argument against perfectionism would actually discredit every alternative ethical theory one can think of, *including his own.* If Regan is arguing that moral considerability and significance must not be linked to characteristics over which one has no control, what theory could escape his argument? Even the sort of "meritorianism" that accords moral significance to effort rather than to one's native abilities would fall afoul of Regan's argument, since it presupposes that one is able to make an effort, able to see the importance of making an effort, and so on. More importantly for Regan, we do not choose to be subjects-of-lives, and amoebas do not choose *not* to attain that condition: nevertheless, Regan clearly sees a rather large moral difference between these dissimilar life forms. More generally, if one believes that justice is not unrelated to the basic interests of a being, and one accordingly denies that inanimate dartboards can be morally significant, one must admit that justice is after all subject to a "lottery" of sorts. Perfectionism is no worse off than Regan's own view in this respect.

Finally, let us consider Regan's rejection of the Kantian view that only rational beings capable of being morally autonomous are "ends in themselves," that is, morally considerable. Regan asks us to imagine deliberately torturing a human child. She is not a moral agent, so, given Kantian doctrine, we do no direct wrong to her at all. (Let us also stipulate that she will never be a moral agent, due to physical disease or severe mental handicap: no moral-agent-to-be is being wronged either.) Let us also imagine that the torturer does not enjoy the cruelty he is inflicting (he is a first-time torturer acting out of intellectual curiosity only) and will never be tempted to torture again; thus, no habit that would imperil *moral agents* is being encouraged. It seems that Kant's theory would exonerate our torturer. (The real Kant, by all accounts a gentle and humane being, would perhaps have gone back to the moral drawing board if presented with such an example.) What conclusions does Regan draw from this?

First, he notes, this is an extremely implausible result. In effect, our reflective intuitions are doing somersaults of indignation. More significantly, however, Regan argues that this result violates the requirement of *impartiality*, "the principle of formal justice," which any adequate moral theory must meet. We all must agree that the child suffers just as a moral agent would, were he to be in the torturer's clutches instead. But this suffering, and this suffering alone, is the morally relevant similarity between the child and a victim who is a moral agent: "But if the suffering is similar, and if causing it in the case of moral agents violates a direct duty to them (as Kant allows), then how can we nonarbitrarily avoid the conclusion that causing suffering to human moral patients violates a direct duty to them? To reply that moral agents can act in accordance with the categorical imperative while human moral patients cannot is true but irrelevant. The issue concerns their *shared* capacity for suffering, not their differing abilities. Otherwise, we flaunt the requirement of formal justice: we allow dissimilar treatment of *relevantly* similar cases."[39]

Perfectionists, who would gauge the degree to which the torturing is wrong by ascertaining how gifted the victim is, would be subject to the same objection. Unfortunately, however, hardened Kantians and perfectionists would be able to reject Regan's argument as question begging. The cases of the child and the moral agent *are* morally relevantly dissimilar, they would reply: according to their views, the capacity for suffering is not the *fundamentally* important moral category. They are quite impartial, given their theoretical commitments. For Regan to deny this is tantamount to his assuming the falsity of their positions.

The trouble is that impartiality is a *formal* requirement that radically different ethical theories can all embrace. Such a principle cannot decide the issue. Regan seems to be aware of this: he points out that a *normative* interpretation of justice is required to specify what counts as a morally relevant similarity or dissimilarity.[40] But how are we to decide between different interpretations of justice? According to Regan, we must apply the tests of scope, precision, and conformity to our reflective intuitions. These intuitions must be cool, clear, rational, informed, and *impartial*— in the formal sense! Perfectionists, utilitarians, Kantians, other rights theorists, and so on, would all claim that their views *do* pass these tests. *How is one to reply to them?*

To show, as Regan does in his chapter 7, that the "equal inherent value of all subjects-of-lives" view passes all the above tests for adequacy simply is not sufficient. Alternatives must be ruled out, as he knows full well. He is absolutely correct in pointing out that arguments are wanting for any view that gives primacy to moral agency, to higher degrees of intelligence-related capacities, to the agent's self-interest, or to units of nonmoral good as opposed to individuals. Followers of such views would counter, of course, that his rights view is no less arbitrary. Once one's reflective intuitions agree with Regan's claim that we owe direct duties to humans who are not moral agents, the rest falls into place: we cannot accept this contention and consistently deny that relevantly similar nonhumans are owed no direct duties. But that initial agreement need never occur—unless we can find an argument to support it.

JUSTIFYING THE RIGHTS VIEW

Alan Gewirth's Argument

I believe that such an argument can be provided. A few years ago, I suggested that the reasoning of ethical theorist Alan Gewirth provides a basis for just such a case, although he does not draw the same conclusions about "marginal" humans and nonhuman animals that I do.[41] After giving considerable additional attention to Gewirth's line of reasoning, I am more convinced than ever that it supplies the missing justification required to resolve what threatens to be a relativistic impasse.

Gewirth's argument is spelled out in meticulous detail in his books *Reason and Morality*[42] and *Human Rights*.[43] He restates his argument in compact form in *Gewirth's Ethical Rationalism*,[44] an anthology consisting of articles critical of Gewirth's reasoning and Gewirth's extended reply to each of them.[45] Gewirth's line of argument has remained intact since his first book. In spelling out the essential steps in his argument, I will for the most part rely on his statement of it in *Gewirth's Ethical Rationalism*, referring to the earlier sources when additional clarification is desirable.[46]

Moral codes are action guides; they can only be addressed to agents. Only agents—who are able to exercise control over their behavior, have knowledge of the relevant proximate circumstances of their actions, and have purposes they want to fulfill[47]—are capable of action. When we take the point of view of any particular, reflective, rational agent, Gewirth holds, we can see how that agent *logically* must accept and respect the rights of others. (Just *who* those others are will be discussed shortly.) Gewirth, of course, does not claim that agents in actuality go through the steps he outlines, "graduating" as *moral* agents as they arrive at its conclusion. I would wager that almost all of us came to have moral regard for others long before we could have waded through *Reason and Morality*, probably influenced far more by emotion than by logic. Nothing Gewirth says is in conflict with our moral experience.

Justification and Judgment

What follows is a rational reconstruction, not a psychological thesis about moral development.[48]

Gewirth's first two premises[49] arise from the conative nature of agency:

(1) "I do X for end or purpose E."

(2) "E is good."

Agents have desires; they have purposes they want to fulfill. An agent reflecting on the fact that she is planning to undertake a certain action in order to achieve a given goal must recognize that she *considers* that goal valuable enough to pursue. "Good" in premise 2 is not a claim about moral goodness; the agent may even regard her purpose as immoral. She may even, on some level, regard the purpose as loathsome. If it is nonetheless her purpose, however, she must find it valuable. Premise 2 is an expression of approbation in this limited sense, purely from the agent's point of view.

When the agent reflects about the nature of agency itself, she will realize that action of any kind has two necessary preconditions or "generic features": (a) the ability to have purposes or goals and (b) the freedom required to pursue those goals. In order to have goals, one must in turn be alive, have a certain minimal quality of life, and have certain basic mental and physical capabilities. Gewirth combines these requirements for the first generic feature of action under the heading of "well-being."[50] The next premise expresses the fact that the reflective agent who wants to pursue her goals must also value her well-being and freedom, and hold that they are good:

(3) "My freedom and well-being are necessary goods."[51]

"Necessary goods" means not only that freedom and well-being are necessary conditions for successful goal pursuit: it carries the agent's approbation. Note that Gewirth is not claiming that the agent's freedom and well-being *are* good: his point is that the reflective agent must *hold* them, as generic features of action, to be good. Even an agent bent on being enslaved or on immolating herself must value the freedom and well-being *needed at that moment* to carry out her purpose.

The agent's realization that her freedom and well-being are requirements for the achievement of any of her goals leads her to the next premise:

(4) "I must have freedom and well-being."[52]

This premise is not just shorthand for "I must have freedom and well-being if I want to act"; it is an expression of the agent's "advocacy" of her own freedom and well-being.[53] She *wants* freedom and well-being because she *wants*—as does every agent, by definition—to achieve her goals. This inevitably leads her, Gewirth argues, to claim that she is *entitled* to freedom and well-being:

(5) "I have rights to freedom and well-being."[54]

Note once again that Gewirth is not arguing that the agent *has* these fundamental, "generic" rights: he is saying that she *holds* or *accepts* that she does, as an agent who wishes to pursue her goals.

Gewirth now uses an indirect proof to show that any agent logically *must* hold that she has these basic rights. If she were to *deny* 5, she would also have to deny:

(6) "All other persons ought at least to refrain from removing or interfering with my freedom and well-being."[55]

Premises 5 and 6 are logical correlatives: rights claims are claims against others.[56] But if the agent denies 6, then she must accept the following substitute premise:

(6′) "Other persons may (i.e., it is permissible that other persons) remove or interfere with my freedom and well-being."[57]

However, 6′ contradicts 2: "I must have freedom and well-being." Remember that 2 is an expression of the agent's *advocacy of* and *insistence upon* her freedom and well-being, not just a descriptive statement about means and ends. Substitute premise 6′ above drops that insistence, replacing it with the agent's admission that, from her point of view, her freedom and well-being are expendable. Premise 6, by contrast, actually entails premise 2. As Gewirth puts it: "For if the agent must have freedom and well-being, then, from the standpoint of his own purposive action, whatever interferes with his having these must be rejected or removed, including interference by other persons."[58] Since agents qua agents must accept 2, they must reject substitute premise 6′. Premise 6′ follows from the rejection of 5; thus the agent must indeed accept 5: she must claim that she has rights to the preconditions for agency.

Before we move on, note that Gewirth is *not* arguing that "Individual S needs freedom and well-being in order to act" logically necessitates "S has the right to freedom and well-being." Obviously, there is a galaxy-wide logical gap between these two statements. The entire argument takes place *within the reflective agent's viewpoint:* From "S *regards* freedom and well-being as necessary goods," it does follow (given that rights claims are correlated with claims to noninterference) that "S rationally *claims* the rights to freedom and well-being."[59] The distinction between the two different pairs of statements is crucial. The first pair of statements provides a blatant example of the notorious "is/ought" fallacy: an evaluative (normative) claim is "deduced" from a mere statement of fact. The second pair of statements avoids any such invalid argumentation.[60]

This completes the first stage of Gewirth's rational reconstruction. Stage two will show why the reflective agent logically must be a moral agent. Up to now, the agent has not made a *moral* claim: her advocacy of her own rights to freedom and well-being, concerning as it does the furthering of her interests alone, is a matter of prudence rather than morality. The shift from the prudential to the moral point of view, according to which others' interests count too, begins with the agent's justification of the rights claim made in premise 5. As Gewirth points out, rights claims, as opposed to bald demands, are claims that one is *entitled to* or *due* certain behavior on the part of others; hence, such claims need to be warranted.[61] The warrant for an agent's claim to basic ("generic") rights is very straightforward: She has purposes she wants to fulfill; that is, she is a "prospective purposive agent." This is the most fundamental "practical justifying reason" that can ever be given. As one who wishes to act, she must claim or advocate that she is entitled to the conditions that make action possible. Thus, she accepts:

(7) "I have rights to freedom and well-being because I am a prospective purposive agent."[62]

The particular identity of the agent is not important here: rank or privilege is wholly irrelevant. Be she Margaret Thatcher, Benazir Bhutto, or Jane Doe, the fact that she has purposes she wants to achieve is what counts. This inevitably leads to the next step in the argumentative shift from the prudential to the moral point of view: the acceptance of the principle of universalizability.

(8) "If the having of some quality Q is a *sufficient condition* of some predicate P's belonging to some individual S, then P must also belong to all other subjects that have Q."[63]

It follows, Gewirth argues, that the agent must hold:

(9) "All prospective purposive agents have rights to freedom and well-being."[64]

Reflective agents accepting premises 1–8, as Gewirth has argued they must, cannot deny 9 without contradicting themselves. To say that Q—being a prospective purposive agent—is sufficient condition for having P—the rights to freedom and well-being—and yet deny that *other* prospective purposive agents have these rights is to say that Q is both sufficient and not sufficient for P.[65] An agent is thus logically obliged to extend basic rights to other agents. This is a *moral* claim, not merely a prudential one, because it implies that others besides oneself are entitled to have their freedom and well-being respected. It logically leads the reflective agent to accept what Gewirth calls "the supreme principle of morality":

(10) "Act in accord with the generic rights of your recipients as well as of yourself."[66] (the Principle of Generic Consistency)[67]

The reader will probably have noticed that there is more than a passing resemblance between the Principle of Generic Consistency and the Golden Rule, popularly rendered as "Do unto others as you would have them do unto you." (Never mind that cynical corollary, "Those who have the gold make the rules"!) What Gewirth has done is to show *why,* in purely logical terms, adherence to this rule is justified.[68] If he is right, refusal by a reflective agent to take the moral point of view is, quite simply, irrational.

As the above indicates, Gewirth's argument allows us to see why ethical egoism is entirely unjustified. It also follows that utilitarianism, a far more plausible consequentialist view than egoism, is mistaken. The Principle of Generic Consistency enjoins us to respect other purposive beings as we do ourselves; it does not impose upon us the overriding duty to maximize utility (happiness or other nonmoral goods), or to act in accordance with rules that do so. Individuals are the primary locus of moral value, not aggregated utility. Unlike egoism and utilitarianism, Gewirth's view has deontological as well as consequentialist features.[69] Perfectionism, which ties degrees of moral significance for individuals to the degree to which intelligence-related capacities are present in those individuals, is also ruled out.[70] Beth may be a far more intelligent, thoughtful agent than Butthead, but that gives her no moral premium. Each is a consciously purposeful being, and this is sufficient, other things being equal, for the full range of basic moral rights. Gewirth's argument also entails the unacceptability of restricting moral considerability or maximum moral significance to moral agents, as Kant and many other full-personhood-view advocates have held (see my section "To Whom Must the Reflective Agent Accord Basic Moral Rights?" below for the elucidation of this point). Thus, Gewirth allows us to extricate ourselves from the quagmire of relativism: die-hard proponents of the respective views above can receive the argument that they deserve instead of having the question begged against them.

Our sketch of Gewirth's argument is now complete. Let us now turn to a key criticism of that argument. Following that, I will show that Gewirth's position supports attributions of full moral significance to so-called "marginal" humans *and*, contrary to Gewirth's assumption, to a great many nonhuman animals.

Is Moral Agency Mandated by Reason?

Many objections have been raised against Gewirth's basic argument. He has anticipated and rebutted most of these objections in *Reason and Morality.* More objections are posed by leading ethical theorists such as R. M. Hare, Marcus Singer, W. D. Hudson, E. M. Adams, Renford Bambrough, and others in *Gewirth's Ethical Rationalism.* Gewirth has replied to them in turn. All of his replies but one are successful, as best I can determine, but even in that one case, Gewirth could have defeated the objection posed. According to that objection, the key move from stage one of Gewirth's argument (steps 1–6) to stage two (steps 7–10)—the move from agency to moral agency—collapses, taking with it Gewirth's justification of moral rights claims.

Frank De Roose argues that, although Gewirth has indeed shown that reflective agents must claim the rights to freedom and well-being *for themselves,* he has not shown that agents must hold that *others* have these rights as well.[71] Paraphrasing R. M. Hare, De Roose charges that Gewirth, who charges that "amoralists" contradict themselves, is himself guilty of a logical fallacy: the equivocation of "having a right" with "claiming a right." From the "relatively uncontroversial" thesis that every reflective agent must *claim* rights for herself, De Roose charges, Gewirth moves, via the (also presumably uncontroversial) principle of universalizability, to "all prospective agents who have purposes they want to fulfill *have* the rights of freedom and well-being."[72] De Roose quotes an early critic of Gewirth, Adina Schwartz, on this seemingly fatal flaw: "Gewirth has only shown that each agent must claim rights for him/herself on prudential grounds. Therefore, each agent is only logically bound to admit that all other agents have sound prudential reasons for claiming those same rights for themselves."[73] Recognizing that others *claim* the rights to freedom and well-being is not tantamount to *according* them those rights. Hence, the rational agent is not inconsistent if she refuses to take the moral point of view. De Roose points out that R. M. Hare later lodged much the same objection: "For if all [Gewirth] had shown was that an agent must claim that there is a prudential requirement on him to seek the necessary conditions for achieving *his* purposes, the universalization of this claim would only yield the claim that there is a prudential requirement on other similar agents in similar situations to seek the necessary conditions for achieving *their* purposes."[74] Clearly, the latter claim is not *moral* at all: it is as resoundingly prudential as the claim from which Hare says it was universalized.

Gewirth does not successfully defend himself against this potentially fatal criticism. In his reply to Hare, Gewirth, for the sake of argument, accepts the terms in which Hare has framed his objection above. Gewirth agrees that (a) "there is a prudential requirement on [an agent] to seek the necessary conditions for achieving his purposes" entails (assuming the principle of universalizability) (b) "there is a prudential requirement on other similar agents to seek the necessary conditions for achieving their purposes."[75] After pointing out that the argumentative move from a to b does not capture the thrust of his argument, Gewirth goes on to argue that Hare's objection fails even on its own terms. Statement b above, *when said by the same agent referred to in statement a,* is actually a *moral* judgment, according to Gewirth. Why? Because it "takes *favorable account of* the interests of persons other than or in addition to [the original] agent."[76] Thus, allegedly, the transition from a prudential to a moral point of view is still accomplished.

Alas, this will not do. An agent who claims that it is in the interests of other agents to seek freedom and well-being takes neither favorable nor unfavorable account of the interests of those other agents: he or she simply acknowledges the facts. Hitler, while probably realizing that it was *in* the interests of his death camp victims to have freedom and well-being, did not exactly take *"favorable account of"* their interests! A much better reply is available to Gewirth, as I shall now go on to argue.

In trying to hoist Hare on Hare's own "prudential" petard, Gewirth concedes too much by accepting Hare's framework for discussion. Gewirth sees that the key to defeating the objection is to stress the agent's standpoint, but he does not appeal to this standpoint in the correct context. The claim to be universalized is *the agent's,* not an outside observer's *description* of the agent's claim. Hare (and Schwartz before him) assumes that "the agent claims the rights of freedom and well-being for herself on prudential grounds" must be Gewirth's prudential starting point on his path to the moral point of view. This initial claim can indeed not be universalized into a moral claim. But they have picked the wrong starting point. The actual claim to be universalized is *the agent's* claim that "As a prospective purposive agent, I have the rights to freedom and well-being" (step 7 in our earlier sketch of Gewirth's argument). When *this* claim is universalized we get step 9: "All prospective purposive agents have the rights to freedom and well-being." This is a *moral* judgment because, by making it, the agent thereby accords rights to others. The agent does not merely observe that others *claim* rights to freedom and well-being because it is in their interests to do so. The novelty and force of Gewirth's argument is due to his insistence that we take the agent's standpoint throughout. Gewirth does not need to show that the agent *has* rights or that all agents *have* rights: he need only show that the reflective agent *must hold* that she has rights. Once this "relatively uncontroversial" (to use De Roose's description) thesis has been established, universalization leads to the agent's *holding* that others with purposes they want to fulfill also have rights. Schwartz, Hare, and De Roose all confuse the agent's claim with a third-person report of that claim.

De Roose's formulation of the objection allows us to see this mistake more clearly. He grants that Gewirth shows that "all [reflective] agents must claim for themselves the right to freedom and well being." The agent, then, is said to judge that "I claim for myself rights to freedom and well-being." De Roose rightly argues that this judgment, when universalized, yields but another prudential claim (presumably, "other prospective agents similar to myself claim rights of freedom and well-being for themselves").[77] But this incorrectly identifies the judgment to be universalized. The statement that "all [reflective] agents must claim for themselves rights to freedom and well-being" does not imply that the agent must think to herself "I claim the rights to freedom and well-being." This adds an additional layer of self-consciousness which need not at all be present. Worse, the core of any rights claim has been omitted in De Roose's formulation. An agent claims the rights to freedom and well-being for herself by saying or thinking "I *have* the rights to freedom and well-being." This statement *is* the rights claim in question! Claiming a right and having a right certainly are two different matters. Since the agent must hold that she has rights, by Gewirth's argument, not merely that she claims rights, the judgment to be universalized is "I [on the grounds that I am a prospective purposive agent] *have* the rights to freedom and well-being." The rest follows just as Gewirth has said. He is not guilty of equivocating "having a right" with "claiming a right." Unless he can be shown mistaken in some other respect, Gewirth appears to have shown that the rational reflective agent logically must hold that others in addition to herself have basic rights.

To Whom Must the Reflective Agent Accord Basic Rights?

Who are these others? Certainly, other reflective moral agents—full persons—who claim rights for themselves are included. As we shall now see, however, this high degree of intelligence is not necessary to warrant rights attributions. Nor must one be able to claim rights to be accorded them.[78]

Preferentially Autonomous Agents

The morally relevant similarity between the reflective agent and others to whom rights are attributed is *having purposes one wants to fulfill.* Gewirth explicitly argues that *this* is the feature that justifies an agent's insistence on generic or basic rights.[79] From the reflective agent's viewpoint (before universalization has led to the agent's taking the moral point of view), as Gewirth puts it, "I must have freedom and well-being in order to pursue by my actions any of the purposes I want and intend to pursue."[80] Individuals lacking the conceptual wherewithal to claim rights can nonetheless be purposive agents. Being able to conceptualize the Principle of Generic Consistency is not the relevant similarity here; thus, the absence of such a capacity cannot be grounds for exile from the moral community. Reflective agents, if they are consistent, must hold that agents who are "preferentially autonomous" in Regan's sense— beings who act to satisfy preferences—also have rights to the preconditions for achieving their purposes. This class of beings is considerably larger than the subclass of reflective, rights-claiming agents. Preferentially autonomous beings need some minimal requirements in order to function, regardless of their level of intellectual sophistication. As Paul Taylor points out with regard to the sense of freedom relevant to this issue, *absence from constraint* is essential to nonhumans and humans alike: "[Absence of constraint] is a concept of freedom that is of central importance for every creature which has a good of its own to realize. For being free in this sense is being in a position to be able to preserve one's existence and further one's good, and being unfree in this sense is being unable to do these things."[81] Equally essential is life and the capacities that allow one to pursue that life when one is given a chance to do so: minimum "well-being." Following Gewirth's line of reasoning, it seems that agents as such, not just conceptually well-developed agents, should have the rights of freedom and well-being attributed to them.

Unfortunately, Gewirth is inconsistent on this very important point. Sometimes he writes as if agents must be highly reflective in order to be agents and to have rights attributed to them; at other times, he seems to deny this. His definition of 'agent' at the outset of his argument— "a being with purposes he or she wants to fulfill who has control over his or her actions and who knows the relevant proximate circumstances of those actions"—includes no reference to the ability to reflect abstractly on the preconditions of actions. Gewirth also pointedly argues that agents with very low-level abilities are nevertheless agents with full moral rights.[82] He repeats this in his later book, *Human Rights,* arguing that "minimal rationality" in the sense spelled out above is all that is required for agency and the rights to freedom and well-being.[83] All preferentially autonomous beings meet this requirement. A dog chasing a ball, picking it up, and presenting it wetly to the thrower wants to engage in the activity, knows what needs to be done, and can control the required movements, just like a small human child chasing a ball (the method of return is different, but the motive for participating does not seem to be!). However, in other passages in which agency is characterized, Gewirth interpolates the requirement that one be capable of reflecting on the preconditions of action and of claiming these preconditions as rights.[84] He puts this very strongly in *Human Rights:* "For a person to have human rights, then, is for him to be in a position to make morally justified stringent, effective demands on other persons that they not interfere with his having the necessary goods of action and that they also help him to attain these goods when he cannot do so by his own efforts."[85] Being "in a position" to make such demands requires a highly developed conceptual apparatus. But this interpolated requirement is omitted in numerous other passages.[86] The interpolation should never have been made in the first place. It is not entailed by any of Gewirth's other contentions, and, as we shall now see, it contradicts his claim that mentally deficient humans are as deserving of rights as reflective agents.

Very Young and Mentally Limited Humans

All consciously conative beings are goal directed; they have preferences or purposes that they want to have satisfied. This holds for very young and mentally limited humans just as much as it holds for the most intelligent of human agents. The intelligent agent must logically recognize, Gewirth argues, that those whom he calls "marginal agents" are individuals striving to survive just as she is, seeking shelter, food, drink, and companionship. As such, they are due full moral consideration. Purposiveness is the key similarity between these others and normal human adults; it justifies the attribution of rights to the former by the latter, *despite* the fact that the individuals compared differ greatly in their ability to fulfill their purposes.[87] However, their temporary or permanent inability to carry out their purposes without endangering themselves or, possibly, others, calls for limitations on their freedom. We do not act justly or respectfully if we dump babies, toddlers, and mentally incapacitated humans on the streets to fend for themselves. Lamentably, this continues to happen in my own country, the United States, where one-third of the homeless, many of them "deinstitutionalized," are estimated to be schizophrenic.[88] In California alone, thirty-five thousand severely mentally ill individuals were evicted from care facilities in the 1980s and left to their own devices.[89] Many, many children are homeless as well (from one thousand to five thousand in the city of Pittsburgh alone).[90] Instead of abandoning those unable to care for themselves, we ought to accord as much freedom as we can to them, nurturing the agency abilities they may have or could develop,[91] while protecting their own and our welfare interests. Our obligations to them increase if we have had any role in their existence or conditions.

Thus, according to Gewirth's view sentient conative beings who are not able to systematically achieve their purposes must have their actions limited at times, but the fact that they do not have a full right to freedom does *not* imply that they are less morally significant than normal human agents. So long as they have desires, even on a very basic level, the reflective agent will see that they are due the same moral consideration that she claims for herself. In fact, it is attribution of full moral status to them that leads agents to limit the freedom of very young or mentally limited humans: recognizing that they are not able to achieve many of their goals, we act to protect them from themselves even when they pose no threat to us. We do not withhold this right because we think they are less worthy of moral consideration than we are. Gewirth reasons that even human newborns, as far from agency as they are, are due this moral status: after all, they immediately display primitive desires and begin acquiring memories relevant to the development and satisfaction of preferences.[92] However, Gewirth is oddly blind to the implications of his own view for many human fetuses and nonhuman animals. Let us first examine his views on the moral status of humans before birth.

Human Fetuses

Gewirth accords reduced moral status to human fetuses because, according to him, (a) they are not physically separate from their mothers, (b) they do not even have the most primitive of purposes or desires, and (c) they have not begun to acquire memories.[93] Why accord any moral status to them at all, given his argument from agency? The fact that they are *potential* agents, and that fact alone, warrants some protection, he holds, but in the case of conflict between the desires of the mother and the existence of the fetus, the fetus automatically comes in second.[94] In my chapter 2, we have already seen that no plausible case for the moral relevance of potential has yet been made; we have also seen that extending protection to the fetus purely for the sake of the morally significant being the fetus *will become* translates into no moral status and precious little protection for the fetus. If those arguments were correct, humans before birth are due no moral consideration—if we agree with Gewirth's claims above.

But why should we? Claim a holds for all fetuses, but its relevance to their moral status is questionable (see below). With respect to fetuses past the midpoint of gestation, claims b and c have been called into question quite successfully by neurophysiologists and cognitive psychologists. In all fairness, some of this information was not known when Gewirth wrote his first book; however, to my knowledge he has not altered his views on this issue through the years. We have good reason to question the old assumption that newborns arrive like a mass of warm smooth wax, innocent of experience, desire, and belief. In fact, newborns are remarkably developed, showing signs of having acquired memories of sounds and perhaps even speech.[95] At least in the last several weeks of their gestation, experiences have occurred that result in some detectable preferences after birth (e.g., a preference to hear their mother's voice). None of this makes any sense if we assume that no desires or memories are present before babies take their first breaths. We know too that neural pathways sufficient for pain perception are present well before birth [96]—like REM sleep, a condition correlated with dreaming in us and present in the second-trimester fetus, this is also the case for all other mammals! Does Gewirth suppose that aversion to pain or unpleasant sensations also springs ex nihilo upon the point of birth?

It is true that opportunities for agency are limited in the womb, even for the full-term fetus: going shopping is clearly out. Aside from kicking, turning, gulping fluid at varying rates, and sucking upon one's thumb, one's goal-directed behavior is distinctly inhibited. In this respect, temporary residence inside the mother (Gewirth's first reason for denying full moral status to fetuses) is a damper on agency. However, this should not be a reason to deny full moral status to the fetus if it is not a reason to deny such status to conscious but machine-dependent patients. Gewirth has already made the case for conation, not full moral agency, as the relevant similarity between reflective agents and those with lesser capabilities. If the newborn's having "desires or purposes" is sufficient for full moral status, as Gewirth claims very plausibly, moral agents should probably attribute that status to fetuses in the last half of gestation (earlier, if evidence warrants it). It may be that sentience significantly precedes the development of preferences, but we simply do not know enough to claim such a thing. We ought to give fetuses the benefit of the doubt, as we generally should whenever there is a significant likelihood that a being might care about what happens to him or her.

It does not follow from what I have said that abortion is always wrong, let alone that it should never be legally permitted. Abortions before sentience is achieved would not wrong a zygote, embryo, or fetus, following the reasoning above. Abortions *after* the unborn human is capable of desires and preferences would clearly be justified if the woman is protecting her own physical or mental health by making this choice. Others may make this choice for her if she is unable to do so, as happened in the case of auto accident victim Nancy Klein: upon medical advice, her husband made the agonizing decision to terminate her pregnancy in the hope that it would allow her to emerge from a deep coma. She did in fact wake up, and has said that she agrees with her husband's decision.[97] Rape victims also cannot be *required* to carry a resulting pregnancy to term, even though the fetus is, of course, not responsible; no one is obligated to undergo months of psychological torture for the sake of an innocent. Sometimes circumstances make it impossible for such women to get early abortions. Witness the female Muslim victims of Serbian rapists in the former Yugoslavia, deliberately impregnated, often abandoned by their own families, hoping to get abortions before it is too late.[98] A woman may also choose abortion to protect a family that she already has, as is frequently the case in mainland China, where persecution and reduced food rations await many violators of the one-child policy.[99] Population Action International, a Washington, D.C.-based policy organization, reports that most third-world women seeking to terminate their pregnancies are already married and have other children whom the parents are barely able to support, but who cannot obtain effective contraceptives.[100] In general, it is permissible to defend oneself and others even at the cost of innocent life, regardless of the age of the victim. Moreover, if the fetus would be condemned to a wretched existence once born, abortion could very well be justified.

If sentient fetuses, like newborns, are granted full moral status, however, they ought not to be aborted for relatively trivial reasons. At the very least, doing so would be "indecent," as Judith Jarvis Thomson puts it.[101] (I doubt very much that girls or women seeking late abortions are motivated by less than extremely serious reasons.) Nor would it be justified to abort such a fetus for tissue or organs, even if such products could save the life of another. Basic moral rights holders are not spare-parts warehouses. (By contrast, an anencephalic fetus, possessed of merely a brain stem, would not be wronged by being killed for its organs, or even for purposes of basic medical research. These are not "handicapped children," as some people misguidedly think; they are flesh and blood automata who will die in any case soon after birth unless "extraordinary measures" are taken.)[102] When it *is* justified to abort a sentient fetus, it follows that we ought to inflict the minimum of suffering. The same, of course, holds for any other innocent whom one cannot avoid killing. It is far from clear that injection of saline solution into the amniotic sac, for example, causes no pain to a well-developed fetus. Moreover, if the D and E procedure (dilatation and evacuation) is used on a second-trimester fetus, and that fetus is sentient, death would be almost unimaginably horrible: the fetus is dismembered within the uterus, then removed piecemeal through the cervix.[103] Surely medical science could deliver a better death than this. Relatively few abortions are performed in affluent countries at a stage late enough for sentience to be a possibility.[104] Nonetheless, even one is too many if painless death could be achieved instead, assuming that such an abortion is justified in the first place.

Conative Nonhuman Animals

Gewirth believes that reflective agents must accord some moral standing to sentient nonhuman animals, but not full moral significance. In large part, this belief of his appears to be based on false empirical assumptions. Although he thinks that full moral standing must be extended to mentally incapacitated and newborn humans, on the grounds that they have desires and have some abilities relevant to agency, he denies that nonhumans are even close to exhibiting such qualities. He does assert, however, that the fact that they have feelings, just as we other animals do, requires us to treat them without "wanton cruelty."[105] We also ought not to kill them without very good cause. Still, like human fetuses in Gewirth's view, nonhuman animals may be killed if the interests of humans conflict with the nonhumans' continued existence.[106] Gewirth says nothing of the sort about conscious but severely mentally handicapped humans: we are never justified in turning *them* into pot roasts or vaccine testers, because they—unlike any nonhumans—are purposive proto-agents, despite their "lesser practical abilities" in comparison to normal adult human agents' abilities.[107] Gewirth reiterates this view in his later "Replies to My Critics." [108]

Gewirth cites no evidence to support his low opinion of nonhuman animal abilities. In fact, as we have seen, nonhuman animals (apart from the extremely young) often eclipse some humans in their mental development and their ability to achieve their goals. Even Peter Carruthers, who quite unlike Gewirth denies all moral standing to nonhuman animals, recognizes that this is the truth: "No doubt human babies, mental defectives, and senile old people may enjoy similar levels of mental activity to animals—frequently lower, in fact." [109] Christoph Anstötz, a professor of special education who works directly with mentally limited humans, points out that some of his charges cannot exceed the awareness level of several-weeks-old infants.[110] Evidence indicates that chimpanzees, gorillas, and orangutans are vastly more mentally complex than these human unfortunates, and a large number of other nonhuman mammals would also compare favorably to the humans in their abilities to conceive and satisfy goals. This is exactly what one would expect, given the fact of evolution; sentient nonhumans who could not satisfy their wants when faced with frequently changing circumstances would literally not be long for this world. The very young and mentally deficient of all species can only survive if capable adults protect them. If vulnerable humans who cannot satisfy their own desires are due full moral respect from reflective agents, on the grounds that *these humans resemble those agents in their capacity to have desires they want to have satisfied,*[111] then sentient, conative nonhuman animals are due the same respect.

Gewirth could accept this amendment to his view without doing any violence to his basic line of argument. It would be advantageous for him to do so, since it would bring his contention into line with the biological and ethological evidence. The only part of Gewirth's thinking that would be adversely affected by the admission that some nonhumans can be fully morally significant is a part that he would do well to abandon: a pervasive homocentric bias. As the title of his book, *Human Rights*, indicates, Gewirth is wedded to such a perspective. In all his writing, he takes himself to be defending the view that basic "generic" rights are *human*,[112] that "all humans are actual, prospective, or potential agents,"[113] that having rights is necessarily connected to being human,[114] and that "for human rights to be had one must only be human."[115]

When Gewirth's views are separated from the prejudice of homocentrism, what remains is a view remarkably like Tom Regan's in its conclusions. Indeed, on the face of it, Gewirth's corrected view goes even farther than Regan's. Regan argues that being a subject-of-a-life is sufficient for full moral considerability. As Regan defines 'subject-of-a-life,' it means "every agent": it includes "the ability to initiate action in pursuit of their desires and goals."[116] Beings with desires who are unable to carry out those desires would seem to be excluded. Gewirth includes them in the moral sphere because they have desires: it is this fact, rather than the abilities of agency itself, that justifies the attribution of rights to others. However, if we look more closely at Regan's characterizations of subjects-of-lives, the apparent difference between the two views disappears. Despite the agency-related formulation above, Regan also states that severely mentally deficient humans, who cannot satisfy even "basic needs and correlative desires," are subjects-of-lives.[117] This puzzle is resolved when one realizes that Regan has given us *another,* less restrictive characterization of his key moral notion: "A sufficient condition of being owed such duties [of justice] is that one have a welfare—that one be the experiencing subject of a life that fares well or ill for one as an individual—independently of whether one has a conception of what this is."[118] Very young and mentally limited humans *are* included in the moral sphere after all, and rightly so. According to Regan's "welfare criterion," one need not be an agent to be fully morally significant. His conclusion is not at odds with the (corrected) view of Gewirth.

According to that corrected view, reflective agents should accord any being capable of caring about what befalls him or her a prima facie right to life. Having desires, even if they are quite simple, that one consciously wishes to satisfy gives one a stake in the next moment's outcome. Even those who are so profoundly depressed that they desire neither life nor death retain the capacity to be more than neutral onlookers in life. It is, however, not always easy to identify a desiring, goal-seeking individual. As I have just argued, we cannot say with full confidence that five-month human fetuses qualify, although the neurophysiological evidence seems sufficient to warrant our giving them the benefit of the doubt. Do we really know enough to say which *nonhumans* are consciously purposive beings?

Much of what follows is speculative. However, we do appear to be empirically warranted in attributing consciously purposive behavior to mammals. Neurophysiological as well as behavioral data support this contention. The part of the human brain shared by all mammals, the limbic system, is related to the capacity to have emotions, including desires.[119] Dualists and materialists dispute the nature of the relationship, but in our own cases, at least, this physiological structure appears to be required for affective response. The hypothalamus, a structure shared by all vertebrates, is also part of this picture. In ways we literally cannot disentangle, the hypothalamus and limbic system are tightly correlated with our experiences of positive and negative emotions. The much abused laboratory rat will exhibit aversive or reward-seeking behavior, depending on which parts of these structures are stimulated by electrodes.[120] Other mammals react in similar ways. Not surprisingly, the experience of pleasure is linked to neural pathways in the hypothalamus and limbic system.[121] Beings with a stake in what happens to them in the next moment are necessarily capable of emotion: they affix positive values to their desired outcomes. A good case can be made, then, for including mammals with the relevant functioning brain states in the class of morally significant beings. Tom Regan's contention that mammals at least one year of age are *clear* cases of subjects-of-lives parallels what I have said, although I would pick an earlier age. (Regan's welfare criterion of being a subject-of-a-life also requires an earlier age, as just discussed.)

Are nonmammalian vertebrates then to be excluded from the realm of high moral significance? Fish, amphibians, and reptiles lack limbic systems, after all, and their behavior is not obviously emotional. On the other hand, each such animal has a hypothalamus, which we know to play a key role in emotional response and pain perception. Reptiles, moreover, appear to be motivated: they establish territory, fight, mate, and hunt for food. Indeed, the part of the human brain shared with all reptiles, the "reptilian brain" or "R-complex," is linked to these same basic drives.[122] Fish and amphibians act in similar ways. Do nonmammalian vertebrates feel anything like emotions when they satisfy their drives? Do they *care* about what is happening when they perform these survival-enhancing actions? We simply do not know.

Birds also pose a puzzle. Like us, these vertebrates have evolved from reptiles: we are on parallel tracks in a sense, with fish, amphibians, and reptiles as evolutionary precursors. We do not share a limbic system, but birds and humans both have hypothalamuses. Could some other system have evolved along parallel lines that would allow birds to experience emotions? They *behave* as if they have emotions such as anger, fear, and pleasurable anticipation (consider the racket ducks make when they paddle double-time toward a food-bearing human!). Animal husbandry experts are now beginning to speak about chicken *preferences*, as discussed earlier in chapter 4. We also have every reason to believe that birds (like all other vertebrates) can experience pain. They avoid painful stimuli as assiduously as we do. Additionally, ethological research suggests that they are relatively intelligent. Can an animal nonmechanically perform a series of actions resulting in her obtaining a meal without having *wanted* such an outcome? This is hard to imagine, but perhaps not impossible. Given the complex behavior avian species appear to exhibit, however, we are justified in giving them the benefit of the doubt. Since they may well be capable of experiencing desires, and they behave as if they do, we should err on the side of caution in our treatment of them.

We should also be cautious in our treatment of vertebrates less complex than mammals and birds. We cannot confidently say that they have desires that they wish to satisfy, so they are certainly not obvious cases of morally significant beings. Nonetheless, they very likely can experience pain, and we ought not to inflict such sensations upon them without very good reason. We also ought not to kill them for frivolous reasons, since they may, for all we know, take an active interest in continuing to live. Perhaps some invertebrates with central (albeit simple) nervous systems do as well. I join Albert Schweitzer and Bernard Rollin here in concluding that we should not kill without good reason.

Justification and Judgment

How good the reason must be depends, of course, on how morally significant the "killee" is. Our problem is that, in the case of sentient nonmammals, we do not know the answer to this question. It does seem clear, however, that if killing must be done and we have a choice of victims, we ought to spare clear cases of consciously conative beings. Following Gewirth's thinking, such beings should be accorded a prima facie right to life. Beings *more likely* to be consciously purposive than others, even if they are not clear cases, should also be spared if we have the option. Assuming that nutritious plants are nowhere in evidence, it is morally preferable for a human to kill and eat a fish than to slaughter and barbecue a chicken (let alone a calf, a monkey, or another human). It is also better to eat clams than fish, for the same reason. Please note that the criterion here is not intelligence: the issue is whether the being has the capacity *to care* about what happens to him or her. One does not have to be tremendously bright to prefer pecking corn to having your head chopped off.

This is not to say that intelligence is unrelated to the *loss* that death occasions for morally considerable beings. In some cases, a higher degree of intelligence will make death more of a tragedy for some beings than for others. I will have more to say about this later. At this point, however, despite the necessarily speculative nature of the foregoing discussion, we are entitled to conclude that many nonhumans should be accorded basic moral rights by reflective agents.

Nonconative or Insentient Beings or Systems

As we have seen, if there are sentient beings with no capacity for preferences of any kind, the Gewirthian line of argument I have been pursuing would not justify extending moral standing to them. The same would hold for living beings who have never had the capacity for consciousness (e.g., bacteria, viruses, plants) and nonliving entities (e.g., boulders) or systems (e.g., ponds, wilderness areas). Full persons—reflective agents—are obliged to extend moral status to beings who are consciously conative like themselves. If beings or systems of beings who cannot truly be described in this way are nevertheless morally considerable, it must be on other grounds.

As the title of my book indicates, my focus is on animals, human and nonhuman. I will not here undertake the additional, book-length task of evaluating the varieties of environmental ethics that have been proposed and vigorously debated over the last few years. I do, however, now want to address a position that is at least on the face of it similar to the view I have been defending: Paul Taylor's "biocentric ethic," according to which *being alive* is necessary and sufficient for maximum moral significance.

Paul Taylor has done an excellent job of defending biocentrism along lines that partially parallel the Gewirthian position. He argues that all living things have a "good of their own" and that "freedom" in the sense of "lack of constraint" is needed for each such being to flourish.[123] Moral agents, who recognize their own needs for freedom and well-being, can recognize decidedly nonconscious analogues in simple animals, plants, and microscopic life forms. Although Taylor prefers not to talk about extending moral rights to such beings—it is perfectly consistent and coherent to do so, Taylor holds, but we are apt to confuse these rights with the sorts of rights persons hold[124]—he believes all living things are equally morally significant. He does not defend his position in the way that Gewirth defends his, arguing instead, as Regan does, that his theory passes the tests of comprehensiveness, coherence, conceptual clarity, and consistency with what we know to be empirically true.[125] He is well aware that such a defense constitutes no proof.[126] Unfortunately, as we have seen in discussing Regan's similar type of justification, reasonable, informed, vividly aware people can disagree about such matters (as Regan and Taylor do, despite considerable common ground).

Perhaps we could argue instead, à la Gewirth, that the morally relevant similarity between ourselves and all other living beings is the struggle to survive as the sort of entity one is. If we believe we are justified in claiming the rights of freedom and well-being for ourselves, should the same not hold for all other living beings? Albert Schweitzer had something like such a justification in mind for his own biocentric outlook: "I am life which wills to live, and I exist in the midst of life which wills to live . . . Ethics thus consists in this, that I experience the necessity of practicing the same reverence for life toward all will-to-live, as toward my own."[127] Taylor calls every living entity a "teleological center of life."[128] Every one of us, from the brightest of humans to the humblest of protozoa, is "goal directed" in the sense that there is "a

constant tendency to protect and maintain the organism's existence."[129]
Of course, only some of us are consciously purposive. According to Taylor's view, a *conscious desire* to live as the kind of being one is turns out not to be necessary for moral considerability. All products of evolution, conscious and nonconscious, must function in order to continue: unlike rocks, we cannot simply *be*. It is this "activity" that warrants our moral concern, as he sees it.

Are certain machines, then, also morally considerable? Machines like heat-seeking missiles are also "teleological centers," as Taylor recognizes. They would be as morally significant as we are if being goal directed is the salient normative feature. Taylor argues that this is not the case, that such entities have no "goals" that can be specified independently of the purposes of their human creators, unlike living beings. As Gary Varner has pointed out, Taylor's counterargument is unsuccessful. One need make no reference to human purposes in describing the "goals" of artifacts.[130] I would add here that whether one has been *fashioned* to function in a given way or one has simply *come to be* that way has no bearing on one's moral status. Suppose each of us has been consciously designed by God to be as we are ("human artifacts" in a sense different from the usual one!). Would this disqualify us from the realm of moral considerability? Although Sartre, for example, has argued that such a happenstance would imply that we are unfree, incapable of making moral choices, and thus that morality itself would be meaningless,[131] he is notoriously mistaken on this head. We could be created as beings who must make choices in order to live—"condemned to be free," as Sartre himself notes![132] Presenting us with one of the more infamous inconsistencies in a philosophical work, Sartre, after declaring that the fact of human freedom rules out the existence of a divine creator, correctly points out at the end of his essay that "[Existentialism] declares, rather, that even if God existed that would make no difference from its point of view."[133] We must make choices regardless of our origins, no matter how much we might prefer to escape our "natures." Religious existentialists are in full agreement with the atheistic variety on this point. If one has moral status, it is because of the kind of being one is, not because of how one came to exist. By analogy, if we humans became able to create a consciously purposive android with desires and initiative, the fact that it has been designed could not justifiably be used to deny—or accord!—moral standing to it. Conversely, if heat-seeking missiles had simply come to be rather than having been designed by us, this fact could have no bearing on the question of their moral considerability. Taylor's view will not allow him to make such a distinction.[134] By the very nature of the case, this is a most unwelcome implication for biocentrism.

Most important of all, the feature that makes Gewirth's argument work is lost in the context of Taylor's position. Reflective agents (full persons) logically must advocate basic rights for themselves because, without the necessary conditions for achieving their purposes, they cannot have what *they regard* as good: they cannot have what they *want*. Universalizability and consistency require that other beings who also could not have what *they regard* as good without these preconditions must also be accorded such rights. Entities lacking desires of any kind simply do not come into the picture. Taylor at one stage argues that each living being has "a point of view," a "standpoint," in a sense in which an inanimate stone cannot: we can imagine ourselves in their positions.[135] But this is *our* point of view, not "theirs"! As nonconscious entities, *they can have no "standpoint."* Taylor, after all, is right not to attempt a Gewirth-type justification of his view. He is best off appealing to our rationality, our knowledge, and our vivid awareness of the world.[136] Even so, I suspect that not many observers with these qualifications will accept the implication he has tried unsuccessfully to avoid, that is, the inclusion of "teleological" nonconscious artifacts within the category of beings who are equally morally significant.

Taylor defends a version of environmental individualism; that is, he accords full moral standing to each unique living entity. Environmental holism,[137] which restricts moral considerability to systems of living entities, according secondary status at best to individuals, and environmental pluralism,[138] which accords moral status on different grounds to individuals and to ecological systems or species, are views utterly unsuited to a Gewirth-like justification. I will not here attempt to explore the different justifications that have been offered for such views. I want to point out, however, that the Gewirth-type view that I have been defending is *compatible* with the view that nonconscious entities or systems of entities may be morally considerable. In an article on environmental ethics I wrote several years ago, I briefly defended

Justification and Judgment

an aesthetically based position.[139] More recently, Eugene Hargrove has explicated and defended just such a view, holding that natural entities and nature itself exemplify aesthetic value.[140] Other things being equal, nonmoral value, of which aesthetic value is a subcategory, ought to be protected. This, I believe, should very significantly constrain the actions of moral agents. Nevertheless, I am convinced that this must not come at the cost of denying the basic rights of individuals who can care about what happens to them.

Immoralists, Amoralists, and Bigots: The Limitations and Value of the Appeal to Rationality

Lamentably, logic cannot guarantee that agents with normal mental capacities will respect the rights of others. Even if Gewirth has success-fully shown, as I have argued, that consistency requires the agent to hold that others have rights, I join Frank De Roose in being skeptical about the *behavior* of agents.[141] All will be well if the reflective agent who is not *already* inclined to extend rights to others is motivated to abide by the dictates of reason, but this is not always the case. An agent may be perfectly able to see that other purposive beings should have the rights that she claims for herself, yet refuse to accord such rights. Plato notwithstanding, one may knowingly do evil: *immoralists* can exist.

Gewirth himself tries to resolve this problem through reason alone. As the reader probably will have already anticipated, this sort of attempted solution is doomed to fail. Let us imagine an agent motivated only by self-interest. If, as David Hume has claimed, reason alone can compel no action, what else can motivate the agent to act morally, Gewirth asks. Why should the agent who realizes that she or he is *logically* committed to the rights of others *act* so as to respect those rights?[142] Gewirth's answer is that the agent "rationally must accept the PGC [the Principle of Generic Consistency] because it is entailed by another judgment he accepts."[143] He adds that: "by virtue of the PGC's being rationally jus-tified the rational agent is in fact motivated to accept it, since, being rational, he accepts what is rationally justified."[144] Well and good, but not all agents are *thoroughly* rational. Unfortunately, that is precisely the problem. An agent already wondering if she should do what reason dictates will be unmoved when told that reason dictates it! We are assuredly conative beings: we have to *want* to be rational.

Another group of problematic agents rejects reason at an even earlier point than the immoralists. Members of this distressing group, while fully believing that they are entitled to the rights of freedom and well-being, *refuse to universalize* beyond their own cases. These are the *amoralists,* so frequently discussed by moral theorists like R. M. Hare,[145] the folk whom Jean-Paul Sartre ferociously condemns as "scum."[146] They alone matter; everyone else is purely expendable. Turning from Sartre's refreshingly vitriolic denunciation to the language of pure reason, we see that Gewirth has devoted considerable dispassionate attention to this group. He succeeds in showing that amoralists do contradict themselves, contrary to Hare's and other critics' contentions.[147] Nevertheless, amoralists exist: logic does not overpower their lack of concern for others.

Bigots are also untroubled by logic. Unlike immoralists and amoralists, they do extend rights to *some* others as well as themselves, but deny them to less favored individuals. They "particularize" rather than "universalize" rights claims. Gewirth would be right in saying that there is no rational defense for such attitudes. Logic *ought* to be compelling to an agent, but it frequently is not.

The bad news (and not just for teachers of logic) is that normal agents very frequently reason illogically. Social scientists have conducted studies indicating that illogical, inconsistent processing of information is extremely common.[148] Plenty of others do not practice what reason preaches. In view of these depressing facts, how can one be surprised by the existence of amoralists, immoralists, and bigots?

Why does anyone take the moral point of view, recognizing the legitimate interests of others, rather than opting for immoralism or amoralism? Why does anyone take that point of view consistently, instead of practicing bigotry? Gewirth is correct in surmising that anyone fully committed to rationality will choose moral agency, and strive for fairness. However, those of us who have at some point taken the moral point of view were probably less moved by logic than by emotion. David Hume anticipated psychologists when he argued that "feeling" rather than reason alone leads us to make moral distinctions.[149] While we may doubt the mechanism he proposes for the operation of "the moral

Justification and Judgment

sense," it is difficult to deny that feeling has a central role in moral agency. Simply put, caring about others motivates our moral concern for them.[150] Psychologists who study moral development have amassed much evidence for the caring trait: it begins to appear not much later than one's concern for oneself does. Sympathy for sentient beings has its psychological basis in *empathy*. Unless one is able to imagine oneself in another's position, taking the individual's point of view—we are speaking here of beings who actually have points of view, unlike bacteria and plants—it is difficult to "feel for" that other. Jerome Kagan concludes on the basis of his cross-cultural research that empathy normally appears around the second year of life, and it immediately reveals itself in children's actions.[151] Lawrence Kohlberg also places the development of a caring orientation in childhood.[152] Alas, he takes the caring orientation to be a rather inferior one, thus earning the rightful criticism of psychologist Carol Gilligan. She has argued at length that Kohlberg's theory is biased against females and excessively narrow in its exclusive focus on justice in allegedly advanced moral thinking.[153]

Generally, the "caring" component of the moral point of view continues to be present as one reaches maturity, assuming that adverse circumstances have not throttled it. Adults of both sexes continue to exhibit empathetic and sympathetic motivation, as psychologists have documented[154] and ordinary moral experience plainly reveals. We do not refrain from torturing innocents simply because torture violates rights that we are logically compelled to respect: we refrain because we cannot bring ourselves to inflict undeserved agony. We do not need to study Gewirth in order to become convinced that we ought to help starving Somalians: seeing the dead, hopeless eyes of an emaciated mother trying to nurse a dying infant is quite sufficient to spur our action. Nor do we need to derive the Principle of Generic Consistency to realize that torturing a calf for a meal of veal parmesan is an abomination. In short, we can put ourselves in others' positions and realize that they live, suffer, and have desires as we do. As I discussed earlier, this ability of ours is a trait we seem to share with many nonhuman animals (see my chapter 1). By contrast, human immoralists, amoralists, and bigots have somehow been "arrested," as psychologists might say, in their moral development.

Why, then, rely upon reason in moral matters? Why not trust our "moral sentiments" instead? Conceptualizing the Principle of Generic

Consistency is not necessary for acceptance of the moral point of view, nor is it sufficient to budge individuals firmly committed to their own self-interest. Should we not try to reach the latter's emotions instead? Tears have probably won more moral battles than appeals to consistency.

This may well be so, but the sad fact is that reliance largely upon feelings has led to many a moral outrage. Bigots are filled with fervent, totally illogical conviction. We are all too familiar with examples of this in our treatment of other humans. When Nelson Mandela was finally released from prison by the white South African government, signaling the eventual end of apartheid, an enraged Afrikaner declared his implacable opposition to what was to come: "According to me, [black South Africans] are not human beings!"[155] So much for reasoning in accordance with the evidence; bigots brandishing their guns substitute frothing mouths for moral deliberation. Speaking of those who are *really* not human beings, one cannot help but notice that they are also often victims of our selective perception. I am reminded of a news report about a man who lost his arm in combat who was reduced to hunting doves one-handed. I woke up to this report on my clock radio one morning; since I thought I might have simply been having a nightmare, I wrote National Public Radio for a transcript.[156] For decades, this man and his other one-armed friends have participated in a Texas dove-hunting competition organized just for them. While simultaneously decrying the inability of others to empathize with his position—"There ain't nobody who's got two arms that, you know, that can say, 'I know how you feel.' They don't know how you feel"—he enthusiastically tries to blow doves to smithereens. Expectably, many doves are wounded ("winged") by the one-armed hunters, who seem completely unaware of how *they* might feel. A skeet competition is also held, but it does not occur to any of the participants to make this anything more than an adjunct part of the competition. Two-armed hunters—of humans as well as nonhumans!—also frequently fail to empathize with their intended prey, of course. Their emotional capacities are intact, but their minds do not tell them about the morally relevant similarities between themselves and their victims.

To very loosely paraphrase Immanuel Kant, reason without emotion may be impotent, but emotion without reason is blind. Without reason, although it can never guarantee morality, one has little chance of avoiding delusion, prejudice, and arbitrariness. Anyone to whom truth and fairness are important should acknowledge the immense value of logic. Properly understood, reason should inspire our passionate devotion.

Herein lies the great value of Gewirth's enterprise. He has shown that what many of us almost automatically *feel* to be true—that individuals who can care about what happens to them are ends in themselves, just as we are—can be *justified* in the most stringent way. Some ears will probably be deaf to the twin appeals of reason and emotion, but others can be reached. More than this we cannot ask.

A Final Appeal to Intuitions: How Can We Accept the Rights View?

Undeniably, however, it helps if the moral arguments presented to one do not clash in a fundamental way with one's strongly held convictions. One might object at this point that rather few human moral agents will find their emotions to be in tune with the Gewirth-based rights view that I have offered in these pages. Can moral agents really be expected to agree with reasoning that tells them that many other animals—mammals and possibly also birds—are no less morally significant than they themselves are? Unquestionably, many moral agents have the "gut conviction" that beings with "richer" experiential lives count for much more than those with simpler concerns. The "richness" in question is, they feel, surely related to intelligence. This is a deeply held, ingrained "intuition" for many, and the view I have been defending runs quite counter to it, despite the fact that it permits killing (as we shall soon see in detail) and is compatible with the view that not every individual with a prima facie right to life is equally harmed by death.

Undoubtedly, the Gewirth-based rights view does clash with some intuitions. Perfectionism dies hard, particularly when we see ourselves —full persons—as the standard of maximum moral significance. But there are other deeply ingrained "intuitions" that clash with perfectionism and cohere with the rights view. Do we not also have the "gut conviction" that young children—quite independently of the fact that they could one day be moral agents!—and mentally disabled but nonetheless consciously purposive people are fully morally significant, and should not be sacrificed for our benefit? Granted, the folks I have termed "normalists," along with their neo-Nazi cousins, do not share this conviction, but the rest of us feel otherwise. Are we not revolted by the notion of imprisoning and experimenting upon such humans, no matter how many moral agents may benefit from such machinations? We are still less inclined to accept the exploitation of less intelligent humans for purposes of food, sport, or raiment. The Gewirth-based view tells us *why* this "gut feeling" of ours is correct, *without* the rationally indefensible baggage of homocentrism and speciesism. It also coheres with the conviction that unwanted suffering or death, whether it be visited upon a dog, a child, or Albert Einstein, is intrinsically *bad*, to be justified, if at all, in the most stringent manner. Empathy quite naturally extends to any innocent apparently in pain or resisting death, regardless of species: this basic part of our emotional makeup is also fully compatible with Gewirth's view—and contrary to our perfectionistic inclinations.

Not surprisingly, our emotions pull us in incompatible directions. Our entrenched "intuitions" do not all cohere. I am arguing that many of them are actually in better accord with the position I have been defending than with the view that sentient, conative mentally limited humans count relatively little or not at all in comparison to moral agents. If all that I have argued in this book holds water, reason should lead us to reject the latter view. Is it not also true to say that almost all of us *want* to reject that view?

RESPECTING BASIC MORAL RIGHTS: OBLIGATIONS AND CONFLICTS

Now let us finally turn to the implications of the rights view I have defended. As Bernard Rollin has argued, biological parameters—telos—must be respected if any individual is to receive respectful treatment. We do chimpanzees no favors if we dress them up and make them television costars. Biology and ethology are needed to enlighten us about the needs and interests of animals of all species, although this research should be conducted in a manner consistent with the rights of its subjects, supposing they are capable of caring about what befalls them.

Suppose we do know enough about the capabilities and needs of these nonhuman animals to accord them appropriate treatment. What obligations would we have to them? A few general points need to be made before proceeding to specifics. As argued earlier, mammals (and birds, giving them the benefit of the doubt) should at the very least be accorded a prima facie right to life by reflective moral agents. Depending upon their abilities and circumstances, they should also be accorded the prima facie right to freedom. Any being capable of experiencing pain, including fish, amphibians, and reptiles, should also not be subjected to that experience at our hands without the best of reasons, although—given our current state of knowledge about their mentality—the Gewirth-based argument cannot be used to show that they have a moral right to life. Despite my conviction that we ought not to kill these simpler animals when this can be avoided, the discussion that follows will be focused on mammals and birds.

Domesticated Animals

According to the Gewirth-based rights view, beings with desires they want to satisfy should be regarded as ends in themselves regardless of their origins. It does not follow from this, however, that moral agents would have exactly the same moral obligations to each of them. Baird Callicott, for one, seems to think that equal moral consideration and significance must translate into equal obligations,[157] a position he rightly rejects, but this is not the case. Duties to morally significant beings may be acquired as well as unacquired. Tom Regan has developed this distinction, made by John Rawls.[158] (See my chapter 3 discussion of this issue in connection with the "kinship" argument for speciesism.) We have the unacquired duty not to interfere with the freedom or well-being of others, unless they pose a threat to us. We have additional, acquired duties to beings whose existence or living conditions have resulted from our choices. For example, we have obligations to our children that we do not have to children under others' care, even though all the children are equally morally significant. By the same token, we humans have special responsibilities to the nonhuman animals our species has domesticated, even though they have no higher moral status than undomesticated consciously purposive nonhumans. Although some have argued that these nonhuman animals originally "domesticated themselves" by deliberately seeking out human alliances,[159] this alleged fact hardly absolves us from responsibility. The characteristics of countless nonhumans born since the initial stage of domestication have been shaped by human choices. For example, turkeys bred for abundant breast meat can no longer fly, unlike their "scrawny" wild cousins; Chihuahuas bear little resemblance to ancestral wolves; and hairless, whiskerless "Sphynx" cats could have no wild counterparts. Even if we have not personally chosen to domesticate members of other species by deliberately breeding them for certain characteristics we find to be desirable, we nonetheless participate in the process of domestication by accepting the benefits of such arrangements. What ought we to do about all the mammals and birds we have used for food, products, experimentation, testing, work, recreation, and companionship?

Simply setting formerly exploited animals free, without regard for their own well-being and the devastating effects such actions would have on other living creatures and whole ecosystems, would be unconscionable. No right is absolute, and this assuredly includes the right to freedom. As I argued earlier, it is grossly immoral to throw a young child or mental patient out on the streets, particularly in the name of "freedom" and "autonomy." The same holds for most domesticated nonhuman animals. Some could readapt to the wild, perhaps, but we cannot contemplate releasing billions. We would be abrogating the responsibilities to them that we have acquired, not to mention endangering ourselves and other animals through ecological devastation, if we were to do so. No rights view worth the name could sanction such idiocy.

If we are convinced that they have basic moral rights, however, then we ought to stop supporting exploitation of these animals. If more and more individuals come to this conclusion, these practices would gradually die. Given present circumstances, we should do our best for those nonhuman animals who are currently suffering and being killed. People in charge of these animals, as well as people at large, need to be engaged in reflection about the effects of their actions as well as of their passivity. In the end, vivid information and rational persuasion does far more good than any alternative course of action.

I do not want to give the impression that I support the eventual demise of all practices involving domesticated nonhuman animals. It is possible, even highly desirable, to enjoy a mutually beneficial, respectful relationship with another animal. Companion animals can benefit at least as much as the human animals who are lucky enough to offer them homes (often, the nonhuman is the one who does the choosing). They are as major a responsibility as any other live-in relative, however, even though we do not have to send them to college. Those not willing to accept the responsibility of adding a full-fledged member to the family should get pet rocks or teddy bears instead. Bernard Rollin has written with deadly accuracy about the sundry ways in which humans violate the telos of "pets,"[160] from routine mutilation of ears and tails to casual abandonment when the humans find it "convenient." None of this is compatible with the Gewirth-based rights view. We also behave irresponsibly if we condemn companion animals and their offspring to endless rounds of reproduction. I once had a discussion with an acquaintance who had just been given two kittens by a neighbor. My acquaintance had just lost his last cat, an adolescent in the throes of the reproductive urge who had been run over by a car. He noted that one of the kittens "would have to go" because both were males, and he did not want to have them constantly fighting while they were around him. He was horrified when I urged him to neuter both cats. Pointing to a picture of *Star Trek*'s Mr. Spock tacked to a bulletin board in my office, he said he believed along with Spock that we should "not interfere" with other life forms. The truth is, of course, that we have *already* interfered by participating in the process of domestication. These animals are not in the wild, participating in the cycle of ecological continuation (upon which countless lives depend) when they fight over mates, suffer, and die; they live in a world of concrete and wheels, dependent upon the humans who have bred their kind. That fact, as well as our willingness to take them in, results in acquired duties on our part.[161] Given this context, deliberately exposing them and their offspring to cars, abandoning them by roadsides and streets, and dumping them in "euthanasia" mills is hardly tantamount to noninterference! It is as deeply irresponsible as allowing one's barely pubescent children to breed other children: "George, we mustn't interfere with little Hortense and her boyfriend! We must respect their autonomy!"

It is also possible to have mutually beneficial relationships with other animals whose milk or eggs we use for food.[162] I know a number of people living on small "no kill" farms who treat their chickens, cows, and goats with respect and care, sheltering them from predation and disease in return for consuming their products. These farms bear no resemblance to large, efficient operations where nonhumans are regarded as living milk faucets or egg factories, of course, and they also differ markedly from the farms that used to be traditional in Western countries. My grandmother had chickens, and she killed them herself (I can never forget the eye-popping prelude to every Sunday's chicken dinner). The small farms I am talking about are closer to some third-world agricultural units in largely lacto-vegetarian countries like India. Gary Varner has argued that, *by the standards of Western "efficiency,"* it is not possible to provide milk (and eggs) for large-scale commercial consumption without occasioning extra deaths to the nonhumans. He holds that it might be possible to avoid this consequence under sustainable agriculture (in third-world conditions, he observes, it can be done).[163] If the relationships between ourselves and these animals can be truly mutually beneficial and respectfully conducted, there can be no objection to it.

This is fortunate, particularly in those parts of the world where milk or eggs play leading roles in human nutrition. Where legumes, vegetables, grains, and fruits are plentiful and a vitamin B_{12} source is available[164] (as well as a vitamin D dietary source if brief exposure to sunlight on a fairly regular basis is not possible), humans[165] can thrive on strictly vegetarian (vegan) diets, according to mainstream nutritional experts (e.g., the American Dietetic Association[166] and the highly regarded nonvegetarian nutritionist Johanna Dwyer).[167] If all of these conditions are not met, or an individual is so unfortunate as to be allergic to most plant foods, milk or eggs save human lives. Nonhuman animals need not suffer and die for us to obtain these products from them.[168]

However, there can be no objection whatever to eating these animals after they have lived well and died natural deaths, provided that consumption is limited to amounts compatible with health. I could not easily do this myself, anymore than I would relish serving up my dear dead granny, but clearly no rights are violated by such a practice. If reason were on the side of making meals of the dead (assuming no disease would be transmitted, of course), emotions could be adjusted. In Robert Heinlein's *Stranger in a Strange Land,* the sipping of broth made from Michael Valentine Smith is an act of humorous homage.[169] Others who already love the taste of, for instance, pork, as I once did before I found

Justification and Judgment

I could no longer look such a dinner in the face, would find it easier to contemplate eating formerly happy, naturally dead animals. If we did decide to eat meat under such circumstances, perhaps we could still find a place for the marvelous, unparalleled domestic pig on a "no kill" farm. A pig living the good life on a farm—I have met many, although the majority of pigs in the United States these days are subjected to the living hell of a total confinement system[170]—is a delight. Iowa State philosopher Gary Comstock knows whereof he speaks when he discusses pigs. Apart from the fact that he lives in a state where the porcine species looms large, he has family intimately involved in raising pigs. He observes that: "Pigs are intelligent, affectionate, and social animals. The only things they seem to love more than having their stomachs and ears rubbed is lying next to their neighbors after having run playfully in circles around them, squealing and barking all the while."[171] Those who know them best, like Dr. David Fraser of the Centre for Food and Animal Research in Ottawa, an acquaintance of mine, have developed a warm regard for them. Fraser has even been inspired to write several poems featuring them, which he regularly recites in their presence, such as "Porkyr! Porkyr!" (sample line: "Did He who made the rose make thee?"). Pigs can lay no eggs and their milk is not prized (except by piglets), but those whose religions and psychological inclinations allow them to eat naturally deceased porkers are welcome to do so, as far as the rights view is concerned.

However, given current planetary resources and the excess numbers of humans now existing and in need of food (see my discussion of the food crisis in chapter 4), we should be eating lower on the food chain rather than continuing to breed large numbers of porcine "protein factories in reverse."[172] (In using such language, I do not mean to suggest that the morally significant beings under discussion are mere machines. No doubt we humans are also "protein factories in reverse!") Pigs are not the most inefficient converters of protein—cattle raised for their flesh have that distinction—but, still, only 12 percent of the feed protein given to them is converted to animal protein (this is the figure for the entire animal; the figure for edible protein would be smaller). Cow milk and hen eggs are a better protein "bargain," but even in those cases, given *current* feeding practices, only 22 percent and 23 percent returns, respectively, can be expected.[173] The figure would be vastly different with respect to cows if they got most of their food in pastures, but one must take care not to devastate the land by grazing large numbers of them. As discussed in the previous chapter, if Brown University researchers are correct, there are already too many of us: Assuming that food could be distributed equally, 5.5 billion humans would be adequately fed, they estimate, but only if meat production is forgone! However, if we do the ecologically and morally responsible thing and reduce our numbers, there could be no moral objection to mutually beneficial, respectful relationships between human animals and some domesticated animals who are eaten after their natural deaths.

Wild Animals

As Tom Regan contends, wild animals with "preference autonomy" are due our respectful nonintervention,[174] unless we acquire duties to them because of other actions we have taken or they pose a threat to us. According to the rights view, it is as wrong to tear an ape, tiger, gazelle, dolphin, and so on, from her home for transportation to a zoo or "recreation" park (let alone a research lab) as it would be to capture and display another human. Once the animals have been captured and bred in captivity, however, supposing that they are able to breed, the duties to them that we have acquired as a result of the wrong we have done require us to behave with careful deliberation. All of them may not be able to readapt to the wild; captive-born animals are especially at risk. It is even possible that some may have come to prefer their new location. How can we try to redress the harm we have done?

Consider the case of Lucy, the signing chimpanzee I mentioned earlier in this book. Born in captivity, Lucy was one of the first chimpanzees to be included in the American Sign Language experiments. She was brought up like a child in a human family (the Temerlins) from the very day of her birth.[175] According to the Temerlins, Lucy became very close to them, and they to her. Alas, by age ten, she was too big and powerful for comfort: she began doing inadvertent damage to the furnishings. After much anguished deliberation, the Temerlins decided it would be best if Lucy were released in Africa to live a "free" life. The trouble was that Africa was as foreign to Lucy as it would be to any ten-year-old who had never been outside Oklahoma. Temerlin last saw her just before her departure, after a separation of some time. He reports that she was wildly happy to see him; he left her with sadness as well as hope. Jane Goodall tells the story of what happened next.[176] In Africa, volunteers fluent in sign language did their best to prepare Lucy for release. She was kept in a large enclosed area at first, with two other (wild) chimpanzees. Horrified by her strange companions and her surroundings, Lucy repeatedly signed "Please help. Lucy wants out. Please help." Sometime after finally being released, Lucy's dead body was discovered—missing her hands and feet. It seems that human poachers had killed another human, albeit in a chimpanzee body.

Koko the gorilla, whom I have mentioned several times in earlier chapters, was also born into captivity—in a zoo—but soon left, like Lucy, to become part of a sign language experiment. She too lived with humans who came to love her. Unlike Lucy, however, Koko has remained with her human best friend, Francine "Penny" Patterson. When the fully grown Koko tore a sink out of a wall (blaming Patterson's 100 lb. assistant by signing "Kate there bad"), Patterson simply reinforced the trailer.[177] Koko has been joined by two male gorillas and her cat Smoky (her first, named All Ball by Koko, was killed in traffic; Koko still recognizes and apparently grieves over All Ball's picture).[178] Quarters are certainly cramped, and nearby traffic disturbs the apes, so Patterson is trying to raise enough money to buy land for a gorilla reserve in Hawaii. She has no intention of abandoning her charges to a "free" life there, however: she will move with them.

Now, according to the rights view, neither Koko nor Lucy should have been born in captivity. However, as a result of their interactions with humans, their well-being came to differ in key respects from the well-being of wild gorillas. Each seemed to be genuinely satisfied with their human "families," enjoying lives full of stimulation. Freedom is not simply the lack of physical restraint: it is having the opportunity to pursue your own goals. How can those goals include a life one has never known, requiring survival skills one has never learned? It seems to me that Penny Patterson's reserve plan is more respectful of Koko than the deliberate separation of Lucy from her people.

The twenty-one-year-old Sugarloaf Dolphin Sanctuary in the Florida Keys provides what appears to be a very ethical approach to the prob-

Justification and Judgment

lem of captive wild animals.[179] The sanctuary is intended to offer captive dolphins a choice: return to the sea or stay in the company of humans. One dolphin lives there: she has chosen to stay, although she can easily swim away whenever she likes. Lloyd Good, owner of the sanctuary, has offered homes to dolphins from closing "recreation" parks like Ocean World and to dolphins trained for war exercises by the navy (fortunately for those dolphins, they have been "decommissioned"). If the plan is well executed—and if the closing Ocean World decides not to accept more lucrative offers for the dolphins from "amusement" parks overseas—Sugarloaf Sanctuary will be a model for responsible human action in this area.

Nonhuman animals whose lives have *not* already been disrupted by us should be permitted to run their own lives. Domesticated nonhuman animals and many captive wild animals need our protection to survive otherwise hostile environments; wild animals live in habitats to which their species have adapted over vast stretches of time. They are far better able to realize their purposes if they and their habitats are unmolested by humans. The lives they lead are hardly free from suffering and early death, but these are inextricable parts of lives resulting from morally neutral evolutionary processes. The well-being and freedom of predators require the killing of others. Even if, contrary to fact, they were able to decide that morally they ought not to kill, any such decision would be suicidal. Should human moral agents try to protect the freedom and well-being of the preferentially autonomous prey? We certainly should try to do that in *our* environments, where wild predators are misplaced, relocating them if this is possible. (As Sapontzis has argued, we should also prevent our well-fed companion animals from helping themselves to other nonthreatening creatures; there are other ways to provide stimulating environments for them.) [180] But any attempt on the part of moral agents to eliminate predation in the wild would not only violate the basic moral rights of those predators; it would lead to the kind of environmental devastation that would cause far more loss of life and misery than it could prevent. Steve Sapontzis has argued that almost all predation by nonhumans is, as a matter of practical fact, such that our attempts to prevent it would *add* to the sum of suffering in the world.[181] Moreover, *freedom, well-being in the broadest sense* (set by biological parameters), and *lives*, not just suffering, are at stake. Baird Callicott correctly points out that the prey as well as the predators would ultimately be destroyed by such meddling, constituting an "ecological nightmare." He uses this as a refutation of Peter Singer's utilitarian animal liberation view and Regan's rights theory, contending that both imply that we should pull out all the stops to prevent predation.[182] On the contrary, we can have no obligation to create such horrific consequences. We would violate far more individuals' rights by wholesale global "rescue" operations than we would safeguard.

Plainly, however, the lives of wild creatures and our own often intersect. We continue to build our own lives in what had been their habitats, and this inevitably leads to conflicts. Our typical solutions have given little significant weight to any interests apart from our own. Consider the case of the deer in Fox Chapel, a wealthy suburb of Pittsburgh, Pennsylvania. Up until recently, hunting has not been allowed in this residential, semiwooded area, but many residents have become very upset by growing numbers of deer grazing in their yards: as a local newspaper report explains, "[t]here is an outcry from residents whose landscaping has been destroyed." [183] Relocation of the deer is not an option, because other counties also have more deer than they prefer. Despite the protests of residents who are appalled by killing as a solution to deer-devastated rosebushes, the county has allowed bow hunters to "cull" the deer. Since the deer are often unafraid of humans, they are easy to target: 120 died by the arrow during the fall and winter of 1993–94.[184] I add here that bow hunting cannot be regarded as "humane extermination." In Texas, studies indicate that only half of all deer hit by arrows are actually "retrieved" by bow hunters. The rate of crippling and septic infection among unrecovered deer is high. Deer who *are* retrieved slowly bleed to death, apparently in great pain.[185] Protesters have urged consideration of deer contraception techniques, pointing out that successful trials have been done with other deer populations. This idea has been repeatedly rejected for Fox Chapel. Why? It is "unproven!" [186] This claim is made despite the fact that ungulate contraception has been actively researched for over twenty years and has been developed to a field-tested noninvasive, effective, reversible form, with no observable adverse side effects.[187] Heaven forbid that one should even try such a technique, when bows and arrows could do the job instead! One of my Penn State philosophical colleagues, Priscilla Cohn, lives in a similar suburb near Philadelphia where the same decision has been reached. (It will be done a little differently there. Deer, never hunted before and semitame, will be enticed to clearings where food is set out, then shot by hunters hiding nearby.) On behalf of a local animal rights organization, Dr. Cohn has offered to foot the bill for an alternative: immunocontraception. Despite her group's written agreement to pay the $20,000 needed, she cannot even get authorities to return her calls. Need I say that we would behave a bit differently if feral humans were tearing up our rhododendrons?

I hasten to add that I would only support resorting to contraceptives in *mixed* human/semiwild nonhuman animal communities, and then only if no better alternative is available that respects their lives, for instance, fencing in one's property or employing benign repellents, using deer-warning devices on one's automobile or constructing deer underpasses, or relocation (although this can be extremely traumatic). We should go to whatever lengths we would consider appropriate to prevent damage and danger from humans with whom we cannot reason. Moreover, we have acquired some duties to these nonhumans whose habitats we have invaded and largely destroyed. We are, after all, the original offenders. Since we have already interfered, the very least we should do is minimize the harm we have caused. As Paul Taylor has argued, "restitution" is called for after we have harmed individuals by our efforts to promote our basic and nontrivial interests,[188] not wholesale slaughter.

This brings us to the topic of sport hunting, an activity that bears no resemblance to restitution. In the United States alone, over two hundred million nonhuman animals are killed every year by hunters, not including illegal kills or animals shot in confinement on game ranches.[189] Even those who deny that nonhuman animals can have basic rights must be troubled by the fact that humans are injured, maimed, or killed in hunting accidents every year. I have no total figures on the number of humans inadvertently hurt or killed by hunters, but it is more than a few. The Pennsylvania Game Commission has reported that from 1988 through 1992, 126 people, on average, were shot *each season* in Pennsylvania by bullets or arrows, eight of them mortally.[190] In my semirural county, we started the 1993 hunting season in typical fashion, with a mother of four, out hunting with her husband and young children, being fatally shot by an accidentally discharged rifle.[191] Often, the victims have no connection to hunting. One such case in Maine received national atten-tion. In 1988, Karen Wood was killed near her house while hanging the family laundry on the line in her backyard—a hunter mistook her white mittens for the flash of a white-tail deer's rump. After the accident, mail in the local paper ran solidly against the *victim*, who was survived by a husband and year-old twins. Why didn't she stay inside during hunt-ing season? Why wasn't she wearing hunter orange? Incidentally, the hunter was found innocent of manslaughter, although he did lose his right to hunt for five years for shooting too close to a residence.[192] Now, there is a blood-curdling punishment sure to discourage future hunter carelessness!

Hunters frequently justify their "sport" by citing benefits for the prey and the environment. The prey, allegedly, are kept from becoming too numerous for their food supplies to support. A spokesman for a hunters' "educational" group put it this way: "The main thing they've got to understand is the hunter is the animals' best friend. He wants them to be there year after year. It's our job to keep our animals healthy and keep them for a next generation."[193]

Normally, anyone who claims that killing is an act of friendship toward his victims, intended to ensure the health and future existence of his pals, would be regarded as just a bit confused. Despite the fine sound-ing appeal to friendship, this hunter has no sense whatever of the prey as *individuals:* the living targets he wants to see running about in the future cannot be the same ones who now die by bullet or arrow. None-theless, hunters would no doubt reply, those who are killed *are* benefited as individuals: surely a quick, clean death is preferable to agonizingly slow starvation! Unfortunately, the hunter-as-mercy-killer scenario is based on false assumptions. As Robert Loftin (a philosopher who by no means rejects sport hunting) has documented, various scientific studies have shown that death at the hand of the hunter is seldom "clean" and frequently prolonged. Crippling cannot be avoided by even the most conscientious of hunters.[194] Even if it could be shown that the hunted animal would otherwise starve, a fact one cannot know, it is far from clear that this fate would be more agonizing. Indeed, the claim that deer, for example, would starve if they were not hunted is itself questionable. Bruce Larson, professor of silviculture at the Yale Forestry School, has conceded that "undernourishment" is a much more accurate description than "starvation."[195] Moreover, allegedly protecting the animals themselves and the environment from their "overpopulation" cannot justify the overwhelming numbers killed, because most hunted species (birds) would not overpopulate if left alone by us.[196]

This is not to say that overpopulation of herbivores such as deer cannot occur, at least temporarily, particularly in areas where habitat has been compromised and natural predators have been removed by humans (as has happened in Pennsylvania, second only to the much larger Texas in the number of hunting licenses sold every year—9 percent of Pennsylvanians are sport hunters).[197] Rather than reintroduce these predators, game commissions actually manipulate conditions so that there will be *more* such animals to kill, further despoiling the environment.[198] In belated recognition of this fact, the Pennsylvania Game Commission has recently moved to permit hunters to kill more female deer. With "best friends" like these, wild animals need no enemies! No, sport hunting is hardly the way to make amends for the damage that we ourselves have caused.[199] It is thoroughly incompatible with the rights view.

I by no means pretend to have all the answers about appropriate treatment of consciously goal-seeking nonhuman animals, supposing, as I do, that they are fully morally significant. However, it does seem clear that our obligations depend in large part on what we have already done or reaped the benefits from in the past. Domestic and wild nonhuman animals with desires they want to satisfy do not differ in their moral standing, but they are not due the same *treatment* from us. Just as we must do when we assess our actions or inactions with respect to other humans, we must ask ourselves if we have acquired duties beyond the fundamental obligation of noninterference. We also need a sound reservoir of empirical information to hand, about the telos of individuals as well as about the ecological consequences various actions of ours would have. Then we might have a better chance of doing the right thing from time to time.

"The right thing" will sometimes require causing death. The rights view is fully compatible with the taking of life under the appropriate circumstances, as we shall now go on to see.

Justification and Judgment

Killing Is Sometimes Justified

The rights to freedom and well-being presuppose a right to life that moral agents are obligated to respect. However, it does not follow from this that killing such a being is always wrong. When we euthanize a companion animal whose suffering can only be alleviated by death, we demonstrate far more respect and compassion for that companion than we would by inaction. The same would hold for a wild animal hit by a car, in agony from mortal wounds. "Mercy killing" is fully justified in such circumstances, and I would go so far as to say it is obligatory when we have assumed responsibility for such an animal. Mortally ill humans whose suffering cannot be eased who clearly want to die should also be granted that wish. Of course, we must not take such actions lightly, lest we create circumstances favorable to unjustified killing. The same attitude of caution should extend to our treatment of suffering nonhumans. "Euthanasia" should be what the word originally means: a "good death" given out of respect and concern, not a matter of convenience ("The damn cat keeps clawing the furniture") or the result of irresponsibility ("The bitch keeps getting pregnant!").

Killing is also sometimes justified when death does *not* benefit the subject. As noted many times before, rights are prima facie, not absolute. Unless one is a strict pacifist, one must acknowledge that it is sometimes morally permissible to kill someone who has the right to life, even when that individual intends us no harm. This holds for our dealings with our own kind, too. One is just as morally justified in killing an insane human brandishing a knife who mistakes one's head for a cantaloupe as one is in killing a rabid dog lunging at one's throat. Similarly, if a homicidal maniac intending mass murder can only be stopped by killing the innocent youngster she is using as a shield, it is permissible to kill the innocent, whether he be a human or a puppy.

But we must not forget that the killing of an innocent threat or shield with a prima facie right to life is permissible only if no feasible alternative course of action can be taken by the moral agent. If the only alternative to killing in such a situation is our own or another's (e.g., one's spouse's or child's) death, endangerment, or risk of severe injury, we are justified in killing. Still, we should not kill the insane attacker, be he human or canine, if instead he can be trapped without great risk, nor

Justification and Judgment

should we cause hostages to die if we can secure their release without endangering other innocents. Moral agents who reflect on these matters generally agree about the necessity of seeking alternatives when humans are involved, but are frequently far less concerned when nonhuman animals are the potential victims. If these animals do have a prima facie right to life, then we should be equally concerned to seek alternatives when they threaten us or "shield" another threat.

We are also justified, it seems, in *allowing* some rights holders to die, if not doing so would threaten our own lives or the lives of those for whom we are responsible. If we are luckless enough to live in a war-ravaged country, possessed of barely enough resources to sustain our small family until the probable date of the next cease-fire, when we can search for more victuals, we may have to refuse twenty starving neighbors' requests to share. If we need to build a shelter and plant a garden in order to sustain ourselves, we should do so, even though we are dooming the nonhumans who formerly lived in that area and now have nowhere to go. Sadly, we may be in competition for resources that cannot sustain all of us. All conative beings will struggle for life, and they can receive no moral censure if some must be allowed to die as the price of that struggle. As Paul Taylor says, such conflicts arising from competing claims cannot be avoided, although we should try to minimize them.[200]

We may very well also be justified in *killing* if we are trapped in a *scarcity of resources* situation.[201] In such a situation, humans or nonhumans who seek our food or water will compromise our survival at the very least, since supplies are not abundant; if we have no other way to stop them, we must kill if we and those who depend on us are to live. They too would be justified in seeking the same end. We are supposing, then, that individuals are confined to an area in which the total food or other resources available are insufficient. If there is not enough to go around for everyone to make it, *those involved have the right to influence the odds in their favor*. As Taylor puts it, why, given such an unavoidable conflict, should anyone assume that another's interests must be *more* morally important than his or her own?[202] (Only moral agents can see the conflict in this way, although all will strive for survival.) Those who intentionally allow others' interests to outweigh their own are either saints or passionately attached to those others, but they cannot be morally *required* to sacrifice themselves.

Justification and Judgment

It might be replied to this that since each of the individuals trapped in such a conflict are, by hypothesis, *equally* morally significant, strict justice requires some such procedure as drawing lots (those who lack the ability to participate in such a plan would have lots drawn for them). This is not the same as automatically subordinating one's interests to someone else's, since everyone would face the same odds. If a procedure of this kind is followed and you are the loser, acquiescing to your death is not an admission that others' interests are *more* important than one's own, it might be argued: it is an acknowledgment that their interests are *no less* important than your own. However, although I have argued this way in the past,[203] I am no longer convinced that this reasoning is correct. Killing an innocent threat (e.g., a deranged human who mistakes you for Satan) instead of being killed oneself would be unjustified given such a view—unless one has had the time to flip a coin and has luckily won the toss! By the same token, it would be immoral to hold on to your small amount of food *instead* of allowing it to be a lottery prize and starving if you do not draw the winning number. This conclusion is, it seems to me, at odds with morality rather than in accordance with it. Moral codes are action guides, as Gewirth has shown, anchored in the conditions we all require to fulfill our purposes. If our purposes are in grievous, inevitable conflict, we agents each have the moral right to protect ourselves as best we can. To substitute chance for action is to forget what a moral code is all about.[204] Although we are not, of course, morally required to fight for our own lives when they are in conflict with those of others, I cannot see how we could be obligated to stand aside while "fate" determines the outcome. Moreover, we *are* required to protect the lives of those we love or for whom we are responsible, when we can do so: our actions and our closeness have led to new, acquired duties which we cannot leave to anyone else. Leaving *their* lives to chance would be unconscionable. Of course, this applies to everyone alike.

Now, one way to survive given a scarcity of *food* resources is to kill *and eat* one of your competitors. In fact, it may be the only way to survive, if you are trapped in an environment too inhospitable to cultivate an adequate amount and variety of plants or to provide food for domestic nonhuman animals whose milk or eggs could sustain you or your family.[205] Wild nonhuman animals are normally in such straits: predators' lives are in direct conflict with the lives of the animals they prey upon. It is not possible for all to survive, given the resources available to them. Even if the predators all die, the animals that otherwise would have been eaten will become too numerous for the habitat to sustain. When we omnivorous humans are added to this mix to try to eke out a marginal existence, decisions to kill must be made if we are to survive. We might find it psychologically easier to let our competitor die by giving him no share of what little food we have and then eating him after he starves to death, but these ways of achieving our ends are not greatly different morally, as James Rachels has argued brilliantly in another context. In fact, as he points out, the passive method may well be more cruel than active killing.[206] In the situation we are describing, the competitor is also trapped in an area where resources are too scarce to sustain all. If he had not died, you or someone else would have done so. There is no dishonor, although there certainly is tragedy, in this way of resolving the conflict, *regardless* of who the survivor turns out to be.[207] (I strongly suspect that some of us—like me, for example—are just not cut out for this kind of conflict resolution. Perhaps I would behave differently than I think if I were put in the scarcity of resources situation and my survival depended upon my actions, but I cannot imagine being able to kill and eat an innocent, including a stranger of another [sentient] species. People like me would have been "selected out" pretty quickly during the Pleistocene era if others had not killed for them.)

The dilemma we are discussing is fully compatible with the equal moral status of all the parties involved. The competitor you kill or allow to die may be another human or a consciously goal-seeking nonhuman, or you might be the one to die. In practice, when humans in such a situation have a choice, they prefer to kill and eat the nonhuman competitor, for prudential reasons as well as psychological considerations. But this in no way implies that these nonhumans have inferior *moral* status. (As I noted earlier, if we have the choice in such circumstances to kill a nonhuman who is not obviously a fully morally significant being, like a fish, amphibian, or reptile, instead of a nonhuman mammal or a human, we should choose the former.)

Justification and Judgment

Lifeboat Analogies and Real Dilemmas

Tom Regan has also argued that the killing of other rights holders is justified in scarcity of resources situations. To make as powerful a case as he can, he resorts to that classic analogy, the lifeboat dilemma. Thought experiments like this make it easier for us to isolate relevant factors, provided that the analogy is apt. I shall argue that Regan does indeed show that killing would be justified in the situations he describes. The analogies he sketches, however, while applicable to a few dilemmas that actually arise, bear little resemblance to most scarcity of resource conflicts. Those conflicts are better represented by a different lifeboat analogy Regan does not consider.

Regan offers us two scenarios. In the first of these, he has us imagine that five survivors of a nautical catastrophe, four humans and a dog, are huddled together on a lifeboat. Unfortunately, the boat is overloaded and sure to sink unless one of the five passengers is tossed overboard to drown.[208] Regan holds that each passenger is equally morally significant ("equally inherently morally valuable"). Clearly, however, unless there is a volunteer, someone—who would die in any case—should be killed to give the others a chance. Before I discuss Regan's notorious resolution of this conflict (the dog gets pitched overboard), let us turn to the second of his lifeboat scenarios. He now has us imagine that four of the five passengers can live if the remaining passenger is killed *and* eaten.[209] If nothing is done, all will die. Again, they are all in the same boat morally, as it were; nevertheless, it would be justifiable to kill one so that the others may live. After all, the one marked for death would have died anyway were no action to be taken, along with everyone else. Once more, the dog is taken to be the sacrificial animal of choice. I disagree quite thoroughly with the argument Regan gives for killing the nonhuman animal in these cases, but let us postpone that issue. How applicable are Regan's particular lifeboat scenarios to scarcity of resource situations that actually exist on our planet?

Regan's first analogy does not seem to be very close to the resource dilemmas faced by humans and nonhumans in various parts of the world. How often must we decide between letting *everyone* die of starvation, thirst, exposure to the elements, and so on, or saving most by eliminating some "mouths to feed"? Still, his analogy does capture another kind of conflict, the kind that exists when conjoined twins sharing inadequate vital organs are born. If nothing is done, both will die, but saving one twin's life will necessitate the other's death.[210] Regan's analogy is also applicable to cases like the following. Suppose that a woman who is nineteen weeks pregnant develops an illness that is sure to kill both her and the (let us assume) sentient fetus if nothing is done one way or the other. Without certain medication, the woman will become irreversibly comatose, then brain-dead. The medication will, however, kill her fetus. Alternatively, the fetus could be saved if the woman is allowed to become comatose, then placed on life-support until the fetus becomes viable and can be delivered by cesarean section. Either both die, or one is saved at the cost of the other. Plainly, one is obligated to save someone; thus, it is justified to allow the other to die or be killed. Given the Gewirth-inspired (and corrected) rights view, both have full moral status. The judgment about who must go will have to turn on other factors. For example, if the woman is still conscious, she has the moral right to defend herself against the disease by taking the medicine that will kill the fetus. She might instead decide to sacrifice her life for the sake of her baby and refuse the medication, as women sometimes do: this too is her moral right. If she is not in a position to make a decision, and has not previously made her wishes known were such a situation to occur, others will have to do it. They may try to decide on the basis of what the woman might have preferred if she had been able to speak. If they cannot determine what her wishes would have been, they must let other considerations decide the issue. They may decide that the consequences for other rights holders of one individual's dying would be worse than in the case of the other, and choose to save the first on that account (e.g., in our case, the woman might have another young child who would be badly harmed by her death). They might decide on the basis of age (the fetus, unlike the woman, has had little chance to enjoy life or set goals) or the disruption death causes to a life plan (here, the woman comes out ahead). They may even flip a coin, or—and this is rather more likely—allow emotion to break the tie. Just as when two people are drowning and only one can be saved, third parties are morally permitted to rescue those to whom they feel a stronger emotional tie. They may even be *obligated* to do this, if they have acquired duties to one individual but only unacquired duties to the other (e.g., one's own child versus the neighbor's child, one's spouse versus a stranger). (See my chapter 3 on the bearing of kinship and emotional bonds on moral decisions.) Whatever is decided, however, no disrespect is shown to the individual who is killed or allowed to die; no lesser moral status is attributed to that individual.

The same holds for Regan's second lifeboat analogy, in which either all will die or one will, saving the others by becoming their meal. This, too, is not especially close to the actual dilemmas faced by individuals trapped with too few resources for all to survive, although it does apply in some cases. The draconian decisions imposed on communities devastated by invasion can lead to such a dilemma, as can natural disasters like avalanches or floods. One can be trapped and cut off from normal sustenance in many ways. Of course, *if* we must choose between letting *all* of us die or bringing about the premature death of one to feed the rest, it would seem to be permissible to take action. But we are more likely to be faced by a different dilemma. As Hugh Lehman has pointed out, a different sort of lifeboat analogy strikes closer to home.[211]

Imagine that we are adrift in our boat, hoping for rescue, but lack enough food for all aboard. If it is shared equally, making allowance for body sizes, and so on, some will muddle through, but we know that some will not. This analogy applies to many scarcity of resources situations. Typically, we are not in situations where *everyone* dies *or* some are sacrificed for the sake of the others. More often, we do not have enough for *all* to survive. If some are allowed to die, or are killed and eaten, the rest can manage. This is the kind of situation I was describing earlier. Unfortunately, more than a few moral agents and equally morally significant beings are caught in such a position, especially in very poor communities in extremely inhospitable climates.

It seems obvious that killing would be justified in Regan's dilemmas, though we may quarrel about the choice mechanism Regan uses to determine the victim. As I have argued, killing would also be justified, if less obviously so, in the more realistic scarcity of resources situation. In that situation, as in the third lifeboat analogy, every individual is innocently trapped in an area where lack of supplies puts *each* at very high risk for dying prematurely. Some, in fact, *are sure to die*, although we may not know yet who they are. We can either do nothing to prevent these deaths—*which could come to anyone, including us*—or we can try to influence the odds as I have earlier described. In such a position, the lives of all involved are placed in conflict: they are competitors for survival.

How Not to Decide Who Should Die

Suppose we now take a detached position. If we were impartial arbitrators instead of very "undetached" unfortunates fighting to survive, how would we choose among lives? Since we are assuming that all involved in our third lifeboat (and real!) dilemma, human and nonhuman, are equally morally significant, each having a prima facie right to life, if we are indeed justified in causing death to some for the sake of others, our choice of victim will not be easy. Regan does not hesitate to conclude that the nonhuman animal (the dog, in his examples) should be the one to be killed and eaten. Following is a reconstruction of his argument.

Regan reaches his conclusion by appealing to two premises. The first is the "worse-off" principle, which he claims to be derivable from the "respect" principle (according to which inherently valuable beings should be treated as ends in themselves):

1. When one *must* cause harm either to one innocent individual or to another, and one has the choice to either inflict greater harm on the one or lesser harm on the other, one should inflict the lesser harm.[212]

To this very plausible premise, he adds the following claim:

2. Any other sentient nonhuman that we know of would be harmed *less* by death than would a human.

It follows that:

3. *Therefore,* a nonhuman should be sacrificed instead of a human when their lives are in conflict.

For those of us who do not find Regan's second premise to be obvious, he supplies an additional argument. He contends that:

2a. "[T]he harm that death is, is a function of the opportunities for satisfaction it forecloses,"[213] or, more specifically, "of the number and variety of opportunities for satisfaction it forecloses."[214]

Let us call this the "harm of death" premise. Next, Regan contends:

2b. Humans have a greater number and variety of opportunities for satisfaction than any nonhumans we know of.

Of course, "number and variety of opportunities" must mean the same thing in premise 2a as in premise 2b. Although Regan does not offer any further clarification of "number and variety of opportunities for satisfaction," he must mean more by this than simply "lots of opportunities for different kinds of satisfactions." Regarding the "number" of satisfactions, I do not believe that he is simply making a point about longevity. A seventy-year-old human may have fewer satisfactions ahead than a puppy. "Variety" seems to be the major factor here. But what does this mean? Dogs normally have a number of different preferred activities, as many as some humans do, yet Regan takes it to be obvious that their experiences are much less variegated. For premise 2 to be true, he must intend "variety" to entail "richness" and "complexity," as opposed to "simple-mindedness." Given such a view, chasing and catching Frisbees would count for much less than reading an Emily Dickinson poem. He concludes that:

2c. *Therefore,* any other sentient nonhuman that we know of would be harmed *less* by death than would a human (premise 2 in the first argument above).

If we grant the premises in Regan's first argument, his conclusion certainly does follow. In every scarcity of resources case, nonhuman animals should be the ones who die for the sake of humans. However, Regan's second premise, the claim that nonhumans are harmed less by death than humans, is questionable, both in terms of his own egalitarian theory and in itself, as I shall now argue.

The key support for that premise is the "harm of death" premise in his second, supporting argument. The harm that death occasions is said to depend upon the "number and variety of satisfactions" one might have if one were not to die. The latter phrase is, as we just saw, interpreted as "number and richness or complexity of positive experiences." On the face of it, Regan's "harm of death" premise does not appear to be consistent with the tenets of his rights theory. He repeatedly argues that those with a prima facie right to life are equally inherently valuable, *regardless* of the comparative richness of their experiences. Gewirth makes the same contention: All consciously purposive beings are due respect and protection in equal measure, regardless of how simple or complex their desires may be. We owe all of them respect as ends in themselves, Regan says: the ultimate disrespect is to treat them "as if they were mere receptacles of valuable experiences."[215] We must never confuse the value of an individual's life with the value that attaches to his or her pleasures and satisfactions, he warns us; all rights bearers have equally valuable lives.[216] Yet, he seems to do precisely this when he reasons that the dog should be killed for the sake of beings who are capable of a richer and more complex experiential life. Is he not saying that their lives are *worth* more?

Regan would probably answer that his way of resolving the lifeboat dilemmas is not in conflict with his claim that human and nonhuman subjects-of-lives are equally inherently valuable. It shows no disrespect to inflict a lesser harm on an innocent being in a lifeboat situation rather than inflict a greater harm on another being sharing the same plight. For example, suppose three people are being held hostage by armed, sadistic captors. The captors give one of the hostages a choice: she must either kill hostage A or shoot hostage B in the leg (let us suppose that hostage B is guaranteed medical treatment afterwards and that all three are threatened with death if hostage C does not act). If she abides by the "worse-off" principle, she will shoot hostage B in the leg. Her action in no way shows lack of respect for B, whose life is just as valuable as A's. It would simply be grossly unfair, and utterly disrespectful of A, to inflict the far greater harm on him. Similarly, Regan could say, in the lifeboat cases we do not treat the dog as a mere receptacle of experiences when we kill him. We are simply choosing to inflict the least amount of harm on an individual.

The "worse-off" premise is indeed reasonably and fully compatible with an egalitarian rights view. The difficulty is that Regan's way of assessing the harm that *death* allegedly imposes with respect to different individuals does not work, even supposing—as many philosophers do not—that the concept of being harmed by death is logically coherent. Returning to the hostage analogy I posed above should help us to see this.

Rational people would agree that being killed is far worse than being shot in the leg and then being given medical treatment. But now imagine that hostage C is instructed to kill either A or B; otherwise, she knows that all three are set for execution. Let us stipulate that A and B are both in the prime of life and would greatly prefer to stay alive. What sense does it make to ask whether the one would be harmed more by death than the other? While an individual who is merely shot in the leg is better off than one who is killed, and the same individual is better off being shot in the leg than killed, A and B above would be equally harmed by death inasmuch as *each would lose everything.*

It might be replied at this point that one could have more to lose by death than the other. If A's life is full of rich experiences, replete with opportunities for many varieties of satisfactions, and B's rather dim-witted life by contrast allows for a much more limited smorgasbord of satisfactions, does it not make sense to say that A would lose more, and thus be harmed more by death, than B would?

I do not think so. Suppose that we alter our case one more time. Instead of being threatened with death, both A and B are snatched from their homes and thrown undeservedly into prison, where they will languish in chains for the rest of their lives. Consider what each has lost. Individual A is sundered from his family and friends, as well as from all his favorite activities. He will never again play the piano, travel, read Dostoevsky, write poetry, paint landscapes, listen to Gorecki's Third Symphony, play chess, engage in gourmet cooking, eat in Indian restaurants, or meditate in a Japanese tea garden. Individual B is also ripped from the company of his friends and loved ones. Moreover, he can no longer engage in his favorite activities: washing down cheese nachos with Iron City beer, watching football games, and listening to "Drop Kick Me, Jesus, Over the Goal Posts of Life" (I am *not* making up this song title) on his preferred country music station. Surely it would be wrong to say that A has been more harmed by imprisonment than B has! Although one might say that A has lost a more complex, variegated way of life than B has, as well as a greater number of satisfactions, it would not be true to say that B valued his way of life less than A valued his. They are equally bereft, because each has lost all that made life satisfying. Exactly the same point applies if B is, for example, a dog. He would never again know the joys of running across a meadow, feeling the warm sunshine on his back, being nuzzled by his mother, being bombarded by tantalizing smells in a forest, eating his favorite food, wrestling with buddies, and having his ears scratched. Our canine B might be considerably less intelligent than A, but his joie de vivre does not appear to be any less! The comparative richness of A's and B's experiences and interests is simply not relevant in this context: the degree of harm suffered is a function of how much what has been snatched away matters *to them*. So it is, one might say, with death, which forecloses all further experiences and thwarts all opportunities for satisfaction. If A and B both value living and are in the prime of life, they would be harmed equally by death, no matter how "dull" B is in comparison to A.

Nonetheless, Some Rights Holders Are Harmed More by Death Than Others Are

Despite my criticism of Regan's reasoning, I think that we can discover circumstances in which one individual would be harmed more by death than another with equal moral standing. Death, after all, is inevitable, and it does matter just when it comes. As Joel Feinberg says, "[y]oung deaths are more tragic than old ones."[217] An octogenarian who has had a lifetime to formulate and fulfill goals is harmed less by death than a teenager, even if the teen has developed far fewer interests at that point. (However, we must also consider the ability of surviving individuals to carry on with life. A child we choose to spare who is deprived of an adult's assistance, or, worse, subjected to an actively abusive environment, may be harmed more by living than by dying.) Moreover, death can sometimes be *in* one's interests. If our hostage A is in the unrelievedly painful final stages of a terminal disease and is begging for death, he might be benefited rather than harmed by its occurrence. If we apply the "worse-off" principle in such lifeboat cases, a terminally ill or elderly passenger should be killed rather than a healthier or younger one. (We take the same thing into account when we decide how to allocate another scare resource: donated organs.) Note that this would still follow if the *dog* is the one who is healthy and young!

Another consideration must be taken into account at this point, however: Someone with enough intelligence to grasp the tragedy and finality of death may for that reason be more distressed when killed than, for instance, a young child or a dog unable to understand the situation. The first, unlike the second two, is able to realize that everything of value is about to be lost. Greater intelligence may, therefore, very well translate into greater suffering, and this surely must be included in our estimation of the harm death can cause. On the other hand, as Steve Sapontzis has argued,[218] understanding one's fate and the reason for it may allow one to face death with serene acceptance, a state of mind very unlike the terrified incomprehension of, say, a fox caught in a trap unable to avoid the trapper's descending club. (Bernard Rollin has made the same point with regard to experiencing pain:[219] knowing why one is suffering and being able to anticipate the cessation of that experience may well make pain easier to bear than it would be for a baby or a cat.) Nevertheless, death frequently inspires no serene acceptance in its intelligent victims: this is particularly the case when violence ends life. Here it is plausible to say that such a victim may experience even more distress than an individual who cannot grasp the enormity and senselessness of her loss. Depending on circumstances, then, it seems that intelligence may either ease or exacerbate the burden of impending death. In the very situations we are here discussing, namely cases of killing to resolve conflicts, the distress factor is probably greater for beings intelligent enough to understand what is to occur. We must take this factor into consideration without *also* forgetting the even more weighty factors of advanced age and well-being. Calculating the harm of death can be no simple matter!

The distress factor can be eliminated if death occurs without forewarning. Even in those circumstances, however, we must remember that anyone with desires he or she wants to satisfy (and who does not want to die) suffers a terrible loss at death. As Sapontzis has also pointed out, the "misfortune" of death is a matter of losing all opportunity to have fulfilling experiences, experiences that one values.[220] A bright, young human adult loses a complex network of relationships and has her life plan aborted. A significantly retarded human of the same age loses just as much, *from his perspective.* Each loses all that is precious, all that matters *to him or her.* In fact, the mentally limited young man in my example may have lost the opportunity for many more fulfilling experiences than his normal counterpart would have had! Humans afflicted as he is are so often transcendently happy, able to take joy in the simplest of matters. As we explored in the previous chapter, a life filled with many satisfactions of short-term desires may have more overall satisfaction value than one governed by a "struggle for the big pay-off" strategy. Some say, with horror, that the life of a conscious but mentally retarded person would not be worth living: this is unconscionably arrogant, given the obvious enjoyment life brings to such individuals. If the distress death may cause a victim can be eliminated, therefore, considerations other than intelligence will determine the harm that death inflicts.

If one persists in believing that the richness or poverty of individuals' experiences should decide the issue in scarcity of resources situations, one should be clear about one's actual reason for believing this. It is not that one individual will lose more—be "worse off"—than the other, assuming that age and well-being are not issues. One is really presupposing that some lives are *worth more* than others, regardless of the value those lives have for their subjects. *Make no mistake about it, this exceedingly common view implies that mentally impoverished humans, not just nonhumans, should be sacrificed for the sake of their normal human "superiors."* Although one could take this view and still hold that all purposive sentient beings have a prima facie right to life, one would have to hold that some individuals' right to life is more easily overridden than others'.

This view is, of course, incompatible with any pretense at egalitarianism: for that reason, I have called it "the unequal rights view."[221] Philosophers Michael Tooley and Ruth Cigman have supported this view by arguing, roughly, that one must be able to conceive of X in order to have a right to X.[222] Nonhuman animals and some humans have no concept of life or of the overall loss death would cause, they hold, therefore they cannot have a right to life. There are many problems with this line of argument, including the assumption that none but a fairly mature normal human can have a concept of life. I will not here repeat Steve Sapontzis's masterful critique of Cigman's complex version of the argument I have greatly simplified above.[223] He succeeds in showing that no good case exists for the presumption that rights are tied to the intellectual prowess needed to comprehend the objects of rights, as opposed to one's capacity to benefit from the extension of such rights. Moreover, there is a very strong argument *against* the unequal rights view: Gewirth's. If we consistently trace the implications of his (as I have argued) sound argument, we are logically compelled to reject the perfectionism enshrined in that view. (I take for granted that Regan would also reject the unequal rights view.)

If one adopts the Gewirth-based rights view instead, as I have argued that we should, then scarcity of resources dilemmas must be resolved without appeal to the intelligence of the parties involved, apart from individuals' ability or inability to survive on their own or the distress they might feel at impending death. One's right to protect one's own interests and the interests of those one loves or is responsible for must weigh heavily, as should considerations of age, vulnerability, and any other factors relevant to the fairest resolution of a tragic conflict. If we do throw the dog out of the boat, it should be for reasons other than his inability to do calculus.

When a Lifeboat Analogy Does Not Apply

Lehman has argued that lifeboat situations are actually not all that exceptional. In affluent parts of the world where food is available, at least if it is evenly distributed, we must still sometimes choose *between* human and nonhuman animal lives.[224] Certain types of fatal medical experimentation on nonhumans could save some humans' lives, and a transspecies organ transplant may be the only hope for some humans (assuming, contrary to current fact but for the sake of argument, that such transplants can be done successfully [from the human point of view]). Either the nonhuman will die or the human will die; we must choose who gets to remain in the "lifeboat." If both are equally morally significant, does the human not have the right to fight for her or his own survival, even at the cost of the nonhuman, just as I was arguing above?

No, indeed: we do not have a lifeboat situation here. There is more to such a situation than the fact that one or another individual will die, depending on what action is taken. The parties involved must both be innocently caught in a situation where there are not enough resources to sustain both their lives, although there are enough supplies to support one. Each is at risk: either could die if nothing is done. These individuals truly are competing for life.

These conditions are not present when we are considering killing a consciously goal-seeking nonhuman animal for her organs or for other medical purposes intended to save a human life. The human and nonhuman animal are not *each* at risk of dying if nothing is done.[225] We could only claim there to be a scarcity of resources if we include the nonhuman's healthy, independently functioning body among those resources; by no stretch of the imagination is this compatible with the attribution of full moral rights to that animal. We are not, after all, considering the dilemma of conjoined twins sharing a heart and a liver, both doomed to die if one is not killed. Consider the following parallel. A dying woman has this conversation with a healthy young man who has been kidnapped and brought to her bedside: "Sanchez, you and I are competitors for a scarce resource: your liver. My liver is riddled with disease, and I will soon die without a transplant. No suitable cadaver organs are available, but tests show that your liver would be excellent for me. Either I will die or you will die: our lives are in conflict. I have the right to protect my own life, so I am justified in having you killed so that I may harvest your lovely liver." Of course, she is *not* justified, given that her victim has the same basic moral rights that she does. Anyone who performs the operation on her behalf is likewise not justified. Only one party in this little story is innocent, and we know who it is.

It might be replied that the nonhuman animals who are used for allegedly life-saving medical procedures are (usually) not snatched off the street, like our young man, but kept captive for this very purpose. If they are not used for human purposes they will be killed; no one will keep feeding and sheltering them if this function is not fulfilled. So, since they will die anyway, they may as well die to save another's life. Is this not after all parallel to a lifeboat situation? Either both will die or only one—the nonhuman animal—will.

As is so often the case, when we recast this argument in human terms any plausibility instantly vanishes. If it is wrong to pilfer the liver of a healthy young individual who would prefer to live, it is also wrong to breed him from others to serve as an organ bank, *and* wrong to kill him if his liver turns out to be off-limits. The only difference between my imaginary case and the nonhuman animal "donor" case above is that the wrongful captivity has taken place at a different point. Instead of being held captive in the hospital, Sanchez could have been imprisoned earlier somewhere else for this very purpose. (In fact, my example is horrifyingly close to reality. As I mentioned in chapter 3, there is evidence that political prisoners in some South American dictatorships have been killed and their organs given to extremely wealthy patrons.) His great-great-grandparents might even have been the ones originally captured as a breeding pair for organs, tissues, and so on. Giving the captivity a longer history in no way improves the moral stature of the woman who covets the healthy young man's liver. It may even make it worse:

Justification and Judgment

at least the original captive had a life of his own before the fateful day. The argument that we may as well take his liver and save a life because he would also be killed if we do not presents us with a false dilemma: either the organ snatcher lives and the "snatchee" dies, or both die. These are hardly the only options. Given the wrong already done to him, the young man should be either released or cared for until his natural death, if he has been rendered unable to survive on his own. (In the latter case, noninvasive, nonharmful research involving him, to which he does not object, would be permissible.) This is at least an attempt at restitution, quite unlike the decision to kill him in any case. Declaring him a "useless eater" if he does not become fodder for someone else is hardly respectful.

The same holds for the millions of consciously goal-seeking non-human animals we imprison and kill for our own benefit. If we as consistent moral agents are obliged to extend to them the same prima facie right to life that we claim for ourselves, we are wrong to continue "harvesting" their bodies. Not long ago, I read that researchers at the University of Minnesota are trying to develop a new, genetically engineered pig subspecies that could be used to supply hearts for humans in need of that organ. The pig's blood is designed to contain human proteins, to lessen chances of organ rejection after transplantation.[226] Dr. Fritz Bach, the surgeon in charge of the project, is pleased by the closeness in structure between pig and human hearts, but fears that people may be put off by that very fact: "[Pig and human hearts] are distressingly similar, especially when you think that it's a pig," he is quoted as saying. There are multiple ironies here, including the fact that excess consumption of saturated fat is a leading cause of heart disease. We eat our victims, become ill, and breed more victims to replace our fat-clogged hearts!

In short, the continuing practice of killing nonhuman animals for medical purposes, even in those relatively rare cases where human lives are saved as a result, cannot be painted as a party of innocents trapped in a lifeboat. The only lifeboat situation that would be parallel to this one would be one in which a healthy young individual, minding her own business, is forced onto a lifeboat at gunpoint and made to serve as one's lunch, organ supplier, or vaccine tester. We could even breed her first so that we do not have to leave the lifeboat so often. We have a "deathboat" here, not a lifeboat!

Justification and Judgment

Does the "Liberty Principle" Sanction Killing Others Who Are
Not Already at Risk?

Let us consider one last argument that attempts to justify the killing
of nonhuman animals who, like us, have desires they want to satisfy,
when they neither threaten us nor compete with us for life. Earlier we
discussed the fact that Regan's "worse-off" principle does not justify
killing nonhumans rather than humans when one has the choice.[227] Now
let us turn to his "liberty principle": "Provided that all those involved
are treated with respect, and assuming that no special considerations
obtain, any innocent individual has the right to act to avoid being made
worse-off even if doing so harms other innocents."[228] Regan argues that
this principle would justify the killing of other animals for food *if,* contrary to general fact, meat were essential for human health, presumably
even if those other animals are not independently at risk of starvation.[229]
However, the principle would apply much more broadly than this: it
could also apply to the kinds of medical experiments and procedures
that might save human lives.[230] Once again, let us accept the assumption
that dying when this is not your wish makes you worse off than you
were before. If I may keep myself from dying at the cost of harming
an innocent—say, by killing him for his liver—does this principle not
justify my act?

No, it does not, if we assume that the innocents to be harmed have
a claim to life equal to our own. Let us change the bedside speech of
my imaginary liver-needy human to the kidnapped Sanchez: "With the
utmost sorrow and respect, I must kill you for your liver. After all, without mine, which is going fast, I will be considerably worse off. I have
no other options at this point. Out of respect, I have given you the best
of care and sedated you so completely that you do not mind in the least
what I am saying or what is going to happen to you. I know that you
are an innocent with a prima facie right to life equal to my own, but I
do have the right to prevent myself from being made worse off. Sorry!"
Is it not obvious that one is *not* entitled to pluck the liver from another
innocent being, a being who would otherwise live, if his claim to life
is equal to your own? If we construe the liberty principle this broadly,
it is not consistent with an egalitarian rights view. We must reject the
principle in that case (as must Regan, who holds such a view).

At this point, I think Regan would say that we are not justified in construing the liberty principle so broadly. After all, it is qualified by "assuming that no special considerations obtain." Depending on what he means by this, my liver transplant scenario may not be a fair application of his principle. He gives us the following example of "special considerations": "The 'special considerations' proviso explains why I am not at liberty to take my neighbor's Mercedes just because not having it would make me worse-off relative to him. For since it is his car, he has a right, assuming the car was acquired justly, in addition to our mutual right not to be harmed, and the possession of this additional property right is a special consideration that limits my liberty."[231] Regan's example allows us to formulate the liberty principle less vaguely than before: Provided that all those involved are treated with respect, *and assuming that no prior rights in addition to the mutual right not to be harmed would be violated,* any innocent individual has the right to act to avoid being made worse off even if doing so harms other innocents. Given this formulation, where the italicized clause replaces "assuming that no special considerations obtain," we can see that the liver transplant case would not be permissible. If my car has coughed its last and taking my neighbor's Mercedes would allow me to avoid being made worse off, but it would be wrong for me to do so because I would be violating his *property* rights, surely I would be wrong to snatch his liver—even if I cough *my* last without it. If he has the right to keep his Mercedes, he surely has the right to retain his organs. This holds whether the liver source is a human, a baboon, or a pig.

So interpreted, the liberty principle is not at odds with an egalitarian rights view. It is compatible with killing innocent threats and innocent shields, and can even apply in real scarcity of resource situations where *each* individual is at serious risk of dying and we know that death is already inevitable. But it will not sanction other killings. It cannot be used to justify invasive medical procedures that "sacrifice" nonconsenting, sentient subjects of any species on the altar of our own interests.

What, then, is a desperately ill human to do when the drugs or therapies that could save her life were developed unjustly? On the one hand, accepting such treatment is tantamount to benefiting from innocent others' suffering and deaths. On the other hand, those who have been wrongly sacrificed are already dead: Do we honor them by adding our deaths to theirs? Suppose, *very much* contrary to fact, that the horrors inflicted by medical experimenters in Nazi concentration camps had yielded some potentially life-saving information for humans. Many people furiously reject the notion of benefiting from the agony of such victims, and I find myself much in sympathy with that position. However, I can also sympathize with anyone who might choose to accept such a benefit, reasoning that further death is not helpful to those who have already perished. Still, if one does make such a decision, one must be exceedingly careful not to encourage *further* unjust experimentation: "Never again!" must be one's pledge. If the drugs and therapies we are contemplating using are *even now* occasioning the sacrifice of innocents with a right to life, or encouraging other such products to be similarly developed, our partaking of these benefits might contribute to additional wrongful deaths. We may decide to save our own lives anyway. If the question concerns the life of a loved one unable to make his or her own decisions, we are even more inclined to accept whatever salvation is offered. None can blame a parent or spouse for accepting such an offer. Perhaps the harm we do to some innocents in the struggle to save other innocents can be at least partially counterbalanced by our working for alternatives that do not exact suffering and death as their price.

Conclusion

I have argued that there is no justification for moral agents' continuing to routinely "harvest" beings who are vitally interested in what life holds for them. Any such being, human or nonhuman, is fully morally significant, despite the fact that not all rights held by such beings are the same. Those humans who are fortunate enough to be full persons are no more important in moral terms than the humans and nonhumans who do not have quite this exalted status, but care just as much about what happens to them. Acting in accordance with this reasoning would in fact bring some considerable benefits to us. Given the ecological devastation, health problems, and—ironically—hunger attendant upon the following of meat-heavy diets in affluent countries, the choice to follow a well-planned vegetarian diet is the opposite of suicidal. Moreover, as mentioned earlier, Charles Fink has argued that many of the

resources devoted to experimentation on nonhuman animals would save
more human lives if they were used for direct humanitarian assistance
instead.[232]

These facts notwithstanding, it cannot be denied that one might sometimes be adversely affected by the decision to be a consistent moral
agent. An equal moral significance view, *even when confined to humans,*
leaves us with many tragic choices. Some of these choices will result in
the justifiable deaths of other innocents whose lives are in unavoidable
conflict with our own; others may lead us to accept our own deaths
rather than, for example, allowing a political prisoner to be killed so that
you may purchase his liver. If all consciously purposive sentient beings—
mammals and perhaps also birds—have basic moral rights, they must
be included in our deliberations. We should strive to avoid or minimize
conflicts as best we can, exactly as we do when we aim to treat each
other with justice. As I have argued, many of us find that some of our
emotions already cohere with these conclusions, while other emotions
may not. Time and reflection work to alter our emotions and our collective ideals, as we have seen repeatedly in our treatment of one another.
When *all* of our feelings echo our arguments, we will have moved, at
last, beyond prejudice.

Justification and Judgment

Notes

1 HUMAN "SUPERIORITY" AND THE ARGUMENT FROM MARGINAL CASES

1. Paul Taylor, *Respect for Nature* (Princeton: Princeton University Press, 1986), p. 33.
2. Joel Feinberg, "Abortion," in *Matters of Life and Death*, 2d ed., ed. Tom Regan (New York: Random House, 1986), pp. 261–62.
3. Ibid., p. 271.
4. Tom Regan, *The Case for Animal Rights* (Berkeley: University of California Press, 1983), p. 243.
5. Ibid., p. 416 n. 30.
6. For further discussion of different senses of 'person,' see Steve Sapontzis, *Morals, Reason, and Animals* (Philadelphia: Temple University Press, 1987), chapter 4.
7. Taylor, *Respect for Nature*, pp. 33–34.
8. H. J. McCloskey, "The Moral Case for Experimentation on Animals," *The Monist* 70 (1), January 1987, p. 65.
9. Ernest Partridge, "Three Wrong Leads in a Search for an Environmental Ethic," *Ethics and Animals* 5 (3), September 1984, pp. 62–64.
10. Compare the use of 'person,' for example, in Evelyn Pluhar, "Moral Agents and Moral Patients," *Between the Species* 4 (1), Winter 1988, pp. 32–45, and Evelyn Pluhar, "Is There a Morally Relevant Difference Between Human and Animal Nonpersons?" *The Journal of Agricultural Ethics* 1 (1), 1988, pp. 59–68.
11. See, e.g., Jerome Kagan, *The Nature of the Child* (New York: Basic Books, 1984), and Lawrence Kohlberg, "Moral Stages and Moralization," *The Psychology of Moral Development* (San Francisco: Harper & Row, 1984). Major elements of Kohlberg's enormously influential theory have come under attack by critics such as Carol Gilligan, *In a Different Voice* (Cambridge, Mass.: Harvard University Press, 1982), but his placement of the beginning of the process of moral development in early childhood has not been questioned.
12. Regan, *The Case for Animal Rights,* pp. 84–85.
13. Ibid., p. 244. I will argue later in this book that Regan really offers two criteria for moral considerability, both of which he calls "being the subject-of-a-life."
14. Donald Griffin, *Animal Minds* (Chicago: University of Chicago Press, 1992), p. 10. As Griffin points out, references to consciousness, taboo in psychology for generations after the adoption of behaviorism, are beginning to regain intellectual respectability. See Bernard Rollin, *The Unheeded Cry: Animal Consciousness, Animal Pain, and Science* (Oxford: Oxford University Press, 1989),

for a thorough discussion of behaviorism's impact on the biological and social sciences.

15. See, for example, R. G. Frey, *Interests and Rights: The Case Against Animals* (Oxford: Clarendon Press, 1980), and Peter Carruthers, *Introducing Persons* (Albany: State University of New York Press, 1986), pp. 230–32.

16. Rollin, *The Unheeded Cry: Animal Consciousness, Animal Pain, and Science,* chapter 6.

17. Ibid., p. 140.

18. Jean-Paul Sartre, *The Transcendence of the Ego,* trans. Forrest Williams and Robert Kirkpatrick (New York: Noonday Press, 1971), p. 75.

19. Marvin Minsky, "The Intelligence Transplant," *Discover Magazine,* October 1989, pp. 52–58. Minsky does go on to claim that we humans are not all that different: "The vast majority of the things you do in a day, you do completely unconsciously . . . When you recognize a friend on the street you don't consciously think: 'This appears to be Jim; I recognize the face and gait . . .' " (p. 58). Clearly, however, it does not follow from this that one is not conscious when recognizing one's friend! Minsky's comment about humans only makes sense against a background of consciousness. He admits that even the most sophisticated computers cannot see, understand, or know.

20. As we shall soon see, however, some contemporary philosophers have concluded that *neither* dogs nor human infants are conscious (see my discussion of "the sentience defense of homocentrism" in this chapter)!

21. See Steven Rosen, *Food for the Spirit* (New York: Bala Books, 1987), and Tom Regan, ed., *Animal Sacrifices* (Philadelphia: Temple University Press, 1986), for very interesting discussions of the various implications religious worldviews have regarding nonhuman life.

22. Taylor, *Respect for Nature,* chapter 3.

23. J. Baird Callicott, *In Defense of the Land Ethic* (Albany: State University of New York Press, 1989), p. 10.

24. "Animal Rights Nonsense," *Nature* 305, October 13, 1983, p. 562.

25. Ibid.

26. A. I. Melden, *Rights in Moral Lives* (Berkeley: University of California Press, 1988), pp. 51–72. Shortly, however, we will explore the radical view (defended by Descartes and some contemporary philosophers) that sentience is restricted to humans. At this point in our discussion, I will leave the assumption that many nonhumans are sentient unchallenged.

27. Ibid., p. 57.

28. Ibid.

29. Ibid., p. 58.

30. Ibid., pp. 57–58.

31. Alan Gewirth, *Reason and Morality* (Chicago: University of Chicago Press, 1978), pp. 103, 317.

32. St. Thomas Aquinas, *Summa Contra Gentiles,* book 3, part 2, chapter 112, *Animal Rights and Human Obligations,* 2d ed., ed. Tom Regan and Peter Singer (Englewood Cliffs: Prentice-Hall, 1989), pp. 6–9.

33. Ibid., p. 8.

34. Ibid., p. 7.

Notes

35. Charles C. Ryrie, "The Inspiration of the Bible," in *The Ryrie Study Bible* (Chicago: Moody Press, 1976), pp. 1956–57.

36. See, e.g., Andrew Linzey, *Christianity and the Rights of Animals* (New York: Crossroad Publishing Co., 1987); Regan, ed., *Animal Sacrifices;* Peter Singer, *Animal Liberation,* 2d ed. (New York: Random House, 1990), chapter 5; and Bernard E. Rollin, *Animal Rights and Human Morality,* (Buffalo: Prometheus Books, 1992), pp. 28–32.

37. The objection that the argument is weak because one is reasoning from only one case—one's own—confuses *analogical* with *enumerative* inductive reasoning. Since *one* type of analogical reasoning does indeed call for enumeration of several cases in its premises, it is easy to see how the confusion arises. (For the two types of analogical inference, see, e.g., Howard Kahane, *Logic and Contemporary Rhetoric,* 6th ed., [Belmont, Ca.: Wadsworth Publishing Co., 1992], p. 297.)

38. Letter from Descartes to Henry Moore, reprinted in *Animal Rights and Human Obligations,* 2d ed., ed. Regan and Singer, p. 18. The belief that other *human* minds exist, by contrast, is apparently "clear and distinct" enough to be warranted in Descartes's terms.

39. For trenchant criticism of Descartes's view, see Singer, *Animal Liberation,* chapter 5; Regan, *The Case for Animal Rights,* chapter 1; and Daisie Radner and Michael Radner, *Animal Consciousness* (Buffalo: Prometheus Books), 1989, chapter 6.

40. Rollin, *The Unheeded Cry: Animal Consciousness, Animal Pain, and Science,* p. 154.

41. Ibid., p. 154.

42. James Rachels, *Created from Animals* (Oxford: Oxford University Press, 1990).

43. Rollin, *The Unheeded Cry,* chapters 9, 10.

44. Peter Harrison, "Theodicy and Animal Pain," *Philosophy* 64 (247), January 1989, pp. 79–92.

45. Peter Carruthers, "Brute Experience," *The Journal of Philosophy* 86, 1989, pp. 258–69. He presents the same arguments in the last chapter of his book *The Animals Issue* (Cambridge: Cambridge University Press, 1992): see chapter 8, "Animals and Conscious Experience."

46. Singer, *Animal Liberation,* pp. 201–2.

47. Rachels, *Created from Animals,* p. 129. Animals subjected to procedures without anesthesia or analgesia still sometimes have their vocal cords tied. See Singer, *Animal Liberation,* p. 29.

48. "The Growth of Anti-Vivisection," *The Animals' Agenda,* September/October 1988, p. 50.

49. Mary Midgley, *Animals and Why They Matter* (Athens, Ga.: The University of Georgia Press, 1983), p. 28.

50. Bernard Rollin, "The Moral Status of Research Animals in Psychology," *The American Psychologist,* August 1985, p. 924.

51. It is retitled "Animal Pain" in *Animal Experimentation: The Moral Issues,* ed. Robert Baird and Stuart Rosenbaum (Buffalo: Prometheus Press, 1991), pp. 128–39.

Notes

52. Carruthers, *The Animals Issue*.

53. For example, Carruthers was an invited guest at Iowa State University at the Fall Colloquium of their bioethics program. Roughly one hundred students and faculty witnessed his debate with William Robinson on the existence of nonhuman animal suffering. See *The Ag Bioethics Forum* 4 (2), December 1992, for the debate presentations.

54. Harrison, "Theodicy and Animal Pain," p. 92. Harrison tells us that he does not support the beating of pets and the like. He believes, along with Aquinas and Kant, that wanton (apparent) cruelty toward nonhumans (as opposed to "painful" but not maliciously motivated treatment of nonhuman animals, e.g., probably most instances of factory farming and experimentation or testing) might lead to abuse of humans: see his "The Neo-Cartesian Revival: A Response," *Between the Species* 9 (2), Spring 1993, pp. 71–76. Peter Carruthers expresses a similar view in his *The Animals Issue*, chapter 7.

55. Carruthers, "Brute Experience," p. 268. He allows us to indulge in the belief that animals are conscious only when this belief has no "morally significant" effect on other humans (p. 269). Although Carruthers cautions us in his 1992 book that, since he could be mistaken, "it may be wiser" to treat nonhuman animals as if they could feel pain (pp. 192–93), his idea of "caution" is not to *worsen* our treatment of these nonhumans. He continues to support commercial operations that cause nonhuman animals great suffering (supposing they could experience it). This position follows from his version of contractualism, briefly sketched below.

56. Carruthers, *The Animals Issue*, p. 168.

57. Ibid. See, e.g., pp. 107, 166–68, 194. Carruthers at least grants that these folk may have "admirable" character traits such as kindness and abhorrence of cruelty, however misdirected their concerns supposedly are (p. 168).

58. Ibid., p. 195.

59. Ibid., pp. 160, 166.

60. Ibid., p. 196.

61. Steve Sapontzis, "Review of Peter Carruthers' *The Animals Issue*," commissioned by the *Canadian Philosophical Review*. I am grateful to Professor Sapontzis for giving me an advance copy of this review.

62. Carruthers does not address the issue of mentally defective humans in his article, but he does discuss it at length in his book, arguing that his version of contractualism can avoid the implication that humans who are not rational agents can justifiably be exploited. I will state and refute his arguments on this head in my chapter 2.

63. Edward Johnson, "Carruthers on Consciousness and Moral Status," *Between the Species* 7 (4), Fall 1991, pp. 190–92.

64. William Robinson, "Can Animals Feel Pain in the Morally Relevant Sense? Yes," *The Ag Bioethics Forum* 4 (2), December 1992, pp. 4–5. I thank Professor Robinson for providing me with the expanded version of his article, "Some Nonhuman Animals Can Have Pain in a Morally Relevant Sense," an as yet unpublished essay.

65. Harrison, "Theodicy and Animal Pain," p. 80.

66. Ibid., p. 81.

Notes

67. R. Baird and S. Rosenbaum, *Animal Experimentation: The Moral Issues.*
68. Harrison, "Theodicy and Animal Pain," p. 81. He does not take note of the fact that the same problem arises, notoriously, for the assumption that other humans can have pain experiences. If he were asked about this, he might follow Descartes in adopting a language criterion of consciousness. Although we are not the only animals who scream, he might say, we are the only ones who scream "God, that hurts!" There are many well-known difficulties with the language criterion (see Rollin, *The Unheeded Cry,* chapter 6), but there is an extra difficulty for Harrison, should he try to use it: he concedes that some nonhumans are capable of learning a language (p. 82 n. 8).
69. Harrison, "Theodicy and Animal Pain," p. 86.
70. Ibid., p. 82.
71. Stephen Jay Gould, "Evolution as Fact and Theory," *Discover,* May 1981, p. 36. For more discussion, see his "Darwinism Defined" in the same science magazine (January 1987, pp. 64–70), and his book *Ever Since Darwin: Reflections in Natural History* (New York: W. W. Norton, 1977).
72. Niles Eldridge, *The Monkey Business: A Scientist Looks at Creationism* (New York: Pocket Books, 1982), p. 115.
73. Gould, *Ever Since Darwin,* p. 11.
74. Harrison does at least consider (then dismiss) the view that a pain mechanism would have survival value for nonhumans, as discussion below of his premise 3 will indicate.
75. Harrison has replied to an earlier version of my criticisms of his position (Evelyn Pluhar, "Arguing Away Suffering: A Neo-Cartesian Revival," *Between the Species* 9 [1], Winter 1993, pp. 27–41) that my example of grieving behavior after the death of a companion can be handled by a sociobiological explanation making no reference to conscious states. The explanation: The surviving member of a "superannuated breeding pair" is now past breeding; fasting would free resources for use by younger conspecifics. Thus, such a behavior would be favored by evolutionary processes. He goes on to generalize that all seemingly complex nonhuman animal behavior can in principle be explained in this nonmentalistic way. (See his "The Neo-Cartesian Revival: A Response.") Without going into the well-known problems with sociobiological explanations, let me just point out that Harrison's explanation makes no sense of the apparently grieving behavior of much younger nonhumans at the death of individuals who are not even members of their own species. As Donald Griffin convincingly argues, mentalistic explanations of complex nonhuman animal behaviors are far more economical than nonmentalistic explanations. See his *Animal Minds.*
76. Singer, *Animal Liberation,* p. 122. I observed this first-hand as an ethics discussant at the First International Conference on Farm Animal Welfare, sponsored by the University of Maryland's departments of animal and poultry science (held at the Aspen Institute, the Eastern Shore of Maryland, June 7–10, 1991). Those industry spokespersons and animal husbandry faculty who were not particularly sympathetic to concerns about nonhuman animal welfare had no problem admitting that farm animals suffer from intense confinement; they disputed the *importance* of this fact.
77. Harrison, "Theodicy and Animal Pain," p. 82.

Notes

78. Allan C. Wilson, "The Molecular Basis of Evolution," *Scientific American* 253(4), 1985, pp. 164–73.

79. In a remarkable footnote, Harrison himself appears to concede that non-human animals can be intelligent, creative, and even learn genuine languages ("Theodicy and Animal Pain," p. 82 n. 8). He makes no discernible attempt to square this admission with the claims made in the text of his paper.

80. Ibid., p. 84.

81. Harrison has replied to this criticism of mine (first made in my "Arguing Away Suffering") by saying that the problem of making sense of uncaused decisions is solved when *agents* are identified as the causes of these decisions and resultant actions. Alas, this proposal merely pushes the problem back one step: it is difficult to see how agents who choose randomly can be said to be free. By the way, compatibilists, who hold that causation is compatible with free will, would agree that agents are causes of their choices.

82. In this context, see Harrison's discussion of reflex behavior on p. 84 of "Theodicy and Animal Pain." I will address this discussion separately below in the context of nonhuman animal learning.

83. Donald Griffin has written extensively on this topic. See, e.g., his *Animal Thinking* (Cambridge, Mass.: Harvard University Press, 1984) and *Animal Minds*. See also Daisie Radner and Michael Radner, *Animal Consciousness;* Rollin, *The Unheeded Cry;* and Rachels, *Created from Animals.* For an excellent review of the ethological evidence and its ethical implications, see Marc Bekoff and Dale Jamieson, "Reflective Ethology, Applied Philosophy, and the Moral Status of Animals," chapter 1 of *Perspectives in Ethology,* vol. 9, ed. P. P. G. Bateson and P. H. Klopfer (New York: Plenum Publishing, 1991).

84. He has finally done so in his reply to an earlier version of my criticisms. He now holds that *any* attribution of conscious mental states to nonhumans is mere "linguistic confusion." Allegedly only other humans, who can verbalize their mental states, can *properly* be said to make choices, experience sadness, reason, and so forth. Any such claims about nonhumans should be framed in quotation marks to indicate their off-color sense. (See his "The Neo-Cartesian Revival: A Response.") This reply on his part fails. Those who read Harrison's argument for this contention in his reply will see that it turns on his unquestioning acceptance of a version of the verifiability criterion of meaningfulness, according to which any claims not verifiable by publicly observed criteria (e.g., language reports) are literally nonsense. The verifiability criterion is the theoretical heart of logical positivism, and, as mentioned above, is philosophically as dead as a doornail. (One cannot help but wonder why an *occasionalist,* of all people, would want to embrace a position that would construe his own view as gibberish.) (See my "Reply to Harrison," *Between the Species* 9 [2], Spring 1993, pp. 77–82, for details of Harrison's view and its problems.)

85. Harrison, "Theodicy and Animal Pain," p. 84.

86. Ibid.

87. Ibid.

88. Rollin, *The Unheeded Cry,* pp. 145–46.

89. Harrison, "Theodicy and Animal Pain," p. 85.

90. Richard Restak, *The Brain* (New York: Bantam Books, 1984), pp. 156, 162.

Notes

91. Note that this phenomenon, if it could be shown to hold for nonhumans suffering violent attack, would not by itself license moral agents to treat them in these ways, any more than we would be licensed to do the same to humans. Individuals undergoing great physical trauma are gravely damaged, even if they might possibly not be suffering *at that moment.*

92. Harrison, "The Neo-Cartesian Revival: A Response."

93. See, e.g., Gould, *Ever Since Darwin,* pp. 182–85, 207. See also Bruce Bower, "Ancient Ape Suggests Human, Chimp Lineage," *Science News* 142, September 26, 1992, p. 198.

94. Nevertheless, one must not forget that chimpanzees have very large brains in proportion to their body weight in comparison to the average mammal (Gould, *Ever Since Darwin,* p. 187). Allan Wilson notes that birds and mammals are in turn much bigger-brained in relation to body size than less complex nonhuman animals. He argues that the increased intelligence concomitant with this attribute helps to drive evolution itself, as I noted earlier. See his "The Molecular Basis of Evolution," *Scientific American* 253 (4), 1985, pp. 164–73: note his chart on p. 172. Like many other biologists and ethologists, but unlike Harrison, Wilson holds that these complex nonhuman animals have developed primitive cultures.

95. See Gould, *Ever Since Darwin,* p. 208, and Bruce Bower, "Hominid Headway," *Science News* 132, December 19 and 26, 1987, pp. 408–9.

96. Bruce Bower, "Human Brain Reveals the Anatomy of Pain," *Science News* 139, March 16, 1991, p. 167.

97. See, e.g., Robert Langreth, "Pediatric Pain," *Science News* 139, February 2, 1991, pp. 74–75.

98. "Suicide Brains: Naturally Prone to Pain?" *Science News* 138, November 10, 1990, p. 301. See also Bruce Bower, "Brain Images Show Structure of Depression," *Science News* 142, September 12, 1992, p. 165.

99. Harrison, "The Neo-Cartesian Revival: A Response."

100. C. J. Ducasse coined this term in his "Is Life After Death Possible?" in *Philosophy and Contemporary Issues,* 4th ed., ed. J. Burr and M. Goldinger (New York: Macmillan, 1980), pp. 382–91. He himself is an unabashed interactionist. For a far better response to the "impossibility of interaction" criticism than Descartes's notorious "pineal gland as seat of the soul" suggestion, see p. 390 of Ducasse's article. Interactionism, thus defended, is a much more plausible dualistic theory than occasionalism. Occasionalists, who invented their theory to skirt the objection that nonphysical and physical substances are too different to be causally related, must perforce hypothesize a nonphysical spirit, God, who creates (causes) a physical world, then causes some physical creatures in said world to have nonphysical mental states. This hardly solves the original problem!

101. Harrison, "Theodicy and Animal Pain," p. 86.

102. Ibid., p. 87; italics mine.

103. He cites studies claiming, e.g., that opiates affect "the psychological context" of the brain rather than the nerve messages. We now know that opiates work by releasing neurotransmitters that bind with brain receptors. Significantly, all vertebrates share this physiological mechanism.

Notes

104. Rollin, *The Unheeded Cry,* p. 151.

105. Charlene Crabb, "A Touch of Pain," *Discover,* June 1993, p. 41.

106. Restak, *The Brain,* pp. 136–37.

107. A. J. Beitz, "Anatomic and Chemical Organization of Descending Pain Modulation Systems," in *Animal Pain,* ed. C. E. Short and A. Van Poznak (New York: Churchill Livingstone, 1992), pp. 31–62. I thank William Robinson for providing me with this reference. For a very condensed and very clear discussion of the physiological structures underlying pain in human and nonhuman animals, see Robinson's "Some Nonhuman Animals Can Have Pains in a Morally Relevant Sense," an unpublished expanded version of his "Can Animals Feel Pain in the Morally Relevant Sense? Yes." *Ag Bioethics Forum,* 4(2), 1992, pp. 4–5. Note that it does not follow from these facts that the limbic system is required for pain perception. Nonmammalian vertebrates have brain structures and processes sufficient to result in pain experiences for humans with damaged limbic systems.

108. Crabb, "A Touch of Pain." The researcher quoted is Allan Basbaum (University of California at San Francisco).

109. Harrison, "Theodicy and Animal Pain," pp. 84–85.

110. Ibid., p. 84.

111. Ibid., p. 85. As we shall see, although he tries to make sense of nonhumans' apparently learning from what we would experience as pain, he makes no attempt to account for the use of nonhumans in pain research. If he is right, one might as well use daisies. (Sadly, a great deal of our knowledge about pain mechanisms comes from a tradition of research on nonconsenting nonhumans. See Restak, *The Brain,* pp. 157–61.)

112. Harrison, "Theodicy and Animal Pain," p. 91.

113. If Rollin's Kantian argument for the requirement of self-awareness for learning is correct, Harrison would always need to use quote marks when discussing nonhuman "learning." One cannot be self-aware without being aware in the first place.

114. Harrison, "Theodicy and Animal Pain," p. 91.

115. Harrison does also suggest, in the puzzling last section of his original paper, that nonhuman animals can be compared to "chronic amnesiacs," who learn all sorts of things from experience but forget who they are from moment to moment, retaining the lessons but not the identity of the learner (Ibid., p. 89). It is not clear that the concept of such a "learning chronic amnesiac" is coherent. However, much more seriously, this way of trying to understand nonhuman animal behavior seems to attribute consciousness to them. After all, chronic human amnesiacs are aware of the present, even if they do not recall it later.

116. Harrison, "The Neo-Cartesian Revival: A Response." The article responded to is my "Arguing Away Suffering."

117. See, e.g., Restak, *The Brain,* chapter 5; Carol Ezzell, "Memories Might Be Made of This: Closing in on the Biochemistry of Learning," *Science News* 139, May 25, 1991, pp. 228–30, and the same author's "Watching the Remembering Brain at Work," *Science News* 140, November 23, 1991, p. 333.

118. "Occam's razor" (roughly, "what can be done with fewer assumptions is done in vain with more"), used to "shave off" superfluous hypotheses or entities,

is named after English scholastic philosopher William of Occam (1300–1349). Although he was probably not the first to state some version of this principle, he was apparently the first to use it extensively. This principle is basic to inductive reasoning and, thus, to scientific hypothesizing.

119. Harrison, "Theodicy and Animal Pain," p. 85.

120. Ibid., p. 83.

121. Ibid.

122. According to Stephen Clark, more would be going wrong here than double-standard thinking. Beings acting "instinctively," he argues in his *Nature of the Beast* (Oxford: Oxford University Press, 1982), p. 20, must exercise a fair amount of initiative and intelligence. See my discussion of the "autonomy" argument for homocentrism, below.

123. Few would claim that nonhumans, as far as we know, are capable of conceptualizing moral principles and self-consciously choosing to act in accordance with those principles. This does not mean that they cannot act virtuously, however. See Sapontzis, *Morals, Reason, and Animals*, pp. 43–44, on this issue. I will return to Sapontzis's account in my discussion of the moral agency defense of homocentrism, below.

124. Harrison, "Theodicy and Animal Pain," p. 82, footnote 8.

125. That includes some theists. See, e.g., Linzey, *Christianity and the Rights of Animals; Rosen, Food for the Spirit*, and Regan, ed., *Animal Sacrifices*.

126. Harrison, "Theodicy and Animal Pain," p. 88.

127. Descartes, letter to Henry Moore, excerpted in Regan and Singer, eds., *Animal Rights and Human Obligations*, 2d ed.

128. Harrison, "Theodicy and Animal Pain," p. 91. Does this mean that they experience pain, but not in the way we do, or does it mean that they do not experience pain, unlike us? Harrison also equivocates on the meaning of 'pain experience,' as quotes below will show.

129. Ibid., p. 90.

130. Ibid.

131. Ibid.

132. Ibid., p. 90.

133. Ibid., emphasis mine.

134. He appears to be just as wrong about human infants as he is about nonhumans, as will be discussed below.

135. Harrison, "The Neo-Cartesian Revival: A Response."

136. As we shall soon see, if Harrison had made the distinction Peter Carruthers has made between conscious and unconscious experience, he could have avoided any inconsistency. Carruthers, however, is no more successful than Harrison is in making a convincing case for the machine model of nonhumans and mentally simple humans.

137. Harrison claims at one point that he is not denying that nonhuman animals are incapable of remembering past experiences, since then they could not *learn* ("Theodicy and Animal Pain," p. 89; no quotation marks bracket this time). However, the only example of nonhuman learning he gives is the unconscious "learning" of a protozoan, as we have already seen. Moreover, the thought experiments he gives us would be utterly pointless without the claim,

made explicitly, that nonhuman animals are akin to permanent amnesiacs. An amnesiac, by definition, has lost her memory. (A permanent amnesiac, he seems to think, would retain whatever has been "learned" in the past, without realizing that *she* learned it [p. 89]. But this would only be the case for habitual actions, the very kind of actions that no longer rely on conscious recollection. A painful experience the previous day is quite another matter. Amnesiacs, in fact, do not remember persons who have hurt them [unless they regain their memories!].)

138. Rollin, *The Unheeded Cry*, p. 144.

139. Carol Adams, "Abortion Rights and Animal Rights," *Between the Species* 7 (4), Fall 1991, p. 184.

140. Harrison, "Theodicy and Animal Pain," p. 90.

141. Langreth, "Pediatric Pain," pp. 74–75. See also the recent study by S. Anand and P. R. Hickey in the January 2, 1992, issue of *The New England Journal of Medicine*. Some physicians were also concerned about the dangers of anesthetizing such tiny beings; the danger turns out to be in the opposite direction.

142. D. D. Edwards, "Study Supports Easing Circumcision Pain," *Science News 133*, March 19, 1988, p. 182.

143. Langreth, "Pediatric Pain," p. 75.

144. Carruthers, *The Animals Issue*, 174–76. Carruthers does not mention Descartes's name in his briefer article, "Brute Experience." Since Carruthers's arguments against nonhuman animal suffering are essentially the same in his article and in chapter 8 of his book, I will use both sources freely in the following discussion.

145. Carruthers, "Brute Experience," p. 260.

146. Carruthers, *The Animals Issue*, p. 184.

147. Ibid., pp. 56–57. Donald Griffin, to mention but one cognitive ethologist, would disagree with Carruthers's claims about insects. See the works by Griffin cited below.

148. Ibid., p. 186.

149. Johnson, "Carruthers on Consciousness and Moral Status"; Robinson, "Some Nonhumans Can Have Pain in a Morally Relevant Sense."

150. Carruthers, "Brute Experience," p. 258.

151. Ibid., p. 262.

152. Ibid., p. 265. At first, Carruthers says that "most" of nonhuman experience is unconscious, but then he goes on to say that "[t]he experiences of all these creatures will be of the nonconscious variety" (p. 265). The discrepancy might be explained by the fact that he allows for the *possibility* that a few of the higher primates besides ourselves might have some conscious experiences, although he very much doubts it (ibid.) He makes the same point in his *The Animals Issue*, p. 186.

153. Carruthers, "Brute Experience," p. 267.

154. Ibid., p. 268.

155. Carruthers, "Can Animals Feel Pain in the Morally Relevant Sense? No." p. 2.

156. Presently, there are two major rival explanations for this baffling phenomenon; Carruthers mentions only one (see his *The Animals Issue*, p. 172). The

source of Carruthers's explanation is presumably Lawrence Weiskrantz, who has done the most extensive work on the problem. Weiskrantz proposes that blindsight results from optic nerve fibers that bypass the visual cortex to reach the midbrain. This part of the brain is related to unconscious actions. Weiskrantz suspects that stimulation of the visual cortex may be required for *conscious* sight, but not for "unconscious" sight. Michael Gazzaninga proposes, by contrast, that destruction of the affected part of the visual cortex is not complete. He has found some few living neurons in those areas. Gazzaninga hypothesizes that the stimulation is too borderline to trigger conscious sight but sufficient for unconscious recognition. See Denise Grady, "The Vision Thing: Mainly in the Brain," *Discover,* June 1993, pp. 57–66, for a careful but accessible discussion of this issue.

157. Griffin, *Animal Minds,* pp. 259–60.

158. Dennis Senchuk, *Against Instinct* (Philadelphia: Temple University Press, 1991).

159. Carruthers, "Brute Experience," p. 266.

160. I owe this distinction to William Robinson. See his "Some Nonhuman Animals Can Have Pain in the Morally Relevant Sense."

161. Carruthers, "Brute Experience," p. 262.

162. Ibid.

163. Robinson, "Some Nonhuman Animals Can Have Pain in the Morally Relevant Sense."

164. Bruce Bower, "A Child's Theory of Mind," *Science News* 144, July 17, 1993, pp. 40–41.

165. Carruthers, "Brute Experience," p. 269.

166. Johnson, "Carruthers on Consciousness and Moral Status," p. 192. The odious example is my own.

167. Johnson also recognizes this problem (ibid.). Note, however, that Carruthers has gone on in his book to make a differently based case for good treatment of babies, children, and mentally damaged adults, even if they are all automata. See my chapter 2 discussion of his arguments.

168. William Robinson has also pointed out that Carruthers's model of conscious experience is not even able to make sense of suffering by normal human adults. He notes that the experience, which Carruthers holds is not in itself painful, cannot be turned into a painful experience merely by one's possible or actual thought about one's possible or actual thought about it. For the details of his argument see "Some Nonhuman Animals Can Have Pain in the Morally Relevant Sense."

169. Robinson, ibid., gives a sketch of an intrinsic theory of consciousness that avoids the pitfalls of the Cartesian view.

170. Robinson identifies David Rosenthal as the author of such an account. See Rosenthal's "Two Concepts of Consciousness," *Philosophical Studies* 49; 1986, pp. 329–59. As Robinson notes, Rosenthal holds that some nonhumans are able to think about their sensations.

171. Carruthers, "Brute Thought," p. 191. As Rollin points out, the verbal requirement for thought would make language acquisition impossible. See *The Unheeded Cry,* pp. 138–39.

Notes

172. See Donald Griffin, *The Question of Animal Awareness: Evolutionary Continuity of Mental Experience* (New York: Rockefeller University Press, 1981), *Animal Thinking,* and *Animal Minds;* Stephen Walker, *Animal Thought* (London: Routledge and Kegan Paul, 1983); Stephen Clark, *The Nature of the Beast* (Oxford: Oxford University Press, 1982); Bekoff and Jamieson, "Reflective Ethology, Applied Philosophy, and the Moral Status of Animals"; Rollin, *The Unheeded Cry,* and *Animal Rights and Human Morality,* chapter 1; Radner and Radner, *Animal Consciousness;* Singer, *Animal Liberation,* chapters 1, 5, 6; Regan, *The Case for Animal Rights,* chapters 1, 2; Sapontzis, *Morals, Reason, and Animals,* pp. 216–22.

173. Rollin, *The Unheeded Cry,* p. 49.

174. "Biting Flies Flee Elephants' Swatters,'" *Science News* 144, July 31, 1993, p. 70.

175. Griffin, *Animal Thinking.* See also his "A New Science that Sees Animals as Conscious Beings," *The Smithsonian,* March 1985, pp. 67–75, and chapter 5 of his 1992 *Animal Minds.*

176. Griffin, *Animal Minds,* pp. 107–8. For a specific example, see his discussion of a study done on "bright" and "dumb" crows on pp. 105–6.

177. See Gotthart Berger, *Monkeys and Apes* (New York: Arco Publishing Co., 1985), pp. 82, 220–21. See Jane Goodall, *The Chimpanzees of Gombe* (Cambridge, Mass.: Harvard University Press, 1986), for the details of observations made over the course of more than thirty years.

178. Griffin, *Animal Minds,* pp. 1–2.

179. Sue Savage-Rumbaugh and Roger Lewin, "Ape at the Brink," *Discover,* September 1994, pp. 91–98. This piece is an excerpt from the authors' *Kanzi: The Ape at the Brink of the Human Mind* (New York: John Wiley and Sons, 1994).

180. E. Tylinek and G. Berger, *Monkeys and Apes* (New York: Arco Publishing Co., 1985), p. 96.

181. "Monkeying Around With the Relatives," *Discover,* March 1988, pp. 26–27.

182. "Brain Cell 'Coupling' Linked to Memories," *The Pittsburgh Press,* Pittsburgh, Pa., November 1, 1989, p. A15.

183. Charlene Crabb, "Rio, the Logical Sea Lion," *Discover,* February 1993, p. 20. Ronald Schusterman of California State University, Hayward, who conducted the experiments, believes that animals belonging to many other species could probably do the same; so far, none but Rio has been tested for an understanding of elementary logic.

184. Bruce Bower, "A 'Handy' Guide to Primate Evolution," *Science News* 135, January 7, 1989, pp. 10–12.

185. Griffin, "A New Science That Sees Animals as Conscious Beings."

186. Bruce Bower, "Grammar-Schooled Dolphins," *Science News* 126, December 1, 1984, pp. 346–48. Perhaps it is just as well that we have not learned how to ask the dolphins to tell us what they think of our behavior!

187. Dawn D. Bennett, "Making Sense of Animal Sounds," *Science News* 127, May 18, 1985, pp. 314–17.

188. See Sharon Brownlee, "A Riddle Wrapped in a Mystery," *Discover,* Octo-

ber 1985, pp. 85–93; "Kanzi Extends His Speech Reach," *Science News* 134, August 27, 1988, p. 140; "Chimp's Recall Making History," AP report (Atlanta), *The Pittsburgh Press,* July 9, 1991, p. A2; Radner and Radner, *Animal Consciousness,* chapter 7; and Erik Eckholm, "Language Acquisition in Nonhuman Primates," in *Animal Rights and Human Obligations,* ed. Regan and Singer, pp. 66–72.

189. Reported on *Weekend Edition,* National Public Radio, April 23, 1988.

190. See a thorough discussion of the honeyguide literature in Griffin's *Animal Minds,* pp. 164–69.

191. J. Fisher and R. A. Hinde, "The Opening of Milk Bottles by Birds," *British Birds* 42, 1949, pp. 347–57, and A. C. Wilson, "The Molecular Basis of Evolution," *Scientific American* 253 (4), 1985, pp. 164–73. See also Radner and Radner, *Animal Consciousness,* pp. 144–45, and Griffin, *Animal Minds,* pp. 41–42.

192. Griffin, *Animal Minds,* p. 42.

193. Geoffrey Cowley, "The Wisdom of Animals," *Newsweek,* May 23, 1988, p. 56. See also Eugene Linden, "Can Animals Think?" *Time,* March 22, 1993, pp. 58–60.

194. Frey, *Interests and Rights: The Case Against Animals.*

195. For excellent critiques, see Regan, *The Case for Animal Rights,* pp. 38–49, and Sapontzis, *Morals, Reason, and Animals,* pp. 111–29.

196. R. G. Frey, "Autonomy and the Value of Animal Life," *The Monist* 70 (1), January 1987, p. 63 n. 17. (He is referring specifically to Regan's criticisms here.)

197. Loren E. Lomasky, *Persons, Rights, and the Moral Community* (Oxford: Oxford University Press, 1987), pp. 44, 183.

198. Ibid., p. 45.

199. Ibid., p. 223.

200. Clark, *The Nature of the Beast,* pp. 19–22. See also Senchuk, *Against Instinct.*

201. Griffin, *Animal Minds,* p. 208.

202. Michael A. Fox, *The Case for Animal Experimentation* (Berkeley: University of California Press, 1986), pp. 28–29.

203. Ibid., p. 27.

204. Frey, "Autonomy and the Value of Animal Life," p. 61.

205. Frey objects that the senile and the paranoid would count as having "preferential autonomy" in Regan's view. He seriously doubts that such lives have much value, hence he considers Regan's concept "impoverished." Once again, however, Frey's counterargument only works if we assume that "autonomy" must be full-fledged. Why does it not make sense to speak of "minimal" autonomy? To the extent to which the senile and the mentally ill are able to have desires and act upon them, they act purposefully, and have some measure of control over their lives. They are also capable of caring about what happens to them, and of valuing their own lives, even if some others doubt that those lives have much value.

206. Fox reversed himself the same year his *The Case for Animal Experimentation* was published. See his letter to the editor in *The Scientist,* December 15, 1986. For a deeply personal, candid account of his change of mind (and heart),

see "Animal Experimentation: A Philosopher's Changing Views," *Between the Species* 3 (2), Spring 1987, pp. 55–60, 75, 80.

207. McCloskey, "The Moral Case for Experimentation on Animals," p. 79. McCloskey is not a homocentrist, however: he is well aware of the fact that not all humans have the capacity for moral agency, even potentially. We will return to his view later.

208. Melden, *Rights in Moral Lives*. Melden is also not simply describable as a homocentrist, although he does believe that all humans can be gathered into the moral community. His position will also be discussed in detail later.

209. Stanley Wechkin, Jules H. Masserman, and William Terris Jr., "Shock to a Conspecific as an Aversive Stimulus," *Psychonomic Science* 1, 1964, pp. 47–48, and "'Altruistic' Behavior in Rhesus Monkeys," *The American Journal of Psychiatry* 121, 1964, pp. 584–85. See James Rachels's discussion of these experiments in his "Do Animals Have a Right to Liberty?" in *Animal Rights and Human Obligations*, ed. Regan and Singer, p. 215.

210. Experimental psychologist Stanley Milgram has done a number of related experiments, and all have had roughly the same outcome. Other researchers have confirmed his results. See his own description of this body of work in Stanley Milgram, *Obedience to Authority* (New York: Harper & Row, 1974).

211. Joan Dunayer, "The Nature of Altruism," *The Animals' Agenda*, April 1990, p. 29.

212. Ibid., p. 28.

213. Ibid.

214. Melden, *Rights in Moral Lives*, pp. 64–71. However, note that Melden does not really accord the family dog membership in the family: "What a pity it is when the pets die! But they are replaceable. And there is none of the grief felt when a member of the family dies" (p. 62). It is plain that in Melden's view such a dog would be at best a very peripheral member of the moral community.

215. S. F. Sapontzis, "Are Animals Moral Beings?" *American Philosophical Quarterly* 17 (1), January 1980, pp. 45–52. Cf. his *Morals, Reason, and Animals*, pp. 43–44.

216. Immanuel Kant, *Grounding for the Metaphysics of Morals*, trans. James W. Ellington (Indianapolis: Hackett Press, 1981), pp. 35–36.

217. Carl Cohen, "The Case for the Use of Animals in Biomedical Research," *The New England Journal of Medicine*, October 2, 1986, p. 865.

218. Jan Narveson, "On a Case for Animal Rights," *The Monist* 70 (1), January 1987, pp. 31–49. For Kant, of course, moral agency and autonomy are inseparable.

219. The reader will find an excellent introduction to the concepts of ethics in William Frankena, *Ethics*, 2d ed. (Englewood Cliffs: Prentice-Hall, 1973).

220. Ibid., p. 14.

221. Kant, *Grounding for the Metaphysic of Morals*, p. 36. This is one of the formulations of the categorical imperative, the "end-in-itself" formula, as note 21 on the same page points out.

222. Gewirth, *Reason and Morality*, p. 135.

223. W. D. Ross, *The Right and the Good* (Oxford: Oxford University Press, 1930), and *The Foundations of Ethics* (Oxford: Oxford University Press, 1939).

Notes

224. Frankena, *Ethics*, p. 52.

225. Tom Regan, *All That Dwell Therein* (Berkeley: University of California Press, 1982), p. 117. Basic moral rights are contrasted with "nonbasic moral rights": the latter arise from other obligations we have. For example, a being with no basic moral rights at all would have a "nonbasic moral right to life" if we protect it solely because it would deeply distress a being who does have basic moral rights. I think it is quite misleading to refer to such protection in rights terms at all: we would normally only speak in terms of the rights of the "basic" rights holder. Thus, I will not speak in terms of "nonbasic" moral rights. Although strictly speaking "basic moral rights" can be seen as redundant, I will keep the "basic" because it serves to underscore the fact that rights ground obligations. (Deontologists disagree about the precisely correct analysis of 'moral right.' For example, McCloskey and Regan, both deontologists, disagree about whether rights are moral claims or entitlements [see McCloskey, "The Moral Case for Experimentation on Animals," pp. 76–77]. At this point, nothing hinges on these disagreements.)

226. R. G. Frey, "The Significance of Agency and Marginal Cases," *Philosophica* 39 (1), 1987, p. 40.

227. Narveson, "On a Case for Animal Rights," pp. 44–46.

228. See Singer, *Animal Liberation*, pp. 18–20; Rollin, *Animal Rights and Human Morality*, pp. 27–28; and Regan, "An Examination and Defense of One Argument Concerning Animal Rights," in *All That Dwell Therein*, pp. 113–47.

229. Regan, ibid., p. 116. Regan points out that the argument did not get its name from its initial proponents. Jan Narveson, who opposes the argument, was the first to call it an appeal to "marginal" (nonparadigmatic) cases.

230. Regan, ibid.

231. Rollin, *Animal Rights and Human Morality*, pp. 27–28.

232. Singer, *Animal Liberation*, p. 19.

233. Ibid.

234. This argument, contained in "A Vindication of the Rights of Brutes," a satirical pamphlet written by Thomas Taylor, is paraphrased by Singer on p. 1 of *Animal Liberation*.

2 RESPONSES TO THE ARGUMENT FROM MARGINAL CASES

1. Ernest Partridge, "Three Wrong Leads in a Search for an Environmental Ethic: Tom Regan on Animal Rights, Inherent Values, and 'Deep Ecology,'" *Ethics and Animals* 5 (3), September 1984, pp. 62–65.

2. Ibid., p. 62.

3. Charlie Blatz, "Why (Most) Humans Are More Important Than Other Animals: Reflections on the Foundations of Ethics," *Between the Species* 1 (4), 1985, p. 16 n. 13. As I pointed out in my "The Personhood View and The Argument from Marginal Cases," *Philosophica* 39 (1), 1987, p. 25, Blatz's general argument for restricting moral considerability to full persons fails because he mistakenly believes that those who make practical morality possible, namely moral agents, must therefore be the only legitimate objects of moral concern.

Notes

For detailed criticism of Blatz's argument, see Sapontzis, *Morals, Reason, and Animals,* pp. 145–47.

4. Theodore Vitali, "Sport Hunting: Moral or Immoral?" *Environmental Ethics* 12 (1), Spring 1990, pp. 73–75.

5. Reported on the national news program *Morning Edition,* National Public Radio, August 17, 1990. See also "Setting Dogs on Prisoners," *The Animals' Agenda,* October 1990, p. 32.

6. "Death Penalty Interview," aired on National Public Radio's evening news program *All Things Considered* on July 13, 1990. The source of these statistics is Stephen Bright, director of the Southern Prisoners' Defense Committee. It is also estimated that roughly 6 percent of the maximum security prison population in the United States is schizophrenic: see Claudia Wallis and James Willwerth, "Awakenings: Schizophrenia," *Time,* July 6, 1992, pp. 53–57, p. 55.

7. "Execution of the Mentally Retarded," *United States of America: The Death Penalty,* Amnesty International, 1990, pp. 6–7.

8. C. E. Harris Jr., *Applying Moral Theories* (Belmont: Wadsworth Publishing Co., 1986), p. 134.

9. Ibid., p. 143. The emphasis is my own. Also see p. 128: "The idea that equal respect is due all human beings is the basis for the universalization principle."

10. Office of Technology Assessment, *Alternatives to Animal Use in Research, Testing, and Education* (New York: Marcel Dekker, Inc., 1988), p. 77. (As we shall see, the Office of Technology Assessment, the research arm of the U.S. Congress, has another, more serious response to the argument from marginal cases.)

11. Robert Nozick, "Review of Tom Regan's *The Case for Animal Rights,*" *New York Times Book Review,* November 27, 1983, p. 11.

12. Ibid.

13. Ibid., p. 29.

14. Ibid.

15. Alan Holland, "On Behalf of a Moderate Speciesism," *The Journal of Applied Philosophy* 1 (2), 1984, p. 282.

16. Ibid.

17. Roger Crisp, "A Comment on 'On Behalf of a Moderate Speciesism' by Alan Holland," *The Journal of Applied Philosophy* 2 (2), 1985, pp. 279–80.

18. Office of Technology Assessment, *Alternatives to Animal Use,* p. 77. The charge is repeated on p. 83.

19. Ibid., p. 77. They quote Tom Regan: "Thus, if we want to insist that [marginal humans] have an equal right to life . . . we cannot consistently maintain that animals, because they fail to satisfy these [full-personhood] conditions, therefore lack this right."

20. Ibid., p. 83.

21. See the textbook "straw person" fallacies in Robert J. White, "The Facts About Animal Research," *Reader's Digest,* March 1988, pp. 127–32, and John G. Hubbell, "The 'Animal Rights' War on Medicine," *Reader's Digest,* June 1990, pp. 70–76. The latter article is particularly egregious in its suppression and distortion of evidence. *Reader's Digest* mass-produced and advertised reprints of both articles. Not surprisingly, this periodical's policy is to refuse to publish any articles in support of nonhuman animal rights.

Notes

22. Office of Technology Assessment, *Alternatives to Animal Use in Research*, p. 80.

23. Ibid., p. 83.

24. Cohen, "The Case for the Use of Animals in Biomedical Research," p. 865.

25. Ibid., p. 866.

26. Ibid.

27. Sapontzis, *Morals, Reason, and Animals*, pp. 210–13.

28. Cohen, "The Case for the Use of Animals in Biomedical Research," p. 867.

29. Ibid.

30. Ibid., p. 866.

31. Ibid., p. 869.

32. Steve Sapontzis, "Speciesism," *Between the Species* 4 (2), Spring 1988, p. 98. (This short article is a commentary on my "Speciesism: A Form of Bigotry or a Justified View?" *Between the Species* 4 [2], 1988, pp. 83–96.) Sapontzis's major point is that the appeal to the rights of marginal humans is irrelevant to the moral status of animals. See my response on pp. 99–101 of the same issue of *Between the Species*.

33. Ethologists David Wood-Gush and Alex Stolba have demonstrated this in their work. For a good summary of their results, see Marlene Halverson, *Farm Animal Welfare: Crisis or Opportunity for Agriculture?* Department of Agricultural and Applied Economics, University of Minnesota, pp. 11–14, 46.

34. "Chimp's Recall Making History," AP report (Atlanta), *The Pittsburgh Press*, July 9, 1991, p. A2.

35. "Calculating Apes," *Science News*, May 23, 1987, p. 334, and August 27, 1988, p. 140.

36. "Scientists Say Chimps Find Rx in a Leaf," *The Pittsburgh Press*, August 18, 1985, p. A9, and "Do Chimps Practice Medicine With Herbs?" *The Washington Post*, December 27, 1985.

37. "Monkeys Play By the Numbers," *Science News*, June 15, 1991, p. 383.

38. "Machiavellian Monkeys," *Discover*, June 1991, pp. 69–73.

39. C. A. J. Coady, "Defending Human Chauvinism," *Report from the Center for Philosophy and Public Policy* 6 (4), University of Maryland, Fall 1986, p. 14.

40. Maurice Temerlin, *Lucy: Growing Up Human* (Palo Alto: Science and Behavior Books, Inc., 1975), p. 50.

41. A. V. Townsend, "Radical Vegetarians," *The Australasian Journal of Philosophy* 57 (1), 1979, p. 93.

42. Carruthers, *The Animals Issue*, pp. 115–16. This is not the only argument Carruthers gives against the marginal cases challenge. His separate "social stability" argument (pp. 117–18) is a species of the "side effects" appeals made by egoists and utilitarians in their attempts to escape that challenge; these appeals will be discussed later in this chapter.

43. Jane English, "Abortion and the Concept of a Person," *The Canadian Journal of Philosophy* 5 (2), October 1975, pp. 233–43; reprinted in *Ethics for Modern Life*, 4th ed. ed. R. Abelson and M. L. Friquegnon (New York: St. Martin's Press, 1991), pp. 211–18. (My page references will be to the latter publication.)

44. Ibid., p. 217.

45. Ibid.

46. Ibid.

47. Ibid. Italics are mine. Peter Carruthers draws the identical conclusion about early versus late stage abortions. See his *The Animals Issue*, pp. 117, 165.

48. English, "Abortion and the Concept of a Person," p. 217.

49. Carruthers, *The Animals Issue*, p. 114.

50. Ibid., p. 115.

51. Ibid., p. 161.

52. See St. Thomas Aquinas, "Differences Between Rational and Other Creatures," from *Summa Contra Gentiles* (Chicago: Benziger Brothers, 1928), chapter 112 of book 3 part 2; and Immanuel Kant, "Duties to Animals and Spirits," from *Lectures on Ethics*, trans. Louis Infield (New York: Harper & Row, 1963), pp. 239–41.

53. Carruthers, *The Animals Issue*, pp. 159–61. The reader familiar with Carruthers's view of nonhuman animal mentality will remember that "cruelty" to nonhumans is strictly impossible, according to him, since they are allegedly incapable of consciousness (see my discussion of his view in chapter 1). He is speaking here, for the moment, purely in "commonsense" terms, reserving his denial of consciousness for the last chapter of his book. (Fools that we are, we "ordinary" folk persist in believing that a screaming rabbit with detergent in her eyes actually experiences pain.)

54. Ibid., p. 160.

55. Ibid., pp. 160–61.

56. Ibid., p. 118.

57. Peter Singer, "Animal Liberation or Animal Rights?" *The Monist* 70 (1), January 1987, p. 4.

58. Carruthers, *The Animals Issue*, p. 119.

59. Ibid.

60. Ibid., p. 120. Carruthers treats this last point as a separate, third argument against the appeal to anthropology. However, since this "third" point presumes, as does the "second," that societies killing human nonagents to maximize societal survival can do so while fully recognizing those individuals' right to life, it is convenient to treat the two together as one argument.

61. Helga Kuhse and Peter Singer, *Should the Baby Live?* (Oxford: Oxford University Press, 1985), pp. 106–7.

62. Ibid., p. 111.

63. Ibid., p. 110.

64. Srinivasa Prasad, "India Infanticide Is High," AP report, *The Pittsburgh Post-Gazette*, February 14, 1993, p. A7.

65. Coady, "Defending Human Chauvinism," p. 14.

66. Ibid.

67. Narveson, "On a Case for Animal Rights," p. 44.

68. Jesse Kalin, "Two Kinds of Moral Reasoning," *Canadian Journal of Philosophy* 5 (3), 1975, p. 328. See Narveson's acknowledgment in his earlier article "Animal Rights," *Canadian Journal of Philosophy* 7(1), 1977, p. 176.

69. Narveson, "On a Case for Animal Rights," p. 44.

70. Ibid., p. 47.

71. Ibid., p. 46.

72. Ibid.

73. Narveson, "Animal Rights," p. 177.

74. Narveson, "On a Case for Animal Rights," p. 47.

75. Narveson, "Animal Rights," p. 178.

76. Tom Regan, "Narveson on Egoism and the Rights of Animals," *Canadian Journal of Philosophy* 7 (1), 1977, pp. 181–84.

77. Peter Carruthers does not believe that this rule would extend enough protection to loved ones (*The Animals Issue*, pp. 117–18). The latter would be regarded as "property" of caring rational agents, to be respected as such when possible, but to be shunted aside when vital interests are at stake (to use his example, we could blow them up if they are blocking our escape from kidnappers, just as we would dynamite our neighbor's beloved BMW if it were in the way). The obvious answer to this objection is that one would need to strengthen the prohibition against harming beloved marginal humans. The prohibition should be as strong as the sentiment, which would surely eclipse any attachment one would have to a BMW.

78. Narveson, "On a Case for Animal Rights," p. 46.

79. Ibid., p. 47.

80. Some sources of information on this voluminous subject are Thomas Levenson, "The Heart of the Matter," *Discover*, February 1985, pp. 82–87; Harold M. Schmeck Jr., "Fetal Tissue Is Alternative to Marrow Transplants," *New York Times*, May 15, 1986, p. A10; Joe Levine, "Help from the Unborn," *Time*, January 12, 1987, p. 62; Rick Weiss, "Forbidding Fruits of Fetal-Cell Research," *Science News* 134, November 5, 1988, pp. 296–98; Rick Weiss, "Bypassing the Ban," *Science News* 136, December 9, 1989, pp. 378–79; Rick Weiss, "Fetal-Cell Recipient Showing Improvements," *Science News* 137, February 3, 1990, p. 70; and Jack Anderson, "Tissue Use Is Life-and-Death Debate," syndicated column, *The Herald-Standard*, Uniontown, Pa., July 24, 1991, p. B2.

81. Levenson, "The Heart of the Matter"; Emanuel Thorne (Aspen Institute for Humanistic Studies, Washington, D.C.), *The Wall Street Journal*, August 1987, p. 16.

82. L. W. Sumner, "A Third Way," in *The Problem of Abortion*, ed. Joel Feinberg (Belmont: Wadsworth Publishing Co., 1984), p. 86.

83. Harold M. Schmeck Jr., "New Light on the Chemistry of Dreams," *New York Times*, December 29, 1987, pp. C1, C12.

84. Robert N. Langreth, "Pediatric Pain," *Science News* 139, February 2, 1991, pp. 74–75.

85. Edd Doerr and James W. Prescott, eds., *Abortion Rights and Fetal Personhood* (Long Beach: Centerline Press, 1989).

86. Narveson, "On a Case for Animal Rights," p. 47.

87. Lance Morrow, "When One Body Can Save Another," *Time*, June 17, 1991, pp. 54–58. Poll results are on pp. 56–57.

88. He is quoted in "Neomorts: A New Alternative in the Laboratory," *The Animals' Agenda*, March 1987, p. 20.

89. Ibid., pp. 20–21.

90. Evelyn B. Pluhar, "Must an Opponent of Animal Rights Also Be an Opponent of Human Rights?" *Inquiry* 24 (2), June 1981, p. 235.

91. Dale Jamieson, "Rational Egoism and Animal Rights," *Environmental*

Notes

Ethics 3, Summer 1981, pp. 167–71. The quote is on p. 171.

92. Peter Carruthers also uses this sort of appeal, calling it the "argument from social stability" (see his *The Animals Issue,* p. 117.)

93. Sapontzis, *Morals, Reason, and Animals,* pp. 140–43.

94. Ibid., p. 141.

95. Ibid.

96. Ibid.

97. Feinberg, "Abortion," p. 267.

98. Melden, *Rights and Persons,* p. 223. Note, however, that despite this rather distressing characterization of severely defective babies, Melden does not deny moral considerability to them. His reasons for including them in the moral community, as well as other humans who can never be and were never full persons, are primarily speciesist; see chapter 3 for his and others' arguments in this vein.

99. Ibid., p. 221.

100. Ibid., p. 222.

101. Ibid., p. 223.

102. Frey, "The Significance of Agency and Marginal Cases," p. 42.

103. H. J. McCloskey, "Moral Rights and Animals," *Inquiry* 22 (1–2), Summer 1979, p. 42. As we saw in chapter 1, Peter Carruthers, another follower of the full-personhood view, made the same suggestion in his 1989 article, "Brute Experience," p. 269.

104. Melden, *Rights and Persons,* p. 218.

105. Ibid., p. 220.

106. Ibid., p. 219.

107. Ibid.

108. Ibid., p. 220.

109. He suggests something along these lines on p. 218.

110. See chapter 3 for my discussion and refutation of the view that those who have suffered misfortunes like Melden's Smith are thereby deserving of full moral rights, unlike those who have never had the capacity for full personhood. This argument is one of many made to show that speciesism is justified, so it will be taken up in the chapter devoted to that topic rather than here.

111. Joel Feinberg, *Harm to Others* (Oxford: Oxford University Press, 1984), chapter 2, sections 3–7.

112. David DeGrazia, "The Distinction Between Equality in Moral Status and Deserving Equal Consideration," *Between the Species* 7 (2), Spring 1991, p. 75.

113. Kathy Squadrito, "Commentary: Interests and Equal Moral Status," *Between the Species* 7 (2), Spring 1991, pp. 78–79.

114. David DeGrazia, "Response," *Between the Species* 7 (2), Spring 1991, p. 80.

115. DeGrazia, "The Distinction Between Equality in Moral Status and Deserving Equal Consideration," pp. 75–76.

116. DeGrazia, "Response," p. 80.

117. DeGrazia, "The Distinction Between Equality in Moral Status and Deserving Equal Consideration," pp. 75–76. As DeGrazia correctly points out, Tom Regan at times also takes the position that some lives are richer than others, and that as a result, under very restricted circumstances, lesser lives should be

Notes

sacrificed in order to spare richer ones. Although Regan would permit vastly fewer such deaths than Frey, the two do seem to agree in this key respect. I shall argue later in this book that Regan cannot consistently take such a position.

118. R. G. Frey, "Moral Standing, the Value of Lives, and Speciesism," *Between the Species* 4 (3), Summer 1988, p. 197. He makes the same point in his "Autonomy and the Value of Life," pp. 57–58.

119. Frey, "Moral Standing, the Value of Lives, and Speciesism," p. 197.

120. Ibid.

121. DeGrazia, "Response," p. 80.

122. Bernard Rollin, "The Frankenstein Thing," in *Genetic Engineering of Animals: An Agricultural Perspective*, ed. J. W. Evans and A. Hollaender (New York: Plenum Press, 1986), p. 287.

3 SPECIESISM AND FULL PERSONHOOD

1. As discussed in chapter 2, these are the types of humans who pose moral dilemmas for followers of the full-personhood view. That unfortunate designation "marginal" in the argument from marginal cases applies to them alone. Those who have *lost* their moral agency, even permanently, can retain protection if they formerly wished such treatment in case of incapacitation. Respecting the former wishes of individuals who have irretrievably lost full personhood is analogous to respecting the former wishes of dead people.

2. Peter Singer, *Animal Liberation* (New York: Avon Books, 1975). The second edition of this classic in the nonhuman animal ethics debate (New York: Random House, 1990) contains essentially the same treatment of speciesism. (Unless otherwise specified, subsequent references to *Animal Liberation* will be keyed to the second edition.) See also James Rachels, *Created from Animals* (Oxford: Oxford University Press, 1990), p. 181.

3. Singer, *Animal Liberation,* p. 6.

4. Ibid., p. 9.

5. Ibid., p. 19.

6. Ibid., p. 9.

7. See, e.g., Thomas Young, "The Morality of Killing Animals: Four Arguments," *Ethics and Animals* 5 (4), 1984, p. 89.

8. Cohen, "The Case for the Use of Animals in Biomedical Research," p. 867.

9. Leslie Francis and Richard Norman, "Some Animals Are More Equal Than Others," *Philosophy* 53, 1978, p. 527.

10. Cohen, "The Case for the Use of Animals in Biomedical Research," p. 867.

11. Fox, *The Case for Animal Experimentation,* pp. 58–59.

12. *The Animals' Agenda,* March 1991, p. 2. The percentages were 88.8 percent for the civil rights movement, 83.3 percent for feminism, 86.3 percent against apartheid, 83 percent antiwar, 58.2 percent for gay liberation (with 24 percent being "neutral" on this issue; one wishes for more "liberated" attitudes in this regard). No comparison figures were given to document the attitudes of those opposed to nonhuman animal rights, but it is clear that the charge of misanthropy against nonhuman animal rights supporters is highly questionable.

13. *The Animals' Agenda,* January/February 1990, p. 46.

14. Cohen, "The Case for the Use of Animals in Biomedical Research," pp. 865–66.

15. Ibid., p. 867.

16. Sapontzis, *Morals, Reason, and Animals,* p. 85.

17. Fox, "Animal Experimentation: A Philosopher's Changing Views," p. 56.

18. Sapontzis, "Speciesism," p. 98. Sapontzis's article is a commentary on an earlier article of mine, "Speciesism: A Form of Bigotry or a Justified View?" published in the same issue, pp. 83–96.

19. Sapontzis in his commentary above actually denies that Singer construes speciesism in this way, but as we have seen, Singer does indeed explicitly link speciesism to the treatment of marginal cases. See Singer, *Animal Liberation,* p. 98, and my reply, "On the Relevance of Marginal Cases: A Reply to Sapontzis," *Between the Species* 4 (2), p. 100.

20. Office of Technology Assessment, *Alternatives to Animal Use in Research, Testing, and Education.* See my chapter 2 for a discussion of their attempts to defeat the argument from marginal cases.

21. Mary Midgley, *Animals and Why They Matter* (Athens: University of Georgia Press, 1984), p. 99.

22. Ibid.

23. Ibid., p. 100.

24. Ibid.

25. Ibid.

26. "Rap Artist Blasts Elections," AP report, *The Herald-Standard,* Uniontown, Pa., August 17, 1992, p. D4.

27. See, e.g., Lisa Newton's classic article, "Reverse Discrimination As Unjustified," *Ethics* 83 (4), 1973, pp. 308–12.

28. Reported by Carl Rowan in his column "Court Ruling Cruel to Blacks," *The Pittsburgh Press,* January 28, 1989, p. B2.

29. For more reflections on this topic, see my "Preferential Hiring and Unjust Sacrifice," *The Philosophical Forum* 12 (3), 1981, pp. 214–24.

30. Midgley, *Animals and Why They Matter,* p. 100.

31. Rollin, "The Frankenstein Thing," pp. 288–89.

32. Jared Diamond, "Making a Chimp Out of Man," *Discover,* December 1984, pp. 55–60.

33. Rollin, "The Frankenstein Thing," p. 289.

34. Ibid.

35. "Gene Data Place Home of 'Eve' in Africa," *Science News* 140, September 28, 1991, p. 197. See Steven J. Gould's clarification of this hypothesis and its implications in his "Eve and Her Tree," *Discover,* July 1992, p. 32. Scientific controversy over the data continues, but evidence so far suggests that we do have a "common mitochondrial ancestor," even if it remains unclear how the branches of the "family tree" are to be understood. See Bruce Bower, "New Gene Study Enters Human Origins Debate," *Science News* 144, September 25, 1993, pp. 196–97.

36. Michael A. Fox, "Animal Liberation: A Critique," *Ethics* 88 (2), 1978, p. 112 (italics mine).

Notes

37. Stanley Benn, "Egalitarianism and Equal Consideration of Interests," in *Equality,* ed. J. R. Pennock and J. W. Chapman (New York: Atherton, 1967), p. 62.

38. Peter Singer, *Animal Liberation,* pp. 240–41.

39. Rachels, *Created from Animals,* pp. 186–87.

40. Michael Wreen, "In Defense of Speciesism," *Ethics and Animals* 5 (3), September 1984, pp. 53, 56. Wreen couches his view in terms of "personhood," not "full personhood," but the latter phrase is an accurate description of his primary rights bearers. See my chapter 1 on the arguments for calling highly autonomous moral agents "full persons" rather than "persons."

41. Rachels, *Created from Animals,* p. 182. Rachels also distinguishes "unqualified" from "qualified" speciesism. The "unqualified" speciesist holds that mere species membership can be a morally relevant characteristic, whereas the "qualified" speciesist believes that species membership is a marker of sorts for other morally relevant characteristics (e.g., rationality, autonomy, language ability, etc.) (pp. 182–84). Rachels dismisses the first view on the ground that species could not possibly be a morally relevant characteristic, but he does not consider the more sophisticated view linking full personhood to species membership. He rejects the second view because none of the proffered characteristics distinguishes *all* humans from *all* nonhumans. We have already discussed this in chapter 1. For that reason, I will not adopt Rachels's unqualified/qualified speciesism distinction.

42. Singer, *Animal Liberation,* p. 9.

43. Ibid. Rachels, *Created from Animals,* pp. 182–84.

44. Alan White, "Why Animals Cannot Have Rights," in *Animal Rights and Human Obligations,* ed. Regan and Singer, p. 120.

45. Ibid.

46. Ibid.

47. Ibid., p. 121.

48. See Steve Sapontzis's enlightening discussion in chapter 4 of *Morals, Reason, and Animals* of the confusion over different concepts of personhood in moral debates.

49. White, "Why Animals Cannot Have Rights," p. 120.

50. Ibid.

51. Wreen, "In Defense of Speciesism," p. 50 (italics mine).

52. Sidney Shoemaker, *Self-Knowledge and Self-Identity* (Ithaca: Cornell University Press, 1962), pp. 3–4.

53. Ibid., p. 4.

54. Wreen, "In Defense of Speciesism," p. 50.

55. Evelyn Pluhar, "Speciesism Not Justified," *Ethics and Animals* 5 (4), December 1984, p. 123.

56. Michael Wreen, "If At All Humanly Possible," *Between the Species* 2 (4), 1986, p. 191.

57. Ibid., p. 192.

58. McCloskey, "Moral Rights and Animals," pp. 23–54.

59. Ann S. Causey, "On the Morality of Hunting," *Environmental Ethics* 11 (4), Winter 1989, p. 335.

Notes

60. Paul Taylor, *Respect for Nature* (Princeton: Princeton University Press, 1986). Causey cites Taylor on her p. 335.

61. Ibid., chapter 5. This is the very chapter Causey cites in favor of her view.

62. Fox, *The Case for Animal Experimentation*, p. 63. (Fox has since repudiated speciesism, as mentioned above.)

63. Benn, "Egalitarianism and Equal Consideration of Interests," p. 62.

64. Wreen, "In Defense of Speciesism," p. 52.

65. Wreen has replied to this criticism of mine (among others), I have replied in turn, he has responded once more, and I have again commented. Although our debate has greatly increased the complexity of the appeal to fairness, the problem remains basically the same. Readers who want to read the full debate for themselves should read Wreen's "In Defense of Speciesism"; my "Speciesism Not Justified"; Wreen's "My Kind of Person," *Between the Species* 2 (1), 1986, pp. 23–28; my "Speciesism Revisited," *Between the Species* 2 (4), 1986, pp. 184–89; his "If At All Humanly Possible"; and, finally, my "Speciesism: A Form of Bigotry or a Justified View?" pp. 86–87.

66. Feinberg, *Harm to Others*, pp. 79–85.

67. Feinberg, "Abortion," pp. 266–67.

68. Ibid.

69. John T. Noonan Jr., "An Almost Absolute Value in History," in *Philosophy and Contemporary Issues*, 6th ed., ed. J. Burr and M. Goldinger (New York: Macmillan Publishing Co., 1992), pp. 263–68.

70. Daniel Callahan, *Abortion: Law, Choice, and Morality* (New York: Macmillan Publishing Co., 1970).

71. Sumner, "A Third Way," pp. 71–93.

72. Expectations that nonhuman-animal-to-human organ transplants will finally succeed are high precisely because of drugs of this kind. On June 28, 1992, a fifteen-year-old baboon was killed for his liver in a transplant operation at Presbyterian University Hospital in Pittsburgh, Pennsylvania. Surgeons were attempting to save a human whose own liver had been destroyed by the hepatitis B virus. See "Baboon-to-Human Transplant Sparks Debate," AP report, *The Herald-Standard*, Uniontown, Pa., p. A2, and "A Life for a Life," *Time*, July 13, 1992, p. 21. Although the human died after a cerebral hemorrhage on September 6, his transplanted liver functioned well for an unprecedentedly long time ("Doctors Seek Answers in Death of Baboon Liver Recipient," *The Herald-Standard*, Uniontown, Pa., September 8, 1992, p. A2.) More such transplants were planned: although a January 10, 1993, baboon-to-human liver transplant at the same hospital was much less "successful" (the recipient died within three weeks), surgeons hope that a new immunosuppressive drug, K76, will yield better results (for the humans, that is). See Byron Spice, "Baboon Livers Were Damaged by Rejection," *The Pittsburgh Post-Gazette*, September 28, 1993, pp. A1, A5.

73. L. W. Sumner has argued that we ought to extend our concept of harm to include those who had no such prior condition, suggesting that life can be construed as a harm or a benefit to a conceptus. See his *Abortion and Moral Theory* (Princeton: Princeton University Press, 1981), p. 215. This language remains logically puzzling, however. As we shall soon see, Feinberg makes a different, less confusing terminological suggestion.

Notes

74. Feinberg, *Harm to Others*, p. 102.

75. Jesse Birnbaum, "Crybabies: Eternal Victims," *Time*, August 12, 1991, pp. 16–18, p. 17. The man died two years after his revival. His estate was denied the claim by a judge.

76. There will be more discussion of the concept of a moral right in chapters 4 and 5. Note, however, that the current gloss is compatible with both consequentialism and deontologism. The *basis* of the right could be the fact that its recognition maximizes utility or nonmoral good, or it might be grounded in the inherent worth of the individual, etc.

77. Feinberg, *Harm to Others*, p. 99.

78. Ibid., p. 102.

79. Bernard Rollin, *Animal Rights and Human Morality* (Buffalo: Prometheus Books, 1981), especially pp. 52–57. See the revised edition of this book (Prometheus, 1992), pp. 74ff.

80. Holland, "On Behalf of a Moderate Speciesism," p. 284.

81. Ibid., pp. 287–88.

82. Ibid., p. 289. Holland advances additional arguments for speciesism that will be considered later.

83. Ibid.

84. Melden, *Rights and Persons*, p. 214.

85. James Nelson, "Xenograft and Partial Affections," *Between the Species* 2 (3), 1986, p. 123. Unlike Holland and Melden, Nelson believes that sentient nonhumans are morally considerable. His views are actually more similar to Peter Singer's than they are to the views of most speciesists.

86. Benn, "Egalitarianism and Equal Consideration of Interests," p. 62.

87. Fox, *The Case for Animal Experimentation*, pp. 60–61.

88. Midgley, *Animals and Why They Matter*, p. 22. Unlike Fox in 1986, however, she denies that this would require us always to take a "humans first" position. (As we have discussed, Fox himself disavowed speciesism after the publication of his book.)

89. Holland, "On Behalf of a Moderate Speciesism," p. 289. This is his second argument for speciesism. (The previously discussed appeal to misfortune is the first.)

90. Francis and Norman, "Some Animals are More Equal Than Others," pp. 522–27.

91. J. Baird Callicott, "Animal Liberation and Environmental Ethics: Back Together Again," in his *In Defense of the Land Ethic* (Albany: State University of New York Press, 1989), pp. 55–56. Callicott believes that the presumption in favor of those more closely related to us can be overridden: "the outer orbits of our various moral spheres exert a gravitational tug on the inner ones" (p. 58).

92. Christina Sommers, "Philosophers Against the Family," in *Vice and Virtue in Everyday Life: Introductory Readings in Ethics*, ed. Christina Sommers and Fred Sommers (San Diego: Harcourt Brace Jovanovich, 1989), pp. 744–45.

93. Francis and Norman, "Some Animals Are More Equal Than Others," pp. 523–25.

94. John Rawls, *A Theory of Justice* (Cambridge, Mass.: Harvard University Press, 1971), pp. 114–15.

95. Regan, *The Case for Animal Rights*, p. 316.

Notes

96. Peter Wenz, *Environmental Justice* (Albany: State University of New York Press, 1988), p. 325.

97. Peter Wenz, "Concentric Circle Pluralism: A Response to Rolston," *Between the Species* 5 (3), 1989, p. 156.

98. Wenz, *Environmental Justice*, p. 316. Earlier, Wenz also claims that his view "avoids (almost completely) employing species membership as the difference which justifies different treatment" (p. 150). However, he does believe that features connected with species membership can and do justify different treatment. He is what James Rachels would call a "qualified speciesist." See Rachels, *Created from Animals*, p. 184.

99. Ibid., p. 320. If we have not had such an influence upon them, however, we primarily have negative obligations (obligations of noninterference) to them.

100. Ibid., pp. 316–17.

101. Ibid., p. 328.

102. Ibid., p. 327.

103. Ibid., p. 328.

104. He does, however, think there is nothing wrong if Israelis earmark food assistance for Ethiopian Jews rather than other starving Ethiopians (ibid., p. 318).

105. Wenz, "Concentric Circle Pluralism: A Reply to Rolston," p. 156.

106. Ibid., p. 156. Italics mine.

107. Taylor, *Respect for Nature*, pp. 147–52.

108. Midgley, *Animals and Why They Matter*, p. 124.

109. Fox, *The Case for Animal Experimentation*, p. 60.

110. R. Z. Sheppard, "Splendor in the Grass," a review of *The Ants*, by B. Hölldobler and E. O. Wilson (Cambridge, Mass.: Harvard University Press, 1990), in *Time*, September 3, 1990, p. 80.

111. Fox, *The Case for Animal Experimentation*, p. 15.

112. Young, "The Morality of Killing Animals: Four Arguments," pp. 88–101.

113. Ibid., p. 88.

114. Ibid., p. 98.

115. Richard B. Brandt, *A Theory of the Good and the Right* (Oxford: Clarendon Press, 1979).

116. Young, "The Morality of Killing Animals," p. 89.

117. Brandt, *A Theory of the Good and the Right*, p. 113.

118. Young, "The Morality of Killing Animals," p. 98.

119. Midgley, *Animals and Why They Matter*, p. 104.

120. Brandt, *A Theory of the Good and the Right*, p. 41.

121. Midgley, *Animals and Why They Matter*, p. 109.

122. There are exceptions. Domestic cats, unless they are kittens or mothers of young kittens, often seem to prefer humans to their own kind. Ethologists do speculate that these cats regard us as their "mothers," however, so their preference may originally have a species basis. Perhaps here we have a true case of "pseudo-speciation"!

123. Carruthers, *The Animals Issue*, p. 163. A. I. Melden takes the same view in his *Rights and Persons*, p. 209.

124. Column by Ann Landers, *The Herald-Standard*, Uniontown, Pa., September 22, 1986, p. 8.

Notes

125. Bradford Gray, *Human Subjects in Medical Experimentation* (Melbourne, Fla.: Robert E. Krieger Publishing Co., 1981).

126. Marcia Angell, M.D., "The Nazi Hypothermia Experiments and Unethical Research Today," *The New England Journal of Medicine* 322 (20), May 17, 1990, p. 1463. This experiment was exposed in 1966.

127. British Medical Association, *Medicine Betrayed: The Participation of Doctors in Human Rights Abuses* (London: Zed Books, 1992).

128. "Consent to Research on the Aged Questioned," *New York Times,* October 30, 1986, p. A20.

129. Bruce Hilton, "Trafficking in Human Organs Bloodies a Medical Breakthrough," *The Pittsburgh Press,* December 11, 1991, p. B3.

4 UTILITARIANISM AND THE PROTECTION OF INNOCENT LIFE

1. Jeremy Bentham, *Introduction to the Principles of Morals and Legislation* (New York: Columbia University Press, 1945).

2. L. W. Sumner, *The Moral Foundation of Rights* (Oxford: Oxford University Press, 1987).

3. Frey, "The Significance of Agency and Marginal Cases," p. 40.

4. Peter Singer, *Animal Liberation* (New York: Avon Books, 1975), chapter 1.

5. R. G. Frey, *Rights, Killing, and Suffering* (Oxford: Basil Blackwell, 1983).

6. Carruthers, *The Animals Issue,* p. 195.

7. Ibid.

8. Ibid., p. 73.

9. Carruthers does not in fact think that nonhuman animals can suffer, but he is convinced that even if they did, their suffering would not be worthy of our moral concern. See my chapter 1 discussion of his argument against the possibility of nonhuman animal suffering.

10. Later in this chapter, we will examine L. W. Sumner's attempt to build significant rights into a utilitarian framework.

11. Peter Singer, "Animals and the Value of Life," in *Matters of Life and Death,* 2d ed., ed. Tom Regan (New York: Random House, 1986), p. 369.

12. Richard B. Brandt, "Some Merits of One Form of Rule Utilitarianism," in *Mill: Utilitarianism with Critical Essays* ed. Samuel Gorovitz (Indianapolis: Bobbs-Merrill, 1971), pp. 324–44.

13. Frey, *Rights, Killing, and Suffering,* p. 116. However, as we shall see, in another context Frey seems to support an acceptance utilitarian approach.

14. For a clear and thorough discussion of other problems facing acceptance utilitarianism, and other forms of utilitarianism designed to avoid unwelcome implications, see Fred Feldman, *Introductory Ethics* (Englewood Cliffs: Prentice-Hall, 1978), chapter 5.

15. This argument is freely adapted from a statement of "The Replacement Argument" in *Ethics and Animals* 3 (1), 1982, p. 2.

16. For incisive discussion of U.S. law concerning laboratory animals, see Rollin, *The Unheeded Cry,* chapter 7.

17. Ibid., p. 175.

Notes

18. Reported in *The Animals' Agenda*, May 1992, p. 37.

19. Reported in *Vegetarian Times*, May 1992, pp. 24–25.

20. Reported in the quarterly newsletter of the Animal Legal Defense Fund, *The Animal's Advocate*, Summer 1993, pp. 1, 5.

21. Jim Mason and Peter Singer, *Animal Factories*, 2d ed. (New York: Crown Publishers, 1990). Beef cattle, traditionally pasture-grazing animals who could have a bit of freedom before slaughter, are increasingly confined in giant feedlots and grain fed for a major portion of their lives. Mason and Singer note that over 70 percent of the beef produced in the United States, for example, results from cattle jammed into extremely large feedlots (p. 14). This has disastrous environmental consequences as well as diminished quality of life for the cattle: see chapters 5 and 6.

22. Peter Singer, "Ten Years of Animal Liberation," *The New York Review of Books*, January 17, 1985, pp. 46–52.

23. "United States Lags Behind EEC," *The Humane Society of the United States*, 1987, p. 2.

24. *The Animals' Agenda*, January 1989, p. 32. For the quote below from the Swedish government, see *The Animals' Agenda*, May 1988, p. 28. See also *The Animals' Agenda*, April 1988, p. 30, and "Farm Animal Rights Get Push," *The Pittsburgh Press*, February 26, 1989, p. J1. (How all of these European efforts will be affected by unification remains to be seen.)

25. Ragnar Tauson, "Research Approaches to Improve the Technical Welfare and the Environment of Laying Hens," paper delivered at the first International Conference on Farm Animal Welfare, The Aspen Institute, Eastern Shore of Maryland, June 9, 1991.

26. For further discussion of what can and should be done to improve the lot of farm animals, see J. F. Hurnik and Hugh Lehman, "Ethics and Farm Animal Welfare," *The Journal of Agricultural Ethics* (4), 1988, pp. 305–18.

27. Peter Singer, *Practical Ethics* (Cambridge: Cambridge University Press, 1979), p. 100.

28. Singer, "Animal Liberation or Animal Rights?" pp. 8–9.

29. Of all the utilitarians I have read on the subject of replaceability, only R. G. Frey (very courageously) accepts the implications for humans. See his *Rights, Killing, and Suffering*, pp. 161–72.

30. Singer, *Animal Liberation*, 2d ed., p. 229: "I still have doubts about this issue."

31. Singer, *Animal Liberation*, 1975, p. 241, pp. 259–60 n. 16.

32. Henry Salt, *Animal Rights* (Fontwell: Centaur, 1980), p. 186.

33. Singer, *Animal Liberation*, 2d ed., p. 228. He wrote about his doubts well before the 1990 reissue of his book. See, e.g., *Practical Ethics*, p. 101, and his "Animals and the Value of Life," p. 370.

34. Singer, *Animal Liberation*, 1975, p. 241.

35. Sapontzis, *Morals, Reason, and Animals*, p. 194.

36. Ibid., p. 195.

37. Singer, *Practical Ethics*, p. 87. Italics mine.

38. Sumner, *Abortion and Moral Theory*, p. 209.

39. Singer, *Practical Ethics*, p. 87.

Notes

40. Derek Parfit, *Reasons and Persons* (Oxford: Oxford University Press, 1984), sections 134–36.

41. Sumner, *Abortion and Moral Theory*, pp. 209–21.

42. Ibid., pp. 220–21.

43. Ibid., p. 214.

44. Singer, *Practical Ethics*, pp. 87–88.

45. Ibid., p. 87.

46. Ibid. Also see p. 101.

47. Dolores Kong, "Second Contraceptive Revolution Still Far From Reality," Knight-Ridder Newspapers, *The Herald-Standard*, July 3, 1988, p. E2.

48. See Richard Lacayo's interview with Randall Terry, "Crusading Against the Pro-Choice Movement," *Time*, October 21, 1991, pp. 26–27.

49. Parfit, *Reasons and Persons*, chapter 17.

50. Parfit argues that this implication of total-view utilitarianism, despite its repugnance, is preferable to the alternative. "Average-view" utilitarianism, which would bid us to count the overall *average* utility as opposed to the *total* utility of different worlds, would not sanction the mass production of marginally acceptable lives. However, it would imply that a world with a large number of very satisfied sentient beings is worse than a world with a much smaller number of slightly more satisfied sentient beings. It would be wrong, then, for a very happy society to have almost-as-happy progeny, because this would lower the average utility. Parfit, a utilitarian, calls this "the absurd conclusion," and reluctantly accepts its repugnant cousin. See *Reasons and Persons*, chapter 18.

51. Peter Singer, " 'Life's Uncertain Voyage,' " in *Metaphysics and Morality: Essays in Honour of J. J. C. Smart*, ed. P. Pettit, R. Sylvan, and J. Norman (Oxford: Basil Blackwell, 1987), p. 170.

52. These figures were publicized in Joel E. Cohen's "How Many People Can Earth Hold?" *Discover*, November 1992, pp. 114–19. I have verified the reported projections in a telephone conversation with Dr. Robert Chen, who made the calculations.

53. Frances Lappé was the first to publicize the fact that domestic farm animals are "protein factories in reverse." See her updated discussion of this in her *Diet for a Small Planet*, 10th anniversary ed. (New York: Ballantine Books, 1982), pp. 70ff. See also A. B. Durning and H. Brough's *Taking Stock: Animal Farming and the Environment*, Worldwatch Paper 103 (Washington, D.C.: Worldwatch Institute, 1991); and chapter 5 of Mason and Singer's *Animal Factories*. The livestock industry objects to the protein-reversal charge: see all three sources above for refutation of that industry's arguments.

54. Singer, *Animal Liberation*, 2d ed. p. 230.

55. Such changes would have to be consistent with continued long-term human habitation, if utility maximization is to be one's overarching goal. Thus, ecological disaster threatening to human existence would have to be avoided. Baird Callicott has charged that a global human shift to vegetarianism would stimulate human population, cause us to take over ever more resources for food production, and likely ultimately result in ecological devastation. See his *In Defense of the Land Ethic*, pp. 34–35. Vegetarians motivated by concern for sentient beings in general or even just their own future generations would not endorse

Notes

such actions. Neither would total-view utilitarians. Nevertheless, considerable reduction in the numbers of wildlife would be compatible with the continued sustenance of a burgeoning, largely miserable human population.

56. Peter Singer, "Killing Humans and Killing Animals," *Inquiry* 22 (1–2), Summer 1979, p. 151. Also see *Practical Ethics*, chapters 4 and 5. According to Singer, preference utilitarianism is the form of utilitarianism that R. M. Hare believes to be implied by the principle of universalizability. Cf. R. M. Hare, "Ethical Theory and Utilitarianism," in *Contemporary British Philosophy*, ed. H. D. Lewis (London: Allen and Unwin, 1976).

57. Singer, *Practical Ethics*, pp. 102–3.

58. Bruce Bower, "A Child's Theory of Mind," *Science News* 144, July 17, 1993, pp. 40–42.

59. Singer, *Animal Liberation*, 2d ed. p. 229.

60. Griffin, *Animal Minds*, pp. 249–50.

61. "Conversations with a Gorilla," *National Geographic* 154 (4), October 1978, pp. 438–65. The cover picture for this issue is Koko's mirror self-portrait.

62. Griffin, *Animal Minds*, chapter 10.

63. Singer, *Practical Ethics*, p. 99.

64. Rollin, *The Unheeded Cry*, chapter 6. For discussion of this argument, see my chapter 1.

65. Griffin, *Animal Minds*, pp. 248–49.

66. Ibid., p. 162.

67. Ibid., pp. 201–3.

68. See Singer, *Animal Liberation*, 2d ed. pp. 229–30.

69. Singer, "Killing Humans and Killing Animals," p. 153.

70. Frey, *Rights, Killing, and Suffering*, p. 116. See also his "Moral Standing, the Value of Lives, and Speciesism," pp. 196–97.

71. Of the two, Frey has above all been the one to change. At a philosophical conference in which I also participated (the March 1987 American Philosophical Association group meeting of the Society for the Study of Ethics and Animals, held in San Francisco), Singer told his co-discussant Frey in a moment of ironic humor that Frey had "finally seen the light." As I recall, many in the large audience chuckled uneasily at this quip.

72. Jonathan Swift, "A Modest Proposal for Preventing the Children of Poor People from Being a Burthen to their Parents or Country, and for Making Them Beneficial to the Publick" (1729), in *Animal Rights and Human Obligations*, ed. Regan and Singer (Englewood Cliffs: Prentice-Hall, 1976), p. 236.

73. H. L. A. Hart, "Death and Utility," *The New York Review of Books*, May 15, 1980, p. 31. As we have already seen, total-view classical utilitarianism has the same implication.

74. Peter Singer, "Letter to the Editor," *The New York Review of Books*, August 14, 1980, p. 53.

75. Hart, "Death and Utility," pp. 29–30.

76. See Evelyn Pluhar, "On Replaceability," *Ethics and Animals* 3 (4), 1982, p. 101. James White also makes this point in his "Are Sentient Beings Replaceable?" in the same issue, p. 93. See also S. F. Sapontzis, "On Being Morally Expendable," *Ethics and Animals* 3 (3), 1982, p. 64. He has revised this article

Notes

in chapter 10 of his *Morals, Reason, and Animals*. See also Michael Lockwood, "Singer on Killing and the Preference for Life," *Inquiry* 22 (1–2), 1979, pp. 157–69.

77. Singer, "Letter to the Editor," p. 53.

78. Singer, *Practical Ethics*, p. 103. Also see pp. 101–2. (Singer refers Hart to these pages in his reply to him.)

79. Singer, *Animal Liberation*, 2d ed. p. 228.

80. As we shall soon see, S. F. Sapontzis argues that reconsideration of the wretched-child dilemma will show that the extended prior-existence view is morally acceptable after all.

81. Singer, "Letter to the Editor," p. 53.

82. Singer, "Life's Uncertain Voyage," p. 166.

83. Singer, "Animal Liberation or Animal Rights? p. 9.

84. Singer, "Life's Uncertain Voyage," pp. 165–69.

85. Ibid., p. 167.

86. S. F. Sapontzis makes this point in *Morals, Reason, and Animals*, pp. 187–88.

87. Ibid., p. 188. He does not endorse this view, of course.

88. Bruce W. Nelan, "Unfinished Revolution," *Time*, January 8, 1990, pp. 28–34, p. 30.

89. Sapontzis, *Morals, Reason, and Animals*, pp. 190–94.

90. Ibid., pp. 190–91.

91. Interview conducted on the evening news program *All Things Considered*, National Public Radio, broadcast on June 18, 1992.

92. Sapontzis, *Morals, Reason, and Animals*, p. 191.

93. Sumner, *Abortion and Moral Theory*, p. 222. A. I. Melden, a nonutilitarian, agrees with this view of utilitarian character judgments. See his *Rights in Moral Lives* (Berkeley: University of California Press, 1988), p. 35.

94. Singer, "Animal Liberation or Animal Rights?" p. 7.

95. Brandt, *A Theory of the Good and the Right*, p. 113. (For a discussion of the limitations and difficulties of Brandt's view, see my chapter 3.)

96. Frey, *Rights, Killing, and Suffering*, p. 73.

97. Ibid.

98. Kuhse and Singer, *Should the Baby Live?* chapter 5.

99. James Nelson, "Critical Notice of 'Rights, Killing, and Suffering,'" *Between the Species* 2 (2), 1986, p. 75. See his excellent discussion of utilitarianism and rights on pp. 73–75.

100. Frey, *Rights, Killing, and Suffering*, p. 86.

101. Ibid., p. 87.

102. Ibid. See p. 88 as well.

103. Sumner, *Abortion and Moral Theory*, chapter 5.

104. Sumner, *The Moral Foundation of Rights*, p. 197. Sumner argues for the more general thesis that rights can be given a consequentialist foundation. A fortiori, if he is right, they can be given a utilitarian foundation. Sumner himself remains a utilitarian.

105. Ibid., pp. 187–88.

106. Ibid., pp. 204–6. Here he is following what he calls the "interest model"

of rights. By contrast, according to the "choice model" of rights, only autonomous beings would have rights. However, Sumner emphasizes that this does not mean that we would not owe nonautonomous sentient beings full protection in the choice model. The protection would simply not be protection based on their *ability to choose.*

107. Sumner discusses this in his earlier work, *Abortion and Moral Theory,* pp. 218–19.

108. Sumner, *The Moral Foundation of Rights,* pp. 207–8.

109. Ibid., p. 208.

110. Ibid., p. 174.

111. Ibid., p. 200.

112. Ibid., p. 208.

113. Ibid., p. 196. Also see pp. 212–13.

114. Ibid., pp. 212–13.

5 JUSTIFICATION AND JUDGMENT: CLAIMING AND RESPECTING BASIC MORAL RIGHTS

1. Fox, "Animal Experimentation: A Philosopher's Changing Views," p. 57.

2. Michael A. Fox, "Letter to the Editor," *The Scientist,* December 15, 1986. The letter was reprinted in *The Animals Agenda,* March 1987, p. 29. In this remarkable letter, Fox responds to a review of his then recently published *The Case for Animal Experimentation* by repudiating the book himself.

3. Rollin, *Animal Rights and Human Morality,* p. 83 (italics are added by me, except for the final reference to "people"). See also pp. 22–28.

4. Sapontzis, *Morals, Reason, and Animals,* chapter 6.

5. Ibid., p. xv.

6. Ibid., pp. 95–96.

7. Carruthers, *The Animals Issue,* chapter 7. See my related discussions of Carruthers's views in my chapters 1 and 2.

8. Ibid., p. 192. As I argued in my chapter 1, Carruthers's neo-Cartesian arguments against the possibility of nonhuman suffering are failures.

9. Ibid., p. 168.

10. Ibid., pp. 166–67. These interests do not include an interest in conducting cruel behavior. Carruthers believes, probably correctly, that most persons directly involved in causing (putative) suffering to nonhuman animals are not motivated by cruelty.

11. As I discussed in chapter 2, Carruthers uses unsuccessful slippery slope and side effects appeals to try to avoid unpalatable implications for mentally limited humans.

12. Cohen, "The Case for the Use of Animals in Biomedical Research," p. 866.

13. Sapontzis, *Morals, Reasons, and Animals,* pp. 96–103.

14. Charles Fink, "Animal Experimentation and the Argument from Limited Resources," *Between the Species* 7 (2), Spring 1991, pp. 90–95.

15. Carruthers, *The Animal Issue,* pp. 156–57.

16. Sapontzis, "Review of Peter Carruthers' *The Animals Issue,*" forthcoming

in the *Canadian Philosophical Review* See my chapter 1 for a discussion of Carruthers's view and Sapontzis's criticism of it.

17. Sapontzis, *Morals, Reason, and Animals,* p. 110.

18. Tom Regan, *The Case for Animal Rights* (Berkeley: University of California Press, 1983).

19. Joel Feinberg, "The Nature and Value of Rights," *The Journal of Value Inquiry* 4, Winter 1970, pp. 243–57. See Regan's chapter 8 for a full spelling out of this view. Note that a given rights holder need not make such claims, or even be able to make such claims.

20. Regan, *The Case for Animal Rights,* p. 243.

21. Ibid., p. 416 n. 30.

22. Ibid., p. 246.

23. Regan points out that Rawls and Kant sometimes appear not to deny this, holding that humanity as such, not just human moral agents, are morally considerable. However, as Regan argues, consistency requires both philosophers to adopt the moral agency view (what I have called the "full-personhood view"). See Regan's *The Case for Animal Rights,* chapter 5, sections 5.4–5.5.

24. Rawls, *A Theory of Justice,* p. 252.

25. Regan, *The Case for Animal Rights,* chapter 4, sections 4.3, 4.6.

26. Ibid., section 4.2.

27. Ibid., pp. 128–9.

28. Rawls has rather little to say about nonhuman animals, beyond the fact that there is no "natural way" to include them in his theory of justice: "it does seem that we are not required to give strict justice" to beings lacking a concept of justice (*A Theory of Justice,* p. 512). However, in the same connection Rawls supposes that it would nonetheless be wrong to engage in cruelty toward nonhumans. As Regan argues in the discussion cited below, Rawls cannot consistently make the latter claim. If "strict justice" does not apply to nonhumans, we can have no obligation to refrain from cruel treatment of them.

29. Sumner, *The Moral Foundation of Rights,* p. 159.

30. Alan Gewirth, *Human Rights* (Chicago: University of Chicago Press, 1982), p. 44.

31. Sumner, *The Moral Foundation of Rights,* pp. 151–62.

32. Regan, *The Case for Animal Rights,* chapter 5, section 5.4.

33. Ibid., section 5.6.

34. Ibid., p. 162.

35. Ibid., p. 247. See also Regan's chapter 6.

36. Ibid., chapter 7, section 7.7.

37. Ibid., p. 234.

38. Friedrich Nietzsche, *Beyond Good and Evil,* trans. Helen Zimmern (London: Allen & Unwin, 1887) ninth article, no. 265.

39. Regan, *The Case for Animal Rights,* p. 183.

40. Ibid., p. 232.

41. See my "Moral Agents and Moral Patients," *Between the Species* 4 (1), Winter 1988, pp. 38–39.

42. Alan Gewirth, *Reason and Morality* (Chicago: University of Chicago Press, 1978).

Notes

43. Gewirth, *Human Rights: Essays on Justification and Application.*

44. Edward Regis Jr., ed., *Gewirth's Ethical Rationalism: Critical Essays With a Reply by Alan Gewirth* (Chicago: University of Chicago Press, 1984). Gewirth's "Replies to My Critics" appears on pp. 192–255.

45. See also Marcus Singer, "On Gewirth's Derivation of the Principle of Generic Consistency," *Ethics* 95, January 1985, pp. 297–301, and Gewirth's response immediately following in the same volume: "From the Prudential to the Moral: Reply to Singer," pp. 302–4.

46. For variant but compatible statements of the first stage of Gewirth's argument (premises 1–5, detailed below) and his indirect proof of premise 5, see *Reason and Morality,* pp. 79–81; *Human Rights,* pp. 50–51, 68; and "Replies to My Critics," pp. 204–6.

47. Gewirth, *Reason and Morality,* p. 27.

48. J. Baird Callicott has objected that any attempt to show that an agent who claims rights for himself or herself on a certain ground, then is "compelled by the logic of my own moral claim upon others to grudgingly grant their similar claims upon me," simply "generalizes egoism." He believes that this falsifies the nature of moral concern: altruism, not "self-love," is its basis. (See his *In Defense of the Land Ethic,* p. 53.) Anyone who argues as Callicott has described *and* purports to be explaining how moral agency *actually* comes to be is indeed vulnerable to this criticism. However, Gewirth does not make the second claim. (Callicott does not mention Gewirth specifically in making his objection.) See my section "Immoralists, Amoralists, and Bigots" below for further discussion of the roles of logic and empathy in actual moral behavior.

49. Gewirth, "Replies to My Critics," p. 204.

50. Gewirth, *Reason and Morality,* p. 64.

51. Gewirth, "Replies to My Critics," p. 205.

52. Ibid.

53. Ibid. See also *Reason and Morality,* p. 79.

54. Gewirth, "Replies to My Critics," p. 205.

55. Ibid.

56. Gewirth, *Human Rights,* p. 2. Gewirth does not *equate* rights claims and "ought" claims, however: he argues that any duties are ultimately grounded in rights (p. 14). Robert Arrington, in chapter 3 of his *Rationalism, Realism, and Relativism: Perspectives in Contemporary Moral Epistemology* (Ithaca: Cornell University Press, 1989), has argued that step 6 is the "fatal flaw" in Gewirth's argument. Although he agrees with Gewirth that when one claims a prudential right for oneself one also claims that others should not deprive one of that right, Arrington holds that these others, who are by hypothesis also prudential and not moral agents, *have no reason* to accept such a duty: "We cannot charge people with obligations whose grounds they do not recognize *and cannot reasonably be expected to recognize!*" (p. 108). Therefore, as Arrington sees it, any duty claim on the original agent's part would be unjustified. If this is the case, the correlative rights claim also fails, and Gewirth's argument cannot get off the ground.

In fact, however, Arrington misinterprets Gewirth in making this charge. Step 6 merely asserts that the agent must claim or advocate that there be no interference with her freedom and well-being. She can do this without believing

Notes

that others will in fact *accept* her claim of noninterference. As Gewirth puts it in replying to a similar objection by Martin Golding, "[the agent] is advocating for himself. He is also prescribing *to* other persons. But there is this difference between prescribing *to* and prescribing *for* other persons: the latter, unlike the former, suggests that the other persons recognize or accept the prescription . . . there is, so far, no assurance that they will in fact comply with [one's prudential rights claim] . . . further steps are needed for this purpose." (See *Human Rights*, pp. 71–72. Arrington apparently never saw this reply; he has no references to this book at all.) From a purely prudential point of view, of course, no one has any reason to acknowledge or respect the rights of others. It is only at the *end* of Gewirth's entire argument that prudential agency becomes moral agency, for any reflective agent whatever. Intermediate step 6, "Others ought not to interfere with my freedom and well-being," is wholly compatible with these others' rejecting any such duties—until they too realize that they contradict themselves if they claim such rights but deny them to others. Thus, Arrington has not shown Gewirth's argument to be unsound.

57. Gewirth, "Replies to My Critics," p. 206.

58. Gewirth, *Reason and Morality*, p. 81.

59. Ibid., pp. 160–61; italics mine.

60. For more on Gewirth's avoidance of the "is/ought" fallacy charge, see his "The Is/Ought Problem Resolved," in *Human Rights*, pp. 100–127. See also W. H. Hudson's criticism of Gewirth's reasoning ("The Is/Ought Problem Resolved?" pp. 108–27) and Gewirth's reply to Hudson (pp. 206–8, 221–25) in *Gewirth's Ethical Rationalism*.

61. Gewirth, "Replies to My Critics," p. 210.

62. Ibid. On the practical nature of this justification, see *Reason and Morality*, p. 72.

63. Ibid.

64. Ibid. Of course, these rights are prima facie rather than absolute. An agent who threatens an innocent being's well-being or freedom might have to be restrained or even killed, for example. I will have more to say about conditions that would warrant such drastic actions later in this chapter.

65. Gewirth, *Human Rights*, p. 52.

66. Ibid., p. 197. See chapter 3 of *Reason and Morality* for a full discussion of the Principle of Generic Consistency (PGC).

67. See Marcus Singer's argument that Gewirth correctly derives the PGC from the universalizability principle, but only by putting the latter principle "to a moral and not merely a derivational use," thus introducing the moral point of view into the argument instead of briding the gap between prudence and morality (Singer, "On Gewirth's Derivation of the Principle of Generic Consistency," p. 297). Gewirth's "From the Prudential to the Moral: Reply to Singer" successfully parries this charge. The principle of universalizability as used by Gewirth in his argument merely spells out what it logically means for a condition to be sufficient.

68. See Gewirth's "The Golden Rule Rationalized" in *Human Rights*, pp. 128–42. He notes that this rule is "the common denominator of all the world's major religions."

69. Gewirth, *Human Rights*, pp. 11–12: "[The concept of human rights] is de-

ontological in that the rights are correlative with strict duties to forbear or assist, so that performance of the duties can be demanded by all Subjects. It is teleological (consequentialist) in that these duties are for the sake of persons' having certain goods . . . this distribution [of basic goods] to each agent is owed to him, and for his own sake; it is not owed to him only as a consequence of more general social goals." Strictly speaking, this makes Gewirth a deontologist, since he denies that consequences are the *only* morally important consideration.

70. See *Reason and Morality,* pp. 119–25, for an unequivocal rejection of perfectionism. Gewirth reiterates this objection in his later "Replies to My Critics," pp. 225–27.

71. Frank De Roose, "Pluhar on Methods of Justification," *Between the Species* 4 (4), 1988, pp. 255–59. De Roose also argues that Gewirth greatly overestimates the persuasive powers of logic in the moral context. See my section "Immoralists, Amoralists, and Bigots" for more on this charge.

72. Ibid., p. 256 (italics mine).

73. Adina Schwartz, "Review: *Reason and Morality,*" *Philosophical Review* 88 (1979), p. 656.

74. R. M. Hare, "Do Agents Have to be Moralists?" in *Gewirth's Ethical Rationalism,* p. 56.

75. Gewirth, "Replies to My Critics," p. 211.

76. Ibid. (italics mine).

77. De Roose, "Pluhar on Methods of Justification," p. 256.

78. Gewirth, *Human Rights,* p. 46.

79. Gewirth, *Reason and Morality,* pp. 123–24. See especially p. 124: "It is not the generic features or abilities of action as a whole that directly lead an agent to hold that he has rights to freedom and well-being; it is rather that aspect of the features or abilities whereby he pursues purposes he regards as good." This is Gewirth's answer to the question he poses on p. 123: "What aspect of being an agent is the justifying ground for claiming to have the generic rights?"

80. Gewirth, *Human Rights,* p. 49.

81. Taylor, *Respect for Nature,* p. 106. Unlike Regan, Taylor prefers to use the term 'autonomy' in the strictest sense, such that having a "plan for life," complete with higher-order desires, is required (p. 239). Only some humans would qualify as autonomous according to this view, although all humans and other living beings could still be said to be *free* in the sense just sketched. (Cf. my discussion of different senses of autonomy in my chapter 1.)

82. Gewirth, *Reason and Morality,* p. 140.

83. Gewirth, *Human Rights,* p. 8.

84. Gewirth, *Reason and Morality,* pp. 120, 138.

85. Gewirth, *Human Rights,* p. 11.

86. Gewirth, *Reason and Morality,* pp. 124, 133, 180.

87. Gewirth, "Replies to My Critics," pp. 224–27. See also *Reason and Morality,* pp. 120–25, 140–45.

88. Claudia Wallis and James Willwerth, "Awakenings: Schizophrenia," *Time,* July 6, 1992, 55. Depending on conditions, numbers of these people were also badly off in institutions. We do not show any respect for these individuals' rights by abusing or neglecting them.

Notes

89. Reported on *Sunday Weekend Edition,* National Public Radio, November 28, 1993.

90. Ellen M. Perlmutter, "Homelessness for Children Has Its Deepest Roots in Poverty," *The Pittsburgh Post-Gazette,* November 26, 1993, pp. A1, A12. Federal programs to aid the homeless, after being cut during the 1980s and early 1990s, are to be increased during the Clinton administration. One hopes that this will go beyond the "bandaid" stage, but little can be accomplished if functional members of society are not willing to take some responsibility for the most vulnerable in their midst.

91. In the case of children, Gewirth recommends "preparatory rights" to foster future autonomy. See *Reason and Morality,* p. 142. Those who will never be capable of directing their own lives are covered by his "principle of proportionality": "members of these groups approach having the generic rights in varying degrees, depending on the degree to which they have the requisite abilities." For clarification of this principle, see his "Replies to My Critics," p. 226.

92. Gewirth, *Reason and Morality,* pp. 142–43.

93. Ibid., p. 142.

94. Ibid.

95. Bower, "A Child's Theory of Mind," pp. 40–41. See also Dr. Anthony De-Casper's study on newborn's processing of speech, reported to the American Psychological Association (AP report, appearing in newspapers on August 13, 1990: see p. 8 of *The Herald-Standard,* Uniontown, Pa.).

96. Langreth, "Pediatric Pain," p. 75. Some people continue to deny that even infants can experience pain. See my discussion of such a view in chapter 1.

97. "Abortion Aided Woman in Recovery from Coma," AP report, *The Pittsburgh Press,* January 13, 1990, p. A5.

98. Lance Morrow, "Unspeakable," *Time,* February 22, 1993, pp. 48–50.

99. "Chinese Whip Men to Force Abortions," March 24, 1991, *The Pittsburgh Press,* p. A5.

100. See "Illegal Abortions Take Third World Toll," Reuters news service, *The Pittsburgh Post-Gazette,* September 13, 1993, p. A3.

101. Judith Jarvis Thomson, "A Defense of Abortion," *Philosophy and Public Affairs* 1 (1), 1971, pp. 47–66.

102. One anencephalic baby has lived for over a year because of her mother's insistence that she remain on a ventilator. Her lawyer maintains that the mother of "Baby K" is acting out of "a firm Christian belief that all life should be protected." The hospital has taken the mother to court, but the judge has ruled that ceasing to treat the baby would violate the Americans with Disability Act. One's heart goes out to this mother, but those capable of more objectivity should realize that anencephaly is not a "disability." *No one,* in the moral sense, is disabled in such a case. (As I write, a federal appeals court is reviewing the lower court decision.) See Ellen Goodman, "Mother God," syndicated column, *The Pittsburgh Post-Gazette,* October 27, 1993, p. C3.

103. Jean Seligmann et al., "The Medical Quandary," *Newsweek,* January 14, 1985, p. 27.

104. Nearly 90 percent of the 1,396,658 legal abortions done in the United States in 1989 were performed in the first trimester: 1 percent occurred after

twenty weeks gestation, and .01 percent of these were performed after twenty-four weeks of gestation. See Amy Wilson, "A Look at U.S. Abortion Figures," Knight-Ridder Tribune news wire, *The Pittsburgh Press*, February 23, 1992, p. E6.

105. Gewirth, *Reason and Morality*, p. 144.

106. Ibid., p. 145.

107. Ibid., p. 144.

108. Gewirth, "Replies to My Critics," pp. 225–27.

109. Carruthers, *The Animals Issue*, p. 163.

110. Christoph Anstötz, "Profoundly Intellectually Disabled Humans and the Great Apes: A Comparison," in *The Great Ape Project*, ed. Paola Cavalieri and Peter Singer (New York: St. Martin's Press, 1993), pp. 158–72.

111. This includes humans afflicted with autism. Although they may appear not to care about what happens to them, this is an illusion. Autistic persons who have been able to learn to communicate tell us that they have always had *internalized* desires and a sense of pleasure: their brain disorder distorts and at least partially severs their connection to the world of objects and other people. Unlike many other mentally disabled humans, they tend to be highly intelligent.

112. Gewirth, *Reason and Morality*, p. 317.

113. Ibid., p. 64.

114. Ibid., p. 103.

115. Ibid., p. 317.

116. Regan, *The Case for Animal Rights*, p. 243.

117. Ibid., p. 244.

118. Ibid., p. 171.

119. Restak, *The Brain*, p. 136.

120. Ibid., pp. 130–32.

121. Ibid., p. 303.

122. Ibid., p. 136.

123. Taylor, *Respect for Nature*, See, e.g., p. 106.

124. Ibid., chapter 5. See especially pp. 253–55.

125. Ibid., pp. 159–60.

126. Ibid., p. 167.

127. Albert Schweitzer, "The Ethic of Reverence for Life," in *Animal Rights and Human Obligations*, ed. Regan and Singer, pp. 32–33.

128. Taylor, *Respect for Nature*, p. 121.

129. Ibid., p. 122.

130. Gary Varner, "Biological Functions and Biological Interests," *The Southern Journal of Philosophy* 28 (2), 1990, p. 256.

131. Jean-Paul Sartre, "Existentialism Is a Humanism," trans. Philip Mairet, in *Existentialism from Dostoevsky to Sartre*, ed. Walter Kaufmann (New York: New American Library, 1975), pp. 345–69.

132. Ibid., p. 353.

133. Ibid., p. 369.

134. In fact, he is willing to consider the possibility that a sufficiently sophisticated example of "artificial intelligence" would be as morally worthy as any living being (Taylor, *Respect for Nature*, p. 125). I have argued that he would have to attribute the same status to rather simpler mechanical systems as well.

Notes

135. Ibid., pp. 120–23.

136. Ibid., p. 161.

137. J. Baird Callicott is the finest explicator and defender of holism, in my opinion. His position is inspired by Aldo Leopold's *A Sand County Almanac* (New York: Oxford University Press, 1949). See Callicott's *In Defense of the Land Ethic.*

138. See Gary Varner, "No Holism without Pluralism," *Environmental Ethics* 13, Summer 1991, pp. 175–79, for a very clear and strong defense of pluralism.

139. Evelyn Pluhar, "Two Conceptions of an Environmental Ethic," *Ethics and Animals* 4 (4), December 1983, pp. 110–27.

140. Eugene C. Hargrove, *The Foundations of Environmental Ethics* (Englewood Cliffs: Prentice-Hall, 1989), chapter 6.

141. De Roose, "Pluhar on Methods of Justification," p. 257.

142. Gewirth, *Reason and Morality,* pp. 190–96.

143. Ibid., p. 193.

144. Ibid., p. 195.

145. Hare, "Do Agents Have to Moralists?"

146. Sartre, "Existentialism Is a Humanism," p. 366. Sartre contrasts "scum" with "cowards": the latter, terrified of their own responsibility as choosing beings, pretend that they are forced by conditions beyond their control to do as they do. Both types of individual deny, in their different ways, that all humans are "condemned to be free."

147. Gewirth, "Replies to My Critics," pp. 212–15.

148. "How Dare We?" *Science News* 132, July 1987, pp. 57–59.

149. David Hume, *A Treatise of Human Nature,* ed. L.A. Selby-Bigge (London: Oxford University Press, 1888), book 3, part 1, pp. 455–76. See also Part 1: "The Moral (In)Significance of Reason," in Sapontzis's *Morals, Reason, and Animals,* for arguments about reason's limitations in moral contexts.

150. J. Baird Callicott has also argued, quite extensively, that feelings, the "moral sentiments" invoked by Hume and by Adam Smith, underlie our willingness to take the moral point of view. For a very good statement of his position, see, e.g., his *In Defense of the Land Ethic,* p. 53. I agree with his contention, although, unlike him, I see no conflict between it and attempts to rationally justify ethical positions. I must also disagree with his view that Aldo Leopold's holistic environmental ethics, which accords moral considerability to biotic communities rather than directly according such status to individuals, naturally arises from the adoption of the Humean-Smithian perspective. How can empathy and sympathy result in direct moral concern for wholes rather than individuals? (I conveyed this objection to Professor Callicott in a private communication on February 6, 1991.) Gary Varner also raises this criticism in his "No Holism Without Pluralism," p. 179.

151. Jerome Kagan, *The Nature of the Child* (New York: Basic Books, 1984).

152. Lawrence Kohlberg, "Moral Stages and Moralization," in *The Psychology of Moral Development* (San Francisco: Harper & Row, 1984).

153. Carol Gilligan, *In a Different Voice* (Cambridge, Mass.: Harvard University Press, 1982). For examples of philosophical support for Gilligan's position, see Owen Flanagan, "Virtue, Sex, and Gender: Some Philosophical Reflections on the Moral Psychology Debate," *Ethics* 92, April 1982, pp. 499–512; Owen

Notes

Flanagan and Kathryn Jackson, "Justice, Care and Gender: The Kohlberg-Gilligan Debate Revisited," *Ethics 97,* April 1987, pp. 622–37; and Lawrence Blum, "Gilligan and Kohlberg: Implications for Moral Theory," *Ethics 98,* April 1988, pp. 472–91. See also *Women and Moral Theory,* ed. Eva F. Kittay and Diana T. Meyers (Totowa, N.J.: Rowman & Littlefield, 1987). For criticism of other aspects of Kohlberg's theory, see T. M. Reed, "Developmental Moral Theory," *Ethics 97,* January 1987, pp. 441–56. For additional criticism and an exploration of Kohlberg's low scoring of humans who care about nonhuman animals, see my "Kohlberg and Concern for Nonhumans," *Between the Species* 5 (2), Spring 1989, pp. 81–85. My paper is a response to psychologist Dr. Julie Dunlap, who has used Kohlberg's apparatus to probe for the development of moral concern for nonhumans. See her "The Adolescent as Environmental Ethicist," pp. 70–80 in the same volume.

154. Bruce Bower, "Getting Out From Number One," *Science News 137,* April 28, 1990, pp. 266–67.

155. Reported by Bob Simon of CBS News on February 15, 1990. See Robert Bianco, "Networks, CNN Were Swept Along in Celebration of Mandela's Release," *The Pittsburgh Press,* February 21, 1990, p. D7.

156. Story reported on the news program *Morning Edition,* National Public Radio, on September 28, 1993. The report is transcribed on pp. 14–16 of NPR's official transcript of that day's program.

157. Callicott, *In Defense of the Land Ethic,* pp. 55–56.

158. Regan, *The Case for Animal Rights,* chapter 8, section 8.3.

159. Stephen Budiansky, *The Covenant of the Wild: Why Animals Chose Domestication* (New York: William Morrow and Company, 1992). However, according to ethologist James Serpell (University of Pennsylvania), no one really knows how domestication originally occurred; theories such as Budiansky's are dismissed as "just so" stories. (Serpell is quoted in R. Mestel's "Ascent of the Dog," *Discover,* October 1994, p. 94.) Moreover, the moral conclusions drawn by Budiansky—roughly, since domestic animals supposedly chose to submit themselves to human rule in exchange for shelter, food, and protection from predators, we humans are justified in exploiting and slaughtering them—simply do not follow. For a careful examination and refutation of Budiansky's moral argumentation, see Gary Calore, "Evolutionary Covenants: Domestication, Wildlife and Animal Rights," slated to be published in Priscilla Cohn, ed., *Animal Rights and Wildlife,* forthcoming from Edwin Mellen Press.

160. Rollin, *Animal Rights and Human Morality,* chapter 4.

161. These duties do not cancel our duties to other rights bearers, e.g., the ones typically used to feed dogs and cats. Currently, pet food is a by-product of the human-oriented food industry. If more people became serious about respecting the rights of all beings who care about what happens to them, they and their companion animals would no longer have these sources. Dogs, who are omnivores like us, can thrive on vegetarian diets without much trouble, but cats need carefully designed diets that include taurine as a nutritional supplement. See, e.g., James Peden, *Vegetarian Cats and Dogs* (Swisshome, Ore.: Harbinger Press, 1992).

162. The same would hold for sheep whose wool is desired. Clearly, however,

the conditions under which the sheep live and have their wool taken would have to be drastically different from current commercial operations (see Singer, *Animal Liberation,* 2d ed., p. 232).

163. Gary Varner, "What's Wrong with Animal *Byproducts?*" *The Journal of Agricultural and Environmental Ethics* 7 (1), 1994, pp. 7–17.

164. B_{12} is made by bacteria, and it is not found naturally *in* plant sources. It is readily found *on* plants in third world countries, but people in affluent countries where food is very hygienically produced need small amounts of the vitamin (e.g., from fortified cereal) if they contemplate strict vegetarianism. See V. H. Herbert, "Vitamin B_{12}: Plant Sources, Requirements, and Assay," *The American Journal of Clinical Nutrition* 48, 1988, pp. 852–58.

165. Including children after they have been weaned. On The Farm, a very poor but idealistic and self-sustaining commune in Summertown, Tennessee, hundreds of vegan children born to vegan mothers have been followed for over a decade. The children are healthy, and their heights and weights do not significantly differ from those of omnivorous children. Adults on The Farm are very well-educated about nutrition, fortifying their soy milk with vitamin B_{12}, and giving young children and pregnant or lactating women iron supplements (just as omnivores are advised to do). See Jean M. O'Connell et al., "Growth of Vegetarian Children: The Farm Study," *Pediatrics* 84 (3), 1989, pp. 475–80. Nutrition textbooks of the 1980s warning against vegan diets for children base these conclusions on earlier studies of communities where children were not given properly balanced diets or enough calories. As O'Connell points out, none of those other studies approaches The Farm study in terms of numbers of children subjects and the length of time the subjects were followed.

166. American Dietetic Association, "Position of the American Dietetic Association: Vegetarian Diets," *The Journal of the American Dietetic Association* 93 (11), 1993, pp. 1317–19.

167. Johanna T. Dwyer, "Nutritional Consequences of Vegetarianism," *Annual Reviews in Nutrition* 11, 1991, pp. 61–91. Dwyer warns that dietary planning is essential if good nutrition is to result; she gives the same advice to omnivores. She writes that "malnutrition due to poor dietary planning or secondary to disease is largely avoidable or preventable, and is not a necessary concomitant of vegetarian [including vegan] diets" (p. 73).

168. See my "Who Can Be Morally Obligated to Be a Vegetarian?" *The Journal of Agricultural and Environmental Ethics* 5 (2), 1992, pp. 183–215, and my "Vegetarianism, Morality, and Science: A Counter-Reply," *The Journal of Agricultural and Environmental Ethics* 6 (2), 1993, pp. 185–213, for detailed discussion of the moral and nutritional issues involving vegetarian diets. These articles are part of a larger context: my first responded to Kathryn George's "So Human an Animal . . . , or the Moral Relevance of Being an Omnivore," *The Journal of Agricultural and Environmental Ethics* 3 (2), 1990, pp. 172–86, and the second was in turn a rebuttal of her "The Use and Abuse of Scientific Studies," 1992, in 5 (2) of that journal, pp. 217–33. She has responded one final time in her "Use and Abuse Revisited," *The Journal of Agricultural and Environmental Ethics* 7 (1), 1994, pp. 41–76. I have once again refuted her (old and new) contentions in my "Vegetarianism, Morality, and Science Revisited," pp.

77–82 in the same issue. See Gary Varner, "In Defense of the Vegan Ideal," also critical of K. George's position, pp. 29–40 in that issue as well. George also responds to Varner in her "Use and Abuse Revisited," and he has replied to her response, again in that same issue, pp. 83–86.

169. Robert Heinlein, *Stranger in a Strange Land* (New York: Berkeley Medallion Books, 1968).

170. Mason and Singer, *Animal Factories*, rev. ed. (New York: Harmony Books, 1990), pp. 7–10.

171. Gary Comstock, "Pigs and Piety: A Theocentric Perspective on Food Animals," *Between the Species* 8 (3), Summer 1992, p. 122. Comstock is also the author of *Is There an Obligation to Save the Family Farm?* (Ames: Iowa State University Press, 1987).

172. The phrase is Frances Moore Lappé's. See her *Diet for a Small Planet*, p. 67.

173. Mason and Singer, *Animal Factories*, p. 110. The livestock industry objects to Lappé's and Mason and Singer's protein reversal figures. For refutations of the industry's objection, see Lappé, *Diet for a Small Planet*, pp. 87–88; Mason and Singer, pp. 13–14, chapter 5; and Durning and Brough, *Taking Stock: Animal Farming and the Environment*, Worldwatch Paper 103.

174. Regan, *The Case for Animal Rights*, p. 357.

175. Psychologist Maurice Temerlin and his wife Jane adopted Lucy. See his account of the experience in Temerlin, *Lucy: Growing Up Human*.

176. Dr. Goodall's account was part of an acceptance speech she made upon being awarded the 1987 Albert Schweitzer Medal by the Animal Welfare Institute. See "To Jane Goodall from John Melcher: The Albert Schweitzer Medal," *The Animal Welfare Institute Quarterly* 36 (4), Winter 1988, pp. 1–3.

177. Francine Patterson, "Conversations With a Gorilla," *National Geographic* 154 (4), October 1978, pp. 438–65. See also Francine Patterson and Wendy Gordon, "The Case for the Personhood of Gorillas," in *The Great Ape Project*, ed. Cavalieri and Singer.

178. Koko also named Smoky, who is gray. See Wendy Gordon, "A Cat Named Smoky," *Gorilla, the Journal of the Gorilla Foundation* 15 (2), pp. 13–14.

179. Tao Wolfe, "Park's Closing Forces Move for Dolphins," *Fort Lauderdale Sun-Sentinel*, reported in the *Pittsburgh Post-Gazette*, Pittsburgh, Pa., August 1, 1994, p. A8.

180. Sapontzis, *Morals, Reason, and Animals*, pp. 246–47. Bernard Rollin reaches the same conclusion in *Animal Rights and Human Morality*, p. 101.

181. Sapontzis, *Morals, Reason, and Animals*, pp. 246–47.

182. Callicott, *In Defense of the Land Ethic*, pp. 57, 277 n. 15. See also his "The Search for an Environmental Ethic," in *Matters of Life and Death*, 2d ed., ed. Tom Regan (New York: Random House, 1986), pp. 399–400. In his earlier 1986 article, Callicott writes that Regan's and Singer's views "seem" to have such an implication, but in his more recent piece he argues that an antipredation policy follows from their positions.

183. Tom Barnes, "Deer Hunters Get Green Light," *The Pittsburgh Post-Gazette*, October 2, 1993, pp. D1, D6.

184. Wyndle Watson, "120 Deer Killed in Hunt," *The Pittsburgh Post-Gazette*, May 19, 1994, p. B1.

Notes

185. See, e.g., "The American Hunter Under Fire," *U.S. News and World Report* (cover story), February 5, 1990, p. 35; "Bow Hunting: A Most Primitive Sport," *The Animals' Agenda,* May 1990, pp. 15–18; "Bow Hunting Under Attack," *Act'ionLine,* April/May 1990, pp. 16–18; and Jude Reitman, "The Fall of the Wild," *E Magazine,* May/June 1990, p. 64.

186. Barnes, "Deer Hunters Get Green Light," p. D6.

187. John W. Turner Jr., "Remotely Delivered Immunocontraception in Captive White-Tailed Deer," *The Journal of Wildlife Management* 56 (1), 1992, pp. 154–57. Recently, a national symposium was held on the topic of "Contraception in Wildlife Management" (Denver, Colorado, October 26–28, 1993). The meeting was attended by scientists, game commission heads, and educators. One of the speakers, Dr. Priscilla Cohn (see below), has told me that a game commission representative from a western state noted in his talk that "people are getting sick of the killing." I believe that we will be hearing more about wildlife contraception in the future.

188. Taylor, *Respect for Nature,* pp. 304–7.

189. "The American Hunter Under Fire," p. 30.

190. Tim Reeves, "Panel OKs Bill Aimed at Trigger-Happy Hunters," *The Pittsburgh Post-Gazette,* Pittsburgh, Pa., April 9, 1993, pp. B1, B5.

191. Jackie Beranek, "Hunting Accident Kills Local Woman," *The Herald-Standard,* Uniontown, Pa., November 30, 1993, p. A1.

192. Scott Shalaway, "Hunters Must Face Truth: Cleanup Needed to Preserve Sport," *The Pittsburgh Press,* November 25, 1990, p. D17.

193. "Goal of Buckmasters Party Is to Educate Non-Hunters," AP report, *The Pittsburgh Post-Gazette,* August 7, 1994, p. C8.

194. Robert Loftin, "The Morality of Hunting," *Environmental Ethics* 6 (3), Fall 1984, pp. 245–46. Loftin supports sport hunting, despite his devastating critique of the way it is done, because hunters contribute financially and politically to the preservation of natural habitats. However, surely there are other nonfatal and ecologically sounder ways of achieving the same purpose! If the animals are rights holders, any such defense of killing them is, of course, utterly inadequate. Imagine a criminal justifying vicious muggings by boasting that he donates 3 percent of the money stolen to charity. Additionally, the amount of support hunters provide for the preservation of habitats appears to be greatly exaggerated. According to *E Magazine,* most of the money generated for this purpose comes from taxpayers in general ("The Fall of the Wild," p. 64).

195. He is quoted in *The Animals' Agenda,* March 1987, p. 25.

196. Ibid., pp. 244–45.

197. David Guenther, "The Hunting Debate," *The Pittsburgh Press,* Pittsburgh, Pa., November 27, 1988, p. H1.

198. Even pro-hunting sources concede this. See, e.g., Don Hopey, "You Can't See the Forest for the Deer," *The Pittsburgh Post-Gazette,* Pittsburgh, Pa., Science and Health feature, September 13, 1993, pp. A7, A9.

199. For more on the issue of hunting, see my "The Joy of Killing," *Between the Species* 7 (3), Summer 1991, pp. 121–28.

200. Taylor, *Respect for Nature,* chapter 6. Taylor deliberately focuses only on conflicts between humans and wild nonhumans.

201. I am indebted to Hugh Lehman for stimulating my thinking on this kind

Notes

of issue. See his "On the Moral Acceptability of Killing Animals," *The Journal of Agricultural Ethics* 1 (2), 1988, pp. 155–62, and my "When Is It Morally Acceptable to Kill Animals?" *The Journal of Agricultural Ethics* 1 (3), 1988, pp. 211–24. I continue to rethink my position on situations in which killing a moral equal is justified.

202. Taylor, *Respect for Nature*, pp. 293–94.

203. See my "When Is It Morally Acceptable to Kill Animals?", p. 216.

204. This is not to say that moral agents should not resort to lots in desperate situations. In special circumstances, this method may actually be the most prudent for all parties concerned to adopt; e.g., if one were stuck in the proverbial lifeboat, the thing would probably capsize if everyone struggled, fought over food and water, etc.! If "Everyone for herself!" is apt to kill all or most of the trapped victims, a lottery would be preferable. (Not the sort of lottery Shirley Jackson chillingly sketches in her classic story, however! In Jackson's small fictional farming community, lottery losers are stoned to death by their neighbors in an annual ritual whose original purpose has been lost. Tradition rather than scarcity of resources perpetuates the brutality. See "The Lottery," written in 1948 and anthologized in *The Lottery* [New York: Avon Books, 1971], pp. 211–19.)

205. Assuming, as I am at this point, that the rights view is correct, any such domestic animals would have to be treated with full respect, as I discussed above. To treat them as mere commodities is to ignore the valid claims that can be made on their behalf.

206. James Rachels, "No Moral Difference," in *Ethics and Modern Life,* 4th ed., ed. R. Abelson and M. L. Friquegnon (New York: St. Martin's Press, 1991), pp. 167–73. Rachels's topic is active versus passive euthanasia, but his arguments apply to any cases of killing versus letting die.

207. A moral agent ought to do her best to keep off the menu those to whom she has acquired as well as unacquired obligations, however, preferring to win the competition (provided that it is unavoidable!) against someone to whom she has only unacquired obligations. In the scarcity of resources situation, the latter obligation is overridden by one's own right to well-being, but other obligations are not canceled. In actuality, our emotions would probably prevent us from making a meal of those to whom we are closely tied, be they human or nonhuman.

208. Regan, *The Case for Animal Rights*, chapter 8, section 8.13.

209. Ibid., p. 351.

210. One such tragic case was widely publicized in the United States during the summer of 1993. Within a year's time, the remaining infant, Angela Lakeburg, had also died. See "At What Price, Against What Odds?" *The Pittsburgh Post-Gazette,* June 11, 1994, p. B5.

211. Lehman, "On the Moral Acceptability of Killing Animals," p. 159.

212. Regan, *The Case for Animal Rights,* pp. 307–8. See also pp. 248–50 for his elucidation of the respect principle. Regan states the worse-off principle slightly differently than I have: "Special considerations aside, when we must decide to override the rights of the many or the rights of the few who are innocent, and when the harm faced by the few would make them worse-off than any of the many would be if any other option were chosen, then we ought to override the

Notes

rights of the many." However, the principle also applies in situations where we must choose between harming one innocent being rather than another (p. 308).

213. Ibid., p. 324.

214. Ibid., p. 351.

215. Ibid., p. 248.

216. Ibid., p. 235.

217. Feinberg, *Harm to Others*, p. 93. Hugh Lehman has argued that Regan's "number and variety of satisfactions" view actually implies that a fifty-year-old human should be flung overboard rather than a forty-year-old human (see his review of Regan's *The Case for Animal Rights* in *Dialogue* 23, 1984, p. 675). He poses this as an objection to Regan's contention, which may indeed have this consequence. Feinberg's way of looking at such cases does not necessarily have this particular implication, however. Too many other factors could outweigh the ten-year age difference, such as new goals, projects, and other "unfinished business." When the age difference is far greater, however, such as that between an eighty-year-old and a fifteen-year-old, both innocents, the worse-off principle would justify killing the former rather than the latter. This seems to be correct. It is a matter of justice: Other things being equal, every individual should have the opportunity to fulfill as many of his or her goals as possible. The two individuals' lives are equally morally valuable, but the elderly person's life is already approaching completion. The youngster should have the same opportunities that the elderly person has already enjoyed.

218. Sapontzis, *Morals, Reason, and Animals,* p. 169.

219. Rollin, *The Unheeded Cry,* p. 144.

220. Sapontzis, *Morals, Reason, and Animals,* p. 171.

221. See my "When Is It Morally Acceptable to Kill Animals?", p. 216.

222. See Michael Tooley, "Abortion and Infanticide on Demand," in *Ethics and Modern Life,* 4th ed., ed. R. Abelson and M. L. Friquegnon (New York: St. Martin's Press, 1991), pp. 186–96, and Ruth Cigman, "Death, Misfortune, and Species Inequality," *Philosophy and Public Affairs* 10, 1981, pp. 47–54.

223. Sapontzis, *Morals, Reason, and Animals,* chapter 9.

224. Lehman, "On the Moral Acceptability of Killing Animals."

225. Regan makes the same point when he pictures yet another lifeboat case: A healthy dog shares a boat with four sick humans. The humans have the ability to give the disease to the dog and then test an untried vaccine on her. Regan correctly says that this is not compatible with his rights view, because in forcing the dog to run *their* risks they are treating her as a mere commodity. Unlike the humans, the animal can only lose in this situation (p. 385). The situation is quite different when all are initially at risk, as is the case if there is not enough food.

226. "Doctors Creating New Pig Breed to Donate Hearts to Humans," *The Pittsburgh Press,* February 10, 1991, p. A10.

227. For more strong arguments against using the worse-off principle to justify killing, see Charles Fink, "The Moderate View on Animal Ethics," *Between the Species* 7 (4), Fall 1991, pp. 194–200. Fink and I (in my "When Is It Morally Acceptable to Kill Animals?" and my "Who Can Be Morally Obligated to Be a Vegetarian?") have entirely independently argued in sometimes strikingly similar ways to reach the same conclusions on this point.

228. Regan, *The Case for Animal Rights,* p. 331.

Notes

229. Ibid., p. 337.

230. Regan's opposition to all invasive experiments for human purposes indicates that he would not apply the argument in this way. For the reasons I go on to spell out, I think that consistency would also preclude his using the argument to justify raising and killing sentient, conative nonhuman animals (who are not already independently at risk) for their flesh, supposing we were carnivores rather than omnivores. See my "Who Can Be Morally Obligated to Be a Vegetarian?", pp. 193–97.

231. Regan, *The Case for Animal Rights*, p. 331.

232. Fink, "Animal Experimentation and the Argument from Limited Resources," pp. 90–95.

SELECTED BIBLIOGRAPHY

BOOKS OR PARTS OF BOOKS

Abelson, Razial, and Marie-Louise Friquegnon. *Ethics and Modern Life,* 4th ed. New York: St. Martin's Press, 1991.

Adams, Carol J. *The Sexual Politics of Meat.* New York: Continuum, 1990.

Amnesty International. *United States of America: The Death Penalty.* Amnesty International, 1990.

Aquinas, St. Thomas. *Summa Contra Gentiles,* book 3, part 2, chapter 112. In *Animal Rights and Human Obligations,* 2d ed. Ed. Tom Regan and Peter Singer. Englewood Cliffs: Prentice-Hall, 1989, pp. 6–9.

Arrington, Robert. *Rationalism, Realism, and Relativism: Perspectives in Contemporary Moral Epistemology.* Ithaca: Cornell University Press, 1989.

Baird, R., and S. Rosenbaum. *Animal Experimentation: The Moral Issues.* Buffalo: Prometheus Books, 1991.

Bekoff, Marc, and Dale Jamieson, "Reflective Ethology, Applied Philosophy, and the Moral Status of Animals." Chapter 1 in *Perspectives in Ethology,* vol. 9, ed. P. P. G. Bateson and P. H. Klopfer. New York: Plenum Publishing, 1991.

Benn, Stanley. "Egalitarianism and Equal Consideration of Interests." In *Equality,* ed. J. R. Pennock and J. W. Chapman. New York: Atherton, 1967, pp. 67–78.

Bentham, Jeremy. *Introduction to the Principles of Morals and Legislation.* New York: Columbia University Press, 1945.

Berger, Gotthart. *Monkeys and Apes.* New York: Arco Publishing Co., 1985.

Brandt, Richard. "Some Merits of One Form of Rule Utilitarianism." In *Mill: Utilitarianism with Critical Essays.* Ed. Samuel Gorovitz. Indianapolis: Bobbs-Merrill, 1971, pp. 324–44.

———. *A Theory of the Good and the Right.* Oxford: Clarendon Press, 1979.

British Medical Association. *Medicine Betrayed: The Participation of Doctors in Human Rights Abuses.* London: Zed Books, 1992.

Budiansky, Stephen. *The Convenant of the Wild: Why Animals Chose Domestication.* New York: William Morrow and Company, 1992.

Callahan, Daniel. *Abortion: Law, Choice, and Morality.* New York: Macmillan Publishing Co., 1970.

Callicott, J. Baird. "The Search for an Environmental Ethic." In *Matters of Life and Death,* 2d ed. Ed. Tom Regan. New York: Random House, 1986, pp. 381–423.

———. *In Defense of the Land Ethic.* Albany: State University of New York Press, 1989.

Carruthers, Peter. *Introducing Persons.* Albany: State University of New York Press, 1986.

———. *The Animals Issue.* Cambridge: Cambridge University Press, 1992.

Cavalieri, Paola, and Peter Singer, eds. *The Great Ape Project.* New York: St. Martin's Press, 1993.

Clark, Stephen. *The Nature of the Beast.* Oxford: Oxford University Press, 1982.

Comstock, Gary. *Is There an Obligation to Save the Family Farm?* Ames: Iowa State University Press, 1987.

Doerr, Edd, and J. W. Prescott, eds. *Abortion Rights and Fetal Personhood.* Long Beach: Centerline Press, 1989.

Dombrowski, Daniel A. *The Philosophy of Vegetarianism.* Amherst: University of Massachusetts Press, 1984.

Ducasse, C. J. "Is Life After Death Possible?" In *Philosophy and Contemporary Issues,* 4th ed. Ed. J. Burr and M. Goldinger. New York: Macmillan, 1989, pp. 382–91.

Durning, A. B., and H. Brough. *Taking Stock: Animal Farming and the Environment. Worldwatch Paper 103.* Washington, D.C.: Worldwatch Institute, 1991.

Eldridge, Niles. *The Monkey Business: A Scientist Looks at Creationism.* New York: Pocket Books, 1982.

Feinberg, Joel. *Harm to Others.* Oxford: Oxford University Press, 1984.

———. "Abortion." In *Matters of Life and Death,* 2d ed. Ed. Tom Regan. New York: Random House, 1986, pp. 256–93.

Feldman, Fred. *Introductory Ethics.* Englewood Cliffs: Prentice-Hall, 1978.

Fox, Michael A. *The Case for Animal Experimentation.* Berkeley: University of California Press, 1986.

Frankena, William. *Ethics,* 2d ed. Englewood Cliffs: Prentice-Hall, 1973.

Frey, R. G. *Interests and Rights: The Case Against Animals.* Oxford: Clarendon Press, 1980.

———. *Rights, Killing, and Suffering.* Oxford: Basil Blackwell, 1983.

Gewirth, Alan. *Reason and Morality.* Chicago: University of Chicago Press, 1978.

———. *Human Rights: Essays on Justification and Application.* Chicago: University of Chicago Press, 1982.

Gilligan, Carol. *In a Different Voice.* Cambridge: Harvard University Press, 1982.

Goodall, Jane. *The Chimpanzees of Gombe.* Cambridge: Harvard University Press, 1986.

Gould, Stephen Jay. *Ever Since Darwin: Reflections in Natural History.* New York: W. W. Norton, 1977.

Gray, Bradford. *Human Subjects in Medical Experimentation.* Melbourne, Fla.: Robert E. Krieger Publishing Co., 1981.

Griffin, Donald. *The Question of Animal Awareness: Evolutionary Continuity of Mental Experience.* New York: Rockefeller University Press, 1981.

————. *Animal Thinking*. Cambridge: Harvard University Press, 1989.

————. *Animal Minds*. Chicago: University of Chicago Press, 1992.

Halverson, Marlene. *Farm Animal Welfare: Crisis or Opportunity for Agriculture?* Staff Paper P91-1. St. Paul: University of Minnesota, 1991.

Hargrove, Eugene. *The Foundations of Environmental Ethics*. Englewood Cliffs: Prentice-Hall, 1989.

Harris, C. E. *Applying Moral Theories*. Belmont: Wadsworth Publishing Co., 1986.

Hume, David. *A Treatise of Human Nature*. Ed. L. A. Selby-Bigge. London: Oxford University Press, 1888.

Kagan, Jerome. *The Nature of the Child*. New York: Basic Books, 1984.

Kahane, Howard. *Logic and Contemporary Rhetoric,* 6th Ed. Belmont, Ca.: Wadsworth Publishing Co., 1992.

Kant, Immanuel. *Lectures on Ethics*. Trans. Louis Infield. New York: Harper & Row, 1963.

————. *Grounding for the Metaphysics of Morals*. Trans. James W. Ellington. Indianapolis: Hackett Press, 1981.

Kittay, Eva F., and Diana T. Meyers, eds. *Women and Moral Theory*. Totowa: Rowman & Littlefield, 1987.

Kohlberg, Lawrence. *The Psychology of Moral Development*. San Francisco: Harper & Row, 1984.

Kuhse, Helga, and Peter Singer. *Should the Baby Live?* Oxford: Oxford University Press, 1985.

Lappé, Frances. *Diet for a Small Planet*. 10th anniversary ed. New York: Ballantine Books, 1982.

Leopold, Aldo. *A Sand County Almanac*. New York: Oxford University Press, 1949.

Linzey, Andrew. *Christianity and the Rights of Animals*. New York: Crossroad Publishing Co., 1987.

Lomasky, Loren E. *Persons, Rights, and the Moral Community*. Oxford: Oxford University Press, 1987.

Magel, Charles R. *Keyguide to Information Sources in Animal Rights*. London: Mansell Pub., 1989.

Mason, Jim, and Peter Singer. *Animal Factories,* Rev. Ed. New York: Harmony Books, 1990.

Meldin, A. I. *Rights and Persons*. Berkeley: University of California Press, 1977.

————. *Rights in Moral Lives*. Berkeley: University of California Press, 1988.

Midgley, Mary. *Animals and Why They Matter*. Athens: University of Georgia Press, 1983.

Milgram, Stanley. *Obedience to Authority*. New York: Harper & Row, 1974.

Nietzsche, Friedrich. *Beyond Good and Evil*. Trans. Helen Zimmern. London: Allen & Unwin, 1887.

Noonan, John T. "An Almost Absolute Value in History." In *Philosophy and Contemporary Issues,* 6th ed. Ed. J. Burr and M. Goldinger. New York: Macmillan Publishing Co., 1992, pp. 263–68.

Office of Technology Assessment. *Alternatives to Animal Use in Research, Testing, and Education*. New York: Marcel Dekker, Inc., 1988.

Parfit, Derek. *Reasons and Persons.* Oxford: Oxford University Press, 1984.

Rachels, James. *Created from Animals.* Oxford: Oxford University Press, 1990.

———. "No Moral Difference." In *Ethics and Modern Life,* 4th ed. Ed. R. Abelson and M. L. Friquegnon. New York: St. Martin's Press, 1991, pp. 167–73.

Radner, Daisie, and Michael Radner. *Animal Consciousness.* Buffalo: Prometheus Books, 1989.

Rawls, John. *A Theory of Justice.* Cambridge: Harvard University Press, 1971.

Regan, Tom. *All That Dwell Therein.* Berkeley: University of California Press, 1982.

———. *The Case for Animal Rights.* Berkeley: University of California Press, 1983.

———, ed. *Animal Sacrifices.* Philadelphia: Temple University Press, 1986.

———, and Peter Singer, eds. *Animal Rights and Human Obligations.* Englewood Cliffs, N.J.: Prentice-Hall, 1976.

——— and Peter Singer, eds. *Animal Rights and Human Obligations,* 2d ed. Englewood Cliffs, N.J.: Prentice-Hall, 1989.

Regis, Edward, ed. *Gewirth's Ethical Rationalism: Critical Essays With a Reply by Alan Gewirth.* Chicago: University of Chicago Press, 1984.

Restak, Richard. *The Brain.* New York: Bantam Books, 1984.

Rollin, Bernard. "The Frankenstein Thing." In *Genetic Engineering of Animals: An Agricultural Perspective.* Ed. J. W. Evans and A. Hollaender. New York: Plenum Press, 1986, pp. 285–97.

———. *The Unheeded Cry: Animal Consciousness, Animal Pain, and Science.* Oxford: Oxford University Press, 1989.

———. *Animal Rights and Human Morality.* Rev. ed. Buffalo: Prometheus Books, 1992.

Rosen, Steven. *Food for the Spirit: Vegetarianism and the World Religions.* New York: Bala Books, 1987.

Ross, W. D. *The Right and the Good.* Oxford: Oxford University Press, 1930.

———. *The Foundations of Ethics.* Oxford: Oxford University Press, 1939.

Ryrie, Charles C. *The Ryrie Study Bible.* Chicago: Moody Press, 1976.

Salt, Henry. *Animal Rights.* Fontwell: Centaur, 1980.

Sapontzis, Steve. *Morals, Reason, and Animals.* Philadelphia: Temple University Press, 1987.

Sartre, Jean-Paul. *The Transcendence of the Ego.* Trans. Forrest Williams and Robert Kirkpatrick. New York: Noonday Press, 1971.

———. "Existentialism Is a Humanism." Trans. Philip Mairet. In *Existentialism from Dostoevsky to Sartre.* Ed. Walter Kaufmann. New York: New American Library, 1975, pp. 345–69.

Savage-Rumbaugh, Sue, and Roger Lewin. *Kanzi: The Ape at the Brink of the Human Mind.* New York: John Wiley and Sons, 1994.

Senchuk, Dennis. *Against Instinct.* Philadelphia: Temple University Press, 1991.

Shoemaker, Sidney. *Self Knowledge and Self Identity.* Ithaca: Cornell University Press, 1962.

Short, C. E., and A. Van Poznak, eds. *Animal Pain.* New York: Churchill Livingstone, 1992.

Singer, Peter. *Animal Liberation.* New York: Avon Books, 1975.

————. *Practical Ethics*. Cambridge: Cambridge University Press, 1979.

————. "Animals and the Value of Life." In *Matters of Life and Death*, 2d ed. Ed. Tom Regan. New York: Random House, 1986, pp. 338–80.

————. "Life's Uncertain Voyage." In *Metaphysics and Morality: Essays in Honour of J. J. C. Smart*. Ed. P. Pettit, R. Sylvan, and J. Norman. Oxford: Basil Blackwell, 1987, pp. 154–72.

————. *Animal Liberation*. 2d ed. New York: Random House, 1990.

Sommers, Christina. "Philosophers Against the Family." In *Vice and Virtue in Everyday Life*. Ed. Christina Sommers and Fred Sommers. San Diego: Harcourt Brace Jovanovich, 1989, pp. 728–54.

Sumner, L. W. *Abortion and Moral Theory*. Princeton: Princeton University Press, 1981.

————. "A Third Way." In *The Problem of Abortion*, 2d ed. Ed. Joel Feinberg. Belmont: Wadsworth Publishing Co., 1984, pp. 71–93.

————. *The Moral Foundation of Rights*. Oxford: Oxford University Press, 1987.

Taylor, Paul. *Respect for Nature*. Princeton: Princeton University Press, 1986.

Temerlin, Maurice. *Lucy: Growing Up Human*. Palo Alto: Science and Behavior Books, 1975.

Tooley, Michael. *Abortion and Infanticide*. Oxford: Clarendon Press, 1983.

————. "Abortion and Infanticide on Demand." In *Ethics and Modern Life*, 4th ed. Ed. R. Abelson and M. L. Friquegnon. New York: St. Martin's Press, 1991, pp. 186–96.

Tylinek, Erich, and Gotthart Berger. *Monkeys and Apes*. New York: Arco Publishing Co., 1985.

Walker, Stephen. *Animal Thought*. London: Routledge and Kegan Paul, 1983.

Wenz, Peter. *Environmental Justice*. Albany: State University of New York Press, 1988.

JOURNAL ARTICLES

Adams, Carol. "Abortion Rights and Animal Rights." *Between the Species* 7 (4), Fall 1991, pp. 181–89.

American Dietetic Association. "Position of the American Dietetic Association: Vegetarian Diets." *Journal of the American Dietetic Association* 93 (11), 1993, pp. 1317–19.

Angell, Marcia. "The Nazi Hypothermia Experiments and Unethical Research Today." *The New England Journal of Medicine* 322 (20), May 17, 1990, pp. 1462–64.

Bennett, Dawn D. "Making Sense of Animal Sounds." *Science News* 127, May 18, 1985, pp. 314–17.

Blatz, Charlie. "Why (Most) Humans Are More Important Than Other Animals: Reflections on the Foundations of Ethics." *Between the Species* 1 (4), Fall 1985, pp. 8–16.

Blum, Lawrence. "Gilligan and Kohlberg: Implications for Moral Theory." *Ethics* 98, April 1988, pp. 472–91.

Bower, Bruce. "Grammar-Schooled Dolphins." *Science News* 126, December 1, 1984, pp. 346–48.

———. "Hominid Headway." *Science News* 132, December 19, 1987, pp. 408–9.

———. "A 'Handy' Guide to Primate Evolution." *Science News* 135, January 7, 1989, pp. 10–12.

———. "Getting Out From Number One." *Science News* 137, April 28, 1990, pp. 266–67.

———. "Suicide Brains: Naturally Prone to Pain." *Science News* 138, November 10, 1990, p. 301.

———. "Human Brain Reveals the Anatomy of Pain." *Science News* 139, March 16, 1991, p. 167.

———. "Brain Images Show Structure of Depression." *Science News* 142, September 12, 1992, p. 165.

———. "Ancient Ape Suggests Human, Chimp Lineage." *Science News* 142, September 26, 1992, p. 198.

———. "A Child's Theory of Mind." *Science News* 144, July 17, 1993, pp. 40–41.

———. "New Gene Study Enters Human Origins Debate." *Science News* 144, September 25, 1993, pp. 196–97.

Brownlee, Sharon. "A Riddle Wrapped in a Mystery." *Discover*, October 1985, pp. 85–93.

Carruthers, Peter. "Brute Experience." *The Journal of Philosophy* 86, 1989, pp. 258–69.

———. "Can Animals Feel Pain in the Morally Relevant Sense? No." *The Ag Bioethics Forum* 4 (2), December 1992, pp. 2, 5.

Causey, Ann. "On the Morality of Hunting." *Environmental Ethics* 11 (4), Winter 1989, pp. 327–43.

Cigman, Ruth. "Death, Misfortune, and Species Inequality." *Philosophy and Public Affairs* 10, 1981, pp. 47–54.

Coady, C. A. J. "Defending Human Chauvinism." *Report from the Center for Philosophy and Public Policy* 6 (4), University of Maryland, Fall 1986, pp. 12–14.

Cohen, Carl. "The Case for the Use of Animals in Biomedical Research." *The New England Journal of Medicine*, October 2, 1986, pp. 865–70.

Cohen, Joel E. "How Many People Can the Earth Hold?" *Discover*, November 1992, pp. 114–19.

Comstock, Gary. "Pigs and Piety: A Theocentric Perspective on Food Animals." *Between the Species* 8 (3), Summer 1992, pp. 121–35.

Crabb, Charlene. "A Touch of Pain." *Discover*, June 1993, p. 41.

———. "Rio, the Logical Sea Lion." *Discover*, February 1993, p. 20.

Crisp, Roger. "A Comment on 'On Behalf of a Moderate Speciesism.'" *The Journal of Applied Philosophy* 2 (2), 1985, pp. 279–80.

DeGrazia, David. "The Distinction Between Equality in Moral Status and Deserving Equal Consideration." *Between the Species* 7 (2), Spring 1991, pp. 73–77.

———. "Response." *Between the Species* 7 (2), Spring 1991, pp. 79–80.

De Roose, Frank. "Pluhar on Methods of Justification." *Between the Species* 4 (4), 1988, pp. 255–59.

Diamond, Jared. "Making a Chimp Out of a Man." *Discover*, December 1984, pp. 55–60.

Dunlap, Julie. "The Adolescent as Environmental Ethicist." *Between the Species* 5 (2), Spring 1989, pp. 70–80.

Dwyer, Johanna. "Nutritional Consequences of Vegetarianism." *Annual Reviews in Nutrition* 11, 1991, pp. 61–91.

——, and Franklin M. Loew. "Nutritional Risks of Vegan Diets to Women and Children: Are They Preventable?" *The Journal of Agricultural and Environmental Ethics* 7 (1), 1994, pp. 87–109.

Edwards, D. D. "Study Supports Easing Circumcision Pain." *Science News* 133, March 19, 1988, p. 182.

English, Jane. "Abortion and the Concept of a Person." *The Canadian Journal of Philosophy* 5 (2), October 1975, pp. 233–43.

Ezzell, Carol. "Memories Might Be Made of This: Closing in on the Biochemistry of Learning." *Science News* 139, May 25, 1991, pp. 228–30.

——. "Watching the Remembering Brain at Work." *Science News* 140, November 23, 1991, p. 333.

Feinberg, Joel. "The Nature and Value of Rights." *The Journal of Value Inquiry* 4, Winter 1970, pp. 243–57.

Fink, Charles. "Animal Experimentation and the Argument from Limited Resources." *Between the Species* 7 (2), Spring 1991, pp. 90–95.

——. "The Moderate View on Animal Ethics." *Between the Species* 7 (4), Fall 1991, pp. 194–200.

Fisher, J., and R. A. Hinde. "The Opening of Milk Bottles by Birds." *British Birds* 42, 1949, pp. 347–57.

Flanagan, Owen. "Virtue, Sex, and Gender: Some Philosophical Reflections on the Moral Psychology Debate." *Ethics* 92, April 1982, pp. 499–512.

——, and Kathryn Jackson. "Justice, Care, and Gender: The Kohlberg-Gilligan Debate Revisited." *Ethics* 97, April 1987, pp. 622–37.

Fox, Michael A. "Animal Liberation: A Critique." *Ethics* 88 (2), 1978, pp. 106–18.

——. "Animal Experimentation: A Philosopher's Changing Views." *Between the Species* 3 (2), Spring 1987, pp. 55–60, 75, 80.

Francis, Leslie, and Richard Norman. "Some Animals Are More Equal Than Others." *Philosophy* 53, 1978, pp. 507–27.

Frey, R. G. "Autonomy and the Value of Animal Life." *The Monist* 70 (1), January 1987, pp. 50–63.

——. "The Significance of Agency and Marginal Cases." *Philosophica* 39 (1), 1987, pp. 39–46.

——. "Moral Standing, the Value of Lives, and Speciesism." *Between the Species* 4 (3), Summer 1988, pp. 191–201.

George, Kathryn. "So Human an Animal . . . , or the Moral Relevance of Being an Omnivore." *The Journal of Agricultural and Environmental Ethics* 3 (2), 1990, pp. 172–86.

——. "The Use and Abuse of Scientific Studies." *The Journal of Agricultural and Environmental Ethics* 5 (2), 1992, pp. 217–33.

————. "Use and Abuse Revisited: Response to Pluhar and Varner." *The Journal of Agricultural and Environmental Ethics* 7 (1), 1994, pp. 41–76.

Gewirth, Alan. "From the Prudential to the Moral: Reply to Singer." *Ethics* 95, January 1985, pp. 302–4.

Goodpaster, Kenneth E. "On Being Morally Considerable." *Journal of Philosophy* 75 (6), June 1978, pp. 308–25.

Grady, Denise. "The Vision Thing: Mainly in the Brain." *Discover,* June 1993, pp. 57–66.

Griffin, Donald. "A New Science that Sees Animals as Conscious Beings." *The Smithsonian,* March 1985, pp. 67–75.

Harrison, Peter. "Theodicy and Animal Pain." *Philosophy* 64 (247), January 1989, pp. 79–92.

————. "The Neo-Cartesian Revival: A Response." *Between the Species* 9 (2), Spring 1993, pp. 71–76.

Hart, H. L. A. "Death and Utility." *The New York Review of Books,* May 15, 1980, pp. 25–32.

Herbert, Victor. "Vitamin B_{12}: Plant Sources, Requirements, and Assay." *The American Journal of Clinical Nutrition* 48, 1988, pp. 852–58.

Holland, Alan. "On Behalf of a Moderate Speciesism." *The Journal of Applied Philosophy* 1 (2), 1984, pp. 281–91.

Hurnik, J. F., and H. Lehman. "Ethics and Farm Animal Welfare." *The Journal of Agricultural Ethics* 1 (4), 1988, pp. 305–18.

Jamieson, Dale. "Rational Egoism and Animal Rights." *Environmental Ethics* 3, Summer 1981, pp. 167–71.

Johnson, Edward. "Carruthers on Consciousness and Moral Status." *Between the Species* 7 (4), Fall 1991, pp. 190–92.

Langreth, Robert. "Pediatric Pain." *Science News* 139, February 2, 1991, pp. 74–75.

Lehman, Hugh. "On the Moral Acceptability of Killing Animals." *The Journal of Agricultural Ethics* 1 (2), 1988, pp. 155–62.

Lockwood, Michael. "Singer on Killing and the Preference for Life." *Inquiry* 22 (1–2), 1979, pp. 157–69.

Loftin, Robert. "The Morality of Hunting." *Environmental Ethics* 6 (3), Fall 1984, pp. 241–50.

Mangells, Ann Reed, and Suzanne Havala. "Vegan Diets for Women, Infants, and Children." *The Journal of Agricultural and Environmental Ethics* 7 (1), 1994, pp. 111–22.

McCloskey, H. J. "Moral Rights and Animals." *Inquiry* 22 (1–2), Summer 1979, pp. 23–54.

Mestel, R. "The Ascent of the Dog." *Discover,* October 1994, pp. 89–98.

————. "The Moral Case for Experimentation on Animals." *The Monist* 70 (1), January 1987, pp. 64–82.

Narveson, Jan. "Animal Rights." *The Canadian Journal of Philosophy* 7 (1), 1977, pp. 161–78.

————. "On a Case for Animal Rights." *The Monist* 70 (1), January 1987, pp. 31–49.

Nelson, James. "Critical Notice of 'Rights, Killing, and Suffering.'" *Between the Species* 2 (2), 1986, pp. 70–80.

Bibliography

———. "Xenograft and Partial Affections." *Between the Species* 2 (3), 1986, pp. 116–24.

Newton, Lisa. "Reverse Discrimination As Unjustified." *Ethics* 83 (4), 1973, pp. 308–12.

Nozick, Robert. "Review of Tom Regan's *The Case for Animal Rights.*" *New York Times Book Review,* November 27, 1983, pp. 11, 29–30.

O'Connell, Joan M., et al. "Growth of Vegetarian Children: The Farm Study." *Pediatrics* 84 (3), 1989, pp. 475–80.

Partridge, Ernest. "Three Wrong Leads in a Search for an Environmental Ethic." *Ethics and Animals* 5 (3), September 1984, pp. 61–74.

Patterson, Francine. "Conversations with a Gorilla." *National Geographic* 154 (4), October 1978, pp. 436–65.

Pluhar, Evelyn. "Must an Opponent of Animal Rights Also Be an Opponent of Human Rights?" *Inquiry* 24 (2), June 1981, pp. 229–41.

———. "Preferential Hiring and Unjust Sacrifice." *The Philosophical Forum* 12 (3), 1981, pp. 214–24.

———. "On Replaceability." *Ethics and Animals* 3 (4), 1982, pp. 96–105.

———. "Two Conceptions of an Environmental Ethic." *Ethics and Animals* 4 (4), December 1983, pp. 110–27.

———. "Speciesism Not Justified." *Ethics and Animals* 5 (4), December 1984, pp. 122–29.

———. "Speciesism Revisited." *Between the Species* 2 (4), 1986, pp. 184–89.

———. "The Personhood View and the Argument from Marginal Cases." *Philosophica* 39 (1), 1987, pp. 23–38.

———. "Moral Agents and Moral Patients." *Between the Species* 4 (1), Winter 1988, pp. 32–45.

———. "Speciesism: A Form of Bigotry or a Justified View?" *Between the Species* 4 (2), Spring 1988, pp. 83–96.

———. "On the Relevance of Marginal Humans: A Reply to Sapontzis." *Between the Species* 4 (2), Spring 1988, pp. 99–101.

———. "Is There a Morally Relevant Difference Between Human and Animal Nonpersons?" *The Journal of Agricultural Ethics* 1 (1), 1988, pp. 59–68.

———. "When Is It Morally Acceptable to Kill Animals?" *The Journal of Agricultural Ethics* 1 (3), 1988, pp. 211–24.

———. "Kohlberg and Concern for Nonhumans." *Between the Species* 5 (2), Spring 1989, pp. 81–85.

———. "Reason and Morality Revisited." *Between the Species* 6 (2), 1990, pp. 63–69.

———. "Utilitarian Killing, Replacement, and Rights." *The Journal of Agricultural Ethics* 3 (2), 1990, pp. 147–71.

———. "The Joy of Killing." *Between the Species* 7 (3), Summer 1991, pp. 121–28.

———. "Who Can Be Morally Obligated to Be a Vegetarian?" *The Journal of Agricultural and Environmental Ethics* 5 (2), 1992, pp. 189–215.

———. "Vegetarianism, Morality, and Science: A Counter-Reply." *The Journal of Agricultural and Environmental Ethics* 6 (2), 1993, pp. 185–213.

———. "Arguing Away Suffering: A Neo-Cartesian Revival." *Between the Species* 9 (1), Winter 1993, pp. 27–41.

———. "Reply to Harrison." *Between the Species* 9 (2), Spring 1993, pp. 77–82.

———. "Vegetarianism, Morality, and Science Revisited." *The Journal of Agricultural and Environmental Ethics* 7 (1), 1994, pp. 77–82.

Reed, T. M. "Developmental Moral Theory." *Ethics* 97, January 1987, pp. 441–56.

Regan, Tom. "Narveson on Egoism and the Rights of Animals." *Canadian Journal of Philosophy* 7 (1), 1977, pp. 179–86.

Reitman, Jude. "The Fall of the Wild." *E Magazine*, May/June 1990, pp. 36–64.

Robinson, William. "Can Animals Feel Pain in the Morally Relevant Sense? Yes." *Ag Bioethics Forum* 4 (2), 1992, pp. 4–5.

Rollin, Bernard. "The Moral Status of Research Animals in Psychology." *The American Psychologist*, August 1985, pp. 920–26.

Rosenthal, David. "Two Concepts of Consciousness." *Philosophical Studies* 48, 1986, pp. 329–59.

Sapontzis, Steve. "Are Animals Moral Beings?" *American Philosophical Quarterly* 17 (1), January 1980, pp. 45–52.

———. "On Being Morally Expendable." *Ethics and Animals* 3 (3), 1982, pp. 58–72.

———. "Speciesism." *Between the Species* 4 (2), Spring 1988, pp. 97–99.

Singer, Marcus. "On Gewirth's Derivation of the Principle of Generic Consistency." *Ethics* 95, January 1985, pp. 297–301.

Singer, Peter. "Killing Humans and Killing Animals." *Inquiry* 22 (1–2), Summer 1979, p. 151.

———. "Letter to the Editor." *The New York Review of Books*, August 14, 1980, p. 53.

———. "Ten Years of Animal Liberation." *The New York Review of Books*, January 17, 1985, pp. 46–52.

———. "Animal Liberation or Animal Rights?" *The Monist* 70 (1), January 1987, pp. 3–14.

Squadrito, Kathy. "Commentary: Interests and Equal Moral Status." *Between the Species* 7 (2), Spring 1991, pp. 78–79.

Thomson, Judith J. "A Defense of Abortion." *Philosophy and Public Affairs* 1 (1), 1971, pp. 47–66.

Townsend, A. V. "Radical Vegetarians." *The Australasian Journal of Philosophy* 57 (1), 1979, pp. 85–93.

Turner, John W., Jr. "Remotely Delivered Immunocontraception in Captive White-Tailed Deer." *The Journal of Wildlife Management* 56 (1), 1992, pp. 154–57.

Varner, Gary. "Biological Functions and Biological Interests." *The Southern Journal of Philosophy* 28 (2), 1990, pp. 251–70.

———. "No Holism without Pluralism." *Environmental Ethics* 13, Summer 1991, pp. 175–79.

———. "What's Wrong with Animal *Byproducts*?" *The Journal of Agricultural and Environmental Ethics* 7 (1) 1994, pp. 7–17.

———. "In Defense of the Vegan Ideal: Rhetoric and Bias in the Nutrition Literature." *The Journal of Agricultural and Environmental Ethics* 7 (1), 1994, pp. 29–40.

———. "Rejoinder to Kathryn Paxton George." *The Journal of Agricultural and Environmental Ethics* 7 (1), 1994, pp. 83–86.

Vitali, Theodore. "Sport Hunting: Moral or Immoral?" *Environmental Ethics* 12 (1), Spring 1990, pp. 73–75.

Wechkin, Stanley, J. H. Masserman, and W. Terris Jr. "Shock to a Conspecific as an Aversive Stimulus." *Psychonomic Science* 1, 1964, pp. 47–48.

———. " 'Altruistic' Behavior in Rhesus Monkeys." *The American Journal of Psychiatry* 121, 1964, pp. 584–85.

Weiss, Rick. "Forbidding Fruits of Fetal-Cell Research." *Science News* 134, November 5, 1988, pp. 296–98.

———. "Bypassing the Ban." *Science News* 136, December 9, 1989, pp. 378–79.

———. "Fetal-Cell Recipient Showing Improvements." *Science News* 137, February 3, 1990, p. 70.

Wenz, Peter. "Concentric Circle Pluralism: A Response to Rolston." *Between the Species* 5 (3), 1989, pp. 155–57.

White, James. "Are Sentient Beings Replaceable?" *Ethics and Animals* 3 (4), 1982, pp. 91–95.

Wilson, Allan C. "The Molecular Basis of Evolution." *Scientific American* 253 (4), 1985, pp. 164–73.

Wreen, Michael. "In Defense of Speciesism." *Ethics and Animals* 5 (3), September 1984, pp. 47–60.

———. "My Kind of Person." *Between the Species* 2 (1), 1986, pp. 23–28.

———. "If At All Humanly Possible." *Between the Species* 2 (4), 1986, pp. 189–94.

Young, Thomas. "The Morality of Killing Animals: Four Arguments." *Ethics and Animals* 5 (4), 1984, pp. 88–101.

INDEX

Abortion, 3, 88–89, 99–100, 148, 213, 220, 253–54, 339 n. 104; and contraception, 196, 211–12, 253; and rape, 253

Action, generic features of, 241, 338 n. 79

Adams, Carol, xiii, 312 n. 139

Agency, conative nature of, 241, 252

Agents, 16, 79, 88, 239, 240, 249, 256, 262, 283; logically must accord rights to others, 240–48, 256, 259, 263–65; in original position, 234–35; reasons for their according rights to marginals, 90–94, 96, 97–102; should be accorded rights, 249–50, 338 n. 79

Altruism, 172, 175, 336 n. 48

Amoralists, 245, 263–65

Apes, 47, 49–50, 62, 77, 134, 275. *See also* Chimpanzees; Gorillas; Kanzi; Koko; Lucy; Orangutans; Washoe

Aquinas, St. Thomas, 11, 46, 90, 128, 138, 227, 228, 306 n. 54

Argument from analogy to other minds, 13, 17, 20, 23–25, 27, 39, 305 n. 37

Argument from evil, 32, 37

Argument from marginal cases, 63–66, 67–68, 71, 126, 139, 177, 179, 227, 232; alleged inconsistent, 74–77; alleged to be reversible and redundant, 72–74; alleged to underestimate many nonhumans, 81–85; alleged to underestimate marginal humans, 77–81; biconditional version, 64–66, 70, 72–73, 121, 122, 124, 126, 130, 136, 178, 180; cate-

gorical version, 63–64, 73, 75, 77, 81, 85, 103, 120, 122, 178; and the endangerment argument, 87–95; and former full persons, 113–20, 323 n. 1; and potential full persons, 107–13; and self-interest, 95–101; and speciesism, 126–29, 139; and utilitarian side effects, 101–107

Aristotle, 11, 20, 28, 154

Artificial intelligence. *See* Computers

Automata, 16, 19, 33, 34, 38, 44, 52, 254. *See also* Machine model of animals

Autonomy, 2–5, 12, 57, 80, 118, 270, 271, 315 n. 205; and the full-personhood view, 57–58, 62, 110, 141, 205; and homocentrism, 46, 52–55, 338 n. 81; preference, 4, 6, 54, 274; and speciesism, 128

Babies. *See* Infants

Baboons, 83, 130, 149, 150, 152, 153, 155, 157,158–59, 299, 326 n. 72

Bacteria, 8, 9–10, 12, 259, 265

Behaviorism, 7, 14

Benn, Stanley, xiii, 107, 108, 137, 145, 146, 157

Bentham, Jeremy, 180

Bible, used to defend homocentrism, 11–12

Bigotry, 90, 91, 123, 126, 170, 263–66; and allegedly rational preferences, 174–77, 235; and speciesism, 126–35, 136, 139, 170, 172

Biocentric ethic, 260. *See also* Biocentrism

Biocentrism, 9, 260, 262

Birds, 22, 53, 83, 90, 186, 270, 280; African gray parrots, 51; brains of, 309 n. 94; blue tits, 51, 83; chickens, 156; and deceit, 204; and emotions, 258; honeyguides, 50–51; mallards, 53–54; moral significance of, 267, 269, 301; and pain, 258; and self-consciousness, 203; and subjects of lives, 232

Blatz, Charlie, 68, 317 n. 3

Blindsightedness, 38, 40, 43, 312 n. 156

Brain: birds, 51, 309 n. 94; brain death, 100, 115–16, 118; chimpanzee, 25–26, 309 n. 94; fetal development of, 99, 254; human, 26; mammals, 22, 29, 257, 309 n. 94; and language, 48, 64; and memory, 48; opiate receptors, 309 n. 103; and pain, 26, 28–29; permanently damaged, 8, 44, 62, 98, 118–19; reptilian, 258. See also Limbic system

Brandt, Richard B., 173–77, 216, 235

Buddhism, 8, 11

Callahan, Daniel, 147

Callicott, J. Baird, 9, 162, 163, 167, 269, 276, 327 n. 91, 331 n. 55, 336 n. 48, 341 n. 137, n. 150, 344 n. 182

Calves, 91, 97, 116, 138, 187–88, 205

Cannibalism, 99, 205

Carruthers, Peter, xiii, 14–17, 37–45, 88–94, 175, 181–82, 228–30, 255, 306 n. 54, n. 55, n. 57, n. 62, 312 n. 152, 156, 313 n. 168, 319 n. 42, 320 n. 47, n. 53, n. 60, 321 n. 77, 328 n. 9, 334 n. 10, n. 11

Cats, 1, 3, 5, 21, 40–42, 45, 49, 52, 56, 57, 62, 66, 68, 75, 77, 79, 90, 91, 100, 130, 171, 228, 270, 271, 281, 293, 328 n. 122

Cattle, 187–88, 273. See also Calves; Cows

Causey, Ann S., 143

Chickens, 16, 82, 91, 130, 156, 180, 188, 197, 204, 212, 258, 259, 271, 272. See also Eggs

Children, 1, 2, 32, 50, 84, 98, 151, 163–65, 176, 191, 192, 193, 196, 197, 201, 206, 208, 212, 253, 254, 265, 269, 271; comparison to nonhumans, 76, 84; experimentation on, 123; homeless, 251, 339 n. 90; moral status of, 64, 68, 76, 95, 100, 104–105, 113, 211, 220, 267, and pain, 18, 36, 44; and persons, 2, 4, 62; rights for, 140, 250–51, 339 n. 91; and vegetarianism, 343 n. 165. See also Infants; Wretched child, the case of

Chimpanzees, 4, 20, 24–26, 47–48, 50, 53, 65, 75, 82–85, 100, 134, 140, 163, 168–70, 202, 255, 268, 274–75, 309 n. 94. See also Kanzi; Lucy; Washoe

Chomsky, Noam, 48, 49

Cigman, Ruth, 294

Clark, Stephen, 53, 311 n. 122

Coady, C. A. J., 85, 95, 96

Cohen, Carl, 58, 77–81, 82, 126–28, 129, 130, 229

Cohn, Priscilla, 277–78, 345 n. 187

Comatose humans, 8, 62, 64, 77, 78, 79, 114–16, 140, 253, 286

Communication: and homocentrism, 12, 46–51, 55; and nonhumans, 26, 46, 49; as required for moral agency, 2, 60. See also Language

Companion animals, 96, 172, 271, 276, 281, 342 n. 161

Computers: and biocentrism, 340 n. 134; and learning, 7–8, 304 n. 19; and language, 49–50; and nonhuman animal behavior, 41–42

Conation, 241, 250–52, 254–55, 259, 264, 268, 282

Conscious experience: denied to babies and young children, 44; as explanation of nonhuman animal behavior, 41–43; intrinsic theory of, 45; learning without, 20, 23, 30; relational theory of, 43–45; vs. (alleged) unconscious experiences, 38–40, 43. See also Consciousness

Consciousness: and children, 44, 201; denied of nonhumans, 20, 27–28, 30, 35, 37, 43; and evolution, 14, 38, 42; flexibility as hallmark of, 42; and infant pain, 34–36; language allegedly required for, 45; perceptual vs. reflective, 5. *See also* Conscious experience; Mere consciousness; Self-consciousness

Consequentialism, 59, 63, 101, 124, 174, 221–22, 231, 232, 244, 327 n. 76, 337 n. 69. *See also* Egoism; Utilitarianism

Contraception: and abortion, 212; compared to murder, 112, 196, 221; for deer and other ungulates, 277–78, 345 n. 187

Contractarianism. *See* Contractualism

Contractualism, 16, 182, 230, 234

Cows, 187, 271, 273, 274

Crisp, Roger, 73–74

Cruelty, 11, 16, 90–91, 126, 186, 228, 238, 254, 306 n. 54, 320 n. 53, 334 n. 11, 335 n. 28

Death: by execution, 69, 183; disutility of, 60, 209–10; duties applying after, 117; as harm, 267, 268, 288–95; of humans vs. nonhumans, 60, 62, 116, 149, 224, 267, 268, 285, 299–300; legal criteria, 116; as a loss, 259, 294; as in one's interests, 280–81; natural, for farm animals, 272, 274; and natural selection, 22; of non(full)persons, 89, 92, 101, 149, 172, 176; and replacement, 185, 201, 204, 209–10; risked deliberately, 32; and self-defense, 283; and wild animals, 276, 277, 279. *See also* Abortion; Euthanasia; Infanticide; Killing

Deer, 27–28

DeGrazia, David, 121–22, 322 n. 117

Deontological views, 59, 60, 63, 88, 104, 174, 218, 231, 232, 244, 327 n. 76, 337 n. 69

Dependent beings, 193, 194, 211. *See also* Independent beings

DeRoose, Frank, 245–48, 338 n. 71

Descartes, René, 13, 14, 17, 18, 33, 37, 39, 43, 45, 46, 52, 139, 309 n. 100

Desires: and agency, 241, 251; to continue living, 201, 261; and the loss of death, 293; infants, 252, 254; nonhuman, 41, 52, 204, 254–59, 261, 265, 269, 280, 298; and rights, 10, 262, 289; and self-awareness, 202, 207; and subjects-of-lives, 3, 232; unconscious, 38. *See also* Conation

Disutility, 60, 101, 174, 180, 183, 185, 194, 195, 200, 207–209, 211, 213–16, 218, 220

Dogs, 5, 8, 49, 52, 56–57, 62, 66, 68, 69, 75, 82, 90, 91, 116, 137, 160–61, 186, 212, 289, 316 n. 214, 347 n. 225

Dolphins, 49, 129, 274–76

Domestic animals, 161–62, 168, 269–74, 276, 342 n. 159; on farms, 27–74, 331 n. 53, 346 n. 205. *See also* Companion animals

Double-aspect theory, 19. *See also* Dualism, mind-body

Dualism, mind-body, 13, 18, 19, 26, 27, 257; Cartesian, 19, 28, 45; interactionism, 18, 309 n. 100. *See also* Double aspect theory; Epiphenomenalism; Hypophenomenalism; Occasionalism; Parallelism

Duty: acquired, 162, 164–66, 269, 271, 274, 278, 280, 283, 286; to children, 216, 220; to former full persons, 118–19; to future generations, 191; and having rights, 140–41, 256; to humans vs. nonhumans, 199, 239–240; and moral agency, 80; to moral agents, 235, 238; to non-moral agents, 239; and normative moral theories, 104; to reproduce, 196–97; unacquired or natural, 164, 166, 269; and utilitarianism, 132, 136, 244

Eggs, poultry, 47, 187, 188, 271–73, 283. *See also* Chickens

Egoism, 59, 95–96, 104, 232, 233, 234, 236–37, 244, 336 n. 48; and full-personhood view, 60, 63; and treatment of former full persons, 113; and treatment of marginal humans, 87–88, 97–98, 100–101, 102, 105–106; and treatment of nonhuman animals, 97

Eldridge, Niles, 21

Elephants, 46, 47

Empathy, 265, 268, 341 n. 150

English, Jane, 89–90

Environmental ethics, 9, 154, 162, 260–63; and aesthetics, 262–63; and holism, 262, 341 n. 137, n. 150; and individualism, 262; and pluralism, 262. *See also* Biocentrism

Epiphenomenalism, 19. *See also* Dualism, mind-body

Euthanasia: of humans, 88, 194, 195, 281; of nonhumans, 271, 281

Evolution, 19, 21, 22, 24, 27, 29–31, 41, 50, 53, 55–56, 255, 258, 261, 276, 307 n. 75, 309 n. 94, 324 n. 35; theory of, 14, 17, 20–22, 24, 27, 42, 48

Execution: of retarded humans, 69–70, 318 n. 6; of innocents, 183

Experimentation: on marginal humans, 184, 268; on marginal humans vs. on nonhumans, 62, 76, 78–81, 99, 102, 122, 205, 222, 300; by Milgram, 56; by Nazis, 300; on nonhumans, 14, 16, 26, 48, 49–50, 55, 61, 70, 100, 128, 225, 229, 274–75, 295, 298, 301; regulations pertaining to nonhumans, 185–87; on retarded or senile humans, 117, 176; at Tuskegee, 123, 176. *See also* Vivisection

Factory farming, 15, 228, 272; and nonhuman animal welfare, 16, 39, 185, 187, 199, 204; Swedish phase-out, 188; the United States compared to other countries, 187–88

Farms, non-factory, 271–72

Feinberg, Joel, 3, 347 n. 217

Fetus, 62, 89, 100, 105, 148–49, 213, 221, 251, 286; anencephalic, 254; rights, 113, 219, 251–54, 255, 257; tissue and organ transplants from, 99

Fink, Charles, 229, 300, 347 n. 227

Fish, 203, 257–59, 269, 284

Fox, Michael A., 54–55, 127–28, 130, 137, 162, 171, 172, 225, 315 n. 206, 334 n. 2

Francis, Leslie, 126–28, 130, 162, 164

Frankena, William, 59

Freedom: as absence from constraint, 249; as a basic interest, 151, 270; and compatibilism, 31, 308 n. 81; of choice, 31, 261; as a generic feature of action, 241; limitations on the right of, 250–51, 270; for living things, 260; and the problem of evil, 18, 20, 31; as a right, 242–49, 264, 269, 276, 281

Frey, R. G., xiii, 52, 54, 58, 60, 110, 121–23, 180–81, 184, 205, 217–20, 223, 225–26, 233, 236, 315 n. 205, 332 n. 71

Full-personhood view, 57–63, 77, 80, 107–17, 119, 230, 245, 325 n. 40; and the argument from marginal cases, 64, 66–68, 71, 73–74, 76, 84–89, 103–17, 119, 120–23, 124; incompatibility with homocentrism, 61–62, 70; modified in favor of speciesism, 136–39, 179; and utilitarianism, 180–82, 225, 335 n. 23

Gewirth, Alan, 10, 59, 234, 235, 240–56, 259–60, 262–65, 267–69, 271, 283, 286, 289, 294, 336 n. 45, n. 46, n. 56, 337 n. 60, n. 67, n. 69, 338 n. 71, n. 79, 339 n. 91

Gilligan, Carol, 265, 303 n. 11, 341 n. 153

Index

God, 11, 12, 18–19, 27, 30, 32, 45, 46, 61, 196, 213, 214, 261
Golden Rule, 244
Goodall, Jane, 47, 48, 275
Goodpaster, Kenneth, xiii
Gorillas, 48, 134, 202, 255, 275. *See also* Koko
Gould, Stephen Jay, 21, 27
Griffin, Donald, 5, 41, 47, 49, 202, 203, 303 n. 14

Hare, R. M., 245–47, 264, 332 n. 56
Hargrove, Eugene, 263
Harris, C. E., 70
Harrison, Peter, 14–37, 39, 40, 44–45, 306 n. 54, 307 n. 68, n. 74, n. 75, 308 n. 81, n. 84, 310 n. 115, 311 n. 128, n. 136, n. 137
Hart, H. L. A., 206–207
Holland, Alan, 72–74, 155–57, 162
Homocentrism, 10–57, 88, 104, 105, 125, 225, 230, 231, 256; autonomy and intelligence defense of, 46–55; incompatibility with full-personhood view, 61–63, 70, 108; moral agency defense of, 55–57; sentience defense of, 12–46; and speciesism, 126, 130, 136–37, 268; theological defense of, 11–12
Homophobia, 174, 177, 323 n. 12
Hume, David, 263–64, 341 n. 150
Hunting: defense of, 68, 143; of humans, 69–70, 98; by nonhumans, 53, 258; of nonhumans, 11, 15, 32, 62, 86, 96, 167, 185, 266, 277–80, 345 n. 194
Hypophenomenalism, 19, 27. *See also* Dualism, mind-body

Immoralists, 263–65
Impartiality: as formal principle of justice, 233, 238–39; and utilitarianism, 178, 181–182, 186, 194, 196, 218, 219
Independent beings, 193–94, 215. *See also* Dependent beings

Infanticide, 92, 94–95, 99, 196, 111–12, 212, 218
Infants: anencephalic, 8, 339 n. 102; compared to adult apes, 255; denial of rights to, 92, 180; experiments and, 100; moral concern for, 64, 265, 322 n. 98; nonhuman, 130, 203, 205; and pain, 33–34, 36, 44; as (allegedly) replaceable, 206; rights for, 65, 111–13, 140, 219, 250–51, 254; as a stage in the life of a person, 108–10, 114, 117–18; sympathetic interest in, 96–98; underestimated, 252. *See also* Children; Infanticide
Insane humans: and full-personhood, 62, killing in self-defense, 281; moral concern for, 64, protection for, 98
Insects, 38
Instinct, 20, 31, 32, 35, 42, 53, 54
Interests: basic, 151, 178, 238, 278; conflicts of, 16, 99–100, 138, 255, 282–83, 295; and egoism, 236; equal consideration of, 179, 181, 186; of former full persons, 119; of former living persons, 117; and harmful life, 152, 154; and the harm of death, 292; and moral considerability/significance, 1, 2, 10, 81, 160, 226, 228, 291; and the moral point of view, 243, 246–47, 264; of nonexistent beings, 221; nonhuman, 17, 268, 277; and rights, 219; and speciesism, 125, 127, 137–38, 144, 173, 299; ulterior or nonbasic, 151, 161; and utility maximization, 222; on behalf of vulnerable humans, 101; welfare interests, 3, 232, 251
Intuitions, moral, 97, 182, 214, 223, 230; reflective, 233, 235–239, 267–68
Invertebrates, 13, 258

Jainism, 8, 11
Jamieson, Dale, 101

Johnson, Edward, 17, 38, 44, 45
Justice: compensatory, 133; distributive, 157–58; as fairness, 230; formal principle of, 233, 238, 239; moral point of view and, 265; normative interpretation of, 239; perfectionism and, 237–38; Rawls theory of, 234; social, 127; strict, 283, 335 n. 28; having a welfare and, 256. *See also* Impartiality

Kant, Immanuel, 6, 7, 8, 57, 59, 60, 61, 64, 70, 90, 128, 139, 203, 214, 215, 227, 228, 232, 233, 236, 238–39, 244, 266, 304 n. 54, 316 n. 218, n. 221, 335 n. 23
Kanzi, 47–48, 50, 82, 84
Killing: and allowing to die, 282, 284; of children, 165, 206, 218; choosing victims, 60, 148–49, 288–95, by drawing lots, 283, 346 n. 204; due to scarcity of resources, 282–83, 346 n. 207; of the handicapped, 22, 68–69, 89–90, 92–95, 97, 101–102, 126, 144, 180; of humans by hunters, 278–79; of innocents under utilitarianism, 182–84; when justified, 281–88; and the liberty principle, 298–99; of nonhumans by humans, 11, 81, 121, 138, 155, 158, 167–69, 173, 255, 258–59, 269–72; of nonhumans by hunters, 345 n. 194; of old vs. young, 347 n. 217. *See also* Abortion; Euthanasia; Hunting; Infanticide; Replaceability argument
Kinship: appeal to, 162–71; as closeness, 166; as genetic relatedness, 163–64
Kohlberg, Lawrence, 265, 303 n. 11, 341 n. 153
Koko, 49, 202, 275, 344 n. 178

Language: as (alleged) criterion for consciousness, 45, 307 n. 68, 308 n. 84, 313 n. 171; experiments with other species, 26, 37, 49–50, 82, 84,

202, 274–75; and homocentrism, 46–51; as not required for moral concern, 64; as (allegedly) required for rights, 140, 164
Learning: in nonhumans, 29–30, 203, 310 n. 115, 311 n. 137; self-awareness required for, 6–8, 203
Lehman, Hugh, 287, 295, 345 n. 201, 347 n. 217
Liberation movements, 16, 55, 126, 128, 227, 230, 277, 323 n. 12
Liberty principle, 298–99
Lifeboat analogies, 104–105, 285–88, 295–97
Limbic system, 29, 257–58, 310 n. 107
Living nonsentient beings, 8–9, 10, 259–62. *See also* Bacteria; Plants; Protozoa
Logical positivism, 7, 14–15, 308 n. 84
Lomasky, Loren, 52–54
Lucy, 49, 85, 274–75

Machine model of animals, 13, 17, 25, 37, 45. *See also* Automata
Mammals, 3, 22, 25, 29, 36, 48, 202–3, 205, 211, 232, 252, 255, 257–58, 267, 269–70, 284, 301, 309 n. 94
Marginal humans, 77–81, 107–20, 321 n. 77; as disadvantaged, 159–62; name coined by Narveson, 317 n. 229; vivisection of, 121–22. *See also* Argument from marginal cases
Materialism. *See* Physicalism
Mates, our obligations to, 163–65
McCloskey, H. J., 3, 55, 58, 60, 110, 143, 316 n. 207, 317 n. 225
Melden, A. I., xiii, 10, 55, 57–58, 60, 108–17, 113, 156, 316 n. 208, n. 214, 322 n. 98, 333 n. 93
Mentally limited humans, 17, 250–51, 306 n. 62, 315 n. 205, 334 n. 11, 338 n. 88
Mentally retarded humans, 62, 64–65, 68, 76, 84, 95, 103, 123, 126, 140, 217, 293; experiments on the retarded, 67, 121, 176; treatment of retarded criminals, 69–70

Mercy killing. *See* Euthanasia

Mere consciousness, 5–8, 62, 78, 200–201, 203–204, 217

Mice, 46, 56, 186

Midgley, Mary, 130–34, 162, 171, 174, 327 n. 88

Milgram experiments, 56

Milk: and blue tits, 51, 83; on "no kill" farms, 271–72; and nutrition, 272, 283; as protein source, 273; and veal calves, 116, 188. *See also* Calves; Cows

Monkeys, 47–49, 55–56, 83, 100, 259

Moral agency, 2, 3, 4, 75–76, 79–80, 88, 180, 232, 239, 252, 265; and full-personhood view, 58, 68, 70, 106; and homocentrism, 12, 55–57; loss of, 114–15; as mandated by reason, 245–48, 264; potential, 108–9; and speciesism, 136–38, 141, 144, 146, 157, 179; and utilitarianism, 180. *See also* Moral point of view

Moral agents. *See* Agents; Moral agency

Moral codes, 1, 184, 240, 283

Morally considerable being, 1, 60–61, 68, 144–45, 147, 156–58, 166, 167, 231–32, 238

Morally significant being, 1, 60, 65, 68, 75–76, 117–18, 161, 232; and capacities, 84, 107, 147, 169–70, 251; character argument for nonhumans as, 227–29; for conative nonhumans, 254–59; fairness argument for nonhumans as, 227, 230; happiness argument for nonhumans as, 227, 229–30; and perfectionism, 236–38

Moral point of view, 243–44, 246–48, 264–66. *See also* Moral agency

Narveson, Jan, xiii, 58, 60, 95–100, 111, 232, 236, 317 n. 229

Nelson, James, 156, 218, 327 n. 85

Newborns. *See* Infants

Nietzsche, Friedrich, 233, 237

Nonconsequentialist views. *See* Deontological views

Noonan, John T., 147

Normalism, 94, 175–77, 268

Norman, Richard, 126–28, 130, 162, 164

Nozick, Robert, 71

Obligations: negative, 161; positive, 161. *See also* Duty

Occasionalism, 18, 19, 27, 30, 309 n. 100. *See also* Dualism, mind-body

Orangutans, 202, 255

Organs: donated, 292; fetal transplants, 99, 254; infants as source of, 112; marginal humans as source of, 100, 102, 149, 153–59, 163, 176; prisoners as source of, 176, 296; trans-species transplants, 124, 153–58, 163, 295, 297, 299, 326 n. 72

Overpopulation, 196–97, 199, 220; and food, 273–74; of herbivores, 280; and utilitarianism, 196, 220, 331 n. 50, 331 n. 55

Pain: and agricultural regulations, 188; and disutility, 180; in fetuses, 99, 252, 254; and laboratory regulations, 186; claimed absent in mentally undeveloped humans, 18, 36–37, 44; claimed absent in nonhuman animals, 12–45, 306 n. 55, 307 n. 75, 310 n. 111, 311 n. 128; as nonmorally bad, 59; and common-sense personhood, 3; physiological similarities in humans and non-humans, 13, 103, 252, 257–58, 269, 309, 310 n. 107; varying responses to, 293; and subjects-of-lives, 3, 232

Parallelism, 19, 27. *See also* Dualism, mind-body

Parfit, Derek, 194, 196–97, 331 n. 50

Partridge, Ernest, 3, 67–68

Personhood: different concepts of, 2–4; moral relevance of its loss,

Personhood (*continued*)
113–20. *See also* Full-personhood view

Pigs, 21, 62, 65, 77, 82, 171, 187–88, 273, 297, 299

Plants, moral status of, 8–10, 259–60, 265

Potential, the moral relevance of, 107–13, 146–50

Predation, 276–77, 344 n. 182

Prejudice. *See* Bigotry

Principle of generic consistency, 59, 244, 249, 263, 265

Product testing, 11, 15–16

Protozoa, 20, 30, 260, 311 n. 137

Rachels, James, xiii, 14, 55, 137–38, 173, 284, 325 n. 41, 328 n. 98

Racism, 126, 139, 169–70, 174, 177; as allegedly confused concept, 131–34; and alleged disanalogy with speciesism, 126–35, 164, 167; and alleged reverse discrimination, 131–34

Rationality: limitations of, 263–66; value of, 266–67

Rats, 46, 48, 56, 75, 77, 171, 186

Rawls, John, 164, 232–35, 269, 335 n. 23, n. 28

Regan, Tom, xii, 3–5, 54, 60, 63–65, 71, 73, 76, 97, 122, 164, 203, 225, 231–39, 249, 256–57, 260, 269, 274, 277, 285–90, 292, 294, 298–99, 317 n. 225, n. 229, 322 n. 117, 335 n. 23, 344 n. 182, 346 n. 212, 347 n. 225, 348 n. 230

Relativism, 240, 245

Replaceability argument, 185; implications for humans, 189–90; implications for nonhumans, 185–89. *See also* Utilitarianism

Reproduction: in humans, 199, 220; in nonhumans, 271

Reptiles, 203, 257–58, 269

Rights: for conative nonhumans, 254–59, 270–75, 280; endangerment argument, 87–95; for full persons, 248; for human fetuses, 251–54;

negative, 167–68; and nonconative or insentient beings, 259–63; and normative theories, 63, 327 n. 76; for preferentially autonomous agents, 248–50; shadow, 217–18, 223; and telos, 154–55; trumped by utility, 221–23; for young and mentally limited humans, 250–51

Rights view: accepting, 267–68; egalitarian, 290, 298–99; Regan's arguments for, 231–240; Gewirth's arguments for, 240–48, 336 n. 56; unequal, 294

Robinson, William, 17, 38, 44, 306 n. 64, 310 n. 107, 313 n. 160, n. 168, n. 169, n. 170

Rollin, Bernard, xii, 5–8, 14–15, 24, 35, 46, 63–64, 123, 134–35, 154, 203, 225–26, 258, 268, 271, 293, 313 n. 171

Ryder, Richard, 125

Sapontzis, S. F., xiii, 17, 57, 79, 81–82, 85, 103–106, 119, 128–30, 192–93, 210, 212–16, 225–30, 276, 292–94, 303 n. 6, 306 n. 61, 311 n. 123, 319 n. 32, 324 n. 19, 334 n. 16, 341 n. 149

Sartre, Jean-Paul, 7, 261, 264, 341 n. 146

Schweitzer, Albert, 258, 260

Sea lions, 48, 314 n. 183

Self-awareness. *See* Self-consciousness

Self-consciousness, 5–7, 62; and preference utilitarianism, 199–205; alleged irreplaceability of, 206–11, 217

Senchuk, Dennis, 42

Senile humans, 62, 64, 65, 68, 77, 78, 79, 95, 117–19, 126, 255, 176, 315 n. 205

Sentience, 8–9, 10, 82, 99–100, 255; and conation, 251, 254–59, 294, 299; empathy for, 265, 268; as homocentric defense, 12–46; and marginal humans, 83–84, 129, 153, 157–58, 177–78, 230–31; and high moral significance, 74, 114, 226, 251, 294; and presumption against being made to suffer, 61, 138, 254; and telos, 154–55; and utilitarianism, 181–82, 185–86, 189, 193, 197, 215, 217, 219–22, 224, 232. *See also* Consciousness; Self-consciousness; Mere consciousness

Sexism, 126, 135, 174, 177; and alleged disanalogy with speciesism, 126–30, 135, 139

Singer, Peter, xii, 63, 65, 66, 76, 92, 125–27, 129–30, 137–38, 179–80, 181–216, 225, 232, 277, 324 n. 19, 332 n. 56, n. 71, 344 n. 182

Species: affinity for, 103, 105; classification as, 134–35; as a marker for important differences, 130–31. *See also* Speciesism

Speciesism, 79–81, 123–25, 205, 231, 268, 324 n. 19, 325 n. 40; and appeal to benevolence, 144–45; and appeal to emotion, 171–72; and appeal to fairness, 145–46; and appeal to harmful life, 150–55; and appeal to kinship, 162–66, 269; and appeal to misfortune, 155–59; and appeal to opportunities for interaction, 167–71; and appeal to rational preferences, 172–77; and appeal to thwarted potential, 146–50; full-personhood-related, 136–39, 179; history of, 125–26; homocentric version, 125–36; mild, 136; moderate, 173; quasi-definitional defense of, 140–44; radical, 136

Subject(s)-of-a-life: as commonsense personhood, 3; as equally morally significant, 231–40; welfare criterion of, 256

Sumner, L. W., 147, 180, 181, 193, 194, 214, 219–23, 231, 234–35, 326 n. 73, 333 n. 104, n. 106

Swift, Jonathan, 206

Taylor, Paul, 2, 3, 9, 143, 169, 249, 260–62, 278, 282, 338 n. 81, 345 n. 200

Teleological views. *See* Consequentialism

Telos, 154–55, 268, 271, 280

Tooley, Michael, 294

Tool use: by hominids, 26; by non-humans, 26, 46–48

Townsend, A. V., 87–90, 92

Unconscious experience, 38, 42. *See also* Conscious experience

Utilitarianism: acceptance, 184, 217, 329 n. 14; average view, 331 n. 50; classical, 181–85, 187, 189, 191, 193, 199–201; extended prior existence view, 192–95; and the full-personhood view, 180–82; and the killing of innocents argument, 182–84; preference, 183, 199–200, 205–207, 209, 211, 216, 232; prior existence view, 190, 192; and rights, 217–23, 333 n. 104; rule, 232, 236; and self-conscious life, 199–201; side effects argument, 101–102, 121, 183; total-view, 190–92. *See also* Replaceability argument

Utility, principle of, 59, 180, 218. *See also* Utilitarianism

Values: moral, 58, 104, 189, 244; nonmoral, 58–59, 180, 263, and the principle of utility, 59

Varner, Gary, 261, 272, 341 n. 138, 341 n. 150, 343 n. 168

Vegetarian diet. *See* Vegetarianism

Vegetarianism, 55, 179, 181, 198, 205, 229, 272, 300, 331 n. 55, 343 n. 164, n. 165, n. 167, n. 168, 348 n. 230

Vertebrates, 13, 24, 36, 257–58, 309 n. 103

Vitali, Theodore, 68–70

Vivisection, 14–15, 45, 76, 86–87, 121–22, 184, 204–205

Washoe, 49, 50, 85

Welfare, moral relevance of, 3, 5, 16, 106, 180, 182, 184, 186–89, 195, 228, 232, 251, 256–57

Well-being: as generic feature of action, 241; due to the preferentially autonomous, 248–50, 270;

Well-being (*continued*)
killing in view of, 281, 293, 294; and living beings, 260; and predation, 276; accorded as a right, 245–48; claimed as a right, 241–44; due to sentient conative beings, 250–52, 254–56
Wenz, Peter, 167–69, 328 n. 98, n. 104
White, Alan, 140–41, 142
Wild animals, 274–80. *See also* listings for individual animals
Wildlife, 199, 331 n. 55
Wilson, Allan C., 22, 27, 309 n. 94

Wilson, E. O., 172
Wolves, 23, 30, 53, 75, 82, 161, 270
Worse-off principle, 288–290, 292, 298–99, 347 n. 217, n. 227
Wreen, Michael, 137, 141–42, 145–46, 325 n. 40, 326 n. 65
Wretched child, the case of, 193–95, 208, 212–16. *See also* Utilitarianism

Young, Thomas, 173–76
Young humans. *See* Children

Evelyn B. Pluhar is Associate Professor
of Philosophy at Pennsylvania State
University, Fayette Campus,
in Uniontown.

Library of Congress Cataloging-in-Publication Data

Pluhar, Evelyn B.
Beyond prejudice : the moral significance of human and
nonhuman animals / by Evelyn B. Pluhar : foreword by
Bernard E. Rollin.
p. cm.
Includes bibliographical references and index.
ISBN 0-8223-1634-X. — ISBN 0-8223-1648-X (pbk.)
1. Animal rights. 2. Human rights. 3. Philosophical
anthropology. I. Title.
HV4708.P67 1995
179' .3—dc20 95-865 CIP